William Massey

A History of England during the Reign of George the Third

William Massey

A History of England during the Reign of George the Third

ISBN/EAN: 9783741163678

Manufactured in Europe, USA, Canada, Australia, Japa

Cover: Foto ©ninafisch / pixelio.de

Manufactured and distributed by brebook publishing software
(www.brebook.com)

William Massey

A History of England during the Reign of George the Third

A HISTORY OF ENGLAND

DURING THE

REIGN OF GEORGE THE THIRD.

BY

THE RIGHT HON.

WILLIAM MASSEY.

SECOND EDITION, REVISED AND CORRECTED.

IN FOUR VOLUMES.

VOL. I.
1745 — 1770.

LONDON:
LONGMANS, GREEN, AND CO.
1865.

PREFACE.

IN preparing this work, I have been much aided by information derived from private sources. About forty years since, the late Mr. Edward Hawke Locker, a Commissioner of Greenwich Hospital, with the sanction of the Royal Family, and with the assistance of many distinguished persons, collected voluminous materials for a life of George the Third. The progress of the work, however, was stopped, by the interposition of Lord Liverpool, then at the head of the Government, who thought the time had not yet arrived for such a publication. Mr. Frederick Locker has kindly placed at my disposal the papers collected by his father for the important work which he had undertaken; and I have thus been enabled to obtain much curious and interesting information, relating both to the public transactions and the secret history of this reign. Lord Bolton has likewise permitted me to refer to the extensive correspondence of his grandfather, the first peer, who was for many years in office, and in confidential intercourse with Mr. Pitt, especially during the earlier years of his administration. I have also had access to other private collections; but contemporary sources of information, unless corroborated by other testimony, cannot safely be relied on. Party prejudice, credulity, and general inaccuracy, without wilful misrepresentation, which perhaps rarely occurs, are sufficient to mislead those who do not advance with vigilance and caution in the search for historical truth.

CONTENTS
OF
THE FIRST VOLUME.

CHAPTER I.

Introduction—Fall of Sir Robert Walpole—His Successors—Seven Years' War—Pitt's great Administration—Conquest of Canada—War in Germany—Death of George the Second. 1742—1760.

	PAGE
Fall of Sir R. Walpole, 1742	1
Death of the Prince of Wales, 1751	4
Party jealousy	5
The Opposition dissolved	6
Death of Pelham, 1753	6
Character of the Earl of Chatham	6
Chatham's affectation	7
Chatham's reverence for royalty	7
Lord Mansfield	8
The Duke of Newcastle as a statesman	9
Newcastle's policy	10
Newcastle addresses himself to Fox	11
Negotiations with Fox	12
Quarrels among the new ministers	12
Preparations for war. Supineness of the King	13
Timid measures of the ministry	14
Conduct of the King	15
Lord Chatham applied to	16
Fox becomes Secretary of State	16
Pitt, Legge, and Grenville dismissed	16
Hostilities commenced by France, 1756	18
Minorca lost	18
Admiral Byng shot	19

	PAGE
Offensive alliance between France and Austria	19
Dissolution of the ministry	21
A new ministry formed under the Duke of Devonshire	23
Pitt's vigorous conduct	22
Pitt becomes perfectly distasteful to the King	23
Intrigues for a new administration	24
Waldegrave sent for	25
A new administration formed	25
Pitt elevated to power	26
Battle of Kolin	26
Affairs in America	26
Expedition against Rochefort. Its failure	27
Return of the Fleet	28
Cause of failure at Rochefort	29
Plan for recovering Minorca	29
Pitt's vigorous prosecution of the war	30
Hanover recovered	31
Expedition to North America	31
General Abercrombie	32
Cape Breton taken	32
Improvement in affairs	32
Blockade of French coast	32
Expedition to the West Indies	33
Capture of Guadaloupe	33
Expedition to Canada	33
General Wolfe	34
City of Quebec	34
Attack on Quebec	35
Wolfe's despatch	37
English troops land	38
Montcalm defeated	39
Death of Wolfe	39
Death of Montcalm	40
Surrender of Quebec	40
Subjugation of Canada	40
Sir Edward Hawke	40
Naval victory at Belleisle	41
Frederick the Great	42
Dresden bombarded	43
Daun defeated	43

CHAPTER II.

Accession of George the Third—His Character—His Policy—Earl of Bute Chief Minister—Progress of the War—Negotiation for Peace—Family Compact—Pitt advises a Declaration of War against Spain—His Counsel rejected—His Resignation—War with Spain—Triumph of the British Arms—Treaty of Peace. 1760—1762.

	PAGE
National prosperity at the accession	45
Enactment that the judges hold their offices for life	46
Education and early years of George the Third	46
Death of his father	47
Waldegrave's character of George III.	48
George the Third as a king	49
Character of public men	50
Mental capacity of George the Third	51
Power of the crown	51
The Tory party	52
Policy of the King	54
Conduct of Lord Bute	54
The King's treatment of Bute	55
His connection with Scotland	56
Lord Bute as an orator	57
Changes in the ministry	57
Peace policy of the Earl of Bute	58
The royal speech to the Council	58
Negotiations for peace	59
Conditions of the treaty	60
Differences between the Courts	61
Interference of France in Spanish affairs	62
Pitt is offended	63
The Family Compact	63
Our Spanish policy	64
Rigorous policy of Pitt	65
Retirement of Pitt	66
Review of Pitt's policy	66
War policy of Pitt	68
Character of Pitt's agents	69
Provision for the war	69
Results of the war	70
Exultation of Newcastle on the fall of Pitt	71
Misgivings of Lord Bute	71
Influence of Court favour on Pitt	72
Lady Hester created Baroness Chatham	72
Lord Mayor's day	73
Parliament meets	74
A new leader of the House of Commons	74
State of parties	74

Spanish affairs	75
War declared with Spain	76
Spanish professions of peaceful motives	76
Hopelessness of peace	77
Noble conduct of Pitt	77
The Family Alliance	78
Parliament prorogued	78
Our Prussian policy	78
Consequences of the Prussian alliance	80
Engagements with Prussia	80
Newcastle treated with indignity	81
Newcastle resigns	82
Earl of Bute's conduct	83
Policy of Lord Bute	84
Expedition against Martinique	85
Fall of the Havannah	85
Attack on the Philippine islands	86
Humiliation of the House of Bourbon	86
Negotiations for peace	87
Treaty of peace signed. Nov. 3	88
Conditions of the treaty	88

CHAPTER III.

Progress of Commerce—Marriage of the King—Means employed for procuring a Vote in Parliament in Favour of the Treaty of Peace—Proscription of the Whigs—Wilkes and the 'North Briton'—Resignation of Bute—Negotiation with Pitt—The Bedford Administration—The American Colonies. 1757—1769.

Domestic events	92
Increase of the national debt	92
Private life of George the Third	94
Domestic policy	95
Negotiations with Pitt	95
Condition of the Court party	96
Fox applied to	96
Corruption of Parliament	97
Insults offered to the Duke of Devonshire	98
The Duke of Devonshire disgraced	100
Fox excuses himself	101
Parliament meets	101
Appearance of Pitt in the House of Commons	101
Fox's management of Parliament	103
Triumph of the Court	104
Policy of George the Third	105
Corruption extended	106

	PAGE
Financial measures	106
Resignation of Earl Bute	107
Grenville becomes Prime Minister	108
Duration of Bute's administration	109
Final retirement of Fox	110
Character of Lord Holland	111
Fox and Pitt compared	112

CHAPTER IV.

Attempt to form a new Administration under Pitt—Its Failure—Duke of Bedford at the Head of the Government—Conduct of the King—Wilkes and the 'North Briton'—General Warrants—Essay on Woman—Expulsion of Wilkes—Grenville's Financial Measures—The Colonial Question. 1763—1764.

Grenville as Prime Minister	115
Lord Bute's intrigues with Pitt	115
Independence of Grenville	116
New intrigues	116
Pitt proposed as Prime Minister	118
Arrangements of Pitt	118
Bute begins to falter	119
Negotiations with Pitt resumed	119
Endeavour to secure the Duke of Bedford	120
Bedford appointed President of the Council	122
Treacherous conduct of the King	122
Dispute about patronage	123
John Wilkes	124
The North Briton	124
Criticism on the royal speech	125
Validity of general warrants	126
Decision of the King's Bench	127
The question really left undecided	128
Proceedings against Wilkes	129
Vengeance of the Court	129
Parliament appealed to	130
Decision of the House of Commons	130
Conduct of the House of Lords	131
Further proceedings of Wilkes and the Government	132
Theory of libels	133
Popular sympathy for Wilkes	134
Wilkes yields to the storm	135
Sir W. Meredith's motion	136
Grenville's amendment	136
The King is personally interested	137
Wilkes's action against Halifax	137

CHAPTER V.

The Colonial Quarrel—Indiscriminate Suppression of Smuggling —Stamp Act—Right of English Parliament to tax the Colonies —The Equity of Imperial Taxation. 1764.

	PAGE
Increase of the minority	139
Character of colonial smuggling	140
Indignation of the colonists	141
Mistaken policy of the Government	142
Disputes with the Indians	143
Procrastinating conduct of the executive	144
Theory of taxation	145
Lord Coke's opinion	145
Despair of the colonists	147
Innocence of Grenville's intentions	148
Mitigatory measures of Grenville	149
Further arguments	149
Colonies neglected by England	150
Effects of jealousy between France and England	152

CHAPTER VI.

The Stamp Act—Illness of the King—Regency Bill—Misconduct of the Ministry and of Parliament on this Question—Attempt to form a New Administration by the Duke of Cumberland—Unsuccessful Negotiation with Pitt—Marquis of Rockingham Prime Minister—Death of the Duke of Cumberland. 1705.

Meeting of Parliament	155
Preparations for carrying the measure	156
The bill passes the Commons	157
Stability of the ministry	157
Sudden illness of the King	159
The constitution did not provide a regency	159
The Regency Bill	160
Insertion of a new clause	162
The King misled by Halifax	163
Culpable conduct of Grenville and Bedford	164
The King is undeceived	165
Conduct of Lord Mansfield	166
The King and Grenville	167
Intrigues with the Opposition	168
The King sends for the Duke of Cumberland	169
Fate of Morton's clause	170
Final decision of the Lords	172

	PAGE
The King wishes to dissolve Parliament	173
The Silk Bill	174
Riots among the weavers	175
Resignation of the ministry	176
Further negotiations	176
Second application to Pitt	177
The negotiation broken off	179
Lord Lyttelton sent for	180
New arrangements of the ministry	180
Feud between the King and the ministry	182
Bedford remonstrates with the King	183
Duke of Cumberland consulted	184
Failure of the new scheme	184
The King sends for Newcastle	186
A new administration and its members	187
The Marquis of Rockingham	187
General Conway	188
The Duke of Grafton	189
Mr. Dowdeswell	189
Lord Northington	189
Chief Justice Pratt created Lord Camden	190
Death of the Duke of Cumberland	190

CHAPTER VII.

Disturbances in America—Assembly of Congress—Irresolution of the Government—Debates in Parliament—Pitt's Denial of the Right of Parliament to Tax the Colonies—Remarks on this Subject—Franklin's Examination at the Bar of the House of Commons—Repeal of the Stamp Act—The Declaratory Act. 1765—1766.

Reception of the American Stamp Act	192
General Provincial Congress	193
Resolutions of the Congress	193
Proceedings of the Home Government	194
Timidity of the ministry	195
The question agitated in Parliament	196
Indecision of the cabinet	196
Re-appearance of Pitt in the House	197
Burke's maiden speech	198
Speech of Pitt	198
Grenville's reply	200
Pitt called to order	201
Pitt replies to Grenville	201
Advice of Pitt	203
The right of taxing the colonies	204

	PAGE
Theory of self-taxation	205
The representative principle	205
Measures resolved on	205
Franklin's evidence	207
Franklin's dialectic skill	208
Declaratory Bill	208
Lord Mansfield's argument	209
The Declaratory Bill	210
Repeal of the Stamp Act	211
Propriety of the repeal	212

CHAPTER VIII

Measures of the Rockingham Administration—Its Dismissal—Pitt Prime Minister and Earl of Chatham—His Schemes—His Illness and Seclusion—Distracted State of the Cabinet—Townshend's Rashness and Ambition—Ministerial Changes—Nullum Tempus Bill. 1766—1771.

Conciliatory measures towards the colonies	214
Cider duty re-arranged	214
Foreign silks prohibited	215
Various domestic measures	215
Weakness of the Government	215
Insubordination of state officers	216
Overtures made to Pitt	218
Partial resignation of the ministry	218
Pitt forms a new administration	219
Pitt's florid style	219
Interference of Temple	220
Pitt's treatment of him	221
Composition of the new ministry	222
Pitt created Earl of Chatham	222
The Chatham administration	224
Objections to Chatham's ministry	225
Pitt's principles of action	226
Change of political circumstances	227
Proposed alliances	227
Negotiations commenced	228
Impracticability of Frederick	229
Chatham's projects defeated	230
Imperious proceedings of Chatham	230
Vacillating conduct towards Lord Gower	232
Arrangement of places	233
False policy of the Government	233
Indian policy	234
State of Ireland	235

	PAGE
Exportation of corn resisted	236
The question in the Lords	237
The question in the Commons	238
East India Company	239
Breach of parliamentary etiquette	240
Chatham's measure passed	241
Anarchy of the Government	242
Disorder of parliament	243
Revenue from America	244
Chatham taken ill	244
Chatham refuses to consult his colleagues	244
Grafton obtains an interview	245
Movements of the Opposition	246
Lyttelton's proposals to Rockingham	247
The East India question	248
Unsettled state of America	248
Suspension of the New York Assembly	250
Townshend's rash measures	251
Physical prostration of Chatham	252
The King's confidence in Chatham	252
Effect of Chatham's retirement	253
Death of Townshend	253

CHAPTER IX.

General Election—State of the Constituency—Wilkes returned to the New Parliament—Disturbed State of the Country—Resignation of Chatham—Expulsions of Wilkes—Letters of Junius. 1768—1769.

General election	255
Number of electors	257
Influence of boroughs	259
The people awakened	261
Political popularity	262
Wilkes reappears	262
Wilkes elected for Middlesex	263
Embarrassment of the Government	264
Wilkes imprisoned	265
Riots of his partisans	265
Popular discontent increases	267
Universal insubordination	267
Chatham withdraws from the Government	268
Circumstances of his withdrawal	269
Anxiety of the ministry to retain Chatham	270
Internal weakness of the Government	271
Determination of the King	271

	PAGE
Popular orators lost in Parliament	271
Glynn elected for Middlesex	272
Wilkes petitions	272
Lord Weymouth's Letter to the Surrey magistrates	273
Wilkes' mode of defence	274
Expulsion of Wilkes moved by Lord Barrington	274
House of Commons determined to persevere	275
Wilkes elected for Middlesex	275
Colonel Luttrell	275
Colonel Luttrell declared member	276
Motion to erase the name of Wilkes	276
Right of the Commons to expel a member	276
Grenville's remonstrances	277
Public indignation excited	278
The county of Middlesex petition the Crown	278
Power of the press—Letters of Junius	279
Rancour of Junius	279
Mysterious authorship of Junius	280
Unfounded charges of Junius	280
Junius attacks Lord Mansfield	282
Vituperation of the Duke of Bedford	282
Politics of Junius	282
Junius become a classic writer	284
Junius compared to Swift	285
Supposed authorship of the letters of Junius	286
Deficiency in the Civil List	286
Aggravation of public discontent	291
Disastrous colonial policy	291
Lord Hillsborough's threat to dissolve the Assembly	293
The Assembly dissolved	293
Views of Government as to America	294
Disputes with the colonies	294
Attempt to prohibit importation from England	295
Public excitement at Boston	296
Deputies invited to meet at Boston	297
Deputation to the Governor	297
No precedent for the convention	297
Indiscretion of the patriots surpassed by the Government	298
General Gage garrisons Boston	299
The colonists intimidated	299
Opening of Parliament—King's speech	300
State of opinion in Massachusetts	300
General Assembly of Massachusetts	301
Assembly of Virginia.—Resolutions	301
Change of tone in the Government	302
Circular of the Government	303
Crisis of the dispute with the colonies	304

CHAPTER X.

Remnant of the Chatham Administration—The Opposition—Reunion of the Grenville Connection—Horned Cattle Session—Chatham's Re-appearance in Parliament—Dismissal of Lord Camden—Sudden Death of his Successor Yorke—Duke of Grafton's Resignation—Lord North Prime Minister. 1769—1770.

	PAGE
Rump administration of Lord Chatham	306
Reasons for its conduct	307
Duke of Grafton alarmed	308
Reappearance of Lord Chatham	308
Coolness of Chatham to Grafton	308
Attempts at accommodation	309
Secessions from the Government	310
The royal speech	311
Reappearance and speech of Chatham	311
Speech of Lord Camden	313
Conduct of Lord Camden	314
Anomalous position of Lord Camden	314
Camden's want of delicate feeling	315
Lord Mansfield's speech	316
Motion for adjournment	316
The Great Seal offered to Yorke	317
His political history	317
He accepts the seals	319
Death of Yorke	320
Resignation of Lord Granby	320
Rockingham's motion	320
Resignation of Grafton	322
Lord North constructs a new Cabinet	323
Opinions of Lord North	324
Loyalty of Lord North	324

CHAPTER XI.

Disunion of the Opposition—Grenville's Bill on controverted Elections—City Address and Remonstrance—Displeasure of the Court—Renewal of Petitions—The Tea Duty retained in America—Bloodshed at Boston—The Irish Parliament. 1770.

Success of Lord North	326
Mr. Dowdeswell's motion	329
Sir George Saville's attack on ministers	329

	PAGE
Dowdeswell's motion to disfranchise revenue officers	330
Grenville's bill on controverted elections	331
Mode of getting up petitions	332
Transference to committee	332
Rigby and Dyson disparage the measure	333
Corporation of London	334
The Lord Mayor's privileges	335
The City's interposition	336
Address and remonstrance of the City	337
The King's reply	338
The City's address censured by the Crown	339
The anger of the Court	340
Angry feelings of the Crown—Firmness of the City members	340
Lord North's conduct—Wedderburn's speech	341
Westminster remonstrance	342
Popular movements sanctioned by Lord Chatham	342
Chatham's condemnatory bill	342
Chatham's speech	343
Mansfield's speech	343
Camden's speech	343
Chatham proposes a vote of censure	343
Chatham moves an address to the Crown	344
Neglect of the American question	344
Proposed repeal of Townshend's Act	345
Party feeling in the House	346
The Revolution breaks out in Boston	347
Affray between the soldiers and the citizens	347
Immediate results of the tumult	349
The non-importation compact	350
Obstinacy of Massachusetts	350
Affairs of Ireland	351
Duration of the Irish Parliament	352
Debate on Irish affairs	353

CHAPTER XII.

Disunion of the Opposition—Another City Address—Death and Character of Grenville—of Lord Granby—of the Duke of Bedford—The Falkland Islands—Prosecution of the Printers—Quarrels between the two Houses—Shoreham Election. 1770.

Mutual dissensions of the Opposition	355
Determination of the King	356
Address of the City of London	357
Answer to the address	357

THE FIRST VOLUME. xix

	PAGE
Death of Beckford	358
Death of Grenville.—His character	359
Grenville of no extraordinary ability	359
Death of the Marquis of Granby	361
Death of the Duke of Bedford	363
Affairs of Corsica	367
The Falkland Isles	367
Satisfaction demanded by England	369
Popular discontent	370
Parliament assembles	371
Barrington's indiscretion	372
His subserviency to the King	373
Interference of Parliament	376
Independence of the judges	376
Responsibility of the judges	376
Chatham and Mansfield	377
Lord Camden	378
Unworthy proceeding in the Lords	378
Debate in the Commons	379
Speech of Wedderburn	381
Conduct of the Ministry	382
Extraordinary scene in the Lords	383
Excitement of the Commons	384
Burke's opinion of Chatham	385
Electoral corruption at Shoreham	386
Operation of Grenville's Act	387

CHAPTER XIII.

Parties—The Constitution, its Theory and Practice—Loyalty—Political Adventurers—Newspapers and Pamphlets—Parliamentary Eloquence—Manners of the House of Commons—Decay of Party.

Sketch of parties	388
Whigs and Tories	389
Extinction of party	390
Court Whigs and County Whigs	391
Disadvantages and dangers of party	392
Party appeals to the constitution	392
Privileges of the peers	394
The House of Commons	394
Power of the Commons	394
Former character of the Commons	396
Parliamentary preponderance of the landed interest	397
Former loyalty of the people	397
Acceptability of William the Third	398

CONTENTS OF THE FIRST VOLUME.

	PAGE
Government by party	399
Party squabbles	400
The people unrepresented	400
Members by purchase	402
Jealousy of the country	402
Power of the aristocracy	403
Party policy	404
Employment of political partisans	405
Hired writers	406
Dr. Johnson as a partisan	409
The stage a political instrument	410
Satirists employed	411
Parliamentary eloquence	411
Present degeneracy of Parliament	412
Decay of eloquence	412
Rhetoric distinguished from eloquence	414
Chesterfield on parliamentary eloquence	414
Parliamentary nothingness of rant	415
Improvement in parliamentary departments	416
Former rudeness in Parliament	418
Present authority of the Speaker	418
Length of modern debates	419
Necessity for parliamentary discussion	420

A
HISTORY OF ENGLAND

DURING THE

REIGN OF GEORGE THE THIRD.

CHAPTER I.

INTRODUCTION—FALL OF SIR ROBERT WALPOLE—HIS SUCCESSORS—SEVEN YEARS' WAR—PITT'S GREAT ADMINISTRATION—CONQUEST OF CANADA—WAR IN GERMANY—DEATH OF GEORGE THE SECOND.

It was not until the middle of the last century, that the Revolution can be said to have rested on a solid and secure basis. The last battle of Legitimacy had then been fought and lost; and though rumours of a renewed struggle were still rife, the conflict between the principles of absolute and responsible Government was virtually decided.

The great minister, to whose constancy and skill the nation was chiefly indebted for the maintenance of the Protestant succession, had at length fallen before the hostile alliance of Jacobites, Tories, Malcontent Whigs, and the Faction of the heir-apparent.

Fall of Sir R. Walpole. 1742

Walpole has been censured as a minister who ruled by means of bribery and corruption; as if he had preferred that mode of government. The truth is, he had no choice; the Government, during the reign of William, and that of his successor, was considered by the great majority of the nation as merely provisional; and the return of the Stuarts in the direct male line was generally expected, if not desired, at the death of Anne. The undisputed succession of the Elector of Hanover inspired little confidence in the stability of the new settlement; the restoration of the rightful sovereign was thought to be only postponed.

The consequence was an occasional and qualified allegiance to the Government *de facto* on the part of public men. They trimmed their policy with a view to another revolution; and for a long time after 1688, even the confidential servants of the Crown kept up a secret correspondence with the banished family. The selfishness and corruption of human nature were brought out by this state of things; and the sagacity of Walpole clearly perceived that the corruption which could not be cured, must be made subservient to the cause of good government.

A fastidious temper would have shrunk with disgust from the sordid traffic in which Walpole did not hesitate to engage; a squeamish morality would have suffered the Commonwealth to perish rather than save it by such means. Walpole may not have been nice; but to charge him with originating a system of venality in public affairs is to confound cause with effect. A minister who could venture to offer a member of Parliament a bank note must have found venality ripe to his hands; and the utmost that can fairly be alleged against him is, that finding corruption, he did not attempt to repress it, but rather turned it to account. The emergency was his justification. Those were not times for a minister to set about reforming public morals. The noble constitution which had lately been delineated by matchless wisdom and moderation was neither valued nor understood by an ignorant people, given up, for the most part, to the political doctrines which had been so

long and so sedulously inculcated by a self-seeking
Church. Divine, Indefeasible, Hereditary Right and
Passive Obedience were doctrines more popular than
the Original Contract and the responsibility of rulers.
Political purists may cavil at the means by which
the salvation of civil and religious liberty was effected,
but such politicians may be left to their paper con-
stitutions and impossible Utopias. *Quieta non mo-
vere*,—Walpole's favourite maxim,—a wise one at most
times,—was especially suited to that critical period.
Thus it was that he sometimes desisted from a sound
course of policy both in foreign and domestic affairs,
because he would not risk a convulsion, which might
hazard the safety of the state. Walpole's mind was
not superior to the age in which he lived; therefore,
his character and conduct are doubtless open to reproach; but no candid advocate of free institutions
will deny that, in the main, he acted the part of a
great statesman and a true-hearted Englishman.

The chief of the allied opposition, which at last
overthrew this brave and honest minister, shrank
from the responsibility of placing himself at the head
of a new government, and sought an ignoble refuge
in the House of Lords. The inferior men to whom
the Earl of Bath deputed the administration feebly
pursued the same policy which they had so long denounced. The patriots, freed from the coercion of a
chief, were soon divided by a fierce contest for office,
and they chose the time when the country was menaced with invasion and civil war, to bring their
quarrel to a crisis, by leaving the King and the nation
without a government.

The Protestant succession had never been in such
imminent peril; indeed, the country was saved rather
by the fatuity which attended every operation of the
Stuarts, and now prevented them from taking the
obvious mode of profiting by their first success, than
by the energy of its rulers. But the danger happily

passed away, and the cause of the Exile was lost for ever.

<small>Death of the Prince of Wales. 1751</small>

An event which happened a few years afterwards was alone wanting to consolidate the Government. This was the death of the heir-apparent, which, instead of being a calamity to his family and to the nation, was a relief to both. The prince had, from his earliest years, endured the rancorous hatred of both the King and Queen. He reciprocated the animosity of his parents; and, on one occasion, hazarded the life of his consort, and the existence of his yet unborn child, merely for the purpose of wreaking his filial spite. That he caballed against the King's government, and comforted the avowed enemies of his family, at the time when the stability of the House of Hanover was imperilled, might possibly have been owing to faction or folly, and not to the gratification of a base and reckless malignity. These are shades which it is hardly worth while to discriminate in such a character. But without adopting the virulence of his mother,* there is abundant evidence that the character of the Prince of Wales was a compound of frivolity and baseness.

<small>Party jealousy.</small>

The Court of Leicester House maintained a rivalry with that of St. James's; and the aspirants to Court favour were perplexed by the necessity of making their election between the present and the future reign. Every man who paid his respects to the Heir was excluded from employment under the Sovereign; in like manner, the service of the King was disqualification for that of the Prince. The demise of the Crown had been, of course, ex-

---

* 'My dear Lord, I will give it you under my hand if you are in any fear of my relapsing; that my dear first-born is the greatest ass, and the greatest liar, and the greatest canaille, and the greatest beast in the whole world, and that I heartily wish he was out of it.'—*Queen Caroline to Lord Hervey.—Memoirs of Lord Hervey.*

pected by the heir-apparent with the greatest impatience. Eleven years before it took place, and at a time when neither the King's age, nor his state of health, offered any hope of its early approach, the Prince of Wales had taken the trouble to arrange the details of his intended administration.* His sudden death was a sad reverse to the worshippers of the rising sun; but they showed great promptitude and decision in repairing their misfortune. Of the many great and noble persons who had been devoted to the Prince of Wales, not a single British peer, temporal or spiritual, except those appointed to bear the pall, ventured to attend his remains to the grave. None of the royal family were present at the funeral.

The Opposition, which had been loosely held together by the name of the Prince, was dissolved at his death. Parliament ceased for a time to be the arena of party conflict, and the Government was jobbed on under the direction of the Duke of Newcastle and his brother, Mr. Pelham.

<small>The Opposition dissolved.</small>

The death of Pelham, in 1753, disturbed the smooth career of Government by corruption. There were at that time three men of high political mark, either of whom was fit for the lead of the House of Commons. These were Fox, Pitt, and Murray. The first may be described as a politician by profession, and he lived in days when public life was a lucrative calling. For many years he had enjoyed one of the richest places in the Government, that of Paymaster. He had made money; and now, like professional men of a certain standing, he looked to position and advancement. Experienced, able, and ready, Fox was the foremost of that class of public men from which ministers of state are ordinarily selected; and if he was distinguished for any quality, it was, that in a

<small>Death of Pelham. 1753</small>

* Diary of Bubb Dodington.

corrupt age he exhibited a preeminent contempt for public virtue.

The next was of a different mould. William Pitt was a genius for brilliant achievements, for extraordinary emergencies, for the salvation of a country.* As a statesman, Pitt can endure comparison with the greatest names of modern history. As an orator he is yet unrivalled; and to find his equal, we must ascend to the great masters of antiquity.

Such a panegyric may seem loose and extravagant. But the claim of Chatham to the character of a statesman rests no less on his unfinished designs, and on his opposition to the rash and shallow policy of the inferior men who supplanted or succeeded him, than on his political achievements. His fame, indeed, as a master of eloquence can be but imperfectly vindicated. Passages may be quoted, grand, affecting, and sublime; these, perhaps, can be matched in oratorical essays, which fell flat upon their audience;† but who shall do justice to those qualities which constitute the essence of oratory—countenance, voice, gesture—all that the Greek calls Action? Yet these were carried by Chatham to an excellence which has not been equalled in modern times.

Character of the Earl of Chatham. Pitt's character had many faults, and one above all, which is hardly consistent with true greatness. A vile affectation pervaded his whole conduct, and marred his real virtues. Contempt of gain was one of the traits which distinguished him in a corrupt and venal age. But not content with foregoing official perquisites which would have made his fortune, and appropriating only the salary which was his due, he must go down to the House of Commons and vaunt in tragic style how

---

* Pitt's magnanimous boast on a memorable occasion is well known, 'I am sure that I can save the country, and that nobody else can.'

† The oratorical discourses of Burke are performances of surpassing power; but, as speeches, they were hardly listened to, because the speaker had not the gift of delivery,—more rare than that of eloquent composition.

'those hands were clean.' On resigning office after his first great administration, he could not retire with his fame, but must convert a situation, full of dignity and interest, into a vulgar scene, by the ostentatious sale of his state equipages.

Sometimes, to produce an effect, he would seclude himself from public business, giving rare audience to a colleague, or some dignified emissary of the Court. Then, after due attendance, the doors were thrown open, and the visitor was ushered into a chamber, carefully prepared, where the Great Commoner himself sat with the robe of sickness artfully disposed around him. Occasionally, after a long absence, he would go down to the House in an imposing panoply of gout, make a great speech, and withdraw. *Chatham's affectation.*

At a later period, he affected almost regal state. His colleagues in office, including members of the great nobility, were expected to wait upon him; at one time he did not even deign to grant them audience, and went so far as to talk of communicating his policy to the House of Commons through a special agent of his own, unconnected with the responsible Government. The under-secretaries of state were expected to remain standing in his presence. When he went abroad he was attended by a great retinue; when he stopped at an inn he required all the servants of the establishment to wear his livery.*

Yet all this pride tumbled into the dust before royalty. Chatham's reverence for the sovereign was Oriental rather than English. After every allowance for the exaggeration of his style, it is still unpleasant to witness the self- *Chatham's reverence for royalty.*

---

* The story of Lord Chatham's dressing up the waiters and ostlers at the Castle Inn at Marlborough, in his livery, is confirmed by Lord J. Russell, who states that Lord Shelburne told the story to his son, the present Marquis of Lansdowne.—LORD JOHN RUSSELL's *Memoirs and Correspondence of Fox*, vol. i. p. 117.

abasement of such a spirit before George the Second and his successor. 'The weight of irremoveable royal displeasure,' said he, 'is a load too great to move under; it must crush any man; it has sunk and broke me. I succumb, and wish for nothing but a decent and innocent retreat.' * At the time when Pitt used this servile language he was the most considerable man in England, and on the eve of an administration that carried the power and glory of England to a height which it had never approached since the days of the Protector.

If it were just to resolve the character of such a man into detail, it would be easy to collect passages from the life of Chatham which should prove him a time-server, a trimmer, an apostate, a bully, a servile flatterer, an insolent contemner of royalty. All these elements are to be found in the composition, as poisons are to be detected in the finest bodies. But taken as a whole, a candid judgment must pronounce the character of Chatham to be one of striking grandeur, exhibiting the noblest qualities of the patriot, the statesman, and the orator.

Last of this distinguished triumvirate was William Murray, memorable, as long as the laws of England shall endure, by the title of Mansfield. He entered Parliament soon after Pitt, with a finished reputation from the other side of Westminster Hall. During the whole of the fourteen years that he passed in the House of Commons he was a law officer of the Crown; and, though in that subordinate capacity, so eminent were his parliamentary talents, that the defence of the Government principally devolved upon him. This position brought him into frequent conflict with Pitt; and though he yielded, like the rest, to the irresistible ascendancy of the Opposition leader, his concession was that of

Lord Mansfield.

* Pitt to Lord Hardwicke, April 6, 1751.—Chatham Correspondence.

moral, not of intellectual, inferiority. His eloquence
was, indeed, of the most sterling kind; in it knowledge, reasoning, composition, elocution, were combined in harmonious excellence; but it wanted a
coarser quality—that impetuous earnestness which,
whether real or simulated, is requisite for complete
success in a popular assembly; accordingly, it attained
its serene perfection on the judgment seat, and in the
Upper House of Parliament. Still, overborne as he
was by the towering genius of his rival, Murray
failed not to vindicate his high pretensions; and all
men assented to the probability and the propriety of
his advancement to the most important office in the
State.

The choice between these eminent persons rested
chiefly with the Duke of Newcastle, a
man whose absurd manner has exposed *The Duke of Newcastle as a statesman.*
him to ridicule, but who really was not
the strange compound of knave and fool which his
character has been represented. Newcastle was far,
indeed, from being a competent minister, but duller
men have filled his office both before and since, and
obtained a respectable place in history. He was the
successor of Walpole in the management of that
machinery of corruption by which the Government
was carried on. Himself a large borough proprietor,
he had a principal share in the traffic for seats in the
House of Commons. Reserving to his own management exclusively the distribution of places, and the
dispensation of the Secret Service fund, he administered this department with considerable skill and
tact. His maxim was to avoid giving offence to, or
breaking with, any man, however inconsiderable.
Those whom he was unable or unwilling to gratify,
he held on by promises or caresses. He evinced a
shrewd perception of the characters with which he
had to deal. At the time when he was doing everything in his power to supplant Pitt, he affected to

carry on a confidential correspondence with him, to whisper State secrets in his ear, to pay the utmost deference to his judgment, and, above all, to ply the King's name—a spell which never failed in its influence upon the Great Commoner. Newcastle is a remarkable instance of the success which usually attends the unwearied pursuit of one object. Without parts or knowledge, or any higher quality of a statesman; notoriously false, fickle, and timid; grotesque in deportment, and absurd in speech, this man contrived to outwit his competitors, and to maintain his position at the head of affairs during a long official life. His rank, and lavish expenditure in purchasing boroughs, were, no doubt, considerable advantages; but he had little other adventitious aid. He was not, as he has been sometimes represented, the head of the Whig party; for that party, since the Revolution, had been broken up into several sections or clans, as they are termed by a contemporary writer of the highest authority;* and Newcastle influenced only one, although perhaps the largest, of its divisions.

Newcastle's policy. Jealous of power, and conscious, it may be supposed, of intrinsic weakness, it was Newcastle's policy to have no partner in the Government, but to conduct the public business in Parliament through the medium of agents, who, without having access to the Sovereign, or any independent voice in council, should receive their instructions from him alone. While Pelham lived, such an arrangement was practicable; although the Duke's tenacious jealousy of power had, at one time, nearly caused a rupture between the brothers. The difficulty now was to induce either of the distinguished men who stood prominently forward as candidates for office, to accept it on such terms. Newcastle dared

* Lord Waldegrave's Memoirs.

not hint such a proposition to Pitt, and the King's
known repugnance to that statesman was an obstacle,
the force of which he himself had fully acknowledged.
Murray firmly refused any office out of the line of
professional promotion. There remained only Fox,
who, though the least able, was the most eligible of
the three. Public opinion had designated him as the
probable successor of Pelham; and he had, what the
others wanted, a large political following.

To Fox, therefore, the Duke addressed himself,
through the agency of a common friend, *Newcastle addresses himself to Fox.*
the Marquis of Hartington, afterwards
Duke of Devonshire. The terms were
unusually liberal: a secretaryship of state, a seat in
the Cabinet, the lead of the House of Commons, and,
above all, information as to the expenditure of the
Secret Service Money. This fund was then the key
to political power, being chiefly employed in purchasing boroughs and bribing members of Parliament. By these means, Newcastle had procured a
House of Commons subservient to his purposes; and,
at the eve of a new election, it was more than ever
important to retain a firm hold of this potent instrument of corruption. No sooner, therefore, had he
made his proposal to Fox, than he began to fear he
had parted with too large a share of power, and he
hastened to qualify his offer. 'He had meant,' he
said, 'to keep the disposal of the Secret Service
Money to himself.' Fox, with his strong sense, immediately pointed out the inconvenience of such
reserve. 'How was he to manage the House of
Commons, unless he knew who had been bribed
and who had not?' But remonstrance and reason
were in vain addressed to the Duke of Newcastle.
A panic had seized him; and he resolved to retain
the secret service, the patronage of office, and the
nomination of ministerial boroughs entirely in his
own hands.

It was hardly possible for any man of spirit to accept high responsible office upon such conditions. But Fox was not scrupulous, and never thought of hastily breaking off the negotiation upon anything like a punctilio. He consulted his friends, however, and finding them unanimous against his assent to Newcastle's proposal, he wrote to the Duke, resigning the seals which he had agreed to accept the day before. The Duke, delighted no doubt at being relieved from a colleague who, instead of an official hack, threatened to turn out a formidable competitor for power, would have no more to do with statesmen and orators, but forthwith conferred the seals of office upon Sir Thomas Robinson, a diplomatist whose knowledge of public affairs was confined to the petty politics of the German courts, in which he had practised. To conciliate Pitt, places were given to his only followers, Sir George Lyttelton and Grenville. Murray was satisfied by the appointment of Attorney-General, which happily then became vacant. Pitt and Fox consented to remain in the subordinate offices of Paymaster and Secretary-at-War, the new Parliament was constituted pretty much as its predecessor had been, and the Duke and his royal master congratulated themselves on the satisfactory settlement which had been effected.

Negotiations with Fox.

Such an adjustment of places could, however, hardly be durable. Pitt and Fox made common cause against a ministry which excluded them from prominent positions. The Paymaster of the Forces assailed the Attorney-General; the Secretary-at-War turned the Leader of the House of Commons into ridicule; or, as was observed by a spectator, assisted him in performing that office for himself. Acts of insubordination and mutiny, which had been visited, from the highest to the lowest, with prompt and unmitigated severity, when an Imperial mind directed the councils of the

Quarrels among the new ministers.

nation, were now perpetrated with utter impunity, under the weak, irresolute rule of the successors of Walpole. The policy of cowardice and incapacity was resorted to. Overtures were again made to one of the powerful malcontents, through the medium of the Earl Waldegrave, a nobleman who stood high in the estimation of all parties, and possessed what hardly any other public man at that time could boast of, the confidence of the King.

Waldegrave represented to Newcastle the impossibility of carrying on the Government against the alliance of the two great parliamentary chieftains; and he sought to attach Fox to the administration on terms still less favourable than those last offered by the Duke, by assuring him that there was no disposition in the highest quarter to engage his services. Fox, whose appetite for power was not easily disgusted, consented, under such circumstances, to take a seat in the Cabinet, without the post of Secretary of State, and without the recognised lead of the House of Commons.

Events soon occurred to try the vigour and administrative ability of the reconstructed Government. The ancient enmity of France and England threatened an immediate outbreak. The race for empire, which had already commenced on the vast continent of Asia, and on that of the New World, had become bitter contention, and war was inevitable.

Early in 1755, the House of Commons received a message from the crown, asking for a vote of credit, to put the establishments on a war footing. This was readily granted; *Preparations for war. Supineness of the King.* and the King shortly after left the country on his annual visit to Hanover. The impropriety of absenting himself from the seat of empire under such circumstances, was in vain urged upon a selfish and un-English sovereign. The unsettled state of affairs at home, the commencement of war, the weakness of

the Ministry, were considerations which could not
outweigh the personal predilections and convenience
of the German King of England. In peaceful times,
a great nation will maintain its prosperity in spite of
the supineness and incapacity of its rulers, to whom,
in consequence, a thoughtless public opinion attributes the praise of wise government. But when a
state of war demands active and decided measures,
the real character of administration is discovered.
The imbecility of the person who held the first place
in the Council of St. James's, therefore, now became
signally manifest. The British interests at the Court
of France, then the most important, if not the only
important diplomatic post in Europe, had been for
many years entrusted to a fop; and thus, those delicate questions of colonial territory which were in
dispute between the two Governments, and which
might have been adjusted by negotiation, were
necessarily referred to the disastrous arbitrement
of war.

Yet, while the dire necessity was recognised, the
operations were undertaken with a hesitation and timidity which argued little for
the success or glory of England; and, what
was worse, they were characterised by a futile dissimulation, which cast a stain upon her honour.
An expedition was sent out after a French fleet,
supposed to be destined for North America. An
engagement took place, resulting in the capture of
two French ships of the line, and the withdrawal of
the French ambassador from London. A second expedition was despatched under Sir Edward Hawke,
whose instructions were the subject of ridiculous
perplexity to the Government. Newcastle character-
istically proposed a course by which the responsibility should be shifted from the Ministry upon the
brave officer in command. But this being opposed
by Fox, on the ground that the Admiral had too

much sense to act without definite orders, instructions, more intelligible indeed, but falling far short of the stern policy of war, were at last agreed upon. The Admiral was to attack any ships of the line that he might *happen* to fall in with, but he was to spare those of inferior rate, and not to molest trading vessels at all. A pitiful attempt to accommodate naval operations to an impossible condition of compromise between war and peace! However, these absurd instructions were shortly afterwards superseded by orders to attack every Frenchman in the channel; and many captures were consequently made. But these proceedings having taken place without a declaration of war, were treated by the French Government as a violation of public law; and so desirous were they that the whole odium of such an act should attach to the British flag, that they released an English man-of-war which had fallen into the hands of their cruisers.

Meanwhile, it was as Elector of Hanover and not as King of England, that George the Second viewed the prospect of war. England, <small>Conduct of the King.</small> which had no positive interest in maintaining the integrity of Hanover, had for a series of years subsidised other German States for the protection of the Electoral territory. The first thing, therefore, which the King did, without even consulting the English Ministry, was, on the threatened rupture, to enter into a subsidiary treaty with the principality of Hesse, and to open a negotiation with Russia for the same purpose. The Hessian treaty was sent home for official ratification. But public indignation at this gross abuse of the national resources, had now begun to manifest itself in deep murmurs; and one of the ministers, Legge, Chancellor of the Exchequer, whether apprehensive of the coming storm, or arrived at the utmost limit of complaisance, positively refused in Council to attach his signature to the

Treasury warrants for the subsidy, which had already been signed by the Lord Chancellor, by Newcastle, and other members of the Council of Regency.
Lord Chatham applied to. The Duke, astounded and terrified by this unexpected act of insubordination, hurried away, in his crazy manner, to Pitt, and endeavoured to gain him over by tears, by adulation, by an offer of a seat in the Cabinet, and other promises of the most alluring character. But the great parliamentary chief gave the Duke plainly to understand that nothing would satisfy him short of a full measure of ministerial power; that he was ready to support a national war, and to defend Hanover if the enemy's attack should be made on that quarter; but that he did not consider the system of subsidies a proper and efficient mode of carrying on war. He added, however, that if the King's honour was pledged to the Hessian subsidy he would not object to it; but he positively refused to consent to the Russian treaty.

Pitt being found impracticable, it only remained to bid for Fox, whose value was thus raised in the official market. The seals of Secretary of State, with the lead of the House of Commons, were, therefore, yielded to him without further parley; and
Fox becomes Secretary of State. Sir Thomas Robinson was removed to his former and more congenial office of Master of the Great Wardrobe.

The first act of the Government, after Fox's
Pitt, Legge, and Grenville dismissed. accession to real power, was one of mistimed vigour—the dismissal, namely, of Pitt, Legge, and Grenville. By this proceeding, an open breach was made with the men enjoying the largest share of parliamentary fame and of public confidence. But a packed and corrupted parliament reflected dimly, and through a distorted medium, the sense of the nation. In vain was heard the stirring eloquence of Pitt, backed by

the applause of the people. The Government was supported by a majority, the strength of which was in an inverse ratio with that of its merit, or the wisdom of its measures. France threatened, by invasion, to chastise the perfidy of Albion, and insult her weakness. England, acknowledging the danger, instead of relying on her wooden walls and her hardy sons, sought the protection of foreign mercenaries; and an address to the Crown to send for Hanoverian and Hessian troops was carried by as great a majority, as could support a measure the most conducive to the honour and safety of the realm.

The military strength of France was computed, at this time, at two hundred thousand men, besides militia; and she was preparing a naval force of sixty sail of the line.* In America, her colonists, though inferior in wealth and numbers to those of this country, were for the most part trained to arms; and she had a chain of forts in the rear of the English settlements, which lay open and defenceless.†

England had neither soldiers nor sailors. She was forced to send to Germany for the former, and she had not enough of the latter to man the Western squadron.‡ Her possessions in the Mediterranean—Gibraltar and Minorca, each invaluable as a base for naval operations—were all but defenceless. Such was the state to which the country had been reduced by selfish and corrupt factions. The nation itself was sound at heart; and if its feelings and wishes could have been represented in Parliament, the policy of the country would never have been guided by German court cabals, nor her interests postponed to the vile intrigues of the Newcastles, the Foxes, and the Dodingtons.

* Mitchell to Lord Holderness, Dresden, December 9, 1756. Chatham Correspondence.
† Waldegrave's Memoirs.
‡ Ibid.

A French expedition was fitted out at Toulon, destined as it soon appeared for an attack on Minorca; and a declaration of war was at length promulgated in London a few hours before the fleets of both nations came into conflict in the waters of the Mediterranean. Newcastle seemed to have found a kindred spirit in the officer whom he sent in command of the squadron dispatched for the relief of Minorca. I need not here repeat the well-known history of Byng's misconduct. Whether it was owing to imbecility or cowardice that he failed to finish a battle which West, the second in command, had half won; or, that he balanced, with a nicety unusual in a British admiral, the difference in weight of metal between himself and the enemy, is a question of little moment. Certain it is that he abandoned the object of his expedition, which, it must be remembered, was the maintenance of an important possession, not only without adequate cause, but when there was at least a fair prospect of success. Blakeney, the aged veteran, who was left in command at Minorca, did all that military skill and courage could effect with a wholly inadequate force; but, deserted at sea, it was in vain that he protracted the struggle. Minorca was consequently lost.

Hostilities commenced by France. 1756

Minorca lost.

The English nation, impatient at all times of reverses, was transported with rage at the dishonour brought upon their arms. Byng's delinquency was so flagrant that the people were at a loss whether to attribute it to treachery or cowardice; in either case, there seemed to be but one expiation for his offence.

The mismanagement of affairs both at home and abroad had not only imperilled the integrity of the empire, but the stability of social order. Tumult and sedition prevailed throughout the country; and the language of the 'dutiful and loyal addresses' which were brought to the foot of the throne resembled that of 1641.*

The court-martial acquitted Byng of treachery or cowardice, but condemned him to death for a breach of the twelfth article of war in having failed in his duty. Their sentence was accompanied, however, by a strong recommendation to mercy. There can be no doubt that this recommendation ought to have prevailed. The unhappy offender was completely exonerated from the only charge, which, according even to the rigorous exigency of the service, could justly affect life—that, namely, of wilful betrayal of his trust. But the probability is that the life of this incompetent officer was sacrificed not so much to a stern sense of duty and policy, as to a selfish and cowardly concession to that indiscriminating cry for vengeance which, directed full against the prominent offender, passed by those who were, at least, accomplices in his guilt. *Admiral Byng shot.*

A few days before the attack on Minorca, France, departing from her ancient policy, entered into an offensive alliance with Austria. The immediate causes of this great event were, possibly, those usually assigned by historians.† But though Maria Theresa had never stooped to flatter, nor Frederick to insult, the French King's mistress, the altered state of Europe would probably have brought about, at this period, a change in her political relations. The house of Hapsburg no longer possessed that gigantic power against which France had long to struggle for a separate existence. Prussia, from a petty dukedom, had, within little more than half a century, attained the position of a powerful monarchy. Russia, emerged from barbarism, had taken up a foremost place in the European system. *Offensive alliance between France and Austria.*

---

* Waldegrave's Memoirs.
† Frederick's repeated insults to Louis the Fifteenth and the Mistress Pompadour. See Lord Stanhope's History, vol. iv. pp. 74–6.

But the real danger which threatened the balance of power at this moment was not the aggression of Austria, but the ambition and the capacity of the Prussian monarch. He had already wrested Silesia, one of its fairest provinces, from the dominion of Maria Theresa. He had invaded Bohemia and occupied Dresden. The annihilation of this new and formidable power was therefore the object proposed by the union of these ancient rivals now threatened by a common foe. Russia, liberated from her engagements with England, soon after joined the allied powers.

England was thus, by stress of circumstances, forced into an alliance with Prussia, which now stood alone in Europe against the confederation of the three great Powers. If personal feelings had prevailed, nothing could have been more gratifying to the Court of Great Britain than the humiliation of the Prussian monarch, who had thwarted its policy, who had succoured the Pretender,[*] and had harassed George the Second, both by menacing his German dominions and treating him personally with a degree of derision and contumely exceeding even that which he had lavished on Madame de Pompadour. But by the mutability of human affairs, which sets at nought all political prediction, the Sovereign, whose unprincipled ambition had endangered Hanover, was now to be its defender—the upholder of Popery and arbitrary power, although really a professed scoffer at all creeds, was now to be the popular idol under the endearing title of the Protestant hero.

Thus commenced that great struggle known in history by the name of the Seven Years' War. And never, certainly, were the commanding qualities of

[*] 'The King of Prussia is now avowedly the principal, if not the sole support of the Pretender and of the Jacobite cause.'—*Duke of Newcastle to Lord Chancellor, September* 21, 1753.—Coxe's *Pelham*.

the human mind exhibited with more sustained power than by Frederick the Great during this memorable period. Unshaken fortitude under reverses; prompt energy in repairing them; the happiest combination of military talents with administrative capacity,—distinguished this remarkable man, whose whole career is one of the most striking illustrations on record of what resolution, combined with intellectual power, can effect.

The dissolution of Newcastle's administration was the necessary consequence of a state of affairs which demanded able and vigorous councils. Dissolution of the Ministry. The only members of the Government who could have sustained it under such a pressure were determined to withdraw from the unthankful task. Murray, always intent upon professional advancement, claimed the vacant post of Chief Justice, to which he was preeminently entitled. The Duke, seeing the defenceless condition in which he should be left by the removal of his ablest champion from the House of Commons, used all his wonted arts to avert the disaster; but the Attorney-General was immoveable, and threatened to leave the Government, unless he was gratified by the special promotion which he desired. Fox, thus deprived of his able coadjutor, cared not to encounter single-handed the aspiring leader of Opposition, whose appetite for power was now sharpened by recent privation of office. The Secretary, moreover, had little inducement beyond the mere emolument to remain in the Government. The first minister hardly admitted him to a share in council, though willing to impose upon him the fullest measure of responsibility. The King treated him with rudeness and contempt.* Prudence, therefore, concurred with pride, in dictating a retreat from a position which was neither respectable nor tenable.

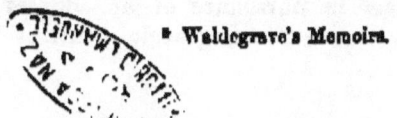

* Waldegrave's Memoirs.

A few days before the meeting of Parliament, Murray was transferred to the Upper House, and Fox ceased to be Secretary of State.

Newcastle still clung, with convulsive grasp, to power. He made a futile effort to gain over Pitt; but the great orator was too sensible of his commanding position to compromise it by a negotiation with the veteran placeman. Lord Egmont, an able speaker, and conversant with affairs, was next applied to; but, like all the other public men of the day, he never thought of postponing a personal object to the exigencies of the public service. He wanted an English peerage, and, as he insisted upon this condition at the very time when his aid was wanted in the House of Commons, it was useless to carry on the treaty. Lastly, the old rival of Walpole—the witty, classic, and accomplished Granville—was offered the post of danger, the Duke proposing to take the Earl's equally dignified, but less conspicuous, place of President of the Council. Granville, however, was no longer susceptible to such temptation.

The Duke had exhausted all his resources; and the dreaded hour of resignation could no longer be deferred. After some negotiation, which resulted in the exclusion of Fox, with whom Pitt refused to act, a new administration was formed under the auspices of the Duke of Devonshire, with Pitt, Secretary of State, and his kinsman, Lord Temple, First Lord of the Admiralty. Pitt, however, was the real minister; and his vigorous councils are discernible in the earliest acts of the new Government. The speech, on opening Parliament, expressly referred to the menacing and almost seditious addresses of the summer in terms of approbation, and announced the dismissal of the German mercenaries who had been brought over in pursuance of an address of both Houses, under the late disgraceful panic of invasion. A national militia was to be substituted as the more becoming and efficient defence of the realm. The forces, both at sea and land, were largely augmented. Another measure was the organisation of the disaffected, half-disciplined, Highland clans into regiments of the line for foreign service. By this fine stroke of policy, sufficient of itself to mark its projector as a master-statesman, a nucleus of rebellion and civil war was eradicated once and for ever—a paralytic member was converted immediately into an arm of strength. From that hour, the cause of the Pretender was extinguished in Scotland.

The King, however, regardless or unconscious of these great merits, could only feel repugnance to the disagreeable manner of his minister. The stability of the throne secured; the honour of his arms vindicated; the confidence of the nation gained:—what were these considerations weighed against errors of tact and taste? Pitt's formal, affected, oratorical style was no doubt wearisome enough when carried into the closet, and Temple's pedantry and arrogance were, perhaps, still more offensive. To His Majesty they were intolerable: 'I must get rid of these scoundrels,' said he to the courtly Waldegrave; 'I do not consider myself a king while I am in their hands.' Accordingly Temple and Pitt were dismissed, and Waldegrave was commissioned to treat with the Duke of Newcastle once more. The Duke, distracted between his love of power and his dread of responsibility, could decide on nothing. On the one hand, he had a secure parliamentary majority composed of his own nominees and mercenaries, closely attached to him for the same reason that all servants are attached to a good place and a liberal master. On the other side he was scared by his consciousness of utter inability to meet the difficulties of public

Pitt becomes personally distasteful to the King.

affairs, and the menacing tone of popular discontent. He had found the great parliamentary leaders impracticable. To ally himself now with Fox, weighed down as he was with odium, would only be to court weakness. Pitt, confident in consummate ability and unbounded popularity, treated his overtures with such contempt, that he pledged his word to the King he would never again propose him as a colleague. At last he resolved to rely upon his parliamentary following. Sir Thomas Robinson was reluctantly dragged once more from his obscurity to be set up again as Secretary of State. The office of Chancellor of the Exchequer, after being refused by Bubb Dodington, was to be conferred on Dr. Lee. This arrangement was about to be carried into effect after the country had been left three months without a government, when the Earl of Chesterfield, who had long retired from the strife of party, and now entertained the most serious apprehension for the safety of the nation, was prompted by public spirit to interpose, for the purpose of combining the only available elements of an effective administration. The parliamentary influence of Newcastle and the commanding ability of Pitt must be united. This was obviously the best, if not the only practicable, mode of carrying on the public service. Lord Bute, as the representative of the Princess of Wales and the heir-apparent, co-operated with Chesterfield in this desirable object. Both Newcastle and Pitt were found accessible to a proposal from a mediation so respectable. The King alone refused his assent, and called upon the Duke to redeem his recent promise never again to act with Mr. Pitt. A pledge by one statesman never to act with another is, to the last degree, rash and short-sighted; but, inasmuch as it is what legists call *nudum pactum*, or a promise made without consideration, it would be a mistaken sense of personal

Intrigues for a new administration.

honour which should allow it to weigh against the
exigency of public duty. Doubtless the Duke of
Newcastle did not trouble himself with the casuistry
of the question; he only saw and eagerly availed
himself of a mode of escape from difficulty. So
far, therefore, from adhering to his promise, if such
it can be termed, he not only repudiated it without
hesitation or evasion, but emboldened by the character and credit of his new supporters, he positively
refused to have anything to do with the administration, *except* in connection with Pitt and his party.

The King, enraged at what he considered perfidy,
as well as personal ill-usage, again sent for
Waldegrave, and laid his commands upon
that loyal friend and servant to place himself at the
head of a new administration. Waldegrave obeyed,
though with sincere reluctance, and had made considerable progress in accomplishing the duty entrusted
to him, when Newcastle, alarmed at the sight of a
government being constructed without his assistance, employed his influence secretly to thwart the
new arrangement, protesting, at the same time, with
gratuitous treachery, both to his royal master and
the new minister, that he should be injured by any
suspicion of such conduct. His intrigues, however,
were successful; the King himself at last saw that
a Waldegrave ministry was impracticable, and that
there was no alternative but to submit to the coalition of parliamentary corruption with statesmanlike
capacity and popular favour.

[margin: Waldegrave sent for.]

The final arrangements were easily made through
the dignified agency of Lord Mansfield and
Lord Hardwicke. The Duke was rein-
stated at the head of the Government, but really
only with the superintendence of that machinery of
corruption by which the routine of Government had
for many years been carried on, but with which
his colleague, with a contemptuous affectation of

[margin: A new adminis- tration formed.]

ignorance in such delicate matters of policy, declined to interfere. All real power was centred in the hands of Pitt, and now his great genius had for the first time ample scope, both in opportunity and in the means of action.

Pitt elevated to power.

At this period, the fortunes of the country were at their lowest point. Chesterfield and other eminent men considered them irretrievable. The administration of public affairs, passing for a series of years through the foul channels of parliamentary corruption, had at last become almost stagnant. The people believed, not without cause, that every politician was a mere self-seeker; and that the interests of the nation were sacrificed to the foreign connections of the reigning family. Pitt alone, of all the public men, possessed the confidence of the country; yet so deficient was its representation in the House of Commons, that, on his accession to office a few months previously, he had great difficulty in procuring a seat in that assembly. The principal cities and boroughs of the empire could present him with their freedom, but the elective franchise was out of their power. That was the property of the Duke of Newcastle, and of the great heads of parties with whom the patriot minister had no connection.

Contemporaneously with Pitt's elevation to power, took place the disastrous battle of Kolin, by which the cause of Frederick, England's only ally, seemed hopelessly ruined. This was followed shortly afterwards by the utter discomfiture of the Duke of Cumberland in Hanover, and the convention of Closterseven, by which his army was disbanded.

Battle of Kolin.

In America, the English flag had been dislodged from a position of great importance. The fort of Oswego, on the Lake Ontario, commanding the great maritime highway of North America, and the communication between the northern

Affairs in America.

and southern colonies of France, was taken, almost without resistance; and with it, sixteen hundred men, one hundred pieces of cannon, together with a great amount of military stores and provisions, fell into the hands of the enemy.

Such was the state of the empire when consigned to the care of Pitt:—Dispossessed of her principal military position in America; of her only harbour in the Mediterranean; driven from the Continent; the seat of empire menaced; her military fame disparaged; the policy no less than the arms of her ancient enemy triumphant in every quarter of the globe. But though politicians were dismayed, the public spirit bore up undaunted under this accumulation of misfortune: and the cry was not for concession or compromise, but for redress of grievances, and the vindication of the national honour.

The season for active military operations was far advanced when Pitt came into power. Nevertheless, immediate measures were taken for relieving the pressure upon the arms of England and of her heroic ally, the King of Prussia, by an important diversion. Early in September, an expedition sailed for the coast of France, with orders to make a descent upon Rochefort, which contained one of her principal naval magazines. But the enterprise wholly failed, in consequence of the jealousies and misconduct of the officers in command. They had every reason to believe that a prompt attack would find the place comparatively defenceless. Yet the General's chief concern was, in possibility of failure, to secure a safe retreat to the ships; and because the Admiral could not undertake to provide for an event, which must always depend upon the winds and waves, instead of an attack, the precious time was occupied by councils of war. While these councils were deliberating, preparations for defence were being made; the opportunity was

Expedition against Rochefort. Its failure.

lost, and the fleet sailed homeward, followed by the derision of the foe.

Some critics, whose judgment is formed by the event, have censured this expedition as rash and ill-planned. But according to the better opinion, the scheme was perfectly feasible, and, in fact, must have succeeded, had the General in command acted with promptitude and decision, or even in accordance with his orders. The French monarch, knowing the defenceless condition of the place, took it for granted that it had fallen, as soon as he heard of the projected attack;* and one of the ablest officers of the expedition, one who afterwards achieved the highest professional distinction, expressed his amazement at the infatuation of its leader.†

Return of the fleet. The return of the fleet without having effected their object, or hardly made an attempt towards it, was greeted, as well it might be, with a burst of public indignation. It was affirmed, and extensively believed, even by persons of ordinary intelligence and information, that Mordaunt and Hawke, the General and Admiral in command, had acted in pursuance of secret orders, without the knowledge of the responsible minister; and that the honour and interests of England had been sacrificed on this occasion, as they were by the treaty of Closterseven, to the sole object of purchasing the immunity of Hanover.‡ But both disasters can be accounted for, without impugning the honour of the officers in command on these occasions. The military incapacity of the Duke of Cumberland was sufficient to mar the prospects of a campaign far more hopeful than that which he directed; but the treacherous and pusillanimous policy, thus attributed

---

* Jenkinson to Grenville, October 18, 1761.—Grenville Correspondence.
† Rodney to Grenville.
‡ Potter to Pitt, October 11, 1757.— Chatham Correspondence. Horace Walpole to General Conway.—Walpole Correspondence.

to him and to his father, was utterly foreign to the
character of the princes of the House of Brunswick.
So far from being a party to the evacuation of Germany, the King refused to ratify the treaty under
which it had been made; and the Duke himself,
though the King's favourite son, and admitted to all
his counsels, was so much aggrieved by the stern displeasure which he experienced on his return, that he
resigned all his appointments and retired from public
life.

The failure of the Rochefort expedition may well
be ascribed to the evils of a divided command. But there were other causes, Causes of failure at Rochefort.
which had long depressed the tone of
military intelligence and energy. The system of
promotion by seniority, which then obtained in the
British service, was not calculated to bring forward
merit; and the evasion of responsibility, which characterised the feeble plans and hesitating orders of
the Government, had taught the routine leaders of
our fleets and armies to consult their own safety, by
a cautious adherence to the strict line of duty, rather
than the pride of their profession and the glory of
their country by a more daring course. But the
fortunes of the empire were now guided by a statesman 'who sought for merit wherever it was to be
found,' and to whose favour or indulgence the only
recommendations were zeal and enterprise in the
public service.

Before the failure of the Rochefort expedition, the
prompt energy of Pitt had devised a plan Plan for recovering Minorca.
for the recovery of that important post
which had been wrested from England under circumstances so disgraceful to her arms. He instructed
the British minister at Madrid to propose the cession
of Gibraltar to Spain, in consideration of her assistance in the recovery of Minorca. The great natural
fortress which commands the entrance to the Mediterranean, is, perhaps, the last military possession

which a government of the present day would think of relinquishing; but it might have been argued, that it was of little use to command the entrance to the Mediterranean when we did not possess a single harbour or haven in that wide sea; and the necessity of regaining Minorca was a primary and urgent consideration. The able and experienced diplomatist,* to whom the treaty was entrusted, was, however, astounded at such a rash scheme; and, certainly, a more improvident device to procure present relief was never conceived by the most reckless speculator. Had it been carried into effect, the object might, indeed, have been immediately gained, but at no distant day must have been entirely frustrated. To maintain any possessions in waters, our only access to which was to be at the pleasure of a power no longer capable of exercising an independent policy, even if there had been reason to suppose that such policy would be in accordance with British interests, was manifestly impracticable; the consequence must have been the conversion of the Mediterranean into a French lake, the annihilation of our commerce with the greater part of the European continent, and ultimately the prevention of that direct communication with our Eastern empire which has so greatly enhanced its value.

The proposition, however, was, happily, not entertained; and it so chanced that its disappointment was owing to the ill humour of that Court of Spain upon the continuance of whose friendly relations the policy of such a measure must have been originally calculated.

This was the only war measure open to any considerable censure. One of the most efficient means of prosecuting the war was to assist the able and indomitable chief,

<small>Pitt's vigorous prosecution of the war.</small>

* Sir B. Keene. — Chatham Correspondence.

who, beaten and apparently ruined one day, showed again victorious the next. Pitt had no soldiers to send the King of Prussia; but he was prompt in procuring him a subsidy. At the same time, he reconstructed the Duke of Cumberland's late army of Hanover; and, luckily, the infraction of the treaty of Closterseven by the French in some important particulars, enabled him to do so without incurring for the country the reproach of a breach of faith. This force, amounting to about fifty thousand men, was taken into British pay, and at its head was placed, on the recommendation of the King of Prussia, his nephew and one of his ablest lieutenants, Prince Ferdinand of Brunswick.

Early in the year following, another expedition was sent to the coast of France; and though the immediate success of this armament was not commensurate with the magnitude of its equipment, its indirect, but main object, the diversion of the French force from a concentrated energy on the Continent, was fully accomplished. While the British fleet was menacing the coast of France, Prince Ferdinand was enabled to recover Hanover. *Hanover recovered.*

At the same time, on the continent of the New World, vigorous efforts were commenced for the entire expulsion of the French. To dislodge them from the island of Cape Breton, commanding the entrance to the great river which formed the highway of North America, was the object of the best-appointed expedition. Admiral Boscawen commanded the fleet; and General Amherst superseded the Earl of Loudoun, an officer of proved incompetence, in the command of the land forces. His second in command was a young regimental officer, who had signalized his zeal and capacity at the siege of Rochefort, the preceding year. This was Brigadier-General Wolfe. *Expedition to North America.*

General Abercrombie, who commanded at New
York, was also ordered to reduce the forts
of Ticonderago and Crown Point, on the
Lakes George and Champlain, and so penetrate into
Canada from the south-eastern point of the American
continent; while a smaller force under Brigadier
Forbes was detached from Philadelphia against Fort
Duquesne, another strong and almost inaccessible
French post.

General Abercrombie.

The most important of these operations was completely successful. After an obstinate resistance, Cape Breton surrendered, as did also St. John's, since called Prince Edward's Island. The attack on the fortified lakes was mismanaged, and ended in failure. But Forbes, by great perseverance and gallantry, captured Duquesne, which, in compliment to the great minister, he called Pittsburg, a name which it still retains, although no longer a possession of the British crown.

Cape Breton taken.

Thus a few months, under the administration of an able and energetic statesman, were sufficient to redeem the country from her depressed and apparently impotent condition. But Pitt did not stop here; having engaged in war, he carried it on with unabated vigour, until success should enable him to conclude a permanent and honourable peace. The nation cheerfully submitted to the unparalleled burdens which their favourite minister unhesitatingly imposed upon it, and seemed to have given him an unlimited commission to restore and maintain its honour and glory.

Improvement in affairs.

Early in 1759, the Government of France, whose coast had been so grievously harassed the preceding year by the British arms, took measures to retaliate by a descent upon England. But the principal ports of the enemy were blockaded or watched by English squadrons. Havre was bombarded by Rodney. Boscawen routed the

Blockade of French coast.

Toulon fleet. Hawke blockaded Brest. A powerful squadron rode in the Channel. The internal defences were amply provided for both by a regular and a militia force.

The offensive operations consisted chiefly of an attack upon the French possessions in the West Indies, and the conquest of Canada, by which England would obtain an undivided empire in the great northern division of the American continent. *Expedition to the West Indies.*

The former, a small expedition, had an adequate result in the acquisition of Guadaloupe, one of the most valuable islands in the West India Archipelago. But the second great enterprise was planned by the minister himself, with the utmost care, and furnished with every means of success. *Capture of Guadaloupe.*

The principle of the scheme was to divert the enemy from a concentration of force upon any given point. Separate attacks were to be made upon Lower Canada by expeditions, one of which was immediately, and the other circuitously, directed against Quebec. A third division of the invading armament was detached upon the distant forts of Niagara, to cut off the communications between Canada and Louisiana. To General Amherst was given the command in chief, with the particular service of accomplishing that arduous duty which had failed the preceding year in the less competent hands of Abercrombie. General Wolfe was to enter the St. Lawrence from the sea, a course now open to an English squadron, in consequence of the reduction of Cape Breton the year before; and was to proceed forthwith to form the siege of Quebec. The ardent mind, which planned this extensive scheme, unfitted to regard difficulties in detail, calculated upon the junction of the forces under Amherst, their task being completed, with those of Wolfe before Quebec. *Expedition to Canada.*

VOL. I. D

Could such a junction be effected, it was not disputed that the capital of Lower Canada must fall. But prudence, as usual, censured a plan, the success of which depended on a favourable concurrence of circumstances. Amherst had not only to encounter the well-appointed garrisons of Ticonderago and Crown Point, elated by the successes of the preceding year; but these overcome, he would probably have to deal with the opposition, hardly less formidable, of the elements and season. And so, in fact, it turned out. The Lakes George and Champlain communicate with each other by a narrow channel, at either extremity of which is a fort. That of Ticonderago covers Lake George; Crown Point is at the entrance of Champlain. These forts were successively abandoned by the enemy, who took up a strong position in a small island at the northern end of Lake Champlain, and commanding the channel, or river, Richelieu, by which it communicates with the St. Lawrence. It became necessary, therefore, to provide naval power to force the passage of this river. Before these preparations could be completed, the season was too far advanced to admit of active operations; and Amherst, after having been twice baffled by storms in attempting to transport his troops up the lake, was obliged to go into winter quarters.

Thus the grand object of the expedition, the taking of Quebec, was left to the unaided resources of the young officer who was second in command; and there can be no doubt, from his having assigned this, the most important duty, to Wolfe, that the minister had fully calculated upon, and was content to abide, such an event.

General Wolfe.

A few words will suffice to show the difficulties which Wolfe surmounted. The city of Quebec is built upon high ground, rising almost perpendicularly from the water. On the north it is bounded by the River St. Charles; on the

City of Quebec.

east and south by the great St. Lawrence. Its fortifications were inconsiderable, its strength being chiefly that of natural situation. The French commandant, Montcalm, an officer of experience and reputation, had entrenched himself in the quarter from which the city was most accessible. Interposed between him and the city was the St. Charles. Deep woods were in his rear, and his lines were completed by the angle formed by the junction of the River Montmorency with the St. Lawrence. By these skilful dispositions, he seemed to have provided alike for the safety of his army and for that of Quebec. Wolfe had taken possession of the Isle of Orleans, a large island opposite Quebec, and opposite, likewise, to Montcalm's position. Having seven thousand good English troops under his command, he was desirous to give battle to the enemy, who, though numerically his superior, had a very small proportion of regular soldiery. But the Frenchman was too well aware of the advantages of his position, to be tempted to quit it by any art or insult.

After having in vain tried various feints and manœuvres up and down the river, and, it must be added, with regret, inflicted much *Attack on Quebec.* injury on the unprotected houses of the town and surrounding country, because the people chose to maintain their allegiance to the crown of France, and to treat the English as invaders, Wolfe determined, at length, to attack the Marquis de Montcalm's lines. He conveyed his troops in boats from the Isle of Orleans across the river to its point of junction with the Montmorency; but the attempt, desperate in itself, seems to have been mismanaged. Many of the transports grounded on a ledge of rocks, an accident which could hardly have happened had proper soundings been taken, or skilful pilotage employed. The Grenadiers, who had first landed, instead of halting until the debarkation of the whole force had been effected, rushed forward with undisciplined valour upon the entrenchments. As might have been expected, they were driven back by the batteries on the opposite heights. The approach of night, accompanied by that of storm and tempest, added to the confusion; and as there was no hope of rallying his troops under such circumstances, the General had no alternative but to avail himself of the turn of the tide to effect a retreat.

It is not surprising that both officers and men were dispirited by a failure so complete. The season was far advanced, and yet there was no appearance of succour from Amherst's or Johnson's divisions. Week after week passed away in inaction. Wolfe himself, during this period, suffered those acute pangs which disappointment and discomfiture inflict on minds of eager and sensitive temperament. His health gave way under the pressure of anxiety and grief; and, doubtless, while stretched on his feverish couch, during those precious weeks of inglorious inaction, his thoughts were occupied by the contrast between what he had done and the magnitude of the task which he had undertaken, his own extravagant vaunts,* and the expectations of his great patron. A few defenceless houses battered down, a quantity of agricultural buildings and produce ruthlessly destroyed—this was the sum of his achievements. The disastrous attempt on Beaufort had not only seriously impaired its effective strength, but demoralised the army, by diminishing their confidence in their young commander. Out of seven thousand men who had appeared before Quebec on the 27th of June, there remained in September scarcely more than half that number available for offensive operations.

* There is a strange story related of Wolfe's vaunting conduct at a dinner with Pitt and Temple, the day before he left England.—LORD MAHON'S *History of England*, vol. iv. p. 228.

On the 9th of September, Wolfe sat down with a heavy heart to write the dispatch which should prepare the minister and the country for the disappointment of their hopes. The only benefit that he could hold out, as the result of the well-appointed expedition under his orders, was that by maintaining their ground, the British force should keep the enemy in check, and so prevent his aiding in the defence of the fortified lakes, in the reduction of which Amherst was supposed to be engaged. [Wolfe's despatch]

Despair, however, had not yet subdued either the faculties or the energies of Wolfe. No sooner had his mind been relieved, by thus preparing his country for the worst, than he resolved upon making the last attempt to accomplish his great object. It is not likely that the plan which he finally adopted with such brilliant success then suggested itself to him for the first time. His eager eye must long since have marked the path which wound along the rugged heights of Abraham. The track, which one man could follow, might be climbed by thousands. On the summit was an extensive plain, upon which an engagement might take place; and the battle won, the victorious General would march unopposed into Quebec. But the difficulties were, to an ordinary capacity, insuperable.

Montcalm himself had been content to leave this precipice under the protection of a company of one hundred and fifty men, a force apparently sufficient to guard a single narrow pass through a cliff—at least until reinforcements could arrive from head-quarters, which were only a short distance in rear of the position. As an additional precaution against surprise, sentinels were posted along the shore. Even supposing the vigilance of the sentinels eluded, and the heights of Abraham scaled, a general action must be fought, without artillery, against a far superior force, and under circumstances which presented victory or destruction as the only alternatives.

That such a design was only justifiable after all other resources were exhausted, must, perhaps, be admitted; but that it was unjustifiable at the time when it was carried into effect can be maintained only by that cold imperturbable prudence which never commits itself to a great and daring deed; and Wolfe knew well that the commission which the great minister had entrusted to him in preference to the accumulated claims of the army list, was not to be satisfied by a mere discharge of duty. Before taking this decisive step, however, the young General held a council of war; and in compliance with the urgent advice of Monckton and Townshend, the two officers next in seniority, some further manœuvres were made for the purpose of drawing the French commander from his impregnable position. Upon the failure of these tactics, Wolfe, with the concurrence of Townshend,* determined to attempt the heights of Abraham.

English troops land. Having directed the Admiral to make demonstrations before Beauport, and at another point some miles up the river, the boats were prepared for the conveyance of the troops to a small bay about two miles above Quebec, and situated at the base of the cliff which led to the heights. As soon as the troops were landed they ascended the cliff, and the boats were sent back for the remaining division of the army.

The landing had been effected without any alarm from the sentinels along the shore, and thus the first difficulty was got over. The passage of the cliffs

---

* Sir Denis le Marchant, in a note to his edition of 'Walpole's History of the Reign of George the Third,' states that Townshend did not, as alleged by Walpole, oppose Wolfe's plan.— Vol. i. p. 21. This note contains some very interesting particulars of the life of Wolfe.

was performed with equal success—the French picquet, scared and astounded at such an unexpected assault upon their post, having run away. Meantime, the reserve of the English had disembarked; and the whole army having scrambled up the hill, each man as he could in the dead of the night, were drawn out in order of battle on the plain above, at dawn of day.

The Marquis de Montcalm, having satisfied himself by ocular observation, that the intelligence which had been conveyed to him *Montcalm defeated.* was not merely another stratagem of the invader to seduce him from his entrenchments, instantly gave orders for his army to pass the St. Charles, and hasten to the battle which he fully anticipated would result in the utter destruction of the daring foe. His arrangements were promptly made, and with the skill which sustained his high military reputation. But the English knew that they must conquer or die, and they saw their heroic chief, having made his final dispositions, station himself in the post of danger. Wolfe adopted the same plan which Nelson, on the other element, always employed with such terrible and decisive effect. He reserved his fire until the enemy should approach within close range. Then their career was suddenly arrested by one general volley of musketry; and, upon the disorder and carnage produced by this discharge, Wolfe himself, although already wounded, rushed forward at the head of his Grenadiers to the charge. The confusion of the enemy was then completed, and the English had only to pursue their flight.

But their leader was left behind: pierced by three musket balls, two of them mortal wounds, *Death of Wolfe.* his dim eyes, over which the veil of death rapidly gathered, were still anxiously strained, in the intervals of agony, towards the raging conflict. He lived to hear the joyful tidings of victory. 'God be praised!' said he with his last breath; 'I die happy.'

A similar fate befell the French General, the gallant Marquis de Montcalm: struck down, in the act of rallying his disordered troops, he was borne from the field into the town. When informed of his approaching death, he expressed satisfaction at the intelligence. 'It is well,' said the high-spirited Frenchman, 'I shall not then see the surrender of Quebec.'

Death of Montcalm.

General Monckton having also fallen, the command devolved upon Townshend, who received the capitulation of the city.

The intelligence of the surrender of Quebec arrived in England only three days after the publication of that despatch by which Wolfe had prepared his country for the failure of the service entrusted to him. The revulsion of the public mind was therefore the greater at this glorious disappointment of their General's gloomy anticipations. The enthusiasm was indeed unbounded. The people voluntarily put on mourning: and every public honour was heaped upon the memory of the departed hero.

Surrender of Quebec.

The subjugation of the whole of the fine province of Canada was completed in the following year. Montreal, the capital of Lower Canada, surrendered to Amherst, and an ineffectual attempt having been made to recover Quebec, the whole territory was finally evacuated by the French in the autumn of 1760. The Canadas thus became and have since continued a part of the British empire.

Subjugation of Canada.

A few weeks after the conquest of Quebec, all fears of invasion were dissipated, and a decisive blow was given to the naval power of France by the victory of the Channel squadron, commanded by Sir Edward Hawke, over the French fleet under M. de Conflans. The action was fought

Sir Edward Hawke.

under circumstances which showed how the master-
spirit of Pitt had infused itself into this as well as
into the other arm of the service. Hawke was the
officer, who, four years before, had held the same
command under orders, the execution of which became a pirate rather than a British admiral. But
the duty now prescribed to him was not the pursuit
and capture of helpless traders; it was to maintain
the inviolability of England, and to assail the armed
power of her great and formidable rival.

During the summer, Hawke had been engaged in
watching the French fleet, which lay safe in the harbour, under the ramparts of Brest. But having been
driven back upon his own coast by the gales of November, De Conflans took the opportunity of coming
out, for the purpose of cutting out a small detachment of English cruisers, under Captain Duff, which
lay in Quiberon Bay. Hawke, anticipating his de-
sign, put to sea again immediately, and Naval victory at
Belleisle.
having effected a junction with Duff be-
fore the French Admiral could come up with him,
he assumed the offensive. Conflans, however, whose
force was inferior to that of his opponent, by two
ships of the line and six frigates, declining an engagement, withdrew his fleet between the island of
Belleisle and the main land, within a line of rocks
and shoals, which appeared to afford a sufficient protection against any hostile attempt. And so it would
have done, had the English commander balanced the
chances of success and failure according to professional routine. He ordered the signal to be made
for action. The master duly reported the extreme
peril of the navigation. The Admiral's answer was
in the tone and spirit which now directed the councils of Whitehall. 'You have done your duty,' said
he, 'in making this representation. Now obey my
orders, and lay me alongside the French Admiral.'
A complete victory was the result. Four of the

enemy's ships of the line were destroyed; two surrendered. The rest of the fleet were dispersed. The naval power of France was thus disabled for the remainder of the war.

<small>Frederick the Great.</small> While almost unqualified success thus attended the skill and daring with which the British arms were wielded both by sea and land, the war against French ascendancy was carried on upon the continent of Europe with equal courage and conduct, but not with the like measure of success. In the summer of 1759, the King of Prussia experienced a terrible reverse. He was defeated in a pitched battle with the Russians at Kunersdorf, near the city of Frankfort, and his army was almost destroyed. His capital lay open to the enemy, and had they promptly profited by the advantage, the military career of the great Frederick would probably have been closed for ever. He was himself prepared for this catastrophe; he wrote to his chief minister at Berlin, announcing the ruinous disaster which had befallen him, and his determination not to survive it. He gave directions to the general who was his second in command relative to the succession of the crown, and pointed out the means which might yet be available for the defence of the capital. Having made these arrangements, he resigned himself to that philosophy which taught him that self-destruction was preferable to submission, and calmly awaited the event.

But fortune had not abandoned him. The Russian General failed to improve his victory. Frederick, on the other hand, with his usual promptitude, took advantage of a delay which offered him another chance of regaining his lost position; in a few days he had collected an army of thirty thousand men; and though two of his generals severally encountered serious reverses during the same campaign, he went into winter quarters, not materially reduced, nor at all disheartened by the disasters which he had sustained.

The campaign in Germany was renewed the following year. Frederick attempted the siege of Dresden, but being baffled by the resolution with which it was defended, he indulged a brutal spirit of revenge by bombarding the city, and thus inflicting death and ruin upon its defenceless inhabitants. Such an act as this deprives the Prussian monarch of all the sympathy which arises in favour of the undaunted defender of his country, and reduces the applause of history to a cold acknowledgment of those great mental and moral qualities which he displayed throughout his eventful career. *Dresden bombarded.*

Leaving Dresden partially destroyed, the King of Prussia marched into Silesia, followed by the Austrian Marshal Daun, at the head of a great army, with two other armies of Austrians and Russians to oppose his progress. Over one of these corps he obtained a victory which saved Silesia. But a body of combined Austrians and Russians pushed forward to Berlin, which, after a gallant resistance, was forced to capitulate. The allies retired, however, at the approach of Frederick, whose energy relieved his capital in three days.

Having effected this object, Frederick determined to attack the allies in their stronghold, Saxony, of which they had entire possession. A more daring movement can hardly be conceived. Daun, the ablest of Frederick's antagonists, was posted in a strong position at Torgau on the River Elbe, with an army greatly superior in numbers and in artillery. From this position there was no chance of dislodging him but by an action; yet, hazardous and almost hopeless as this would be, the alternative presented so many certain evils and probable calamities, that the Prussian monarch decided upon an *Daun defeated.*

engagement as the more expedient course to take. The hardest winter that had been experienced for many years had now set in; his troops were harassed by long and rapid marches; and so devastated had his own country been by war, that it could not afford subsistence to his army during the winter; exhausted by conscription, it could no longer supply recruits; nor did it offer any position where he could lie secure from the attacks of his numerous enemies.

Under these desperate circumstances was fought the bloodiest battle of the whole war. The Prussians, who had previously been informed by their great commander of his determination to dislodge the enemy or perish in the attempt, replied with the devotion of an army which has confidence in its leader. The loss, on both sides, in killed and wounded was said to have been upwards of thirty thousand. But the energy of the Prussians finally prevailed; and the Austrians were forced to retreat. Saxony, with the exception of Dresden, being thus recovered, Frederick retired into winter quarters at Leipsic.

Prince Ferdinand, during this campaign, being greatly over-matched in numbers, could do little more than keep the French in check. But all his efforts, though well planned and ably executed, were insufficient to protect Hesse; and the French army established their winter quarters before the city of Cassel.

Such was the state of the war at the close of its fifth campaign, and at the demise of the British crown by the death of George the Second.

CHAPTER II.

ACCESSION OF GEORGE THE THIRD—HIS CHARACTER—HIS POLICY—EARL OF BUTE CHIEF MINISTER—PROGRESS OF THE WAR—NEGOTIATION FOR PEACE—FAMILY COMPACT—PITT ADVISES A DECLARATION OF WAR AGAINST SPAIN—HIS COUNSEL REJECTED—HIS RESIGNATION—WAR WITH SPAIN—TRIUMPHS OF THE BRITISH ARMS—TREATY OF PEACE.

THE THRONE of these realms was never filled under happier auspices than those which attended the accession of the young King. The pretensions which, during the previous seventy years, had menaced the dynasty of the Revolution were at length utterly extinguished, and George the Third began his reign not only with an undisputed title, but without those disadvantages of foreign birth and manners, which were so distasteful to the people. The King himself, with a happy recognition of his good fortune, in his speech to the Parliament, boasted of his English birth and education, a topic which seemed to revive in the nation that generous sentiment of loyalty which had remained in abeyance since the expulsion of the lineal race of kings. A constitutional and gracious act, supposed to emanate from the young King himself, was also well calculated to recommend him to the respect and affection of the people. A generation still existing could almost recollect the tyrannical outrages perpetrated under the forms of law through the instrumentality of the judicial bench. The Stuarts had always employed these formidable tools, which were entirely at their command, for the

National prosperity at the accession.

violation of the laws of the land, and the ancient rights and liberties of the subject. The supreme administration had consequently become, during that period of misrule which preceded the Revolution, the object of terror, hatred, and contempt, throughout the kingdom. An act of William the Third, by which the judges were to hold their offices during good behaviour, instead of during the pleasure of the Crown, went far to remedy this enormous grievance; but it was reserved for George the Third to inaugurate his long reign by the complete emancipation of justice from its baneful dependence on the Court. In pursuance of a royal message to Parliament, it was enacted that the judges, whose commissions expired by a demise of the Crown, should thenceforward hold their offices for life, subject only to removal, as already provided by the statute of William, upon the joint address of both Houses. Since that time, the conduct of a judge has seldom been the subject of public animadversion, or of inquiry in Parliament. In former reigns, a state trial was a safer and more effectual mode of assailing the life, liberty, or property of the subject than a direct stretch of prerogative. During the last century, state trials have taken place under circumstances of extraordinary excitement; yet in no instance has there been any well-founded complaint that the presiding judge has attempted to strain the law for the purpose of obtaining a conviction.

{Enactment that the judges hold their offices for life.}

Yet the hopes of the new reign arose, for the most part, from that loyal faith and generous confidence which are ever ready, upon the smallest promise, to give ample credit to a new sovereign. The little that was known of the education and early years of George the Third was, however, hardly calculated to justify much expectation of constitutional or enlightened rule.

{Education and early years of George the Third.}

Deprived of his father at an early age—a bereavement, however, which cannot be considered a misfortune—he was brought up under the eye of his surviving parent, a princess *Death of his father.* who had deeply imbibed the exaggerated notions of sovereignty which prevailed in the petty courts of the Continent. Her chief object, apparently, was to establish her own influence over the mind of the heir-apparent. It must have been with this view that she kept him always at home, seldom allowing him to go to Court, or to associate with young people of quality. For the same reason, the dignified governors, whom the King placed about his grandson, were treated by the princess with marked coldness and reserve, while their authority was set at nought by the sub-preceptors, who had been appointed by her royal highness. Lord Harcourt, the Bishop of Norwich, and Lord Waldegrave, successively resigned the office of Governor to the Prince. In vain did these eminent noblemen represent to the King that the heir-apparent was in the hands of persons who insinuated unconstitutional principles into his mind. In vain did many of the leading Whigs express their apprehensions on this subject. The King declined to interfere, and even rebuked the officiousness which reported such scandal.*

There appears, however, to have been good ground for these reports. Scott and Cresset, two of the preceptors, had been recommended by Bolingbroke, an illustrious patron, indeed, but a dangerous guide for the education of an English prince. Stone, the other sub-preceptor, had been implicated, with a much greater man, Lord Mansfield, in a charge of having professed jacobitical opinions; and, though he was formally acquitted with the other parties, there is reason to believe that he

* Coxe's Pelham.

had instilled into the mind of his pupil the doctrines of the exiled dynasty.* A book, containing a defence of James the Second, and compiled by his confessor, the celebrated *Père d'Orléans*, was found in the Prince's possession. Upon inquiry being made, he said his brother Edward had given it to him; but his royal highness was not always scrupulous on the point of veracity.†

Lord Waldegrave, a shrewd observer, and a devoted adherent of the House of Hanover, has drawn the character of his royal pupil.

Waldegrave's character of George III.

A less amiable portrait has seldom been delineated. The Prince is described as not altogether deficient in ability, but wholly without power of application; strictly honest, but without the frank and open behaviour which makes honesty amiable; sincerely pious, but rather too attentive to the sins of his neighbours; resolute, but obstinate, and strong in prejudices; having his passions under command, but with a certain unhappiness in his temper:—' Whenever he is displeased, his anger does not break out with heat and violence, but he becomes sullen and silent, and retires to his closet; not to compose his mind by study and contemplation, but merely to indulge the melancholy enjoyment of his own ill-humour. Even when the fit is ended, unfavourable symptoms very frequently return, which

---

* Lord Campbell's Life of Lord Mansfield.—Lives of the Chief Justices, vol. ii. p. 373.

† 'A trifling incident which occurred on his accession showed the power he had acquired over his countenance and manner. He had arranged beforehand with one of his grandfather's attendants, that a particular message or note should signify to him the death of George the Second. The note was brought to him when he was riding. He showed no emotion; but, observing that his horse was lame, turned his head homewards; when he got off his horse, he told the groom, in a whisper, that he had said the horse was lame, and desired that he might not be contradicted.'—LORD J. RUSSELL's *Introduction to Bedford Correspondence,* vol. iii.—From WALPOLE's *Memoirs of George the Third.*

indicate, on certain occasions, that his royal highness has too correct a memory.'* Another passage shows how accurately Waldegrave had read the Prince's character. Having mentioned the extreme indolence of his nature, he adds:—'When the Prince shall succeed to his grandfather, he will soon be made sensible that a prince who suffers himself to be led is not to be allowed the choice of his conductor. *His pride will then give battle to his indolence, and having thus made a first effort, a moderate share of obstinacy will make him persevere.*'†

Such were the leading outlines of the Prince's character when, at the age of twenty-two, he ascended the throne of Great Britain. <small>George the Third as a king.</small>
Time may have softened some of the harsher traits, but the prominent features, as drawn by this masterhand, can be distinctly traced in after life. The indolence giving way to a stubborn tenacity of power; the reserve and dissimulation; the intolerant prejudices; the lively recollection of injuries; the more than royal forgetfulness of services—all these qualities are to be found in the great and powerful monarch, as they were discovered and noted in the youthful and secluded heir to the throne. George the Third, when he began to reign, had little or no knowledge of either books or men. With the latter he necessarily became acquainted afterwards; but, unfortunately, kings look upon the least amiable side of human nature. This king was not, indeed, doomed to experience the extreme of sordid treachery, which some of his predecessors had proved; but though none of his confidential servants were in secret correspondence with a pretender to his crown, he found, at least in the earlier years of his reign, a dull uniformity of selfishness among politicians, more

* Lord Waldegrave's Memoirs.
† This passage is not in the printed book, but was seen in the MS. by the writer in the 'Edinburgh Review.'—*Ed. Rev.* vol. 37.

depressing to a spirit of any generous instincts than occasional or even frequent instances of rapacity or bad faith. Whether they professed to be his friends, or to be independent of his pleasure, the public men of the day for the most part preferred personal objects to every other consideration, and, which would be intolerable to men of nice and jealous honour, were even ready to claim and accept the favours of the Crown under any circumstances, and without any sense of obligation. Even Pitt himself, while he proudly declined the perquisites of office, did not consider it beneath him to ask for a peerage and a pension, when he could no longer retain his post as a minister of state. Nor can men of exalted rank— the great chiefs of party—be fairly quoted as exceptions to this rule. Wanting nothing for themselves, they were, nevertheless, exorbitant in their demands on behalf of their friends and followers. Thus then it was with all—whether they were nobles of the land, as the Bedfords and the Buckinghams, or professional statesmen, as the Foxes and the Grenvilles, or spies and runners of the Court, as the Jenkinsons and the Dysons,—all were alike; peerages, ribbons, pensions, places, were the cry of all, from the highest to the lowest.

Character of public men.

Such was the scene presented to George the Third when he ascended the throne of his ancestors. Nor did the youthful Sovereign turn from it with disgust. On the contrary, he soon learned to ascertain every man's price, and to calculate his value. Whether it was a badge of chivalry or a city knighthood; the seals of a secretary of state, or the commission of an ensign in the line; his Majesty condescended to weigh the merit of the candidate, or the merit of those by whom he was recommended. Frugal and provident in the dispensation of offices and rewards, he bestowed the patronage at his disposal with a view to future service, and still reserved, when he could, a control over the object of his bounty.

The character of George the Third will unfold itself in the course of this narrative, and, as happens to human nature, will be found to undergo modifications and changes during a protracted, a troubled, and a varied life. But whatever opinion may be formed of his public conduct at different periods, his demeanour in every domestic relation, though not unexceptionable, was, upon the whole, respectable and creditable to his position. The defects in his education were never supplied. His understanding, naturally sound and not below mediocrity, was enlarged neither by study, nor travel, nor conversation; of letters and the arts he was wholly ignorant. But on matters, the discussion of which does not require much cultivation of mind, administrative and political details, he generally went to the point; and according to the measure of his capacity and information, acquitted himself with shrewdness and good sense.

Mental capacity of George the Third.

The commencement of this reign was remarkable for an attempt on the part of the Crown to recover that power and influence which since 1688 had been appropriated by the Parliament. Nor was the adventure so hopeless or so devoid of plausibility as it would appear to a generation fully reconciled to that system of parliamentary government, in which the constitution has long since practically determined. The mode in which parliamentary government first developed itself in this country was not such as to entitle it to the respect and confidence of the nation. The ancient prerogative, which, though often oppressive, was still regarded with reverence and affection by the people as a rightful rule, and as a simple and intelligible principle of government, was now superseded by a new form of policy, which enabled factions, and even individuals, to exercise supreme power by means of a packed and venal House of Commons. The result

Power of the Crown.

E 2

of this mode of administration had been imbecility in the national councils, and the abuse of the public service throughout every department. But of the four sovereigns who had filled the throne since the Revolution, three were foreigners and strangers, and every one of them had reigned by a title *de facto* rather than *de jure*. It was in vain for princes so situated to appeal to the loyalty of the people against the dictation of a cabal. But the case was now altered. The new King was avowedly an Englishman both by birth and education, and in his person the lawful demise of the Crown was at length practically admitted. The present, therefore, seemed to be a favourable opportunity to raise the Crown from the powerless and dependent condition into which it had fallen. The Whigs had hitherto assumed to take the House of Hanover under their exclusive protection; and almost every public man who had held high office since the accession of that family was a member of the great Whig connection.

But it was neither expedient nor becoming that the King of England should always depend upon The Tory party. one party, however great their services might have been. The necessity for doing so had undoubtedly ceased. There was no longer any reason why the Tories should not be admitted to power and employment. Many years had passed since they had withdrawn altogether from correspondence with the exiled princes; and it is obvious that no policy could more strongly recommend itself to the young King than that of encouraging and welcoming the returning allegiance of so considerable a body of his subjects. That George the Third, fortified by the support of this great party, thus happily reconciled to the Crown, should assert the regal authority in a tone which his immediate predecessors were not in a condition to assume, seems to be perfectly intelligible, without resorting to any far-fetched theory for an explanation.

The Tories might also be justly called 'King's Friends,' because their tenet had been ever that of loyalty and implicit obedience.

But the term 'King's Friends' has been ascribed to a class of courtiers, the members and agents of a secret interior cabinet, which was the real council of the Sovereign; where the real policy of the Government was dictated, and from whence all rewards and honours were dispensed. According to this scheme, the ostensible administration, consisting of the great officers of state, was a mere pageant; its policy thwarted, its credit undermined, and its existence terminated, at any time, in the face of Parliament and the country, by an unseen, mysterious power. There was some foundation, in fact, for this ingenious theory. The King certainly showed no favour to ministers neither chosen by himself, nor recommended to him by the confidence of Parliament, but brought into office by the force of party connection. He made no secret of his repugnance to such ministers. Occasionally, perhaps, to suit a temporary purpose, he might wear a face of dissimulation towards them; but his fixed and avowed purpose, from the commencement of his reign, was to break up party connection, and to emancipate his government from the domination of great lords. With this view, he hurried on the peace, and openly defied the whole Whig connection. After the peace was concluded, though willing to take back Pitt as his minister, he preferred the humiliation of entreating Grenville, whom he had dismissed, to remain in his service, rather than submit to the yoke of the party which Pitt insisted on bringing with him. Some years later, again, he gave his whole confidence to Chatham, on the sole ground that he consented to take the administration without a party following. When compelled, in 1765, to admit the Marquis of Rockingham and his friends into employment, he did so with undisguised reluctance, and dismissed them within the year. And he ever acknowledged, as the most signal service that had been rendered to him during his reign, the devotion of Lord North, in standing by him when the Cabinet was deserted by the Duke of Grafton, and assailed by the whole Whig alliance.

There is no doubt he intrigued against the ministers he abhorred, and that he employed irresponsible agents to communicate with his loyal friends in Parliament, as well as with others who were disposed to his service from less honourable motives. But the deep-laid, complicated scheme of a double cabinet, as described by Burke, would have been unintelligible to the limited and practical understanding of George the Third. If he resorted to mystery and secret influence, it was not for the purpose of setting up a cabinet within a cabinet: but simply to disperse the haughty cabals which had enthralled his predecessors, and to recover what he thought fairly belonged to a king,—the right, namely, of choosing his own servants, and being their master, instead of a puppet in their hands. The double cabinet was a romance which sprang from the imagination of the great Whig orator, and Burke pays far too great a compliment to the capacity of the King's 'Friends,' when he attributes to them a design of such admirable order and consistency as that which he describes in the 'Thoughts on the Cause of the Present Discontents.'

Neither was the conduct of the Earl of Bute, the reputed author and manager of this abstruse policy, consistent with the part attributed to him. Instead of keeping in the background, and retaining the direction of that secret interior cabinet, in which alone real power was to reside, he put himself forward with intemperate haste as a candidate for that exposed and prominent post which is the object of a statesman's legitimate ambition. He was sworn of the Privy Council the day after the King's accession. At the first opportunity, he became Secretary of State; and a few months later, he assumed the name and office of First Minister. All this time his language and conduct were those of a High Tory. So far from seeking to dissemble his master's views, he astonished and alarmed the Duke of Newcastle by quoting the King's personal pleasure as a reason for everything that was done or ordered to be done. He named the Court candidates at the general election; and rated the First Lord of the Admiralty for having presumed to dispose of the Admiralty boroughs without the King's express directions.* All this might be arrogant and unconstitutional, but nothing surely could be farther removed from subtle intrigue and clandestine management.

Bute and his system were unpopular; the vulgar clamour, however, was raised, not against the unconstitutional chief of a dark cabal, but against the upstart Scot, the favourite, the minion of the Princess-mother. Yet the scandal implied by the latter epithet appears to have had no other foundation than the fact, that Bute had been for many years the confidential friend of the Princess, and the chief officer of her household. Neither was Bute a favourite in the sense in which Gaveston and Carr and Villiers were favourites; although the jealousy and rage of faction did not hesitate to countenance such a prejudice. The King had, from his earliest years, been taught that his first duty as a sovereign was to cast off the thraldom in which his grandfather had been held by political combinations. Bute had no doubt inculcated this precept; and it was almost a matter of course that the chief political instructor

The King's treatment of Bute.

* Dodington's Diary.

of George the Third should be the minister on whose
counsel and aid he first relied in bringing the new
system of government into operation. To this extent
Lord Bute enjoyed favour and credit; but when
he proved incompetent for the task he had undertaken,
the King cast him aside and sought for abler
services. It is now well ascertained that, instead of
being the ruling genius of a court cabal for years
subsequent to his retirement from office, Bute had
scarcely any communication with the court after that
period, and complained, not without reason, of the
King's neglect and ingratitude.

His birth, indeed, could not be denied; and was,
<small>His connection with Scotland.</small> perhaps, a more serious offence than his
supposed favour with the King or the
Princess. Twice during the century, almost during
an existing generation, had the countrymen of
Bute risen in arms against England, and menaced
the capital itself with an irruption of barbarians.
Nor was the misfortune of his birth redeemed
by personal merit. The Earl of Bute had passed
some of the best years of his life in domestic retirement,
and in a remote part of these islands.
In 1750, he was appointed to the household of the
Prince of Wales; and, after Frederick's death, he
continued in the service, and rose high in the confidence
of the Princess. He was the channel of
communication between Leicester House and the
eminent public men with whom it was the interest
of that little court to maintain friendly relations;
but with none of whom does it appear that he obtained
credit for any political capacity. Lord Bute
had once, for a short time—soon after he became of
age—filled an accidental vacancy in the representation
of the Peers of Scotland. Since that period he
had not sat in Parliament. At the dissolution, which
necessarily ensued on the demise of the Crown, he was
again returned to the House of Lords as a represen-

tative peer, and took his seat in that assembly where he had never uttered a word, and of which he had little or no experience, virtually, as Prime Minister. Such a position was of itself unprecedented. Good sense, under these circumstances, would have dictated the plainest, most unassuming style of oratory in transacting the public business. Bute, however, affected a solemn, sententious elocution, than which nothing could be more foreign to the tone and taste of an English Parliament. A knowledge of affairs would nevertheless have overcome even this formidable disadvantage. But his matter was as jejune, as his manner was ridiculous. The process of reducing an able and powerful cabinet to a junto of loyal and subservient placemen was thus commenced.

<small>Lord Bute as an orator.</small>

No change of importance was made before the dissolution of Parliament in the ensuing spring. Legge, the most experienced financier of the day, was then dismissed; and Lord Barrington, who had no other pretension to the office than devotion to the King, succeeded him as Chancellor of the Exchequer. Charles Townshend, a man of brilliant parts, but whose habitual levity of conduct, and want of judgment, seemed to exemplify the favourite maxim of office politicians, that men of genius are unfitted for business, was appointed Secretary-at-War. Bute himself, long intent upon high office, became Secretary of State in the room of Lord Holdernesse, whom he had induced to resign by the offer of a rich sinecure.

<small>Changes in the Ministry.</small>

Pitt was not dismissed, but his power was at an end. Even on the first day of the new reign, he was kept waiting two hours before the King admitted him to an audience. He afterwards had an interview with Bute, who offered him his protection; but Pitt plainly intimated, though with profuse expressions of loyalty, that he would be satisfied with nothing less than the entire direction of the war; and they parted with mutual reserve and distrust.* The great minister, however, determined not to give the Court the advantage by a precipitate resignation, awaited the event with dignity and temper. He was not kept long in doubt as to the policy of the new system. Bute, with a portentous ignorance of public opinion, fancied that he should win popularity to the side of the Court by putting a summary period to the war, and was only afraid lest Pitt, or some other statesman, should anticipate him in this master-stroke of policy.

<small>Peace policy of the Earl of Bute.</small>

So eager was he to effect this object, that in the speech to be delivered by the King to the Privy Council, on his accession, and which was framed by Bute alone, without consulting any of the responsible advisers of the Crown, the war was referred to as 'a bloody and expensive war,' speedily to terminate in 'an honourable and lasting peace.' Such were the terms in which the Groom of the Stole thought fit to speak of that great struggle, which had raised the country from a state of dejection at once perilous and despicable to a position of honour and safety. And it was not without the greatest difficulty that Pitt himself, to whom it properly belonged to frame that portion of the speech which related to the war, could prevail upon the courtier to consent to a decent modification of it in the printed report.†

<small>The royal speech to the Council.</small>

Pitt was not perversely opposed to peace; but the peace which he sought was something more than a mere hasty cessation of hostilities. It was not enough for him that his country was no longer in danger of insult. He thought that England was in a position to circumscribe the power of that ancient

---

* Lord J. Russell's Introduction to vol. iii. of Bedford Correspondence.

† The words, as altered by Pitt, were 'an expensive but just and necessary war,' and a 'peace in concert with our allies.'

enemy, which, after long depression, had attempted to avenge the chastisement inflicted by Marlborough. Expelled from Asia and Africa, pushed to extremity in America, it still remained that France should be dispossessed of that important acquisition in the Mediterranean Sea, the retention of which must give her too great a preponderance in the balance of Europe.

Negotiations for a general peace had in fact commenced soon after the close of the last campaign, and it was settled that the plenipotentiaries of the great belligerents should hold their congress at Augsburg. But as the war involved two quarrels, one exclusively concerning Great Britain and France, and another in which the great European powers were particularly interested, it was agreed between the Courts of London and Versailles that it would be convenient to arrange their differences by a preliminary and separate treaty, to which no other parties should be admitted but their respective allies. For the purpose of facilitating this particular negotiation, two diplomatic agents, M. De Bussy, on the part of France, and Mr. Hans Stanley, on the part of England, were respectively accredited to the Courts of London and Versailles. The preliminary discussion as to the basis upon which the treaty should proceed, was protracted by Pitt with the view of gaining time for the capture of Belleisle, which he contemplated as an additional security for the recovery of Minorca, in the exchanges which would be discussed at a more advanced stage of the negotiation. Belleisle was taken: and though it was urged with truth that this place could not be compared with Minorca as a military possession, yet the occupation of an island almost within the headlands of the coast of France, and naturally belonging to her as much as the Isle of Wight does to England,*

---

* Duke of Bedford to Lord Bute.—Bedford Correspondence.

would be an intolerable memorial of her humiliation and defeat. Accordingly, after this event, the negotiations were resumed on the 17th of June, with every appearance of an early and satisfactory issue. The Court of Versailles assented without hesitation to two important preliminaries proposed by the British Government. The first was, that the pending treaty, when concluded, should be absolutely final and independent of the future negotiations at Augsburg. Secondly, that the definitive treaty, or at least the preliminary articles, should be signed and ratified before the ensuing 1st of August.

The details of the treaty were distributed under six principal heads; and upon these De Bussy delivered a paper containing the propositions of his government. They were, for the most part, moderate and reasonable, and presented nothing likely to prove a serious difficulty to parties sincerely desirous of effecting a common object. With regard to America, France could do no less than relinquish the Canadas absolutely; some conditions for which she stipulated, being refused, were at once withdrawn. As to Africa and India, she was in the same predicament; and, therefore, her demands, with reference to those quarters, were not insisted upon. It was agreed that, in the West Indies, Guadaloupe and Maria-galante should be restored to France in exchange for Minorca; that France should be repossessed of St. Lucia, and that England should retain Tobago. The independence of the neutral islands of Dominica and St. Vincent was to be guaranteed. The next article gave rise to serious disagreement. France had been deprived of Senegal and Goree, her two trading settlements on the coast of Africa, during the war; one of these she wished to have restored. It was of importance, to her honour at least, that she should be repossessed of Belleisle, which was utterly useless to this country, except for the purpose of the negotiation then pending. The

French proposition was, that Belleisle and one of
the African stations should be given up; and that,
on the other hand, Hesse, Göttingen, and Haynau should
be evacuated by their armies. There can be no
doubt that this proposition offered an ample equivalent for the concessions required. Pitt, however,
not only refused to restore either of the settlements
in Africa, but required from France the surrender of
her conquests in Westphalia and on the Rhine, in
addition to those she was willing to relinquish. With
this exorbitant demand, France could not be expected
to comply. The conquests in Prussia had been
gained by her as the ally of the Empress-queen, to
whom they properly belonged. It is clear, that they
could not have been made the subject of treaty with
England, in accordance with the terms upon which
Austria had assented to the engagement, by France
in a separate treaty with Great Britain; and by which
it was expressly stipulated that such treaty should
contain no provision detrimental to the Imperial
interests. The difference between the two
Courts became still wider when the re- *Difference between the Courts.*
maining articles came to be dealt with.
These were, that England should restore to France,
or give her compensation for, all the captures made
previously to the declaration of war; and, secondly,
that both powers should withdraw their troops from
Germany. The first of these demands seems no
more than equitable. If the comity of nations re-
quires that hostilities should be preceded by formal
notice, it is plain that the belligerent who has violated
this rule cannot justify the retention of any acquisition so obtained on entering into a treaty of peace.
Civilised warfare would cease to exist, and nations
would descend to the practice of pirates if no distinction was to be made between conquests seized
before, and those which have been made after, a
regular proclamation of war. The unconditional
restitution of these captures would seem, therefore,

to have been an affair which concerned the honour of England rather than that of France. Had the question been determined on its own merits, it is hardly to be conceived that the high-minded probity of Pitt could for a moment have hesitated as to the course which it became him to take. The last proposition of the French Government, which referred to the war in Germany, properly belonged to the general treaty which was to be discussed at Augsburg; and on that ground the English minister would have been justified in his refusal to entertain it in this stage of the negotiation. Still, if the treaty had been really, as it was ostensibly, broken off on these grounds, the conduct of Pitt might have been questioned. But if he was satisfied, from the circumstances with which he had long since been acquainted, as well as from the conduct of France herself, that she was not sincere in her offers,* these grounds might serve as a pretext for putting an end to a futile negotiation. On the 15th of July, De Bussy, the French envoy, presented to the Secretary of State *two* papers; the one contained a draft of the articles for the proposed treaty as above enumerated; the other document purported to be a statement of certain claims which the Catholic King preferred upon the Government of Great Britain, and urged the settlement of these claims concurrently with the conclusion of the treaty then pending, and as a guarantee for its stability.

Interference of France in Spanish affairs.

This interference in matters which exclusively concerned the relations between England and another Court, and in the presence too of the ambassador of that Court, was sufficiently significant of the connection which had

---

* 'I can hardly persuade myself that she [France] is in earnest to conclude such a peace; or, should she be willing to do it, that it is only to take breath in order to break it, when she shall again have recruited her strength!'—*Duke of Bedford to Bute, June 13th, 1761.*—BEDFORD *Correspondence*, vol. iii.

taken place between France and Spain, and of the spirit which actuated the new alliance.

A proceeding so insolent, was sure to receive its merited treatment at the hands of Mr. Pitt. He returned the offensive paper, in- Pitt is offended. forming the Frenchman, that his government must not 'presume to intermeddle' in the disputes between Great Britain and Spain; and peremptorily forbade him to introduce such a topic into the negotiation of peace between the two Crowns. At the same time, he instructed the Earl of Bristol, the ambassador at Madrid, to inform that Court, that their claims could not be for a moment entertained on the representation of France; to demand a disavowal of De Bussy's conduct, and likewise an explanation of the armaments preparing in the Spanish ports. Wall, the Spanish minister, admitted, but in soothing and deprecatory terms, that he had authorised the interposition of France in the matter of the Spanish claims; and added a great many pacific assurances, which effectually imposed upon the credulous Bristol. A few days after the Family Compact was signed.

By this famous treaty, the Crowns of France and Spain entered into a perpetual alliance, The Family Compact. for the mutual defence and guarantee of their respective dominions. Peace and war were to be made by common consent; and the same commercial privileges were to be enjoyed by the subjects of both Crowns. There were several other articles, all tending to create the closest connection that could exist between independent sovereignties. It was stipulated, that none but princes of the house of Bourbon should be admitted to this alliance; and in accordance with this provision, the privilege of acceding to it was reserved to the King of the Two Sicilies, and the infant Duke of Parma. It was agreed that the treaty should not take effect until after the termination of the existing war. Such a compact was sufficiently formidable to all the powers of Europe; but it contained one provision, the aim of which could not be misunderstood. Spain was not to be obliged to aid France by arms, except in case of invasion, *or her being engaged in war with a maritime power.*

Pitt has been censured, as if his intolerable arrogance had revolted the French Government, and driven them to seek a new alliance. No doubt the tone of the great minister's diplomacy was haughty and uncompromising, like that which he assumed in the senate, in the council, and sometimes even in the closet of royalty itself. His peremptory demands might have precipitated, they certainly did not suggest those engagements, into which the Court of France now entered. The Family Compact was simply the consummation of that policy which France had steadily pursued for a long series of years, and which this country had resisted with arms more than half a century before. The futility of that resistance had been acknowledged by a peace, which Pitt had declared should not be his model for the treaty which he was prepared to negotiate.

Still it must be admitted, that except by war no attempt had ever been made by this country to avert the alliance between France and Spain. Five years before, Sir Benjamin Keene, the able and experienced ambassador at Madrid, had reported to Pitt the extreme irritation of that proud and sensitive Court at the ill-treatment she had received from England. And it is certain that many of her complaints were well founded. They referred chiefly to violations of her flag during the war with France, and for which England did not afford prompt reparation: to breaches of her fiscal laws by British traders, in carrying on a contraband traffic with the colonies,

and which England took no pains to repress. The
Spanish Government had also preferred a claim
founded on an article in the treaty of Utrecht, to fish
on the banks of Newfoundland; and long conferences
had taken place both at London and Madrid upon
this point, but evidently with little care on the part
of the former Court to bring it to a determination.
Yet all these matters were capable of ready adjustment; and without regard to motives of particular
policy, should have been fairly entertained by virtue
of those broad rules of right and justice, which are
as obligatory on governments as they are on individuals. But the resentment of Spain was no longer
formidable; and, according to a state-morality, sometimes as short-sighted, as it is always ignoble, her
remonstrances were therefore disregarded.

Having made his decision, Pitt took prompt
measures for the renewal of hostilities. *Rigorous policy*
He dismissed the French envoy, and re- *of Pitt.*
called Mr. Hans Stanley. He then assembled the
Council, and urged an immediate declaration of war
against Spain. But the reluctant and hesitating
support which he had received from his colleagues
ever since the commencement of the new reign, now
became open opposition. They saw only the boldness of his policy; and boldness ever appears
temerity in the eyes of ordinary men. It was
possible, they urged, that Spain might yet be con-
ciliated, and detached from her new alliance.
Bristol believed that her intentions were pacific.
Such is the tone which weaker minds assume when
they dare not look inevitable danger in the face. It
was in vain that Pitt endeavoured to convince the
Butes and the Newcastles. His brother-in-law, Lord
Temple, alone supported him, and accordingly he
closed the deliberations of the third council, which
had assembled to debate his proposition, by announcing in his lofty style, that he held himself accountable

to the people who had called him to power, and that he would not be responsible for measures which he could no longer control.

A few days afterwards, Pitt resigned the seals of office. Thus, after a duration of four years, was terminated the most splendid and successful administration that had ever directed the fortunes of Great Britain. I say the administration was at an end; for though Temple was the only minister who accompanied the Secretary in his retirement, the whole genius and policy of the Government began and ended with Pitt. All the other members of the Cabinet were merely officers of state, who were required to concern themselves only with the routine business of their respective departments. If Pitt condescended to acquaint his colleagues with his measures after they had been matured and decided upon, it was as much as he did, or as they expected.

Retirement of Pitt.

But after all, did the policy of the great statesman confer any substantial benefit upon his country? For that is the question which the historian, far removed from contemporary passion and prejudice, must consider and endeavour to determine.

The public life of Pitt extended to nearly half a century; but the eventful part of it was crowded into these four years. All the rest, though containing some noble and splendid passages, was disfigured by faction, by pride, and during some part clouded by mental aberration. But if Chatham's conduct, previous to 1756, was deeply marked with the traits of overbearing ambition, it is assuredly not chargeable with any of the difficulties in which the country was involved at that period. While the Duke of Newcastle was intent only on the maintenance of mere political ascendancy; while the other members of the Government, with limited power and responsibility, were chiefly bent on personal aggrandisement, the interests of

Review of Pitt's policy.

the nation, little regarded or understood, were treated as subservient to these selfish objects. The consequence was, that the Government lost all vigour and respect both at home and abroad. Indignant at seeing his country thus sacrificed, Pitt declared that he, and he alone, was able to save her.

His remedy was war. And it is plain there was no other remedy. Loyalty, the ruling sentiment of those times, had for upwards of seventy years remained in a state of suspended animation. This alone would have sufficed to deprive public spirit of all energy; but, in addition, the upper classes had become so enervated by a long course of corrupt and feeble government, that the distant menace of a French invasion, instead of, as in better days, inspiring a genuine spirit of resistance, became a subject of exaggerated terror and alarm. Pitt had endeavoured to rouse Parliament to a sense of duty; but eloquence, the like of which had not been heard since the days of Greece, was in vain lavished on a packed and venal assembly. Some faint echoes of this patriotic oratory reached many who were not unworthy of the name of Englishmen, and, propagated by report, caused thousands to fix their affections on that Great Commoner, who they fondly hoped was destined to become the saviour of his country. Peace is a great, but not an inestimable, blessing; and when war is the only alternative to a state of national prostration, it is readily to be preferred. Nay, even an appeal to the old animosity between England and her great neighbour was better than the demoralising rule of Newcastle and his Parliaments. But, apart from these higher considerations, this country could not then, at least, safely permit her great rival to attain a military preponderance. Moreover, it was evident that England must submit to the dictation of France, and surrender a portion of her foreign dominions,

unless she was prepared to vindicate her rights and
her honour by the sword.

The principal scene of war had been determined
by the enemy. It was in the new world
that France strove for mastery with her
old rival. We have seen how Pitt provided for the
conflict in America, and the great results of his wise
and energetic measures. He formed, at the same
time, extensive schemes for harassing the enemy at
sea, on his own soil, and on the continent of Europe.
The expeditions to Rochefort and St. Malo have
been censured, as if their object had been incom-
mensurate with their vast expense; but, in fact, these
adventures formed part of an extensive scheme of
operations, the principle of which was to distract the
attention and divide the resources of the enemy.
Nor was Pitt to be deterred by any idle charges of
inconsistency from availing himself of every means
for the successful prosecution of the war. His early
parliamentary fame had been chiefly acquired by
denunciations against the mode of carrying on war
by subsidising petty military states; but the practice
so reprobated was a gross abuse of a system which,
under appropriate circumstances, might be highly
recommended to a war minister. For England to
take into her pay a petty chieftain, who might or
might not bring into the field his contingent of all-
appointed troops [*]—was one thing: to aid a great
military monarch, of consummate ability, and already
in the field at the head of a splendid army—was
another. There could be no just comparison between the waste of a hundred thousand pounds upon
the Elector of Hesse, and the grant of half a million
to the King of Prussia. The Great Commoner had
well and wisely denounced Hanoverian wars for the
sake of Hanover; but when England was to be

---

[*] Pelham to Duke of Newcastle, Oct. 25, 1748.—Coxe's Pelham.

attacked through the side of Hanover, he as well and as wisely declared that the protection of Hanover should be as dear to this country as that of Hampshire.

Still, it was to little purpose that skilful plans were devised, unless fitting agents could be found to carry them into execution. The genius of a great minister is never more signalised than in discovering such agents. Pitt may almost be said to have created his captains. In defiance of all military usage and etiquette, he selected a young regimental officer for the conduct of the great enterprise, which was the leading feature of his plans; and the fame of Pitt must for ever be associated with that of Wolfe. Such cautious veterans as Loudon and Holbourne, who never committed themselves, were not the men for him. Even Hawke and Amherst were different officers under Pitt and under Newcastle. The whole public service was animated by his zeal and energy. *Character of Pitt's agents.*

If, then, it is admitted—and it can hardly be questioned—that England at this time had no alternative but war or submission, it surely follows that such a war must be undertaken on a scale of magnitude proportioned to the great contending powers, and the cause for which they fought. On the one side it was a war of aggression, which, if suffered to proceed unchecked, might have reduced the empire to a province; on the other, not only our colonial possessions, but the civil and religious liberties of the nation, were placed in jeopardy. To carry on a war according to such exigencies, must necessarily involve a vast expenditure. But, though he spent enormous sums, it was the singular fortune of this minister to have it recorded of him that the very treasure applied to the purposes of war at the same time promoted those pursuits which are supposed to be fostered only by peace. *Provision for the war.*

The merchants of London have commemorated the rule of their revered statesman as one 'which united commerce with, and made it flourish by war.' And in days when the principles of free exchange had hardly been broached save in the writings of some French theorists, and when the navigation laws were in full force, foreign conquests were valuable as affording markets for home manufactures, and consequently employment for shipping.

It must be agreed, therefore, that this great administration was beneficial as it was glorious. Not only was the national honour vindicated, and the best security for peace taken, in the assurance that England was still, as ever, willing and able to resent an insult, but the physical power of the enemy was, for a time at least, crippled. His fleets were driven from the British waters—dispersed or destroyed. We had conquered all his important possessions in the Atlantic and the Caribbean Sea, besides his great dependencies on the St. Lawrence. India was also wholly lost to him, though this was a happy coincidence in which Pitt had no concern. It only remained that the united house of Bourbon should be prostrated, and there can be little doubt that this would have been accomplished, had not the minister been checked in his career. His plans for an attack on the Spanish dominions in the West Indies and in the China seas were all matured, and would probably have been as successful then, as they afterwards were, when their success was attended with less important consequences than must have resulted from prompt hostilities. But mediocrity and intrigue had regained their ascendancy in the British councils,* and Pitt was

---

* 'The favourite, united with the minister of numbers, bore down the minister of measures, and, by that means, in effect removed him from the King and Council, and deprived him of the

prevented bringing his great work to an appropriate conclusion.

The Duke of Newcastle, who had maintained a prudent neutrality during the earlier deliberations of the Cabinet upon Pitt's proposition, and had only ventured to pronounce against it when he found that it was sure to be rejected, gave utterance to much exultation at the fall of his great colleague.* A minister who avowed his responsibility to the people, and whose policy was directed only to the public good, must have appeared to the last degree mischievous and dangerous to a politician whose only notion of government was the coarsest management of the House of Commons. But Lord Bute, though he probably entertained the same opinion of Pitt, had many misgivings as to the success of the bold step which he had taken in dismissing the popular minister; nor could he be re-assured by the congratulations of Newcastle, or even by the magnanimous offer of Bubb Dodington to brave public obloquy by filling the vacant office of Secretary of State.† There was indeed every reason to apprehend that in his fall Pitt would drag the Government with him. The ominous murmur of public indignation was already audible. The only chance of averting the danger was to discredit the popular idol by making him an object of Court favour. That imperious spirit who could dictate his will to Europe, had, as his enemies well knew, a weak and vulnerable part. He could not withstand the blandishments of royalty. Accordingly, a scheme

margin: Exultation of Newcastle on the fall of Pitt.

margin: Misgivings of Lord Bute.

means of further serving the public.'—*Earl Temple to Wilkes,* Oct. 16th, 1761.— GRENVILLE *Papers.*

* 'I never saw the Duke in higher spirits than after Pitt, thwarted by the Cabinet in his proposal of declaring war against Spain, had given notice of resignation.'—SIR E. COLEBROOKE's MS., *quoted by Sir Denis le Marchant, in his edition of* WALPOLE's *History.*

† Lord Melcombe to Bute.

was laid for his ruin. When he entered the closet to lay the seals of office at the feet of his Sovereign he was received with the most gracious affability and kindness. Civil expressions of regret at his retirement were accompanied by the offer of rewards and honours. It is pitiful to reflect that this great public servant, who had but the day before used such noble language in quitting the association of a low-minded cabal, should be so unmanned on finding that he had not, by doing his duty to his country, lost the favour of his youthful Sovereign, as to weep. His tears were aptly accompanied by his words. 'I confess, Sire,' he is reported to have said, 'I had but too much reason to expect your Majesty's displeasure. I did not come prepared for this exceeding goodness. Pardon me, Sire, it overpowers, it oppresses me.'

Influence of Court favour on Pitt.

The success of this experiment encouraged the Court to persevere. An intimation was made of His Majesty's gracious desire to bestow large emoluments and honours on his late minister. These offers were received with abundant gratitude, and it was humbly signified by the Great Commoner that a peerage and a pension conferred upon his wife would be acceptable. Lady Hester Pitt was immediately created Baroness Chatham, with a pension of three thousand pounds a year for three lives.

Lady Hester created Baroness Chatham.

Thus did the Court faction succeed, for the moment at least, in disparaging their illustrious rival, and in averting the danger which threatened their own existence. The populace, of course, exclaimed that Pitt was a traitor and a hireling; preparations which had been made for offering him public honours were countermanded, and for a few days nothing was heard but the clamour of invective and scurrility.

It is needless, at the present day, to vindicate the fame of Chatham from any imputation in respect of these honours and rewards. Every taint of sordid corruption was repelled by the bright integrity of his character. Had money been his object, he might long since have enriched himself by what were then considered the fair emoluments of office, but which his unsophisticated honour did not hesitate to reject. But he did not hold himself precluded from accepting such an acknowledgment of his services as his Sovereign might think fit to offer. It is indeed a mean doctrine, and one essentially dangerous to monarchical government, that a man who has done good service to his country, cannot, without injury to his fame, accept the favours which it is in the power of the Crown to bestow. Though titles and pensions cannot purchase signal service, that is surely no reason why such merit should contemn inadequate rewards. Honours, which are of no intrinsic worth, but have their value only in public opinion, must be depreciated and ultimately rendered worthless, if genius and virtue will not condescend to wear them.

The vulgar clamour against the Chatham peerage and pension soon subsided, and when Pitt went into the city on Lord Mayor's day, *Lord Mayor's day.* a month after his retirement from office, he was received with every mark of attachment and veneration. His appearance on that occasion, in the royal procession, in an humble equipage, was a part of that stage play and study of effect, which formed so strange a blemish in his character. The parade of poverty is as unworthy as the parade of wealth; and it was quite beneath Pitt's great position to descend into the streets of London, and bid for the shouts of the populace against the young King and his consort. It is a satisfaction to add, that he was afterwards ashamed of the part he had taken in that day's proceedings, into which he had been led, against his better taste, to gratify the vulgarity of Beckford and the spite of Temple.

Parliament met early in November, but the Government had no cause to trouble itself as to the judgment that assembly might pronounce on recent events. It was the same abject and complaisant Parliament which, in the pay and under the guidance of Newcastle, had listened with apathy to the eloquence of Pitt in opposition;—had afterwards passed his measures without question, when he was in office, and was ready again to disregard his eloquence, now that he was out of power. The lead of the House of Commons was entrusted to George Grenville, a brother of Lord Temple—a man who, by unwearied assiduity and slow degrees, had obtained a considerable position in the House of Commons. His portrait has been handed down to us by the masterly strokes of his great contemporary, and has been again delineated by the no less skilful hand of a living historian.* Grenville had been destined for the chair of the House of Commons; his knowledge of parliamentary business—his devoted attachment to the House, and the decorum of his manners, would have well qualified him for that dignified position; but his evil fortune and that of the nation placed him in a very different post; and the firmness of temper which, under the restraint of law and precedent, might have been well adapted to moderate the debates of a popular assembly, was afterwards signalised by a fatal perseverance in a quarrel, which he had wantonly provoked, and a policy which he did not comprehend. Even on the present occasion, when he was not advanced to the responsibility of First Minister, his want of tact was remarkable.

According to the classification of a temporary observer, there were at this time four political parties: first, Newcastle and his

---

* Burke's speech on American taxation.—Macaulay's Review of the Life of Chatham; Edinburgh Review.

parliamentary following; secondly, Pitt and popularity; thirdly, Lord Bute and the Crown; fourthly, the Duke of Bedford and Fox.* Grenville was consulted by Bute in making the new arrangements consequent upon Pitt's resignation; he must have known, therefore, that it was intended to get rid of Newcastle on the first opportunity. Yet he, himself, must further reduce the strength of the Government, which was already weak enough, by refusing the friendly overtures of Fox and his powerful connection.† A Whig himself, it was with his entire concurrence, if not at his instance, that the administration was recruited almost exclusively from the Tory party.

Lord Egremont, the son of the celebrated Sir William Wyndham, inheriting his father's politics, and some portion of his talents, was, on Grenville's recommendation, appointed Secretary of State in the room of Pitt.‡

No sooner was the change in the Cabinet of St. James's known at Madrid than the tone of that Court was altered. The pacific *Spanish affairs.* assurances with which the stern interpellations of Pitt had been answered by the Spanish minister, were unceremoniously discontinued. Reparations for the wrongs which had been asked of Pitt in a tone never rising beyond that of earnest expostulation, were now peremptorily demanded; while the modest request of the British Government for information as to the nature of the treaty which had just been concluded between France and Spain was as promptly refused. The form of friendly relations was soon after discarded. The Earl of Bristol was ordered to leave Madrid, and the Condé de Fuentes was recalled from London. The Spanish ambassador, in announcing to the Secretary of State the revoca-

* Symmers to Mitchell.— Chat. Corr.
† Narrative in Mrs. Grenville's handwriting. — Grenville Corr.
‡ Ibid.

tion of his credentials, affected to appeal to the British nation against the policy of the Government, and railed against Pitt, by name, in a strain of bitter invective.* This insolence was reproved by Egremont with spirit and dignity. A declaration of war was immediately, and almost simultaneously, published at London and at Madrid.

<small>War declared with Spain.</small>

Thus, within a few weeks after the policy of Pitt had been condemned by the all but unanimous voice of the Cabinet, that policy was forced back upon England, under circumstances of disadvantage, and almost of shame. To all eyes not blinded by jealousy, nor incapable of following the course of events, it must have been manifest from the note on Spanish grievances, presented to the Government by De Bussy, in the month of July, that there was already an understanding between the two great branches of the House of Bourbon hostile to this country. The English Government was to be amused until the annual flotilla of merchandise should have arrived from the West Indies. That important event took place during the deliberation of the Council on Pitt's proposition for an immediate declaration of war; and on the 2nd of November, when the two remaining treasure-ships arrived in the port of Cadiz, the flimsy professions of peace which had throughout imposed on Bristol, were laid aside as no longer necessary. Had the counsels of Pitt been promptly adopted, the two rich galleons, which did not reach Europe till November, must certainly have been intercepted by the English cruisers, and thus the wealth of the enemy would have been made to contribute to the cost of the British armament.

<small>Spanish professions of peaceful motives.</small>

Peace, the political principle upon which the go-

---

* In 1727 the Emperor's resident, Palm, had committed a similar breach of diplomatic decorum. The insult was resented by the House of Commons; and Palm was ordered to quit the kingdom.

vernment of Bute sought to found itself, had indeed vanished at the outset. But there remained a subordinate principle of a much more plausible kind; that, namely, of renouncing German connections. The nation regarded the continental possessions of the Hanoverian princes with great aversion; and nothing more effectually retarded the advancement of those princes in the goodwill of their new subjects, than the yearning which they naturally evinced towards the home of their youth, and the inheritance of their fathers. The early denunciations of Pitt against German alliances and German subsidies, had contributed to his popularity more even than his advocacy of war with France. The plain distinction between the system of subsidies which Pitt reprobated in opposition, and that which he adopted in power, has been already noticed; but the people, who seldom discriminate, or comprehend more than one view of a question, could hardly tolerate what was not, perhaps, the least efficient part of their own minister's war policy. Bute addressed himself to this prejudice—to which it is probable enough his own capacity and information descended. The organs of Government, both in Parliament and in the press, argued the question on the narrow, invidious, and false assumption, that England could have no other object in engaging in war on the soil of Germany than the particular benefit of Hanover. It was probably, therefore, the intention of Bute at all events to discontinue the subsidy to the King of Prussia.

Now was the time when Pitt might have exulted in the vindication of his policy, and retorted upon the jealous and ignorant cabal by which he had been overruled. Human nature could not altogether forbear under such temptation; but the illustrious statesman, without affectedly abstaining from the topic, showed no desire to indulge in the mortification of his late colleagues. The malignity of his detractors he utterly disregarded. 'Time of war,' he said, 'was no season for personal altercation. In the face of the common enemy, England should be united as one man. To bring the war to a glorious end, to exalt the power and reputation of his country was enough for him.' The preparations which he had made, and which the Government had not had time to frustrate, probably insured the result. The spirit which he had infused into the public service could not be immediately quenched. The officers whom he had placed at the head of our fleets and armies were still at their posts.

Meanwhile, the Family Alliance had been seeking to strengthen themselves by the support of some of those European Powers which had as yet maintained neutrality. Having made overtures to Holland without success, they sought by intimidation to detach Portugal from her ancient connection with this country. The Court of Lisbon, helpless itself, could only appeal to England for protection. This appeal could not be evaded; and in pursuance of a royal message, a subsidy of a million was granted by the Commons to His Faithful Majesty. A body of British troops was likewise sent to the Tagus. Parliament was, however, prorogued, without having voted the usual aid to that 'magnanimous ally,' whose services had been distinguished by such honourable mention in the speech from the Throne at the commencement of the session.

The Family Alliance.

Parliament prorogued.

But circumstances had lately occurred which materially affected any claim that Frederick might have preferred to a continuation of the annual subsidy. Early in the year, the Czarina Elizabeth had died, and her successor, a passionate admirer of Frederick, immediately abandoned the

Our Prussian policy.

Austrian alliance, and attached himself zealously to the cause of the Prussian monarch. Sweden had become neutral. On the other hand, England was engaged with a new and powerful enemy; and in compliance with the positive obligation of treaty, as above mentioned, had been called upon to aid her ancient ally, Portugal, with money and arms, to a very great extent.* It was undoubtedly competent to this country at any time to discontinue those subsidiary treaties which she had annually concluded with Prussia, ever since the commencement of the war; and, however binding the terms of these treaties might be in respect of alliance, they imported no engagement to grant pecuniary aid beyond the obligation specifically incurred in each particular year. And even as to the compact of alliance, it would have been absurd to construe the language in which that compact was created, in its strictly literal sense; for if neither party was to be at liberty 'to conclude any treaty of peace, truce or neutrality,' without the concurrence of the other, the wilfulness or particular interest of either might keep the war alive as long as he pleased. A treaty is to be interpreted, like every other contract, in a reasonable sense. But though the English Government was bound by public faith not to entertain the proposition for neutrality in the German war, unless Prussia had been a party to the negotiation, the continuance of the subsidy was entirely an open question.

* See Bute's letter to Mitchell, of May 26, 1762. Bute, though incapable of coming up to Pitt's bold and statesmanlike counsel of immediate war with Spain, on the discovery of the Family Compact, differed strongly from the Duke of Bedford, who urged an immediate conclusion of peace; and, in his answer to Bubb Dodington's congratulations on the retirement of Pitt, he says that he will be a party to such a peace only as the country had a right to expect from her victorious position; and he alludes, with becoming spirit, to 'the infamous prevarications of our most treacherous enemy.' He did not afterwards, however, adhere to this bold resolution.

The alliance of this country with Frederick was obviously of an occasional and selfish character. We found him engaged in a war provoked by himself, and in its commencement hostile to British interests as far as they were affected by Hanoverian connections. His own petulance had alone prevented that alliance with the French, which it was his obvious policy to cultivate. The Convention of 1756, which was the only engagement subsisting between Great Britain and Prussia, merely bound the two powers to resist the entrance of foreign troops into Germany during the continuance of the American war; the object of Great Britain being to protect Hanover from France, and of Frederick to guard his dominions against the invasion of Russia. England had amply fulfilled her part of this compact by the military contingent which she had placed at the disposal of the Prussian monarch, as well as by the other succours she had rendered him in the shape of subsidies and muniments of war. During the entire length of the Seven Years' War, an army in the pay of England had kept the French so well employed that, except in the short interval between the Convention of Closterseven, and the return of Pitt to power, when Frederick fought the great battle of Rosbach, he never encountered a French army. And it is to be observed that, loudly as he inveighed against the treaty of Closterseven, as exposing him to utter destruction, the Prussian monarch never impugned it as a breach of faith.

The war in America being at an end, the terms of the Convention of 1756 would have been literally satisfied, whatever the circumstances in which the departure of the British forces from Germany might have left the King of Prussia. And it can hardly be questioned that the spirit of that treaty would have been sufficiently consulted by stipulating at the same time for the withdrawal of

the French army. It is true that Frederick would
be left in a desperate condition; but it did not appear that his position could be amended by the
maintenance of the war between France and England
on the soil of Germany: he would still be left, as
heretofore, to maintain an unequal conflict with the
united power of Austria and Russia. The result of
that conflict was a matter of no great moment to
this country, which was but little concerned in pre-
serving the integrity of Prussia. It might, indeed,
have been agreeable to a sentiment of chivalrous
generosity not to desert a gallant ally in his struggle
with an overwhelming force; but to expend blood
and treasure in such a cause was certainly not consistent with those sound maxims of policy, which
alone ought to guide the conduct of a great nation.

The Duke of Newcastle, however, availed himself
of this occasion to anticipate the last in-
dignity which remained to be offered to *Newcastle treated with indignity.*
him in a dismissal from office. Every
slight, short of positive contumely, had been heaped
upon him since the commencement of the new reign.
Nominally prime minister, he had never been consulted upon any point of policy. Even Pitt had
thought it necessary to go through the form, at least,
of taking the opinion of his colleague upon the measures which he adopted. But he had left to the
First Lord of the Treasury the entire control of that
department of administration with which he was perfectly familiar, and in which he took the greatest
delight. The whole of the ordinary patronage of
the Government was dispensed by Newcastle. The
important art of 'gratifying' members of Parliament and distributing places was unknown to the
Leader of the House of Commons. But it was quite
incompatible with the designs of the Earl of Bute
that this arrangement should continue. Pitt had
been removed from the direction of the State; but

the object of the Court was only half accomplished while Newcastle had the management of that great engine of corruption by means of which the King's government was, in those days, carried on. This province, which Newcastle had jealously retained in his own hands, through the successive changes of administrations since the time when he refused to admit his brother, Pelham, though chief minister in the Lower House, to any share in it, was now rudely invaded. Boroughs were disposed of, places were given away without his knowledge, or in opposition to his wishes. His complaints were unheeded; and his recommendations were met with significant hints that power had passed into other hands. Convinced at length that such was the fact, Newcastle prepared for the dreaded hour of resignation. The opportunity which he chose was at least decent and consistent. He had always supported the German subsidies, and if they were to be withdrawn, it might be argued that the time was not very well chosen, when another great European power had joined the alliance of the enemy. No part, indeed, of the Duke of Newcastle's public life became him so much as his retirement from it. He had trafficked more largely in jobbing and corruption than any minister before or since; yet, as far as he was personally concerned, his hands were as clean as those of that spotless colleague, who was somewhat too fond of vaunting their purity. Not only was the whole of his own official emolument thus expended in the public service, but the greater part of his private fortune had been lavished in the same way. We learn from competent authority[*] that a landed estate worth twenty-five thousand pounds a year was reduced to the value of six thousand at his

Newcastle resigns.

---

[*] Symmers to Mitchell, December 31, 1762. — Mitchell MSS. — Chatham Correspondence.

final retirement from office; but when the King, on that occasion, referred to the pecuniary sacrifices which he had made to the house of Hanover, and offered him a pension, the Duke replied with dignity, that he was sufficiently rewarded by His Majesty's acknowledgment of his services, and begged leave to decline any compensation.

Bute, being thus wholly released from those connections which had repressed his giddy ambition, immediately placed himself at the head of the Government, and still more to disgust public opinion, always adverse to the sudden exaltation even of distinguished merit, he accepted the blue ribbon of the Garter, which, if not always conferred upon those most deserving, is esteemed the highest personal honour which the Crown has to bestow. Grenville was appointed Secretary of State, and Sir Francis Dashwood was made Chancellor of the Exchequer. The great ability and experience of Walpole, backed by the unbounded confidence of the Crown, and by the staunch adherents of the Revolution settlement, were unable to withstand that opposition which had been created by his arrogance of power. But the Court favour which Walpole enjoyed was founded entirely upon his merit as a public servant; that of Bute had no other origin than royal caprice. There had been no royal favourite thrust into State affairs since the ill-omened precedent of George Villiers; and Bute had none of the brilliant qualities which dazzled the people in the person of Buckingham. There was another serious objection to this Lord of the Bedchamber;—he was a Scotchman; and the prejudice of race, which has hardly disappeared even in these liberal and enlightened days, was at that time strongly prevalent; and the presumptuous upstart was perhaps more frequently and bitterly reviled for his birth than for his many real demerits.

[margin: Earl of Bute's conduct.]

The principles upon which Bute professed to conduct the administration were, as we have seen, plausible enough. His foreign policy was to be that of peace, and the abandonment of continental connections. At home, prerogative was to be rescued from the hands of faction, and restored to independence; while the system of government by bribery and corruption was wholly to cease. We shall now see how these principles were carried out. The first step towards the emancipation of prerogative, it is to be supposed, had been already taken, by the dismissal of the chiefs of parties and the introduction of new men into the principal offices of the State. Bute's reprobation of those odious means which former administrations had employed for the purpose of securing parliamentary support equally to the most wise and beneficial as well as to the worst principles of policy, seemed to evince a sincere reliance on the efficacy of his principle of government by prerogative; and it must be admitted that he did not resort to those means until he found he could not go on without them. The design of restoring peace, and severing England from a connection with German politics, was to be commended; not so his mode of carrying it into effect. In those enterprises, for the accomplishment of which he relied upon his own resources, he signally failed. But he succeeded in bringing about a peace, and detaching England from German connections, because the genius of his predecessor had foreseen, and provided the means of successfully prosecuting, the war which Bute had vainly thought evitable. The impulse which Pitt had given to the war in fact continued as long as his successor was disposed to carry it on; and thus, perhaps, in a great measure, prevented any disaster or mischance which might have resulted from inferior management.

'After the conquest of Canada, Pitt had projected

an expedition against Martinique, the most important French possession in the West India islands, purposing, with a view to the Spanish war which he saw impending, that the same force should afterwards be directed against the Havannah. A squadron, under the command of Admiral Rodney, and the land forces which had been employed in North America under General Monckton, were despatched on this service; and early in the year 1762, intelligence arrived in England that Martinique, and with it, Grenada, St. Lucia, St. Vincent, and a chain of islands extending from Hispaniola almost to the continent of South America, had surrendered. Thus the whole of the French possessions in the Caribbean seas were reduced, for the island of Dominica had fallen a few months before. The fall of Martinique, which had been pronounced impregnable by the French engineers, produced a deep impression at Paris, and even throughout Europe.* Still it was thought that the Havannah, from its great strength, might be successfully defended. But a reinforcement arriving from England, this great enterprise was undertaken with that zeal and energy which Pitt may be said to have restored to the British arms. All the difficulties which the art of the engineer could oppose to invasion, and a garrison equal in numbers to the British assailants, were not, perhaps, the most formidable obstacles which they had to encounter. A climate and a season destructive to the European frame, caused more havoc in the British ranks than the resistance of the enemy. But success at length rewarded indomitable perseverance, and the Havannah—the richest prize of the whole war, and one which determined its event as far as Spain was concerned—yielded to the British flag. Fifteen

Expedition against Martinique.

Fall of the Havannah.

---

* Sir R. Lyttelton to Pitt.—Chatham Corr.

sail of the line, besides smaller ships and merchantmen, together with treasure to the amount of three millions sterling, formed a part of this conquest.

Attack on the Philippine islands. Within a few weeks after this great event, an attack upon the Philippine islands belonging to Spain in the Indian Archipelago, which had been planned by Pitt, was carried into execution, with success, by Sir William Draper, the English officer commanding at Madras.

Thus, without a single reverse, except the occupation of St. John's, Newfoundland, by the French for a few weeks, had a series of victories effectually *Humiliation of the house of Bourbon.* humbled the pride and insolence of the allied house of Bourbon. On the continent of Europe, likewise, the family encountered defeat. The Spanish forces had made considerable progress in Portugal; but on the appearance of the British auxiliaries they were forced to retreat; and, in a short time, they evacuated the Portuguese territory. Frederick, with Russia at his side, instead of opposed to him, was enabled to retrieve the position he had lost the year before; and though the aid of Russia was withdrawn in the middle of the campaign, in consequence of the demise of the Crown, and another change of policy at St. Petersburg, he was still, as he had always been, more than a match for Austria alone. In Westphalia the British and Hanoverian army, under Ferdinand, were victorious. They recovered Göttingen, and thus the French were driven out of Hanover. Defeated in a pitched battle, the French army took shelter under the cannon of Cassel. The siege of Cassel was formed, and that strong garrison which formed a base for the French operations in Northern Germany, surrendered to Ferdinand. With this operation the war in Germany terminated.

Bute, whose eagerness for peace would probably have found as ready an argument in disaster as in triumph, now made overtures to France and Spain, through the medium of the Sardinian minister, and meeting with a ready response, the preliminaries were actually arranged before intelligence could arrive in England of the result of that great expedition to the Havannah, which had been despatched by Bute himself, although planned by his predecessor. The conquest of the Philippine islands in like manner reckoned for nothing. Undertakings which had tasked the greatest abilities of both services were regarded as of no account in the negotiation; for it was agreed that any conquests made by the British arms, and not yet known—a term which was of course meant to apply to these particular enterprises—should be unconditionally restored. Grimaldi, the Spanish minister, was not so improvident. He delayed signing the preliminaries until advices should arrive from the West Indies; willing, in case of favourable tidings, to improve the position of his court in the negotiation, and calculating, as well he might, from the conduct of the British Government, that, however great the success of their fleets and armies, they would still be willing to conclude a peace upon the same terms. Nor was he altogether mistaken. Had it rested with Bute, no advantage whatever would have been demanded, in consideration of restoring all those invaluable possessions of Spain in the Indian seas, from which she derived one of her proudest titles. What were the Havannah and Manilla against the remotest chance of missing the peace? Happily, however, councils somewhat more in accordance with sober policy prevailed in the English cabinet. It was insisted upon that, for the sake of appearances at least, some equivalent should be required for such important concessions. An equivalent—a nominal one, indeed—though perhaps the best that Spain could afford, was readily yielded in the extensive but barren and useless province of Florida; for, notwithstanding that the French Court had endeavoured to frighten the Duke of Bedford and Lord Bute with the wrath of the Marquis Grimaldi, in the event of the smallest compensation being required from Spain for the restitution of Cuba, there can be little doubt that both De Choiseul and Grimaldi were as anxious for peace as Bedford and Bute, although the Bourbon ministers acted with too much discretion and regard for the dignity of their respective courts to make it quite so manifest.

As there could be no real difficulty in the way of negotiation when the party, who was in a position to dictate its terms, declined this advantage, and was prepared to make almost any concession, the treaty of peace was signed at Fontainebleau on the 3rd of November. The principal articles were the same as had been proposed by the French Court the year before, and modified by Pitt. The whole of the French provinces in North America were ceded, with liberty to the French settlers to retire, or, if they remained, to enjoy the unrestricted exercise of their religion. The French were confirmed in the right of fishing on the banks of Newfoundland, which they had acquired by the treaty of Utrecht. In the West Indies, England retained Tobago, Dominica, St. Vincent, and Granada; and restored Martinique and St. Lucia. In Africa, the French obtained the restitution of one of their settlements, Goree, which Pitt had refused. In the East Indies, the French were to have no military occupation, but their factories were restored.

Treaty of peace signed Nov. 3.

With regard to Europe, it was agreed that France and England should withdraw altogether from the German war. Hesse and Hanover were to be evacuated by the French troops, together with Wesel and Gueldres, her retention of which had in the former negotiation been made a

Conditions of the treaty.

point of honour by France, being held for the Empress Queen, as the ally of that sovereign. Minorca and Belleisle were to be exchanged, and the fortifications of Dunkirk reduced, in conformity with the provisions of the treaty of Aix-la-Chapelle.

Spain was compelled to submit to still deeper humiliation. For a series of years, that court had preferred complaints against Great Britain, founded upon three capital points. The first referred to the captures which had been made by British cruisers. The second to the claim asserted of cutting logwood in Honduras. The third to the right of the Spanish to fish on the banks of Newfoundland. These grievances formed the subject of that famous memorial which De Bussy had ventured to tack on to the manifesto of his own government; and were subsequently made the grounds of the Spanish declaration of war. Every one of these points was now given up. The question as to the captures was referred to the English Court of Admiralty. The right of British subjects to cut logwood at Honduras was recognised and protected. The claim of the Spanish to fish on the banks of Newfoundland was formally abandoned.

Had Pitt remained in power, it is probable that, instead of concluding the peace of Paris, he would have profited by the complete success of his own policy to strike a final and fatal blow at the united House of Bourbon. But there is a point beyond which even triumph and success may be unsafely pushed; and it was better perhaps that Bute should bring a glorious war to an abrupt and undignified termination, than that a minister of surpassing genius and patriotic pride should stimulate his country's appetite for conquest and military fame. The despair too of a great enemy is formidable, and it was as well to stop short of extreme provocation. England might perhaps at that time have retained Belleisle and taken Minorca; kept possession of the

Havannah, and dissolved the Family Compact. By
such a course of proceeding, France might have
been insulted and Spain injured, but no permanent
benefit could have been secured to the haughty conqueror. On the contrary, the internal resources of
those great nations, and the gallant spirit of their
people, must at no distant day have led to a renewal
of the conflict, when England, no longer possessed
of her Chatham to direct her councils and rally her
powers, might in her turn have experienced the
vicissitudes of human affairs. It was better as it
was. The details of the treaty are open to criticism;
but it secured to this country everything worth
having, or that she was likely to maintain.

A general pacification followed. Austria and
Prussia, left alone on the battle-field of Europe,
exhausted by seven years of war, deserted by their
respective allies, and finding that neither had gained,
nor was likely to gain, any advantage over the other,
were at last content to cease from strife. The terms
were short and simple. Each party consented to
withdraw within his own territory, which was to have
the same limits as before the war. It would have
been well if so much energy and ability as had been
displayed on this great theatre had been merely
thrown away; or even if the mischief had been confined to the blood and treasure actually expended in
the conflict. But profusely as these were lavished,
they were the least in the amount of evil inflicted on
the human race by this desolating strife. All the
nobler ends, nay, even the ordinary purposes of civil
government, were neglected or abandoned in the
countries, where this glorious game of war was
played; the peaceful inhabitants were ruined; in
many districts their homes were plundered, dis-
honoured, and destroyed, and themselves left to
perish; the fruits of the earth trampled down, and
the soil itself devastated. We are fain to hope that

the present generation entertain juster views than the world has hitherto recognised; and that religion and reason may henceforth find themselves adequately reinforced by education and interest in averting, whenever possible, the enormous wickedness and retributive calamities of war.

CHAPTER III.

PROGRESS OF COMMERCE—MARRIAGE OF THE KING—MEANS EMPLOYED FOR PROCURING A VOTE OF PARLIAMENT IN FAVOUR OF THE TREATY OF PEACE—PROSCRIPTION OF THE WHIGS—WILKES AND THE NORTH BRITON—RESIGNATION OF BUTE—NEGOTIATION WITH PITT—THE BEDFORD ADMINISTRATION—THE AMERICAN COLONIES.

THE domestic History of England during the administration of Pitt was almost a blank. The nation was absorbed in the prosecution of the war. In Parliament, the rage of faction was hushed, and the House of Commons confined itself mostly to its ancient province of granting aids and subsidies to the Crown. If a member was so venturesome as to utter a word of remonstrance against the prodigious sums he was called upon to vote, the great minister would instantly put him down with a word, or even with a glance.* Sometimes it would please him to come down to the House with demands of unprecedented supplies, himself anticipating opposition by exaggerating their magnitude, and challenging an objector to 'stand forth' and be branded as an 'Austrian.'

The expenditure was indeed immense, and the daring minister himself had moments of uneasiness and apprehension, when, amidst the excitement of military triumphs, he cast his eyes upon the gigantic growth of debt by which they were accompanied. The public debt, at the accession

---

* Butler's Reminiscences, vol. i.

of George the Second, amounted in round numbers to fifty-two millions. At the conclusion of the peace of Paris, it had reached nearly to one hundred and thirty-nine millions. After deducting about thirty-one millions and a half, the cost of the Spanish war of 1739, which was got up by the patriots for factious purposes, the difference of upwards of fifty-five millions is to be charged to the Colonial and German wars just terminated.* By far the greater proportion of these sums was raised by way of loan. At the peace of 1763, the floating debt was something under fourteen millions, the greater part of which was funded in the following year.

Many men were appalled at the vast pressure thus accumulated on public credit, and not without reason. No doubt commerce had received an impulse from the war, and conquests might open fresh markets to manufactures; the increase of commerce, however, was in no proportion to the permanent charge upon the national income which the war had created. But if the wealth of the nation did not increase in proportion with her burdens, it was manifest that the latter could not be sustained. It was from the resources of commerce chiefly that this augmentation of wealth must be derived. Corn had been hitherto a considerable article of exportation; but this, the staple produce of the soil, was not increased in proportion to the increase of the population. Manufactures had made but slow progress: and the cotton trade, which now constitutes a full half of the exports of the kingdom, was then comparatively insignificant. The home markets languished for want of internal communication. The wonders of the steam engine were unknown. It was the genius of Hargreaves and Arkwright, Brind-

* Hamilton on the National Debt (3rd edition), p. 100.— Smith's Wealth of Nations; Art. Public Debts.

ley* and Watt, far more than that of the elder or younger Pitt, that has carried England safely through the struggles in which she has been engaged.

<small>Private life of George the Third.</small> The young King had set himself an arduous task; he was to purify both the moral and political atmosphere of the Court. Corruption and faction were to be abolished by withholding bribes, and by elevating new men, unconnected with party, who should derive their consequence and authority from the pleasure of the Crown. But though this experiment did not answer, the still more laudable design of promoting decency of manners by the highest example was attended with better success. George the Third, unlike his two immediate predecessors, brought no disreputable connections with him to the throne; though in the bloom and vigour of youth, he resisted the temptations to which he was exposed by reason of his exalted rank. The people were pleased to see their prince of native birth forsaking the gross habits of his predecessors, and, instead of shutting himself up with foreign paramours, appearing in public, and showing a desire to cultivate the acquaintance of his subjects and countrymen. A happy marriage soon after confirmed him in these habits of continence. A bride was chosen for him, almost as of course, from one of the royal houses of Germany with which he was connected by political

---

* The Bridgewater canal was opened July 17, 1761. It is instructive, as well as amusing, to note some of the contemporary objections to this great project which has contributed so largely to the wealth and industry of the nation. 1. The breed of those noble animals, the draught-horses, would be diminished. 2. The coasting trade would be affected; and, consequently, the supply of seamen to the British navy (the same reason was urged, in the year 1852, against the conveyance of coal, from the north, by rail). 3. Vast sums of money would be sunk. 4. The natural navigation of rivers would be neglected for these new-fangled canals. And, lastly, quantities of land would be withdrawn from the more profitable cultivation of agricultural produce.—MACPHERSON's *History of Commerce*.

as well as family ties. Homely in person, of narrow and uncultivated understanding, Charlotte of Mecklenburg-Strelitz seemed little qualified to engage or retain the affections of a youthful husband. Nevertheless, the union was productive of domestic happiness, and the homely manners of the Court went far to mitigate the unpopularity which the King in his public character too frequently provoked.

The attempt to set up a courtier for Minister of State excited a storm of public indignation; and had not its fury been broken by the Chatham peerage and pension, the fair prospects of the new reign might have been blighted at the outset. It was not, however, against government by prerogative that the rage of the people was directed; this was an idea too abstract and refined for vulgar excitement. It was the Scotch minion of the Princess Dowager who was so odious. From the commencement of the reign, petticoat government and Scotch favourites had been the subject of incessant scurrility. The progress and success of the war allayed for the time, but did not extinguish, discontent. Peace being established, the full tide of obloquy returned upon the Government. At the same time it began to encounter opposition of a still more formidable character. It had now become manifest that it was the fixed resolve of the Court to exclude from employment the whole Whig connection, and to bring in those men only who would be subservient to the high pretensions of the Crown. *Domestic policy.*

Under these circumstances, the great Whig party which had been split into factions ever since the schism of 1716 began to reunite. The Duke of Cumberland, whose name had great political weight, entered into close correspondence with Devonshire and Rockingham. The Duke of Grafton joined them. Newcastle, whose parliamentary influence, though impaired, still rendered him of *Negotiations with Pitt.*

importance, was busily employed in rallying his followers. It only remained to manage Pitt; and Mr. Thomas Walpole, a gentleman of some political consideration, was deputed to sound him. The great orator, as usual on such occasions, entered into a long discourse, vindicating his conduct from the death of the late king until his resignation, at which period he said that, 'out-Toried by Lord Bute, and out-Whigged by the Duke of Newcastle, he had nobody to converse with but the clerk of the House of Commons.'* He professed his unalterable attachment to Whig principles; but added, that the conduct of the leader of the party had so committed them to the peace, that it was difficult to take any consistent line of opposition. Always haughty, sarcastic, and wilful, Pitt offered little encouragement to any overture. All he would say positively was, that he would be no party to any arrangement which substituted the Duke of Newcastle for Lord Bute.

Condition of the Court party. The Court were aware of the formidable resistance which was making head against them; but though determined not to shrink from the conflict, they were ill prepared for it. They had no champion to defend their policy. Grenville wanted neither courage nor firmness; in a subsequent part of his public life, he gave signal, though disastrous, proofs of these qualities. But he was hardly equal to the task of facing Pitt, elated by the fulfilment of all his predictions, supported by a powerful party in Parliament, and by unbounded popularity out of doors. Bute, therefore, had recourse to more vigorous and experienced agency. It was to *Fox applied to.* Fox that the chief minister now addressed himself. Nothing, indeed, short of dire necessity could have induced him to seek for aid in such a

* Lord Albemarle's Memoirs and Correspondence of the Marquis of Rockingham.

quarter. No public man was so obnoxious at Court as the Paymaster. He was suspected of having presumed to think it possible that his lovely kinswoman, Lady Sarah Lennox, might ascend the throne of England.* A still greater offence, he had been a Whig, closely connected with the Duke of Cumberland, and prominent in opposition to Leicester House. Only the year before, Grenville had been asked to forego his claim to the chair of the House of Commons, and to take the lead in that assembly expressly to protect the King from the necessity of employing Fox. But the necessity was now inevitable; and the veteran statesman, ever bold and ready, and his terms agreed to, did not hesitate a moment to accept the post of danger. He reckoned too hastily, however, on the support of those powerful friends with whom he had been hitherto connected. The Duke of Cumberland, his constant patron, highly resented his alliance with the Court, and all intercourse between them ceased. The Duke of Devonshire, and other members of the Whig party to whom he applied, including even Newcastle, would have nothing to do with him.

And now the struggle between prerogative and parliamentary government began in earnest. It was understood that the first conflict would take place on the preliminaries of the treaty of Paris—a ground certainly not very favourable for the Whigs, since all of them, who were members of the Cabinet Council at the time, had voted against Pitt on the momentous question of the war. But the battle-ground of party is not often happily selected.

Finding that the Government could not calculate on support from any branch of the Whig connection, except perhaps the followers Corruption of Parliament.

---

* A few months before his marriage, the King was remarkable for his attentions to this young lady; and it is said he would have married her but for the influence of his mother.—HORACE WALPOLE'S *Memoirs of George III.* vol. i. p. 64.

of the Duke of Bedford, the new leader of the
House of Commons set to work to fabricate a
majority in the coarsest, though the most effectual
mode. Retaining his lucrative place of Paymaster;
and declining the more dignified post of Secretary of
State, which Grenville, in rage and mortification, had
been unceremoniously forced to give up, he commenced a system of wholesale bribery. Members of
Parliament were invited to his office. There, under
the dispensation of one of the joint secretaries to the
Treasury, the officer who, at this day, manages the
patronage department of the administration (though
in a very different manner), votes were purchased for
cash, the lowest price being, we are told, two hundred
pounds. To such an extent was this traffic carried,
that the payments of the King's bedchamber were
stopped for want of funds.*

Bribery and intimidation commonly go together.
<small>Insults offered to the Duke of Devonshire.</small> The vote of the House of Commons having
been secured by money, those whom money
could not reach were to be deterred by
fear; while men of greater mark, who were accessible
neither to money nor fear, were subjected to the ven-

---

* 'I humbly informed His Majesty that it was with great concern that I saw the tendency of the counsels which now had weight with him; that this event [the insult to the Duke of Devonshire] fully showed the determination that those persons who had hitherto been always the most steadily attached to his royal predecessors, and who had hitherto deservedly had the greatest weight in this country, were now driven out of any share in the Government in this country, and marked out rather as objects of His Majesty's displeasure than of his favour; that the alarm was general among His Majesty's most affectionate subjects, and that it appeared to me in this light; it might be thought, if I continued in office, that I either had not the sentiments which I declared, or that I disguised them, and acted a part which I disclaimed.

'His Majesty's answer was short, saying that he did not desire any person should continue in his service any longer than was agreeable to him'—*Marquis of Rockingham to Duke of Cumberland, November 3.*—LORD ALBEMARLE's *Memoirs of Rockingham.*

geance of the Court. The system of proscription
against that illustrious party which had put the
family of Hanover upon the throne, and kept them
there, was well commenced with the head of the
house of Cavendish. Though disliking public life,
the Duke of Devonshire had thought it his duty to
support the Government by holding office. In the
last reign, he was Lord-Lieutenant of Ireland, and
had been summoned from that dignified post by the
express command of the Sovereign, to accommodate
the ministerial difficulties of 1756. On that occasion,
his conduct was marked by high public spirit as well
as discretion. The rivalry for power lay between
Pitt and Fox. The Duke's personal predilections, as
well as his political relations, were with the latter:
but the country was in a critical state; and finding
public confidence entirely reposed in Pitt, he at once
placed that minister in the commanding position
which would give scope to his talents, himself assuming the office of highest responsibility. When
that administration, so full of promise, was dispersed
by the ill-temper of the King, Devonshire, so far
from wishing to indulge resentment, or to embarrass
the King's service, when he gave up the Treasury,
accepted the gold key of Lord Chamberlain. In this
office, with a seat in the Cabinet, he had ever since
continued; but, seeing the tendency of public affairs,
he had taken occasion, on the resignation of Newcastle, to acquaint the King that he could no longer
take any part in councils conducted on principles
which he did not approve; though, from respect to
His Majesty, he was willing to retain his place in the
household, which he did not consider one of political
importance. Upon these terms, as he inferred from
the absence of any intimation to the contrary, the
Duke remained in office until the autumn, when he
received an official summons to attend the Cabinet
Council, assembled for the purpose of considering

the proposed treaty of peace. His Grace respectfully declined complying with this summons, for the reasons he had before stated, and seems to have thought no more about the matter. The Court, however, were of a different mind, and readily availed themselves of this opportunity to put that affront upon him, which had no doubt been previously meditated. The Duke, coming to London a few days afterwards, proceeded, according to etiquette, to pay his respects to the King; but on presenting himself at the back stairs, he was rudely repulsed by the express order of His Majesty. Astounded as he was, His Grace had, nevertheless, sufficient presence of mind to send back the page in waiting to take the royal pleasure with respect to his gold key of office. The answer was, that he would receive the King's orders on the subject. The Duke instantly resigned, and with him his brother, Lord George Cavendish, the Comptroller of the Household. When the former waited upon the King with his wand of office, His Majesty put it aside with a contemptuous gesture, and an ungracious expression of indifference. The Marquis of Rockingham, another great Whig nobleman, resenting the indignity offered to the Duke of Devonshire, came to resign his place of Lord of the Bedchamber, and was dismissed with a similar answer—one more fitting for a menial than a great officer of state. But royal insolence and ingratitude received a severe though dignified rebuke from the descendant of Strafford.* The King's revenge was at once mean and puerile. On the same day, he sent for the Council-book, and with his own hand struck the Duke of Devonshire's name out of the list of Privy Councillors. Such a signal mark of displeasure had never been visited but on delinquency of the gravest

The Duke of Devonshire disgraced.

* See *ante*, p. 96, note.

character. The latest precedents were Pulteney and Lord George Sackville. There was nothing to justify the act in the present instance. The Duke's conduct and demeanour towards his Sovereign had always been perfectly dutiful and respectful. His morals even were unimpeachable. The country itself felt outraged at this insult offered to a great English nobleman by a Scotch and German junto.

Fox, though burning with the hatred of an apostate against his former friends, was too shrewd a man to commit such a blunder as this. He immediately wrote to the Duke of Devonshire, disclaiming any knowledge or suspicion of an intention to strike His Grace's name out of the list of the Privy Council.* Nevertheless, he followed up the work which his royal master had so inauspiciously begun. The grossest corruption that had ever been known in England was succeeded by the most ruthless civil persecution. But this was reserved until after the parliamentary triumph of the Court.

Fox excuses himself.

Parliament assembled on November 25. The great question for discussion was the treaty, of which the preliminaries had been signed a few days before. The result of the debate was amply secured by the transactions which had taken place at the Pay Office; still it was desirable for ministers in the present temper of the nation that it should pass off smoothly. There was not much cause for apprehension in this respect in the absence of Pitt; and he was supposed to be disabled by gout.

Parliament meets.

In the House of Lords, the treaty underwent an elaborate criticism from the two great law lords, Hardwick and Mansfield. Bute appears to have replied with unusual spirit and ability, and the debate closed without a

Appearance of Pitt in the House of Commons.

---

* Note by the late Mr. Allen, on the MS. copy of Walpole's Memoirs.—Sir Denis le Marchant's edition of Walpole.

division. In the Commons, Beckford proposed that the preliminaries should be referred to a committee, with the view of postponing the debate. This was, of course, resisted by the government, and the discussion had proceeded some time, when it was interrupted by the acclamations of the populace in the lobby. The door of the House was thrown open, and Pitt himself, crippled and wasted by the cruel malady which seldom allowed him a respite from suffering, was borne to the bar in the arms of his servants. The consummate orator, who knew how to make his very infirmities subservient to his eloquence, was dressed, and muffled, and bandaged, as usual, with theatrical art; every gesture studied, almost every spasm under regulation. Thus he hobbled slowly to his seat with the help of his friends and his crutch, and accompanied by the titters and jeers of some of the least decent of the hired majority. But on this occasion gout was more his master than his slave. He spoke indeed for three hours and a half, but physical pain nearly overpowered him. He was obliged to pause frequently, and have recourse to cordials; during a part of the time he obtained the unprecedented indulgence of being permitted to address the House in a sitting posture. The speech, though it emitted flashes of the ancient fire, was generally languid, and palled towards the close. He vindicated his war policy, however, with complete success, and justified the war in Germany on the ground that it had divided the strength of the enemy, and diverted him from the defence of the Canadian provinces. Then, referring to his celebrated vaunt on a former occasion, the orator affirmed that he *had* conquered America in Germany. His defence of the Hessian subsidies, on the plea of the elector's relationship to the King, and his indigent condition, was not so happy. Neither did his argument on behalf of the German war go the length of demonstrating that England should enter into a family compact with Prussia. The German war, according to his own showing, had fulfilled its object; and to continue it after the conquest of North America, was to place it on an entirely new footing. As to a family alliance with the King of Prussia, a more extravagant idea could hardly be broached. There was no analogy between a coalition of the two great branches of the House of Bourbon, and a union of England with the House of Brandenburgh. It might be very convenient to an ambitious prince like Frederick to have his dominions guaranteed by England, and thus be enabled with impunity to prosecute any wild and unprincipled plans of aggression upon his neighbours. But it is difficult to understand what reciprocity could exist in a compact of this kind. It would be idle to dwell farther on the absurdity of a suggestion which after all might have been no more than a rhetorical flourish.

Soon after he had finished his speech, Pitt left the House, whether from physical inability to remain, or from a desire to mortify Fox, who had immediately risen to reply. The division showed a majority of nearly five to one in favour of the peace.

Fox's plan of parliamentary management was founded on rewards and punishments. The former had been lavishly bestowed; the latter were inflicted upon an equal scale of magnitude. Every placeman who had voted against the peace was dismissed; a rigorous proceeding in an age when official discipline was not so strict as it is at present. Still, if punishment had been confined to delinquency of this description, the minister might have justified his conduct by the authority of Sir Robert Walpole. Even the dismissal of Newcastle, Rockingham, and others from the lieutenancies of their respective counties, might have found some semblance of a

Fox's management of Parliament.

precedent in the intemperate conduct of the great
Whig statesman when enraged at the factious opposition
which his Excise scheme had encountered.
But it was enough to involve a man in this latter
proscription that his relation or his patron had given
cause of offence. The vengeance of the Court could
condescend upon the humblest victims; and individuals
in the lowest departments of the public service,
excisemen and tide-waiters, were deprived of their
bread because they had procured their appointments
through the interest of some Lord or Member of
Parliament who did not approve of the preliminary
treaty. To these proceedings, Fox had the baseness
and cruelty to lend himself; nor was his mercenary
zeal for persecution restrained except by the limits of
the law itself. He would have gone on to annul the
patents of the last reign had he not been stopped by
the warning of the law officers.

The Court, triumphant, believed that their object
was finally attained. 'Now, indeed, my
son is King!' exclaimed the Princess
Dowager, when she heard of the suborned vote of
the House of Commons. 'Never more,' said the
son, 'shall those Whig grandees be admitted to
power.' But though Parliament had been tampered
with, the great nobility insulted, and small men
ruined, prerogative, so far from having its ascendancy
secured, was in fact not advanced a step.
These measures had, indeed, an effect just the contrary
to that for which they were intended; instead
of erasing party distinctions, and teaching public
men to look for preferment to the Crown alone, they
revived that old party spirit which had languished
for nearly half a century. The entire predominance
of the Whig interest at the accession of the House of
Hanover left room for jealousies to spring up in the
bosom of the party itself; and the schism which took
place in the year following that event, under the

Triumph of the Court.

guidance of the Earl of Sunderland, had never yet been healed. The opposite party, divided again into Tories and Jacobites, were unable to profit by these dissensions, and whatever changes took place in administration, whether Walpole or Newcastle were driven from power, their places were generally supplied from the great Whig connection. George the Third, coming to the throne with advantages which neither of his predecessors possessed, might, indeed, have abolished those old party distinctions which there was no longer any plausible pretence for maintaining. But instead of inviting to his service able and eminent men, without reference to the obsolete banners under which they had been ranged, the course which His Majesty pursued made it sufficiently plain, that his idea of suppressing party distinctions meant no more than the suppression of that great constitutional party whose leading principle it was to restrain monarchical power. Even this design was not hopeless, had it been attempted with caution and tact. The nation was disgusted with party, which, for the last twenty years, had meant an unprincipled struggle for place and power. The Whigs had no hold on public favour; they were considered, not without justice, as a proud and selfish aristocracy; and George the Third might have calculated on popular sympathy in shaking off the irksome domination of a few great families which had oppressed his predecessors, if he had not outraged popular prejudices by the means which he employed. A combination of two characters most odious to the English taste—a reputed minion and a Scot—was set up as the minister whom the King delighted to honour.

That Great Commoner, as the people loved to call him, who owed his elevation to the favour of his countrymen, and who had justified their confidence by elevating the English name to the height of power and grandeur, was set aside, to make way for this worthless upstart. A man whose public life had been an unbroken tenor of rapacity, and who had neither done, nor affected to do, aught for the benefit of his country, was put forward as the unscrupulous agent of a system founded on the ruin of all that was great and noble. Such was the repulsive form which government by prerogative had been made to assume.

Corruption extended.

The Earl of Bute, sensible at last of the formidable hostilities which he had provoked, courted popular approbation in support of his policy. The same means by which a parliamentary sanction had been obtained, were now put in force to procure addresses from municipal corporations in favour of the peace. Five hundred pounds were stated to be the lowest price of an address.* The city were offered a bribe in the shape of fourteen thousand pounds towards the expenses of their new bridge; but that great corporation, which had taken a leading part in supporting the war policy of Pitt, and had made large profits by the war, was uncompromising in its opposition to the Court.

Financial measures.

It devolved, also, upon the new administration to provide means for defraying the expenses of that war, in the glory of which they had no participation. The Chancellor of the Exchequer was Sir Francis Dashwood, a profligate man of fashion, without official or even ordinary political experience. A loan of three millions and a half was negotiated with so much ignorance of the money market, that the new stock rose almost immediately ten per cent.; and thus a sum of three hundred and fifty thousand pounds so easily became the profit of the speculators, that the public, not improbably in those times, were as much disposed to attribute such a result to malversation, as to incompetency on the

---

* Anecdotes of the Earl of Chatham, vol. i.

part of the Government. The Ways and Means by which the interest of the new debt were to be provided for, were devised with similar folly. Upon cider, a home product of a particular district, was to be imposed the burden created by the late war; and this tax, equally impolitic and unjust, was to be raised by means of the Excise—a machinery so obnoxious, that the attempt even to make use of it had almost overthrown the great administration of Walpole, in the plenitude of its power. The voice of the country was loud against the new scheme of taxation; but, like the clamour of 1733, was directed chiefly against its interference with the liberty of the subject. Pitt, who knew little or nothing of finance, instead of exposing the real objections to the measure, represented with great eloquence the popular prejudice; but the House of Commons being so constituted as to be equally impervious to clamour from without and eloquence within, adopted the proposition of the Government by a majority which would have been sufficient to sanction the wisest and most patriotic measures.

At this juncture, to the surprise of all men, the chief of the administration, and the founder of that system of government upon which it was based, announced his resignation. *Resignation of Earl Bute.* The reason, publicly assigned by Bute, for a step so abrupt and unexpected, was ill health—a pretence which appears to have been without any foundation. Want of support in the Cabinet of his own selection was stated by him, in a private letter, as the real cause of his retirement. But his motives, like those of other men in other actions of life, were probably a mixture of reasons and feelings which he himself could hardly define. The difficulties of Government must have been painfully sensible in his inexperienced and incompetent hands. A formidable opposition was growing up in Parliament; the unpopularity of the minister out of doors was so great that he thought it necessary to go abroad in disguise, or attended by a body-guard of pugilists. Libels—which have tormented even the loftiest minds—assailed him with pitiless rancour. On the other hand, the inducements held out by office were much diminished. From a poor Scotch lord, to whom the emoluments of a place in the household of the Prince of Wales had been a principal means of subsistence, he had become, by the death of his wife's father, Mr. Wortley Montague, one of the wealthiest among the nobility; and his personal ambition had been gratified by the highest distinction which his Sovereign could confer. Yet, with all these reasons for retirement, it is probable that Bute intended only to withdraw for a time, until the storm should have blown over. This construction of the favoured minister's sudden retreat from power, would seem to be borne out by the nomination of his successor. George Grenville was, at his instance, and by previous concert, immediately appointed to the head of the Government; and Bute, who had, a few months previously, unceremoniously thrust this minister out of the Cabinet for the convenience of his temporary arrangement with Fox, might well have calculated on displacing him again, if it suited his purpose to do so; while Grenville's talents and political position could hardly have suggested any apprehension of rivalry to his patron.

Grenville becomes Prime Minister.

The prevalent opinion of the time was, that Bute's retirement was simulated; that he merely withdrew behind the scenes, directing everything as before, but preferring irresponsible to responsible power. It seems certain that Bute did not intend to resign power with office. He calculated on his influence with the King,* and, for a certain period after he

---

* 'Mrs. Ryde was here yesterday; she is acquainted with a brother of one of the yeomen of the guard, and he tells her the

had ceased to be minister, that influence continued. Finding that Grenville was not likely to prove the pliant tool he had expected to find him, it seems that, within a few weeks after his resignation, he made overtures to Pitt * with the view of supplanting his own nominee; and Grenville appears to have remonstrated strongly with his royal master for permitting Bute's interference with public affairs.† This clandestine correspondence continued, however, for some time, but is stated, on good authority, to have wholly ceased with the dissolution of the Grenville government.

Bute's administration must be dated from the retirement of Pitt in October, 1761, although he became nominally First Minister on succeeding Newcastle, at the head of the Treasury, in the following summer. He resigned in April, 1763.‡

Duration of Bute's administration.

K. cannot live without my Lord B.; if he goes out anywhere, he stops, when he comes back, to ask of the yeomen of the guard if my Lord B. is come yet, and that his lords, or people that are with him, look as mad as can be at it. The mob have a good story of the D. of Devonshire, that he went first to light the K., and the K. followed, leaning upon Lord B.'s shoulder; upon which the Duke turned about, and desired to know which he was waiting upon?'—*The Countess Temple to Earl Temple, December 17, 1762.—Grenville Correspondence.*

* Duke of Newcastle to Earl of Hardwicke, June 30, 1763.—Rockingham Correspondence.

† 'Lord Bute makes many hugger-mugger visits to Richmond, in a way neither creditable to his master nor himself.'—*Earl of Hardwicke to Hon. C. Yorke, July 20, 1764.—Rockingham*

Correspondence.

‡ 'The opinion of the first Lord Holland that, subsequently to the formation of the Rockingham administration, Lord Bute was not consulted in private by the King, was most decided; and as he lived in intimacy with Bute, his belief on that point is of value.' Mr. Allen in Lord John Russell's recently published Memoirs and Correspondence of Right Hon. Charles James Fox, vol. i. p. 67.—See also in the same page Lord Holland's letter to Mr. Ellis, November 11, 1765, to the same effect. This is corroborated by Bute's complaint of the King's ingratitude. The system of governing by secret influence, of which Bute was the first minister, if not the original author, was carried on by other agents long after Bute had ceased to have any connection with the politics of the Court.

The principal act of this short administration has been already discussed; and if an indifferent peace is preferable to the most successful war, the successor of Pitt so far conferred a benefit upon the country. In the other great object of his policy he was not equally fortunate. We are ill-informed as to the extent to which Bute proposed to carry his scheme of prerogative. To suppose that he meant to follow the example of Strafford in superseding parliamentary government, and setting up the will of the Crown in its stead, is to deny him credit for ordinary knowledge of history, and of the temper and character of the times in which he lived. But a politician so shallow as Bute, might have thought that the exercise of a wide discretion by the Sovereign in the choice of his public servants, was compatible with the character and pretensions of a popular legislature. In fact, he did believe, at first, that the strength of the public men of England really lay in the corruption of the House of Commons; and, consequently, that by restoring purity and freedom to the electoral system, he should obtain a representative assembly submissive to the pleasure of the Crown. On discovering his mistake, he went into the opposite extreme.

Bute's resignation was happily accompanied by the final retirement from public life of that notorious minister, whose practised hand had lately been employed in carrying through the Government measures by such violent and shameful means, as would, in sterner times, have cost him his head. But, instead of impeachment, Fox was to retire with honours and rewards. Some dispute, indeed, arose between the contracting parties as to the terms upon which Fox had undertaken to carry the peace. Bute considered that a peerage, together with a sinecure office for life,* which he had received

Final retirement of Fox.

---
* Writer of the Tallies and Clerk of the Rolls in Ireland.

on assuming the management of the House of Commons, was sufficient reward for the services of a few months, and that he was bound to resign his place of Paymaster. Fox, however, insisted that the peerage was simply the consideration for carrying the peace, and that this contract did not affect his vested interests in office. Lord Shelburne, a young man just entered upon public life, and who had been employed in negotiating the bargain between Bute and Fox, was appealed to, and admitted that, in his zeal for the public service, he had wilfully misrepresented to his chief the terms upon which Fox had consented to act. Bute excused his falsehood as a pious fraud. The fraud indeed, as Fox observed, was plain enough, but the piety was not so obvious. The result of course was, that Fox retained the lucrative place of Paymaster, out of which he had made his fortune, in addition to the peerage and the sinecure.

It has been the fashion of historians to deal leniently with the character of the first Lord Holland. The splendour of his son's reputation, the associations which surround the memory of the late inheritor of his title, and the softening effect of time, relieve the harsh traits of the principal figure in this family of statesmen. Fox has, indeed, been described as a political adventurer; and this is the epithet usually employed when it is intended to cast the most offensive contumely upon a public man. But it is not easy to understand why it should be disreputable to take to public business as a profession, any more than to law, or medicine, or science, or art, or even letters. A tradesman's son who becomes Lord Chancellor is not necessarily assumed to have risen by unworthy means. Why should the same person be vilified if, by giving his talents and industry another direction, he should have attained the position of a Secretary of State? Can it be suggested that political science is a less arduous

Character of Lord Holland.

study than law or physic; or that no one can undertake it with credit who has not a certain position in society? If this term, 'political adventurer,' is intended to apply to every man who enters upon public life without private fortune, or any occupation which may enable him to maintain an independent position, it includes many of the greatest statesmen the country has produced since the Revolution. We may instance such names as Craggs, Walpole, Chatham and his son, Burke, Canning, Horner, and Huskisson. These men, and many others, who might be named, were in this sense political adventurers. The class of politicians to whom the phrase, in its opprobrious sense, is more appropriate, comprises those persons who, without any vocation for public business beyond the accident of birth or family connection, betake themselves to political pursuits, often for no other purpose than that of being provided for by employment in the public service. The public offices have always been occupied chiefly by such persons; and nothing but the jealousy of Parliament, and the increased vigilance of public opinion, have checked their intrusion into the higher departments of the State in preference to unpatronised merit. In fact, any man who enters upon political life with the same object that he would enter upon a regular profession, is an adventurer; but of this class, as many start from a position as from previous obscurity. History affords no ground for an invidious distinction in the quality and character of the public men who have come from different classes of society. The elder Fox and his great rival both entered upon public life as adventurers, inasmuch as neither was independent in respect of fortune. Fox had already dissipated his small patrimony; and the private fortune of Pitt was 100*l.* a year. Each of these men successively filled an office, the irregular emoluments of which, in time of war, were sufficient

Fox and Pitt compared.

in a few years to create a considerable fortune. The Paymaster was entitled by usage of office to receive, in addition to his salary, a per centage upon all subsidies granted to foreign powers, and to retain in his hands, at a time when the rate of interest was five per cent., a balance of public money amounting to at least one hundred thousand pounds. The average perquisites of this office during the periods when it was held by Pitt and Fox can hardly have been less than 20,000*l.* a year. The salary was two thousand. Pitt, on his accession to this office, declined to receive any more than the salary; he directed the balance of public moneys to be transferred from the private credit of the Paymaster to the Exchequer; and the per centages on the subsidies he altogether renounced. Yet when he quitted office, his necessities obliged him to accept an allowance of 1,000*l.* a year from his brother-in-law, Lord Temple. The perquisites of office during a single twelvemonth would have sufficed to realise the capital value of this annuity. But Pitt, with notions of honour and delicacy too pure and refined for the comprehension of ordinary men, scorned to touch public money to which he felt that he had no legitimate claim, and preferred, for the relief of his necessities, to endure the weight of private obligation. Fox pursued a different conduct. The enormous gains of the Pay Office were to him, throughout his public career, a paramount consideration; the example of Pitt, whom he succeeded in this office, had not the slightest effect upon his coarse and venal nature; the self-denial of a noble integrity would appear to him as a freak of romance or ostentation; and the low morality of the times would rather admire the worldly wisdom of Fox than appreciate the magnanimity of his predecessor in office. Fox realised a large fortune from the profits of the Pay Office; and it is certain that he took to public life as a means of repairing his shattered fortunes.

He was, therefore, in the strictest sense, a political adventurer, because it was impossible for him, consistently with his object, to maintain that independence which is essential to a useful and respectable position. But that this position can be maintained by men who enter upon public life without any advantages of private fortune is a fact of ordinary experience.

Having acquired rank and wealth by political pursuits, Lord Holland had gained his objects; and consequently, from this period, he ceased to take an active part in public affairs. The venality and self-seeking which, under his auspices and those of Newcastle, had been impressed on the character of public men, continued to embarrass and discredit representative government for a long time after those potent agents of corruption had retired.* Instances of shameless rapacity in public men are within the experience of the present generation; it is only within latter years that an improved tone of political morality has been recognised, and that those who must ever be corrupt have been constrained to observe some decency in their intrigues for place and power.

* In a letter to Lord Mansfield, in 1765, Grenville says: 'The cure must come from a serious conviction and right measures, instead of annual struggles for places and pensions; and that cure ought not to be delayed.'—*Grenville Papers*, vol. iii. p. 99.

CHAPTER IV.

ATTEMPT TO FORM A NEW ADMINISTRATION UNDER PITT—ITS FAILURE—DUKE OF BEDFORD AT THE HEAD OF THE GOVERNMENT—CONDUCT OF THE KING—WILKES AND THE 'NORTH BRITON'—GENERAL WARRANTS—ESSAY ON WOMAN—EXPULSION OF WILKES—GRENVILLE'S FINANCIAL MEASURES—THE COLONIAL QUESTION.

GRENVILLE took the lead of the Government as First Lord of the Treasury and Chancellor of the Exchequer, the two principal Secretaries of State being the Earls of Egremont and Halifax. There was nothing in the composition of the new government to conciliate public confidence or favour; and the general opinion was, that Bute had merely withdrawn from official responsibility, but that his policy and influence remained as before. The administration, indeed, could put forward no claim to public support beyond the King's pleasure; and this pretension was already sufficiently disparaged by the manner and the circumstances with which it had been preferred.

<small>Grenville as Prime Minister.</small>

It has been already mentioned that within a few weeks after he had placed Grenville in power, Lord Bute made an overture to his great rival. His reason for seeking to disturb the arrangement which he had so recently made does not very clearly appear; the incapacity of the new minister had not yet been so manifest as to call for a change; indeed, except the prosecution of Wilkes, in which Bute concurred, no public business of any importance had arisen since Grenville's accession to power. The probability is, that the independence and not the incapacity of the minister had offended

<small>Lord Bute's intrigues with Pitt.</small>

and alarmed the patron. During the negotiation which was to place Grenville in office as the ostensible chief of the Government, nothing could be more submissive than his deference to the ruling power; and, if he ventured to object to an arrangement, it was only by way of suggestion, and not at all as assuming any claim to dictate in the matter.* But no sooner had Grenville gained his object than this tone was altered. Grenville had no political attachment to Bute. He was a Whig of long experience both in Parliament and in office; and his habits and character led him to regard Lord Bute, when out of office, as having no more right to consideration than any other courtier. Moreover, he disliked Bute personally. He had a mean opinion of his veracity and good faith; and he had neither forgotten nor forgiven the slight which had been put upon him the preceding autumn, when, in spite of his remonstrances, he had been unceremoniously thrust aside to make way for Fox. So far, therefore, was Grenville from acting under the direction of Bute, that he took the earliest opportunity, after his accession to office, of objecting most strongly to his interference in public affairs, and he exacted from the King a pledge that none but his responsible ministers should be consulted in the public business.

The King and Lord Bute have been accused of duplicity and treachery in carrying on a clandestine correspondence with the members of the Opposition. But it is proved, on the authority of Grenville himself,† that His Majesty, so early as the middle of July, had announced to the Cabinet his intention of offering office to Lord Hardwicke and the Duke of Newcastle; and that this

* Grenville Correspondence, vol. ii.—Grenville to Bute, March 22, 1763.

† His own narrative.—Correspondence, vol. ii.

resolution was taken contrary to the advice of Grenville himself, and of the two Secretaries of State, Egremont and Halifax. If any further proof were wanting that the conduct of George the Third, in this particular at least, was open and straightforward, it is supplied by the fact that Lord Egremont was directed to convey the King's offer to the Earl of Hardwicke. The answer returned by that nobleman, through the same regular channel, was a refusal to take office without Mr. Pitt and the Whig party. The King desired ten days to consider Lord Hardwicke's proposal; and, upon this intimation, the ministers suspended their deliberations as a cabinet, and confined themselves to mere matters of routine, according to the practice of an out-going government holding office only until the appointment of their successors. Grenville left London. Public affairs continued in this state of suspense for a month. On the 18th of August, Grenville returned to London and had an audience of the King, but nothing beyond ordinary business was mentioned. The next day, however, the minister thinking, not without reason, that sufficient time had been allowed the King to make up his mind, took the liberty of laying before His Majesty very distinctly that the consequence of a change in the Government must be a reversal of the policy in every particular which had hitherto received his approbation.* The King replied that he had no wish to change his ministers; but a few days afterwards, on the sudden death of Lord Egremont, His Majesty announced to Grenville his determination to place Pitt at the head of affairs; at the same time expressing his wish to do so upon terms, and to make as few changes as possible in the composition of the Government. Grenville expressed his surprise and concern, but must have quitted the

---

* Grenville's Diary.—Correspondence, vol. ii. p. 195.

closet with the understanding that his short term of power was on the point of expiration.

The next day, Mr. Pitt received the King's commands, through the Earl of Bute. Whatever might have been wished, the haughty chief of the Opposition was not the man to enter the Palace by a back door. With the ostentation which belonged to his character, he was carried to court in open day through the streets of London, in his well-known gouty chair, that all the world might know what was going forward. Grenville found this ominous chair set down at Buckingham House when he went there, as usual, to transact business. After waiting two hours, he was ushered into the closet. The King was agitated—but he made no mention of the important visitor who had just left him. Grenville complained and remonstrated in his usual tiresome manner, until the King cut him short, wishing him 'good morrow' in a significant manner. Grenville retired with the impression that his fate was sealed.

Pitt, on the other hand, had quitted the royal presence with the understanding that he was to be minister, and immediately communicated, upon that footing, with Newcastle, Devonshire, Rockingham, and Hardwicke. In an audience of three hours, he had developed his plan of administration, in accordance with the terms which he had previously stated in his interview with Bute. The King could, therefore, have hardly been taken by surprise, although the terms were certainly rigid. He required that the great revolution-families should be restored to power, and parcelled out the principal offices of State principally among the Whig connection. Almost every man in office who had supported the peace was to be removed. The Duke of Bedford, as having taken the chief part in negotiating the treaty, was to be disqualified for office. Lords Mansfield and Holland were also to be excluded from the Cabinet. The peace itself was not to be broken, but to be *ameliorated*. The King listened to these imperious demands with apparent acquiescence. He spoke of saving his honour, indeed, and discussed some points of detail, but he suffered Pitt to depart with the belief that no insuperable difficulty was offered to his proposed arrangements.

Bute, in the meantime, had begun to falter. Two of his agents, Elliott and Jenkinson, strongly represented to him the danger of the course he was pursuing in letting in the great Whig party, with Pitt at their head. It was better, they urged, to endure the ingratitude and mediocrity of Grenville, and await the chapter of accidents, rather than make the certain sacrifice of power and influence by giving up the King and the Government to the most powerful and capable body of men in the State. Bute hurried to the King, retracted all the counsel he had been giving for months past, and urged His Majesty to dismiss Pitt, and replace his confidence in Grenville. In the morning, the King had been advised to pledge himself to Pitt: a few hours after, he was advised to withdraw from his engagement. Distracted by such vacillation, His Majesty once more sent for Grenville, who found him greatly agitated. In the conversation which ensued, the King disclosed all that had passed between himself and Pitt, declared that he could not submit to the terms on which that statesman insisted, and threw himself upon the mercy of his minister. Grenville, though he had little faith in the professions of his Sovereign, consented to remain in office on the repeated condition that there should be no 'secret influence.' This the King readily promised, and dismissed his minister, with renewed assurances of his undivided confidence and support.

Bute was, of course, immediately informed of the stipulation upon which

Grenville had insisted; and consequently made another effort towards an accommodation with Pitt. Early the next morning, he sent for Beckford, the confidential and devoted friend of Pitt, and proposed, through him, a modification of terms; but Pitt, though willing to reconsider details, would consent to no compromise of the principle he had laid down of taking office only in company with the great Whig families. The King himself was not prompt in coming to an explanation; and whether from a spirit of insincerity towards Pitt, or towards his minister, he proposed, and even pressed, that 'poor George Grenville' should be included in the new arrangements in his former subordinate office of Paymaster. At length His Majesty brought this shameful scene of dissimulation to a close by declaring that his *honour* could not admit of Mr. Pitt's propositions.*

<small>Endeavour to secure the Duke of Bedford.</small> The negotiation with Pitt being finally abandoned, the King and his minister were desirous of strengthening the Government by the accession of the Duke of Bedford. But that nobleman having, on the formation of the Grenville cabinet five months previously, refused to preside at its council-board, because he considered it impossible that such an administration could last,† it was

---

* Grenville mentions, with just indignation, the King's duplicity in continuing to treat, or pretending to treat, with Pitt, after his solemn promises and engagements the night before. Yet Grenville would probably never have known this proof of George the Third's duplicity, had it not been for the treachery or gossip of Elliott, Bute's confidant, who mentioned the fact to him some weeks after. I have taken the account of these transactions from Grenville's own narrative, the Hardwicke, Chatham, and Bedford Correspondence.

† In a letter dated April 7, 1763, in answer to one from Bute announcing his resignation, and earnestly entreating the Duke of Bedford to accept office as President of the Council, the Duke says he should deserve to be treated as a madman, should he join an administration which he knew could not last. And he

not to be expected that, on the prompt fulfilment of his prediction, he would lend his aid to the re-construction of the Government out of the same frail materials. A shameful mode of overcoming this difficulty was resorted to by the King. In those private audiences with which Mr. Pitt had lately been honoured, the Duke of Bedford had been named by His Majesty as eligible for office. But inasmuch as Pitt had avowed his intention to modify, if not to reverse, the policy of the peace, he did not consider it expedient to act with those statesmen who had taken a leading part in the promotion of that policy; and on that plain ground he had declined to nominate the Duke of Bedford as a member of his cabinet.

The King took advantage of what had passed in the confidence of the closet to gain over a public man of great mark, who, but for the means so employed, would certainly not have entered His Majesty's service. The Earl of Sandwich was the fitting instrument employed by the King to communicate to the Duke of Bedford not only the fact of his having been specially excepted by Mr. Pitt from the list of his proposed administration, but the very terms of disparagement in which the exception had been made.* Indignant at what seemed a personal slight,

---

recommends that the Dukes of Newcastle, Devonshire, Grafton, and Lord Hardwicke should be called again into His Majesty's service.—BEDFORD *Correspondence,* vol. iii.

* 'I repeated to him [the King] most of what I had said to your Grace by his order; but, in one point, he set me right, and told me I had not expressed myself strong enough; I had said that Mr. Pitt had insisted that the Duke of Bedford should have no *efficient* office in his service; but his words were, that he *might have no office at all*; perhaps some years since he might be admitted to an employment of rank about the Court, but that now no confidence must be shown to those who had been concerned in so disgraceful a measure as the peace.'—*Earl of Sandwich to the Duke of Bedford, Sept.* 5, 1763.—BEDFORD *Correspondence.*

as well as at the apparent ingratitude, if not treachery, of Pitt, who had been sent for at his instance,*

Bedford appointed President of the Council. Bedford was now easily prevailed upon to accept the office of President of the Council. Lord Sandwich was made Secretary of State, and Lord Egmont succeeded Sandwich at the head of the Board of Admiralty. Lord Hillsborough was appointed President of the Board of Trade on the resignation of Lord Shelburne.

The King, having thus succeeded in propping up the administration, proceeded by a further breach of confidence to impair Pitt's means of opposition. His Majesty condescended, either personally or through some sure channel of communication, to inform every gentleman, whose pretensions to employment had been interdicted by Pitt, of the slight which had been put upon him, and even to insinuate the ill-will of that statesman towards individuals of whom he had said little or nothing.† All this was faithfully reported to Pitt by Wood, the Under-Secretary of the department which he had lately filled; and though Pitt's letter in reply is unfortunately lost, it would seem from his answer to Lord Hardwicke, who questioned him directly on the subject, that His Majesty's statement of what had passed in the closet relative to the proscriptions, as they were termed, was not strictly true. Pitt, however, appears to have taken no further notice of

---

* Bute had studiously concealed this fact from Pitt.

† 'What is certain is, that the King, who had hitherto been so cautious and reserved, spoke openly of Mr. Pitt's conditions, and took pains to inflame the anger of the proscribed. In particular, he told Lord Hertford that Mr. Pitt proscribed several, particularly his friend Lord Powis, *had said little of Mr. Legge, and still less of the Duke of Grafton.'*—LORD J. RUSSELL's *Introduct. to 3rd vol. BEDFORD Correspondence.* (See also the GRENVILLE *Correspondence, to the same effect.*)

Well might Lord Shelburne congratulate Pitt on the rupture of a negotiation, 'which carried through the whole of it such shocking marks of insincerity.'—CHATHAM *Correspondence, from Shelburne to Pitt.*

the matter. A noble nature is seldom quick in its perceptions of meanness; and the profound loyalty of the Great Commoner could not have resented, even if it had been alive to, the treachery of his Sovereign. The Court were short-sighted indeed, if they calculated upon ruining such a man by such means as they employed. His power was quite independent of party connection, resting entirely upon the public confidence in his integrity, ability, and success. By the strong pressure of public opinion, he had been elevated to supreme authority in spite of parties and the Crown itself; and his last words on quitting the Government, had been to tell the astonished council that he had been called to office by the voice of the people, and that he considered himself accountable to them alone.

The administration, as re-constructed, was called by the name of the Duke of Bedford; but Grenville jealously insisted on keeping the direction of affairs in his own hands. Within four days after the new arrangements had been completed, a dispute arose as to the dispensation of patronage. Grenville was unwilling to concede the Duke's claim to a share of what he considered the test of power; and even appealed to the King for support against His Grace's pretensions. A few weeks after, the two Secretaries of State, Halifax and Sandwich, preferred similar claims; the latter especially asserted his right to the same patronage which had been enjoyed by his predecessor, Lord Egremont. Grenville, however, prevailed so far as to retain exclusively the distribution of those offices which were required for the management of the House of Commons.

The popular dislike to the new system of Government by courtiers had found vent in a scurrilous press, the annoyance of which continued unabated by the sham retirement of the minister whose ascendancy had provoked this grievous kind of opposition. The leader of the host of libellers was John Wilkes, a man of that audacity and self-possession which are indispensable to success in the most disreputable line of political adventure. But Wilkes had qualities which placed him far above the level of a vulgar demagogue. Great sense and shrewdness, brilliant wit, extensive knowledge of the world, with the manners of a gentleman, were among the accomplishments which he brought to a vocation, but rarely illustrated by the talents of a Catiline. Long before he engaged in public life, Wilkes had become infamous for his debaucheries, and, with a few other men of fashion, had tested the toleration of public opinion by a series of outrages upon religion and decency.* Profligacy of morals, however, has not in any age or country proved a bar to the character of a patriot. The favourites of the people seem to be chosen with as little regard to merit as the favourites of the Court; but in the one case they are commonly selected by caprice; in the other, they are almost always the accidental representatives of a grievance or a principle.

Wilkes' journal, which originated with the administration of Lord Bute, was happily entitled 'The North Briton,' and from its boldness and personality soon obtained a large circulation. It

The North Briton.

* I need only allude to the orgies of Memdenham Abbey, an old Monastic building on the banks of the Thames, where Wilkes and his friends assumed the habits of Franciscan monks, and amused themselves by a mockery of religious rites. It is said that they went through the form of administering the Eucharist to an ape. Sir Francis Dashwood, the late Chancellor of the Exchequer, was one of this party.

The historian of the Roman Empire, who was his contemporary, thus speaks of Wilkes:—

'He is a thorough profligate in principle, as in practice; his life stained with every vice, and his conversation full of blasphemy and indecency. These morals he glories in, for shame is a weakness he has long surmounted. He told us himself that, in this time of public dissension, he was resolved to make his fortune.'—Gibbon's *Miscellaneous Works*.

is surpassed in ability though not often equalled in virulence by the political press of the present day; but at a time when the characters of public men deservedly stood lowest in public estimation, they were protected, not unadvisedly perhaps, from the assaults of the press by a stringent law of libel. While a latitude of invective, which the parliamentary decorum of the present time would not tolerate, was permitted and even encouraged by applause in the Great Council of the nation, the law of privilege, as well as the law of the land, was strictly enforced against a printer who should venture to divulge or comment on the proceedings of either House of Parliament. It had been the practice since the Revolution, and it is now acknowledged as an important constitutional right, to treat the Speech from the Throne, on the opening of Parliament, as the manifesto of the minister; and in that point of view, it had from time to time been censured by Pitt, and other leaders of party, with the ordinary license of debate. But when Wilkes presumed to use this freedom in his paper, though in a degree which would have seemed temperate and even tame had he spoken to the same purport in his place in Parliament, it was thought necessary to repress such insolence with the whole weight of the law. A warrant was issued from the office of the Secretary of State to seize—not any person named —but 'the authors, printers, and publishers of the seditious libel, entitled the North Briton, No. 45.' Under this warrant, forty-nine persons were arrested and detained in custody for several days; but as it was found that none of them could be brought within the description in the warrant, they were discharged. Several of the individuals who had been so seized, brought actions for false imprisonment against the messengers; and in one of these actions, in which a verdict was entered for the

[margin: Criticism on the royal speech.]

[margin: Validity of general warrants.]

plaintiff under the direction of the Lord Chief
Justice of the Common Pleas, the two important
questions as to the claim of a Secretary of State to
the protection given by statute to justices of the
peace acting in that capacity, and as to the legality
of a warrant which did not specify any individual by
name, were raised by a Bill of Exceptions to the
ruling of the presiding judge, and thus came upon
appeal before the Court of King's Bench. The case
was argued on behalf of the plaintiff in error (the
defendant in the action) by the Solicitor-General
De Grey; and on behalf of the plaintiff below, by
Dunning, one of the greatest Banc lawyers ever
known in Westminster Hall. He showed that a Secretary of State was not a conservator of the peace within
the meaning of any act of Parliament, and had no
authority to issue a warrant for the seizure of persons
and papers except in the case of high treason; and
that even if he had such authority, the warrant under
which the defendant justified, was altogether invalid.
He argued if 'author, printer, and publisher,' without naming any particular person, be sufficient in such
a warrant as this, it would be equally so to issue a
warrant generally 'to take up the robber or murderer
of such a one.' This is no description of the *person*,
but only of the *offence*; it is making the officer to be
judge of the matter in the place of the person who
issues the warrant. Such a power, he contended,
would be extremely mischievous, and might be productive of great oppression. He concluded by citing
the principal text-writers on Crown Law to show
'that there must be an accusation; that the person to be apprehended must be named, and that
the officer is not to be left to arrest whom he
thinks fit.'

The counsel for the Crown seems to have made
little more than a colourable show of maintaining
the efficacy of the warrant, either as intrinsically good,

or as emanating from competent authority. He relied rather upon an inferior, but much more tenable position, that the *officer*, the defendant on the record, was at all events bound to act in obedience to his warrant, and was, therefore, justified in what he had done. An act [*] of the last reign had given protection to officers ' for anything done in obedience to *any* warrant,' notwithstanding any defect of jurisdiction in the justice by whom it was issued. And it might well have been argued that the officer was not to concern himself with a question as to the legal sufficiency of the instrument which he was ordered to enforce; still less to raise a doubt as to the title of the great functionary from whom, in this instance, the authority proceeded. The Court of King's Bench, however, intimated a strong opinion against the Crown upon the important constitutional questions which had been raised, and directed the case to stand over for further argument; but when the case came on again,[†] the Attorney-General Yorke prudently declined any further agitation of the questions, and submitted to the judgment of the Court upon the bye-point that the defendants had not acted in 'obedience' to the warrant, inasmuch as the plaintiff did not come within the description of 'author, printer, or publisher,' therein mentioned.

Decision of the King's Bench.

These proceedings were not brought to a close until the end of the year 1765, long after the administration under which they were instituted had ceased to exist. It would be unfair, however, to charge the Government over which Grenville presided with any design of invading the liberty of the subject by issuing this general warrant; since it was an unquestionable fact, and, indeed, it had been expressly found by the Bill of Exceptions, that 'several

[*] 24 Geo. II. c. 44. [†] 3 Burrow's Reports, p. 1706.

of the like warrants had been granted at different times, from the time of the Revolution to the present time, by the principal Secretaries of State, and had been executed by the messengers in ordinary for the time being.' Such a warrant might, therefore, have been issued in the ordinary course from the office of the Home Department, without any sinister design; but as there could be no question as to its illegality, it was the duty of the Crown lawyers to have withdrawn it, and made amends to the parties against whom it had been enforced, as soon as their attention was directed to the defect which rendered it a nullity. Nor was this illegal practice a mere topic for declamation. Such a power, as had been argued by Dunning, might be productive of great oppression; and in this case had actually led to the apprehension and detention of a great number of persons who never could have been molested, had the process been confined to certain individuals against whom a probable cause of complaint could have been made out.

The question of the validity of general warrants,
The question really left undecided. though deliberately raised by the Crown lawyers in their Bill of Exceptions, was not decided, in consequence of the case being determined on another point. But no warrant of this description has since been issued; and no writer has since attempted to maintain the legality of such a proceeding.

The prosecution of Wilkes himself was pressed with the like indiscreet vigour. The privilege of Parliament, which extends to every case except treason, felony, and breach of the peace, presented an obstacle to the vengeance of the Court. But the Crown lawyers, with a servility which belonged to the worst times of prerogative, advised that a libel came within the purview of the exception, as having a *tendency* to a breach of the peace; and upon this perversion of plain law, Wilkes was arrested, and brought before Lord Halifax for examination. The cool and wary demagogue, however, was more than a match for the Secretary of State; but his authorship of the alleged libel having been proved by the printer, he was committed close prisoner to the Tower. In a few days, having sued out writs of habeas, he was brought up before the Court of Common Pleas; and, perhaps, it is not too much to say, that on this occasion the salutary effect of that law—the earliest offspring of the Revolution—which provided for the independence of the judges, was signally manifest. At a time when political morality was at the lowest ebb, and when high prerogative principles were asserted and enforced, liberty might hardly have been safe in the hands of judges deliberating under the terror of dismissal. But the fear of royal displeasure being happily removed, the judges could pronounce the law with fairness and decision. The argument which would confound the commission of a crime with conduct which had no more than a tendency to provoke it, was at once rejected by an independent court of justice; and the result was the liberation of Wilkes from custody. But the vengeance of the Court was not turned aside by this disappointment. An ex-officio prosecution for libel was immediately instituted against the member for Aylesbury; he was deprived of his commission as colonel of the Buckinghamshire militia; his patron, Earl Temple, who provided the funds for his defence,* was at the same time dismissed from the lord-lieutenancy of the same county, and from the Privy Council.

---

* Letters from Wilkes to Lord Temple, May 25, June 5, and July 9, asking loans to the amount of 1200l. for this purpose.—Grenville Corr. vol. ii.

When Parliament assembled in the autumn, the first business brought forward by the Government was this contemptible affair—a proceeding not merely foolish and undignified, but a flagrant violation of common justice and decency. Having elected to prosecute Wilkes for this alleged libel before the ordinary tribunals of the country, it is manifest that the Government should have left the law to take its course unprejudiced. But the House of Commons was now required to pronounce upon the very subject-matter of inquiry which had been referred to the decision of a court of law; and this degenerate assembly, at the bidding of the minister, readily condemned the indicted paper in terms of extravagant and fulsome censure,* and ordered that it should be burned by the hands of the common hangman. Lord North, on the part of the Government, then pressed for an immediate decision on the question of privilege; but Pitt, in his most solemn manner, insisting on an adjournment, the House yielded this point. On the following day, Wilkes, being dangerously wounded in a duel with Martin, one of the joint Secretaries to the Treasury, who had grossly insulted him in the House, for the purpose of provoking a quarrel, was disabled from attending in his place; but the House, nevertheless, refused to postpone the question of privilege beyond the 24th of

---

* The resolution was as follows:—'The paper intituled "The North Briton," No. 45, is a false, scandalous, and seditious libel, containing expressions of the most unexampled insolence and contumely towards His Majesty; the grossest aspersions upon both Houses of Parliament, and the most audacious defiance of the authority of the whole legislature; and most manifestly tending to alienate the affections of the people from His Majesty, to withdraw them from their obedience to the laws of the realm, and to excite them to traitorous insurrection against His Majesty's government.' Pitt moved to omit the last member of the sentence as utterly exaggerated; but, upon a division, it was retained, by a majority of 273 against 111.

the month. On that day, they resolved 'that the privilege of Parliament does not extend to the case of writing and publishing seditious libels, nor ought to be allowed to obstruct the ordinary course of the laws in the speedy and effectual prosecution of so heinous and dangerous an offence.' Whatever may be thought of the public spirit or prudence of a House of Commons which could thus officiously define its privilege, the vote was practically futile, since a court of justice had already decided in this very case, as a matter of strict law, that the person of a member of Parliament was protected from arrest on a charge of this description. The conduct of Pitt on this occasion was consistent with the loftiness of his character. Despising alike the servility of the Commons, and the profligacy of the demagogue whom they wished to offer up as a sacrifice to the vengeance of the Court, the illustrious orator reprobated the facility with which Parliament was prepared to relinquish its privileges; and, at the same time, denounced the whole series of 'North Britons' as 'illiberal, unmanly, and detestable,' not, indeed, retorting upon Wilkes the vague scurrility of the Commons' vote, but denouncing, in language of reprehension not too severe, the base and mischievous spirit of publications which fomented discord and hatred between the different races of the United Kingdom.

The conduct of the Lords was in harmony with that of the Lower House. While the latter had been eager to surrender their privileges and to invade the province of the courts of law, the Lords seemed desirous of showing the same spirit of complaisance to the Court. On the first day of the session, under the pretext of privilege, a new charge was brought forward against Wilkes. The way in which this charge had been got up was not merely dishonourable to the individuals concerned in it, but really dangerous to the liberty of the subject.

The body of publishers, intimidated by the arbitrary proceedings of the Government, had refused to print Wilkes's productions; and he had consequently set up a private press at his own house, for the purpose of printing an edition of 'The North Briton,' and some other compositions. Among the latter was one of an indecent and blasphemous character, called 'An Essay on Woman, with Notes by Bishop Warburton.' This performance was in the form of a parody on Pope's poem, and intended to ridicule the distinguished prelate, who was the pretended editor. It was written by Mr. Potter, himself the son of a primate, and a gentleman well received in political and fashionable society, although notorious for his dissolute habits. A copy of the 'Essay on Woman' was found among the private papers belonging to Wilkes, which had been seized under the illegal warrant of the Secretary of State; and the Government sought to make use of this discovery for the purpose of assisting them in the ruin of their opponent. They could not, however, for very shame, make use of the copy which they had obtained in such a manner. They therefore employed one Kidgell, a parson, and chaplain to the Earl of March,* to tamper with Wilkes's compositor. A copy being by these means obtained, Lord Sandwich, the new Secretary of State, who, up to the time of his accession to high office, had been the companion of Wilkes's looser hours, undertook, or was selected,† to bring this matter before Parliament, as a breach of public morals, as well as of privilege. It was

---

* Well known for his scandalous life, by this title, but still more celebrated in the same way as the Duke of Queensberry.

† It properly belonged to the department of the other secretary, Lord Halifax.

proved, on examination of the man who had betrayed his employer, that the whole impression of this ribald production extended only to thirteen copies, and there was no evidence that any one of these had been circulated or seen by any person. The complaint was similar in this respect to that infamous charge which, a century before, had been the pretext for the judicial murder of Algernon Sidney. It was, indeed, a stronger case than that of Sidney; for a paper found in the possession of an accused person is unquestionably admissible to explain the character of his acts and intentions; but in the case of libel, the paper itself is a dead letter, until a criminal character is communicated to it by the act of publication; or, to borrow a fine illustration of this point, a man may keep poisons in his closet, but has no right publicly to vend them as cordials. It is publication, therefore, which constitutes the guilt; but a copy, surreptitiously obtained, cannot constitute publication.

Theory of libels.

Having entered upon the subject in this spirit, it was not to be expected that the Lords should be restrained from concurring in the votes of the other House of Parliament by any consideration of their particular character, as the Supreme Court of Appeal, and of the possibility that they might be called upon to pronounce judicially, after solemn argument at their bar, on the very questions which were now brought before them in their legislative capacity. So far, indeed, were they from any such misgiving, that they would have adopted the proceedings of the Commons with indecent alacrity: for, had not the Duke of Richmond reminded them that it was not usual to transact any business of importance without being specially summoned, their lordships were prepared to assent to the resolutions of the Commons on the same day that they were communicated. But on the following day the vote was passed, not, however, without strong arguments against it, and a protest,* signed by seventeen peers. The House then proceeded to vote the 'Essay on Woman' a breach of privilege and a blasphemous libel; and to order that Wilkes should be prosecuted by the Attorney-General.

The session was principally occupied by the proceedings against this worthless demagogue, whom the unworthy hostility of the Crown and both Houses of Parliament had ele-

<small>Popular sympathy for Wilkes.</small>

---

* This document, which, according to Walpole, was drawn up by Chief Justice Pratt, is an able and elaborate exposition of constitutional and common law, as well as of common sense, upon this question. But the simple point is forcibly and shortly put in the following passage:—' Nor is this case of the libeller ever enumerated in any of their writings among the breaches of the peace; on the contrary, it is always described as an act "tending to excite, provoke, or produce breaches of the peace." And although a secretary of state may be pleased to add the inflaming epithets of "treasonable, traitorous, or seditious" to a particular paper, yet no words are strong enough to alter the nature of things. To say, then, that a libel possibly productive of such a consequence is the very consequence so produced, is, in other words, to declare that the cause and the effect are the same thing.' The protest thus concludes:—' For these, and many other forcible reasons, we hold it highly unbecoming the dignity, gravity, and wisdom of the House of Peers, as well as their justice, thus judicially to explain away and diminish the privilege of their persons, founded in the wisdom of ages, declared with precision in our standing orders, so repeatedly confirmed, and hitherto preserved inviolable by the spirit of our ancestors, called to it only by the other House on a particular occasion, and to serve a particular purpose, ex post facto, ex parte, et pendente lite in the courts below.'—*Lord's Journals*.

Lord Campbell, in his life of Lord Camden, expresses his approval of the resolutions, on the ground that privilege of Parliament should not interfere with the execution of the criminal law of the country. But whatever objection might be urged against a privilege so extensive, it is certain that, by the law of the land, the person of a member of Parliament was and is protected in every case, except that of treason, felony, or breach of the peace. It is equally certain that a seditious libel comes within neither of the excepted cases. It might be competent to either House of Parliament to circumscribe its privilege; but it can hardly be contended that they could have a right to give a retrospective operation to their vote for the purpose of depriving an individual member of the protection which had already attached to him under the existing law.

vated into a person of the first importance. His name was coupled with that of Liberty; and when the executioner appeared to carry into effect the sentence of Parliament upon 'The North Briton,' he was driven away by the populace, who rescued the obnoxious paper from the flames, and evinced their hatred and contempt for the Court faction by burning in its stead the jack-boot and the petticoat, the vulgar emblems which they employed to designate John Earl of Bute and his supposed royal patroness. The Common Council of the City so far countenanced these riotous proceedings as to refuse a vote of thanks to the Sheriffs who had exerted themselves to quell the tumult, and who had already received the approbation of both Houses for endeavouring to enforce the execution of their orders. Wilkes himself, however, was forced to yield to the storm. Beset by the spies of Government,* and harassed by its prosecutions, which he had not the means of resisting, he withdrew to Paris. Failing to attend in his place in the House of Commons on the first day after the Christmas recess, according to order, his excuse was eagerly declared invalid; a vote of expulsion immediately followed, and a new writ was ordered for Aylesbury. A month after he had thus ceased to be a member, the House entered upon the consideration of his complaint of privilege, which had been made on the first day of the session, and which in accordance with precedent, and high constitutional principle, should have been immediately entertained. Even then they avoided the real question, which was simply whether privilege extended to the protection of a member of Parliament from being held to bail on a charge of seditious libel. But the Opposition, instead of confining the

Wilkes yields to the storm.

* Grenville Correspondence, p. 155.—Reports made to the Secretaries of State from the persons employed by them to watch the movements of Mr. Wilkes and his friends.

discussion to the complaint of privilege which Wilkes had submitted, and which exclusively concerned the House of Commons, must needs make the question of the legality of general warrants, which properly belonged to the courts of law, the prominent topic of debate. Sir William Meredith's motion, 'that a general warrant for apprehending and securing the authors, printers, and publishers of a seditious libel, together with their papers, is not warranted by law,' might well have been met by one of those ordinary amendments to which the House has recourse, when it is expedient to dispose of a question without putting it to the vote. To affirm or negative a mere question of law—and such was the proposition of Sir William Meredith—would have been equally improper; since a resolution of the House of Commons on such a matter must have been without authority, as without effect. But the Government preferred, and for their own immediate purpose, perhaps not unwisely, to deal with the question; and while they did not dispute the principle advanced by their opponents, they proposed to qualify it by an assertion as undeniable, namely, that such warrants were in accordance with the usage of office, and had never been condemned in a court of justice.

After a debate of unprecedented duration, Grenville, who, from his knowledge of parliamentary and general law, must have been aware of the real bearing of the question, attempted to get rid of the complaint of privilege by limiting the question to the legality of a general warrant. He succeeded in carrying his amendment, but by so narrow a majority that had the Opposition been content to lay the stress of their argument upon the one point which concerned the House, namely, the violation of privilege in executing a warrant, whether in itself legal or illegal, upon the person of a member of Parliament, it is probable they would have prevailed. In the end, the real question was negatived without a division; the motion, with the amendment proposed by the minister, was carried, and this matter, which had been long and carefully considered by the Opposition before it was brought forward, resulted in a futile vote.*

The King had taken a strong personal interest in all the proceedings relative to Wilkes. Grenville, by His Majesty's order, had written and despatched to the palace an account of each debate immediately on the rising of the House.† Every member who voted against the Court was marked; the placemen were by this time habituated to the rigour of parliamentary discipline; but the arbitrary policy of the Court went further; and the act of cashiering military officers for their votes in Parliament, which had been so much and so justly reprobated when resorted to upon a particular occasion by Sir Robert Walpole, was now to be reduced to a practice. Lord Shelburne, Colonel Barré, and General Conway, were, among others, deprived of their commissions for their votes on the question of general warrants. These extremities were pursued with the like arbitrary and inflexible temper which had urged the sovereigns of the line of Stuart to their ruin.

The King is personally interested.

There is one other circumstance in the conduct of the Government relative to the business of the general warrants which ought not to pass unnoticed. Wilkes had brought an action against Halifax, the Secretary of State, who had signed the warrant under which his house had been broken open and his papers seized. This action had been commenced in the spring of 1763; but the minister availed himself of every dilatory proceeding which the practice of the Court permitted to delay its progress; and in November in the fol-

Wilkes's action against Halifax.

---

* The numbers were 207 to 197.   † Grenville Correspondence, p. 234.

lowing year, upon Wilkes being outlawed for not surrendering to final judgment in the criminal information upon which he had been prosecuted to conviction by the Attorney-General, Lord Halifax came in, appeared for the first time to Wilkes's action, and pleaded in bar the outlawry of the plaintiff. It is difficult to say whether such chicane was more disgraceful to the great officer who resorted to it, or to the law itself, which permitted an abuse of its process* so oppressive to the suitor.

* This state of the law of procedure continued until 1852, when the scandal was partially remedied by 15 and 16 Vic. c. 76.

CHAPTER V.

THE COLONIAL QUARREL—INDISCRIMINATE SUPPRESSION OF SMUGGLING—STAMP ACT—RIGHT OF ENGLISH PARLIAMENT TO TAX THE COLONIES—THE EQUITY OF IMPERIAL TAXATION.

DURING the discussions relative to Wilkes, the minorities had on one or two occasions attained such an extent as to create serious alarm for the stability of the Government; but when that exciting question was disposed of, they subsided to their former level, and there was a fair prospect that public business would, for some time at least, pursue a smooth though sluggish course. But storm and peril suddenly arose from a quarter where appearances were most serene.

At the termination of the war, it became necessary to take vigorous measures for the suppression of a host of smugglers which infested the British coasts, and rendered the Customs' laws nearly inoperative. The royal navy were for the occasion employed as revenue cruisers, and the commanders of ships of war were regularly invested with commissions as customhouse officers. It is easy to believe that men, accustomed to the exercise of arbitrary authority, armed with these extraordinary powers, and ignorant of the usages of commerce, should sometimes perform the new duties assigned to them with a vigour beyond the law. For such excesses, however, when committed in the British waters, prompt and effectual redress was attainable. But when this system was extended to distant dependencies, grievous cases of oppression and wrong were practically without remedy. And the same system which was resorted to for the purpose of clearing St. George's Channel and the Irish Sea from piratical adventurers was deemed equally applicable throughout the wide Atlantic. It is hardly possible to state a stronger instance of the improvidence of the administration than their conduct in this particular. Contraband was, in strict law, the same on the coast of Norfolk as of Newfoundland; but, in fact, there was no comparison between such cases. Smuggling on the British coasts caused a serious injury to the fair trader and to the revenue, while it afforded occupation to the most lawless and desperate of mankind. But the contraband carried on by the American and West Indian colonies was beneficial to the mother-country, in a degree which more than compensated for the inconsiderable loss of revenue which it entailed; it was contraband only in name, and unless one nation is bound to respect the revenue laws of another—a position which at least is very questionable—there was nothing immoral in the traffic. For a series of years, America had sent large quantities of the manufactures which she imported from Great Britain to the Spanish colonies, receiving in exchange bullion, live stock, medicinal drugs, and other commodities. The beneficial effects, to all the parties concerned, of this trade, which the blind policy of rulers would have repressed, are sufficiently obvious. To England, especially, it was advantageous; for while it created an extraordinary demand for the products of her industry, it enabled the colonists to adjust the balance of trade, which was always greatly adverse to them, by remittances in specie.[*] Thus it was by her free trade alone that America was in a condition to carry on that regulated

Character of colonial smuggling.

[*] Petition of the Merchants of New York to the House of Commons, 1767.

commerce which the mother-country prescribed for her own exclusive benefit. No intimation whatever was given by the Home Government of their intention to prohibit this traffic, which, having been connived at for so many years, had, in the estimation of the colonists, almost lost the character of contraband, and was carried on with the punctuality of legitimate commerce. In the midst of its prosperous and harmless career, the colonial trade was suddenly and violently suppressed as a scandal and a nuisance. Such a blow naturally produced the utmost consternation and resentment. Under a rule, ever strict, if not somewhat harsh, the conduct of the colonies towards the mother-country had been, for the most part, dutiful, loyal, and even affectionate.* If they sometimes murmured at her authority, they still had confidence in her justice; and whatever might have been the feelings of a few restless and ambitious spirits, we are assured, on the best authority,† that, up to this time, the Americans had no desire for independence. But now their welfare was assailed, as it would seem, in the mere wantonness of power, by a blow not less deadly than any which the vindictive rage of a conqueror could inflict. Their trade and shipping were in a moment threatened with ruin; and the very means of performing their current engagements with the mother-country were taken away from them. Under these portentous circumstances, necessity, as well as resentment, dictated a measure which tended immediately to alienation. The colonists resolved to abstain as far as possible from the use of English manufactures, and were prepared to practise the utmost self-denial rather than have any dealings with a nation which

---

* Franklin's Examination before the House of Commons, 1766.

† Franklin in conversation with Lord Chatham.

had visited them with such cruel insult and oppression.*

Mistaken policy of the Government. It probably would have been no easy matter to reconcile the colonies to their ancient loyalty and allegiance, even if this grievous error had been promptly rectified on the part of Great Britain. But the policy which the Home Government pursued was fatally consistent. While the British cruisers were sweeping the seas of colonial merchandise, the Parliament, to which the colonists had always looked up as the ultimate guardian of their liberties, was giving its sanction to a succession of measures which seemed to have been conceived in a spirit hostile to their prosperity and freedom. By one of these acts, the preamble of which asserted for the first time the right of the imperial legislature to impose taxation on the colonies, customs' duties were charged upon the importation into the colonies of various articles of foreign produce, partly for the purpose of raising a revenue, and partly for the protection of the newly-acquired sugar-growing plantations. The proceeds of these taxes were, by an entirely new regulation, to be paid in specie into the imperial exchequer, and to be applied, under the direction of Parliament, towards defraying the 'necessary expenses of defending, protecting, and securing the British colonies and plantations.† This act was accompanied by another,‡

---

* 'They entered into general combinations to eat no more lamb, and very few lambs were killed last year.

'They considered the Parliament as the great bulwark and security of their liberties and privileges, and always spoke of it with the utmost respect and veneration. Arbitrary ministers, they thought, might possibly at times attempt to oppress them; but they relied on it, that the Parliament, on application, would always give redress. They remembered, with gratitude, a strong instance of this, when a bill was brought into Parliament with a clause, to make royal instructions law in the colonies, which the House of Commons would not pass; and it was thrown out.'—FRANKLIN's *Examination*, 1766.

† 4 Geo. III. c. 15.

‡ 4 Geo. III. c. 34.

which substituted throughout America a metallic for the paper currency to which the colonists had been forced to resort, because they had not money enough, after making their remittances to England, to meet the exigencies of their internal trade and commerce. To complete this perverse scheme of policy, a resolution was proposed by the Chancellor of the Exchequer, and readily assented to by the House of Commons,* affirming the propriety of raising a new and additional revenue in the colonies, by means of a stamp duty.

If any accidental circumstance could aggravate the irritation produced by these accumulated wrongs, that circumstance was not wanting. *Disputes with the Indians.* At the time when the British men-of-war appeared off the coast of America in the character of revenue cruisers, a great part of the country was suffering devastation from one of those cruel wars which occasionally broke out between the European settlers and the native Indians. The French, more amiable in manners, and less aggressive than the English, aided besides by the insinuating priesthood of that politic Church which can recommend itself to every condition of human society, had maintained a better correspondence with the natives than the British settlers ever attempted to cultivate. The savage tribes, or nations, as they were termed, had been rapidly compelled to retire before the progress of civilisation, under the vigorous conduct of the Anglo-Saxon; and the intruders had not been scrupulous in trespassing upon the hunting grounds still remaining to the original inhabitants, or in resorting to fraud, as well as force, to dispossess them. The natives had always, therefore, favoured the French rather than the English settlers; and were now

---

* It was proposed and agreed to in a thin House, late at night, and just at the rising, without any debate.—ALMON's *Collection of Papers.*

easily persuaded to view with jealousy and apprehension the triumphs of these formidable settlers over a kindred race, as well as over themselves. Silent and crafty in design, rapid and merciless in execution, the Indians accommodated or suspended their internecine conflicts, and prepared to make common cause against the foreign foe. At the approach of harvest, a simultaneous attack was made upon the principal provinces in the middle and southern parts of the continent, and upon the Canadian forts. The travelling traders were everywhere robbed and murdered; merchandise, to the amount of one hundred thousand pounds, was plundered—a loss which fell chiefly on the towns which carried on their internal trade by sending their goods round the country. The back settlements of Virginia, Maryland, and Pennsylvania, were, for several miles, laid waste and depopulated. Many forts were taken, and the garrisons butchered. At length, after a cruel destruction of life and property, the savages were reduced by an army composed of regular troops and colonial militia.

It was just when they had escaped from this struggle for existence, that the colonists were harassed by the still more grievous, because unprovoked, attack on their trade, their commerce, and their freedom, by that sovereign power to which they had a right to look for favour and protection. The last and most formidable blow was, indeed, withheld for the present. The stamp duty having obtained the sanction of Parliament, the minister was content to postpone carrying it into effect until the ensuing year, in order that the colonial assemblies might have an opportunity of considering his proposition, and if it should prove objectionable, of suggesting some equivalent form of taxation. It may be doubted whether any scheme of finance, or any capital measure of policy could be carried, even in England, after having

<small>Procrastinating conduct of the Executive.</small>

been subjected to the ventilation of public opinion for a year. Certainly such a course of proceeding would be ill calculated at any time to strengthen the hands of administration. The tone and tendency of public opinion in a free country can, for the most part, be ascertained by ordinary observation; and with the peculiar means of information which Government possesses, it is in a condition to mould its policy. In a country where the utmost degree of freedom obtains, there must still be a ruling power whose duty it is to give a practical exposition of its policy. A government which invites the people to suggest measures, deserts its proper functions, and creates disorder in the Commonwealth. Yet, had this tax, novel as it was, been imposed in the ordinary course, without formally consulting the assemblies, or had the experiment been tried at a more convenient season, it is not improbable that the colonies would have quietly submitted. _{Theory of taxation.}

It has been usual to represent the Americans as driven to revolt from British rule by the attempt to impose taxation upon them, contrary to the theory and practice of the constitution, which permit the people to be taxed only by their representatives. But the position of the people of Great Britain and that of the colonists widely differed in this respect. Lord Coke has demonstrated [*] that Customs' duties originated in England _{Lord Coke's opinion.} with a grant of Parliament early in the reign of Edward the First, and that monarch afterwards expressly renounced the right of imposing these taxes without the sanction of Parliament.[†] The illegal exaction of tonnage and poundage by Charles the First were charged as capital offences against the fundamental laws of the realm. But in the charters granted to Virginia and the first New England

---

[*] 2 Institute, pp. 58, 59. [†] 25 Edward I. c. 7.

settlement of Massachusetts bay, while the rights of the emigrants to the privileges of natural-born subjects were conceded in the fullest terms, a *temporary* exemption from taxation, both external and internal, was alone granted. Even the Long Parliament, though in the warmest sympathy with the Puritan adventurers of New England, took care to reserve the same right of sovereignty, by granting these colonists exemption from export and import duties only until the House should take further order to the contrary.* It is true that the colonial assemblies frequently passed declaratory acts asserting the immunity of the colonies from taxation, except by their own representatives; but these acts were always disallowed by the Imperial Government. The Navigation Laws, which placed the trade of the colonies under the restrictions of import and export duties for the benefit of Great Britain, had ever been regarded as an oppressive code,† and, had they been strictly enforced, would probably have encountered similar opposition to that which met the Stamp Act. Those restrictive laws ‡ which so materially retarded the prosperity of the colonies, and failed to effect that selfish and short-sighted object of aggrandising the mother-country in the same proportion, must eventually have produced a rupture between England and America.

* Vote of the House of Commons, 1642.

† Robertson's History of America, book 9, passim.

‡ Franklin states the real grievance of these laws,—'It is not that Britain puts duties upon her own manufactures exported to us, *but that she forbids us to buy the like manufactures from any other country.*'

Franklin was much pressed in his examination by questions having reference to the futility of the distinction between the right to impose external and internal taxation. At length he makes a significant reply,—'Many arguments have been lately used here, to show that there is no difference, and that, if you have no right to tax them internally, you have no right to tax them externally. At present they do not reason so, *but in time they may possibly be convinced by those arguments.*'

The Stamp Act was but the consummation of a perverse and intolerable policy. Their coasts blockaded with a British fleet armed with the authority of the Custom House, more formidable than letters of marque—their only profitable trade entirely stopped—their country threatened with an utter drain of specie;—all this, surely, was enough to stir the spirit of men, whose English ancestors had abandoned the land of their fathers, and sought a home in the unknown deserts of a new world, rather than endure the loss of their civil and religious liberties. And all this had been done long before the Stamp Act arrived in America. That act found the colonies already in a state of passive resistance. They were prepared to retaliate upon England her selfish policy, by abstaining from the use of her manufactures, and taking measures to supply their place by native industry. Had Grenville indulged them in their lucrative trade with the Spanish settlements; could he have abstained from meddling with their monetary system; and been content that the money raised and intended to be applied to their military defence, should be disbursed in the colony, instead of being paid in specie into the British exchequer, he might easily have imposed his stamp duty, or an equivalent, with no more danger of opposition than had attended another inland duty, that of the post-office, which had been submitted to without murmur.

It is easy to state the difference between a port and an inland duty; but the English constitution, which was appealed to, recognised no such distinction in regard of the right of the people to be taxed only by their representatives. The great democratic principle, as it exists in the British constitution, is compromised by an admission of the right of the Government to levy any tax whatsoever. Yet the

American patriot admits the validity * of a Customs' duty, and attempts to distinguish such a tax, by showing that it is paid by the consumer. It is plain, however, that the incidence of a tax is a purely economical question, quite separate from that of the right to impose it; but the reason assigned by this intelligent and well-informed advocate of the colonies shows that the real character of their opposition did not arise from regard to a political punctilio, but from a sense of oppression and practical injustice.

<small>Innocence of Grenville's intentions.</small>

It is perhaps hardly necessary to acquit the minister of any wanton purpose of insult or oppression in thus dealing with the colonies. The most grievous injury which he inflicted on them, the suppression of their contraband trade, was merely part of a system which he had established for the enforcement of the revenue laws indiscriminately throughout the Empire; and his formal understanding, looking only to the statute book, could see no difference between a smuggler at Liverpool and a smuggler at New York. It was just that America should bear a proportion of the charges necessary for her protection and security; but this claim, which had never been disputed, must be asserted as a right, because the Imperial Government had sovereign authority over its dependencies.

The minister said 'he could not understand the difference between external and internal taxes. They were the same in effect, and different only in name.'† That principle conceded, he thought the argument was at an end. If the colonies urged that they were accustomed to duties for the purpose of regulating commerce, but that they objected to taxes directly

---

* 'The authority of Parliament was allowed to be valid in all laws, except such as should lay internal taxes. It was never disputed in laying duties to regulate commerce.'—FRANKLIN's Examination.

† Grenville's Speech on the Address, Jan. 14, 1766.

levied upon them for other purposes, they were to be told their reasoning was unsound; 'that this kingdom has the sovereign, the supreme legislative power over America, and that taxation is a part of that sovereign power.' The proposition is indisputable, the law is clear, and execution is a matter of course. Such is the way in which a lawyer deals with a State question.

But Grenville was not, as he has been commonly represented, of a harsh and arbitrary nature. His Customs' Act had been accompanied by another act,* intended to compensate for the rigour of the first. Thus the timber trade was encouraged by bounties on importation to Great Britain. By the same statute, the duty on colonial coffee was reduced, and it contained other relaxations of the tariff in favour of America. Even in delaying the execution of his plan for raising an inland revenue, against the opinion of his colleagues, Grenville was actuated only by a desire to deal liberally and tenderly with the colonies. The very clause in the Stamp Act which perhaps caused most alarm and discontent, that, namely, which required the produce of the tax to be paid into the Imperial exchequer, was, it would seem, not intended to be enforced.†

Mitigatory measures of Grenville.

Another argument has been maintained in vindication of the equitable right of Great Britain to tax her American colonies. The last war, it is said, was undertaken wholly, and the preceding war chiefly, on their account. If this were true, England would undoubtedly have a right to expect reimbursement, to some extent at least, of the costs which she had incurred. But when the case is examined, the right is by no means so clear.

Further arguments.

---

* 5 Geo. III. c. 45.
† Whately, Secretary to the Treasury to Commissioners of Stamps, April 20. Treasury Minute, April 26, 1765.

The colonies had, for the most part, been originally planted without any assistance either in money or arms from the mother-country. The first settlers were partly adventurers, but principally fugitives from the tyranny which oppressed their native land. They came out, it is true, under the sanction of charters; but it was not by virtue of empty title-deeds that they conquered the savage wilderness; it was by their own courage and self-reliance that they possessed the land; and on a barren sovereignty laid the foundation of a great and enduring empire. Had they depended on the fostering care and protection of the mother-country, the North American colonies must soon have perished; it was only, indeed, when they were in a condition to minister to her wealth, and power, and pride, that England bestowed much attention on her hardy offspring. The writer, whose high authority has been so often quoted in support of the claim of Great Britain to tax the colonies, has, in tracing the political history of these institutions, himself shown that England is not entitled to the merit either of founding them, or of aiding their prosperity; and has marked with just reprobation the selfish and sordid spirit which throughout characterised the conduct of England towards her dependencies.*

Colonies neglected by England

---

* 'The policy of Europe, therefore, has very little to boast of, either in the original establishment, or, far as concerns their internal Government, in the subsequent prosperity of the colonies of America.

'The English Puritans, restrained at home, fled for freedom to America, and established there the four Governments of New England. The English Catholics, treated with much greater injustice, established that of Maryland; the Quakers that of Pennsylvania.

'Upon all these different occasions, it was not the wisdom and policy, but the disorder and injustice, of the European governments, which peopled and cultivated America. When those establishments were effectuated, and had become so considerable as to attract the attention of the mother-country, the first regulations which she made with regard to them had always in view

But it was pretended that the colonies were indebted to England for protection against the foreign enemy. It is certainly possible that these thriving communities in a state of independence might have provoked the cupidity of France or Spain, and that their united means of defence would have proved inadequate to resist the aggression of a great European power. Still, under such circumstances, the jealousy of England could hardly have viewed with indifference the aggrandisement of her ancient rivals by the conquest of the New World; the same principle of British policy which has so often saved Portugal and Turkey, would have sent forth fleets and armies to maintain the integrity of Virginia and New England. But apart from speculative considerations, can it be said with truth that the last war was undertaken wholly for the sake of the colonies? The old animosity between France and England was again rife, and would have broken out, had the existence of the New World been unknown. Disputes had already arisen from the commercial competition of the two great maritime nations for the riches of the East. In accordance with the policy which England had pursued since the Revolution, the pretensions of the

to secure to herself the monopoly of their commerce; to confine their market, and to enlarge her own, at their expense; and, consequently, rather to damp and discourage than to quicken and forward the course of their prosperity. In the different ways in which this monopoly has been exercised consists one of the most essential differences in the policy of the different European nations with regard to their colonies. The best of them all, that of England, is only somewhat less illiberal and oppressive than that of any of the rest.

'In what way, therefore, has the policy of Europe contributed either to the first establishment or to the present grandeur of the colonies of America? In one way, and in one way only, it contributed a good deal. *Magna virum mater!* It bred and formed the men who were capable of achieving such great actions, and of laying the foundation of so great an empire; and there is no other quarter of the world of which the policy is capable of forming, or has ever actually and in fact formed such men.'—SMITH's *Wealth of Nations,* book iv. ch. 7.

house of Bourbon were to be restrained, and the balance of power in Europe was to be preserved. But it would be difficult to show, that America was principally or at all concerned in the question whether France or Great Britain was to have factories on the Hooghly; or whether Prussia was to remain an independent power, or to be divided between Louis and the Empress Queen. Even the question, as it more immediately concerned America, had its limits. There was no necessary connection between the American colonies and the plantations in the West Indies; neither was it indispensable for the welfare of the former that Canada should be united with them under the same head. Nay, if the colonies were disposed to retort the selfish policy of the mother-country, they might have remained indifferent spectators of the struggle between the two great rivals, content that their interest was the same, whether they ministered to the aggrandisement of the one nation or the other. The truth is, that the last war was not undertaken, in the sense in which the term has been used, on account of the colonies at all.* France had long viewed with jealousy and apprehension the great and increasing maritime power of England. That power was founded on an organised system of commerce and navigation, the tendency of which was at once to secure her predominance at sea and in the markets of the world. Accordingly, the French factories in the East Indies were to be destroyed;

<small>Effects of jealousy between France and England.</small>

---

* 'It began about the limits between Canada and Nova Scotia, about territories to which the Crown indeed laid claim, but were not claimed by any British colony; none of the lands had been granted to any colonist; we had therefore no particular concern or interest in that dispute.' FRANKLIN's *Examination*, 1766.

It would be of little moment to the English settlers already in possession of an ample territory with an extensive sea-board and navigable rivers, whether the vast continent of America was to be shared by another race, or to be monopolised by Great Britain.

Minorca, by the possession of which France commanded the trade of the Mediterranean, was to be wrested from her; and above all, those vast and flourishing dependencies in the western hemisphere, which contributed mainly to her wealth and grandeur, were to be assailed, or at least circumscribed. France had no quarrel with Virginia, or Massachusetts, or Connecticut; but the strength of England lay in these noble colonies, and to strike at them was the most effectual way of humbling her pride and power. Thus it was that America became obnoxious to the enmity of France; not on her own account, but as an important member of the British Empire. With what justice, then, or with what grace, could England demand from her colonies a contribution towards the cost of their defence, when they had incurred danger only by their connection with herself? The particular terms of that connection, which were the cause of offence to the other maritime powers, had been prescribed by England for her own exclusive benefit. The colonies had always complained of them as vexatious and oppressive, and had practised every device to evade their operation; nor was it pretended that these regulations, however beneficial to the mother-country, yielded any reciprocal advantage to the provinces upon which they were imposed.

Such appears to me to be the true view of the question as it regards the equity of extending imperial taxation to the colonies for the purpose of providing for their defence. No weight is to be attached to the fact of their having taxed themselves at the requisition of the Government, as an admission of the righteousness of such a claim. It is easy to understand that this people, proud of their British descent, and entertaining a sort of filial affection for the country from which they sprung, should willingly have submitted themselves to a share of her burden, when called upon to do so as an integral part of the British Empire. Taxation, imposed through the channel of a representative assembly, was agreeable to the cherished tradition of English freedom, and a badge of the identity of the colonists with their compatriots, the recognition of which they had asked in their earliest charters. But taxation, imposed by the mere authority of the Central Government, was a badge of subjection and inferiority more suited to a conquered nation than to a race, the brothers and equals of the English people.

CHAPTER VI.

THE STAMP ACT—ILLNESS OF THE KING—REGENCY BILL—MISCONDUCT OF THE MINISTRY AND OF PARLIAMENT ON THIS QUESTION—ATTEMPT TO FORM A NEW ADMINISTRATION BY THE DUKE OF CUMBERLAND—UNSUCCESSFUL NEGOTIATION WITH PITT—MARQUIS OF ROCKINGHAM PRIME MINISTER—DEATH OF THE DUKE OF CUMBERLAND.

PARLIAMENT re-assembled on the 10th of January, and after some party skirmishing, the measure for levying taxes on the colonies, the justice and expediency of which had hardly been questioned either in or out of Parliament, was laid upon the table of the House of Commons. Ever since the colonies had attained stability and importance, the idea of making them contribute to the support at least of the military establishment necessary for their protection had been entertained by successive statesmen. The project had been considered by the ministers of William the Third, of Anne, of George the First; and it was the sagacious prudence rather than the constitutional scruple of Walpole, that deterred him from stirring so dangerous a question.* Pitt would have nothing to do with it.

Meeting of Parliament.

* 'I will leave the taxing of the British colonies,' said he, towards the close of his ministry, 'for some of my successors, who may have more courage than I have, and be less a friend to commerce than I am. It has been a maxim with me, during my administration, to encourage the trade of the American colonies to the utmost latitude; nay, it has been necessary to pass over some irregularities in their trade with Europe; for, by encouraging them to an extensive, growing, foreign commerce, if they gain five hundred thousand pounds, I am convinced that, in two years afterwards, full two hundred and fifty thousand pounds of this gain will be in His Majesty's exchequer, by the

Lord Bute had determined upon the measure, and Charles Townshend, then President of the Board of Trade and Plantations, had undertaken to carry it through the House of Commons. The only sound of opposition which had been raised to the Customs' Bill introduced by Grenville was from a gentleman named Huske, who had passed a considerable part of his life in America, and was, therefore, a great authority on colonial questions; and Huske objected only to the measure being pressed until time had been given for the agents of the colonial assemblies to express their opinions on the subject. But this gentleman, at the same time, asserted the capability of America to contribute largely towards imperial taxation. And with regard to the stamp duty, Grenville asserted* several years after the act had been repealed, that so far from objecting to this tax, many of the agents of the colonial assemblies had recommended it to him as a practicable one. Some of them, indeed, took a distinction between a duty of customs and one of excise, and thought a peculiar objection attached to the latter. Neither was the minister responsible for the ready acquiescence of Parliament in this measure. It was not introduced by surprise, nor in an insidious form calculated to disguise its real character. On the contrary, Grenville, in bringing forward his financial scheme for the preceding year,† had pointedly invited the attention of the House to that part of it which imposed a tax upon the colonies.

Preparations for carrying the measure.

labour and produce of this kingdom, as immense quantities of every kind of our manufactures go thither; and, as they increase in the foreign American trade, more of our produce will be wanted. This is taxing them more agreeably to their own constitution and laws.'—BANCROFT's *History of the United States.*

There cannot be a more striking illustration of the difference between the statesman and the mere minister of routine than the views of Walpole and of Grenville upon this question.

* In the House of Commons, 6th March, 1770.
† 9th March, 1764.

The bill did not pass altogether unopposed, for there was a division on the second reading; but a spectator, who soon after became a foremost actor on that great stage, describes the debate as one of the most languid he had ever witnessed,* and the measure was sanctioned by a great majority. Public opinion entirely approved of the colonial measures. The argument in its favour was so plausible, and coincided so much with the interest of the nation, that it was universally adopted. The last war, it was said, had been undertaken for the defence of the colonies; and, as they had the ability to do so, England had a right to make them contribute towards the expenses. *The bill passes the Commons.*

The administration, thus supported, gave little heed to any opposition which the colonies themselves might be disposed to offer to their policy. The very remonstrances which they had themselves invited, but did not expect to receive, were, when offered by the great States of Massachusetts and New York, withheld from Parliament; and five petitions, forwarded to the House of Commons from as many colonies, were, under pretence of some formal irregularity, contemptuously rejected. The bill became law on the 22nd of March.

The Ministry at this time seemed to rest on a firmer foundation than at any period since the demise of the Crown. The difficulties in which they had been involved by prosecuting the licentiousness of the press with a vigour beyond the law, were now at an end. The courts of justice had avenged the wrongs inflicted on liberty through the sides of Wilkes, and the people were satisfied. The *Stability of the Ministry.*

---

* Burke, 'Speech on American Taxation.' It seems, however, to have been enlivened by a striking burst of oratory from Colonel Barré, who so inauspiciously signalised his first appearance in Parliament by an absurd and insolent attack on Pitt.— Adolphus' *History*, vol. i. p. 171. 2nd edit.

formidable libeller and demagogue himself was overpowered, and driven into exile. A far mightier antagonist, that unrivalled orator and statesman, the idol of the nation, baffled in his recent attempt to regain power, and prostrated by disease, no longer appeared on the scene of strife. The hand of death had lately removed two potent chiefs of the Opposition.[*] Bute had retired to his country seat, under an engagement with the Duke of Bedford not to intermeddle in public affairs.[†]

The state of the nation was, on the whole, satisfactory. The people were reconciled to the peace. The improvement of manufactures and internal commerce occupied the attention of the midland counties. There was no question likely to provoke party conflict. The financial policy of the Government was, in the main part, as we have seen, received with almost unanimous approbation. Some discontent was, indeed, manifested in America; but when was a tax cheerfully accepted by those upon whom its weight was to fall? Worcestershire and Herefordshire had objected the year before to the cider duty; and, in the opinion of their countrymen, with much more reason than Massachusetts or New York could urge against contributing their share to the expenditure of the Empire. But resistance to the decrees of Parliament was no more feared from the American provinces than from the English counties. Such an apprehension never crossed the mind of any English politician; and the most impetuous, as well as the most

---

[*] The Duke of Devonshire and the Earl of Hardwicke died in the autumn of 1764. Since the retirement of the Duke of Newcastle from the Ministry, the Duke of Devonshire became the acknowledged leader of the Whigs.

[†] 'The Opposition is dwindled down to nothing, and Mr. Grenville, for he is the man of consequence, and that does the business. Let them say what they will, Mr. Grenville, I say, will have *champ libre*, and nobody to oppose him.'—*Duke of Newcastle to Marquis of Rockingham, 26th March, 1765.*—*Rockingham Papers*, vol. i. p. 181.

sagacious and prudent, of the colonial patriots admitted the necessity of submission to the imperial legislature.*

Yet it is certain that this measure of taxation for the colonies would have ruined the Ministry which proposed, and attempted to carry *Sudden illness of the King.* it into effect, had not that fate been anticipated by their mismanagement of a question of domestic policy of the simplest character. While the Stamp Act was passing through its last stages, the King was seized with a dangerous illness, the first attack of that fearful malady, by which the later years of his life were wholly obscured.† The cloud, however, on this occasion quickly passed away; but the King, duly impressed by such an awful warning, himself gave directions to his ministers to provide for the Executive Government in the event of his premature decease. The laws of the realm recognised no incapacity in the Sovereign from nonage,‡ or any other cause; therefore it became necessary to make special provision for each particular case. *The constitution did not provide a regency.* In the rude, irregular periods of the monarchy, the mode of appointing a guardian or regent of the kingdom during the minority of the King, had varied according to the circumstances of the time. A powerful subject would sometimes assume the office of Protector, and afterwards procure from Parliament, or from the Privy Council, the confirmation of his authority. But in most instances the regent was appointed by the great barons in Parliament assembled. A statute of Henry the Eighth, vested the Government, during the infancy of the heir to

---

* Such were the counsels of Otis, the eloquent representative of Boston; of Fitch, the Governor of Connecticut, by popular election; of Hutchinson, and of Franklin himself.—BANCROFT's *History of the American Revolution.*

† Adolphus' History of England, vol. i. p. 177, 2nd edition. —Quarterly Review, June 1840.

‡ Co. Litt. 43.

the Crown, in his or her mother, together with such
councillors as His Majesty should, by will or otherwise, appoint; and it was in pursuance of this disposition that the Duke of Somerset afterwards became
Protector of the realm. The next occasion on which
it became expedient to provide for the minority of
the Sovereign was the death of the Prince of Wales
in 1751, when the Princess Dowager was constituted
regent in the event of the demise of the Crown during
the infancy of her son. The course, therefore, which
constitutional usage, as well as natural propriety,
prescribed, was plain and clear. The Queen Consort
had every claim short of absolute right, which no
candidate could have, to represent him. But passing
by this simple and obvious mode of settling the
question, the King and the Ministry between them
dealt with it in such a manner as to cause the most
unseemly discussions in Parliament, and ultimately
the fall of the administration itself.

The whole transaction is one of the most obscure
passages in the history of this reign. The
King desired to reserve to himself the power
of naming the regent by an instrument revocable at
pleasure. Grenville objected to a reservation which
was absurd, as well as unprecedented, for it afforded
no security for the exercise of the power at a time
when His Majesty should be competent to make an
election. The minister advised in accordance with
the last precedent, that the regent should be named
in the speech from the throne, which recommended
a Regency Bill to the consideration of Parliament;
and he reluctantly deferred so far to His Majesty's
wishes as to consent that the choice should be restricted to the Queen and the members of the royal
family usually resident in England. But when a
bill, framed in accordance with this suggestion,
was introduced into the House of Lords, questions
immediately arose as to the meaning of its most

important terms. Who were the royal family? Did it include the Princess Dowager? Was the Queen eligible? And the appropriate result of a debate at once indecent and ridiculous, was to pronounce the King's mother ineligible as not being a member of the royal family; and to refer to the consideration of the Judges the question as to the capacity of his royal consort to hold the office of regent, by reason of Her Majesty being a foreigner. The Judges decided that the Queen was eligible; upon which the Duke of Richmond, with the view of removing any doubt as to the Princess Dowager, moved that the name of Her Royal Highness should be inserted in the bill. This motion should have been carried unanimously. It was respectful neither to His Majesty nor to his mother that Her Royal Highness's position should be a matter of question; and it was a positive insult, that the Princess should be wilfully excluded by a technicality from an honour due to her exalted station.

But there were considerations not wanting in cogency which determined the ministers in opposing the nomination of the Princess Dowager. An opinion prevailed even in the best informed circles, that the King's days were numbered,* and the possibility of Bute's return to power, under the auspices of his royal patroness, had a strong effect not only on Whig place-seekers, but on the minds of statesmen who were above the mere terror of exclusion from office. The Duke of Bedford, for example, who had taken office reluctantly, and had already signified to Grenville his intention of retiring at the end of the session of Parliament, not only entertained, on high constitutional principle, the strongest repugnance to Bute's political system, but also the worst opinion of

* Lord Holland told Horace Walpole that the King was in a consumption, and could not live a year.—WALPOLE'S *Memoirs of Geo. III.*

the man. He therefore opposed the pretensions of the Princess, because he considered them identical with Bute's return to power, and the restoration of the hated prerogative policy. These were, doubtless, the reasons which prevailed with him, when, upon the question being raised in the House of Lords, he stated his opinion, contrary to that of the Lord Chancellor, that the royal family was limited to the persons in the order of succession to the Crown. And when forced by the amendment proposed by the Duke of Richmond, to declare himself plainly, he at once opposed it. The motion was negatived without a division.

But the matter was not suffered to rest here. Halifax and Sandwich, not content with having defeated the attempt of the Princess's friends, must needs assume the offensive, and the plan which they adopted was of the most audacious character. The two Secretaries of State on the following day, without, as it would appear, consulting their colleagues, went to the King and told him that the bill would not pass the House of Commons, unless the persons eligible to the regency were more particularly defined ; intimating plainly that the Princess Dowager would be objected to. The King, anxious that his mother should not be exposed to indignity, himself, it appears, desired that words should be framed for the purpose of excluding Her Royal Highness. Accordingly, the qualification of any regent, other than the Queen, was with His Majesty's sanction, limited to 'any person of the royal family descended from the late King, His Majesty's grandfather.' With these words in his pocket, Halifax hurried down to the House of Lords; and having intimated that he came by special command, he moved the re-commitment of the bill, and inserted a clause containing the words above stated.

It is certain that the King had been taken by

Insertion of a new clause.

surprise, and in the agitation of the moment, from a mere motive of filial respect and affection, had lent himself to a proceeding which might be construed as a mean and heartless desertion of his parent. Of all his ministers, Halifax and Sandwich stood lowest in His Majesty's esteem;* it is to the last degree improbable, therefore, that he would have selected them as his confidential advisers in a matter of the utmost delicacy, and in which he took the deepest personal interest. The conduct of these noblemen cannot be too strongly censured. It was perfidious, fraudulent, unmanly; nor is it possible wholly to exempt the Duke of Bedford and Grenville from blame for failing to disavow this scandalous proceeding. Halifax, indeed, practised deceit upon his colleagues as well as upon his royal master, with reference to this business, but it can hardly be believed with the same success. He made it appear that the exclusion of the Princess had, in the first instance, been suggested by the King, and even asserted that he had endeavoured to dissuade His Majesty from taking such a course.† The most insinuating of all falsehoods is one which is literally true, and such a falsehood was this. It was undoubtedly the fact that His Majesty had urged the insertion of words, which should exclude the Princess, before the bill left the House of Lords; and it is possible that Halifax, having succeeded in possessing the King's mind with the apprehension of an affront being put upon the Princess by the House of Commons, unless this precaution was taken, might have affected to argue that such a precaution was not, absolutely necessary. There would have been nothing incon-

sidenote: The King misled by Halifax.

* Grenville's Diary, 1764, passim.
† 'Lord Halifax repeatedly assured Mr. Grenville that the words 'born in England' had been first proposed by the King to him and Lord Sandwich, and that he had rather held back in it, telling His Majesty that it might possibly not be necessary.' —GRENVILLE's Diary. Correspondence, vol. iii. p. 167.

sistent in such conduct. The great painter of human nature has represented the most subtle of villains clinching his atrocious lies by a feeble pretence of refuting them. It is hardly credible that Grenville, low as he rated the good faith and sincerity of the King, could suppose that His Majesty was indifferent with regard to a subject which affected him upon all the points where he was most sensitive—his filial piety, his personal pride, his prerogative; for all these were aimed at by the alleged hostility to the Princess Dowager. Neither Bedford nor Grenville were capable of devising or of instigating the fraud which had been thus successfully practised upon their royal master; but it is difficult to acquit them altogether of the responsibility which attaches to accessories after the fact. Their eagerness to depress and mortify Bute made them willing to believe any tale, however improbable, which should flatter their animosity. Grenville, indeed, expressed surprise* when Halifax informed him that he had the King's sanction for inserting words to exclude the Princess; but he seems to have taken no pains to inquire respecting the reasons or motives which influenced His Majesty in such an extraordinary determination. A contemporary historian attributes the conduct of the ministers in this transaction to a desire for popularity;† but though no motive could be too mean for the Halifaxes and the Sandwiches, the two principal ministers had little regard to mere popular applause. The Duke of Bedford had never courted it; and now that he was about to relinquish office, it is not likely that he would become a candidate for tribunitial honours. The chief act of his life, the negotiation of the peace of Paris, had been steadily pursued in opposition to public opinion; and while the Regency Bill was passing through Parliament, we

Sidenote: Culpable conduct of Grenville and Bedford.

* Diary—Grenville Corr. vol. iii. p. 148.   † Walpole's History, vol. ii.

shall presently see, that he disregarded popularity, even to the hazard of his life, in procuring the rejection of a foolish, but specious measure, which had received the sanction of the Lower House. Grenville carried his contempt of popularity to a fault. The people, he said, were represented in the Commons' House, and he knew no other exponent of their will. His measures, exactly adjusted to principle and precedent, were never qualified by any consideration of expediency. Had he been in Walpole's place in 1733, he would have braved a revolution rather than give up the excise scheme; and, after the fatal character of his colonial policy had been fully developed in 1770, he declared his opinion unaltered, and his determination, if he had the power, to enforce that policy, confirmed.

The King was soon undeceived. The very day after the Lords had amended the Regency Bill at the instance of Halifax, the Lord Chancellor, who had been no party to these shameful intrigues for the exclusion of the Princess, in an audience of His Majesty, undeceived him as to the grounds upon which he had been induced to give his sanction to the late important alterations of the bill. The King, in the greatest perturbation, sent for Grenville, told him how he had been betrayed, and entreated him to get the obnoxious clause expunged. But the chief minister, having only a few days before rated His Majesty in no measured terms for having presumed, in his absence, to advise with the Chancellor on a clause in the bill,* felt no disposition to

The King is undeceived.

---

* Relative to a proposed alteration in the Council of Regency. The conduct of Grenville, on this occasion, was unreasonable and arrogant. He had been duly summoned to the council at which this matter was discussed, but chose to absent himself on other business. If any apology were called for upon such an occasion, it was due from the minister to his sovereign for what might appear personal disrespect, and was, at least, contrary to etiquette. But the King had condescended to charge Halifax

extricate him from this painful dilemma. He coldly
declined to interfere, on the technical ground that
the alteration in the bill had been made by His
Majesty's authority. He would only go so far as to
say, that if it was proposed in the House of Commons
to insert the name of the Princess, he would not
object to it.

Conduct of Lord Mansfield.
Lord Mansfield, who had been also summoned,
though not a member of the Cabinet
Council, entered the closet after Grenville
had retired. But the Chief Justice was the last man
in the Empire, although perhaps the most able, to
aid his Sovereign in such an exigency. His authority,
derived from established pre-eminence as a statesman, no less than from the great office which he filled
with such distinction, would doubtless have enabled
him, even at this stage of the proceeding, to save
the House of Parliament, of which he was the most
illustrious ornament, from discredit; and his royal
master who, at least, had never betrayed or insulted
him, from unmerited anguish and mortification.
Mansfield, however, was incapable of generosity;
and his conduct, on this occasion, was consistent
with the selfish policy which marked his whole
career. Early in the debate he might have prevented all this scandal, had he supported the
Chancellor in opposing the doctrine of the Bedford
party that the King's mother was not a member of
the royal family. But on that occasion, instead of
at once avowing the only opinion on the subject
which such an intellect could entertain, the Chief
Justice seemed to make a parade of his pusillanimity

with a message to his brother minister, informing him of what had taken place. When Grenville related to Bedford and his colleagues the reproaches which he had vented in the closet, they all, with the exception of the Chancellor, expressed approbation. But Lord Northington seemed disgusted by such unprovoked insolence. — GRENVILLE's *Diary. Correspondence* vol. iii. p. 146.

by declining to reveal the opinion which he admitted having formed. The young King, affected even to tears by the painful position in which he was placed, in vain, therefore, relied on the wisdom and loyalty of an exalted councillor who had long renounced the objects of political ambition. Mansfield's reply to the earnest and touching appeal addressed to him by his Sovereign had been concerted with Grenville before he entered the closet. It was in harmony with that of the minister. The House of Lords could not stultify itself. The First Lord of the Treasury could not ask one House of Parliament to reverse what the Secretary of State had proposed to another House of Parliament by command. Thus, with a refined and heartless mockery, it was made to appear that this unfortunate measure had emanated altogether from His Majesty's will and pleasure. The whole responsibility was to be thrown upon him. It is not surprising that the King was agitated with the strongest emotion. A perfectly sound mind might, under such circumstances, have been distracted; but when it is considered that George the Third had only just recovered from a fit of mental aberration, the wonder is that the excitement to which he was subjected did not produce a return of his malady.

The King, with that tenacity of purpose which belonged to him, still persevered with Grenville. He expressed in gracious and winning terms an entire confidence in his minister's fidelity and zeal. The bill was now in the Commons, and Mr. Morton, Chief Justice of Chester, a gentleman known to be in the confidence of the Princess, had given notice of a motion to insert the name of Her Royal Highness when the bill was committed. Was that motion to be supported or opposed by His Majesty's ministers? And His Majesty desired Grenville freely to give him his opinion upon the question. The reply was that Her Royal Highness had better authorise somebody to say that she was perfectly well satisfied with what had already passed, and to decline this motion.* The King, dissembling his chagrin, affected to acquiesce in the expediency of such a course, though he said he could take no part in the affair. Notwithstanding this rebuff, the King did not yet abandon all hope of melting the obduracy of his minister. On the next day, when Morton's motion was to be made, he treated Grenville with marked attention, and 'expressed more approbation of his conduct than he had done for a long time'†

Intrigues with the Opposition. But while he thus flattered and amused the head of the Government, the King carried on a clandestine correspondence with the Opposition. Thwarted in his views and policy from the least to the most important points;‡ harassed and all but insulted§ in his person, George the Third had at length determined upon making an effort

---

* Grenville Corr.—Diary, vol. iii, p. 158.

† Diary, May 9.

‡ One of the minor causes of disgust was the morose refusal of Grenville to propose a small grant for the purchase of some ground overlooking the Palace Gardens, and upon which Grosvenor Place was afterwards built.

§ Grenville, in his own narrative, sufficiently describes the treatment to which he habitually subjected his Sovereign. Bedford appears to have been more measured in his language, and less frequent in upbraiding; but some insight is afforded into the dictatorial arrogance of his temper by an anecdote unconsciously related by the biographer and eulogist (if these are not convertible terms) of the house of Russell. The Duke had stipulated, as a condition of his taking office, that Bute should not in any way be consulted upon public affairs. He could do no less. But, according to Mr. Wiffen, His Grace considered it an infraction of this compact that Bute should have come to town, in the spring of 1765, and taken his place in the House of Lords. A political rival, with whom, it is to be remembered, Bedford had himself, almost up to that period, sat in cabinet council, was not only to be removed from power, but altogether secluded from public life, and confined to his country-seat, like the disgraced courtier of a mediæval despot!

towards emancipating himself from a thraldom more grievous than that under which his grandfather had groaned. Bute was no longer available for such a purpose; but probably it was by his advice that the King had recourse to his uncle, the Duke of Cumberland; for Bute's son-in-law, the Earl of Northumberland, acted as emissary on this occasion. It could have been no slight pressure which urged either Lord Bute or his royal patron to seek relief at the hands of the eldest prince of the blood. That personage had always maintained an unvarying aversion towards Leicester House. He steadily adhered to the principles which had placed his family upon the throne. He broke off a friendship and political connection of a lifetime with Fox, when that statesman joined the administration of Lord Bute; and had ever since recognised Pitt as the chief of the Whig party. The Princess Dowager and Bute, on the other hand, hated the Duke of Cumberland; and George the Third had been brought up in the same sentiments. To such an extent, indeed, did he carry them, that upon the Duke being struck with apoplexy the year before, the King would not even send to inquire for him, alleging as his reason for this breach of etiquette, if not of common decency, that it would be hypocritical in him to affect any interest in his uncle's welfare.*

Shortly, however, after his own recovery, the King had sent for the Duke of Cumberland under the pretext of communicating to him his intention of providing for a regency, but really with the view of sounding his uncle's disposition relative to the construction of a new administration. The Duke, though on principle loyal and dutiful to the head of his house, could not at once forget the neglect and contumely with which

_{The King sends for the Duke of Cumberland.}

* Grenville Corr.—Diary, vol. ii. p. 490.

he had hitherto been treated, and offered no encouragement to open a matter so important and confidential. But the King showed every desire to conciliate. In deference to the wish of His Royal Highness, and contrary to his own original design, he caused the names of princes of the blood to be included in the Council of Regency. This arrangement was concerted between the King and his uncle without the privity of the Cabinet; and it is alleged by high authority that the idea of excluding the Princess was then suggested to the ministers by way of retaliation for this invasion of their province.* Thus the Duke became reconciled to His Majesty's service; and on the very day the Regency Bill passed the House of Lords, His Royal Highness received, through the medium of the Earl of Northumberland, a commission from the King to communicate with Mr. Pitt, but accompanied with a charge to conduct the negotiation with the utmost secrecy and celerity,† for at this critical stage of the Regency Bill, the King feared to exasperate the ministers by giving them any cause to suspect the loss of his confidence. But five days afterwards, the bill had been returned to the Lords with the amendment upon which the King's heart had been set, introduced in the Commons, and carried triumphantly. The necessity for dissimulation therefore no longer existed: and the Duke of Cumberland was ordered to proceed openly to Hayes.

Fate of Morton's clause.
The fortune which the Regency Bill encountered in the House of Commons completely baffled all the ingenious contrivances which the ministers had employed for the purpose of defeating the just pretensions of the Princess Dowager. Morton and his supporters, of course, disclaimed any authority from Her Royal Highness for the course which they thought proper to take. Grenville, whose

* Lord Hardwicke's Memorial.—Rockingham Corr. vol. i.
† Duke of Cumberland's Narrative.—Rockingham Corr.

reluctance to carry out the King's wishes arose, not
so much from an objection to the nomination of the
Princess as from jealousy that His Majesty should
have consulted any other person than himself, upon
the details of the measure, hardly made a show of
opposition. The truth is, that neither the exclusion
of the Princess from the regency, nor the nomination of the other members of the royal family to
the Council of Regency, had originated with him.
The one had been determined upon by the King,
with the concurrence of the Chancellor, after previous
concert, as has been stated, with the Duke of Cumberland. And the bold measure of exclusion, though
afterwards adopted by Grenville, seems, in the first
instance, to have been altogether the suggestion of
Halifax and Sandwich. If the measure had been his
own, his tenacity of purpose and fearless temper
would hardly have given way at the first adverse
movement of the House of Commons. The probability, indeed, is that he was not ill-pleased to see
the officiousness of his colleagues rebuked by the
House of Commons. In the result, Morton's motion
was carried in the Committee without a division;
and though the sense of the House was taken on
bringing up the Report, the dissentients found themselves in a small minority.*

* The numbers were, 167 to 37. The difficulty mainly arose from naming the *royal family* in the bill. If the regent had been named, according to Grenville's original advice and according to precedent, this unseemly discussion would hardly have arisen. But the King's jealousy of power, and the minister's jealousy of Bute, involved the question in artificial difficulties. If the Queen only had been named, the bill would probably have passed without much discussion; but the nomination of the royal family seemed to contemplate the ascendancy of the Princess Dowager and Bute. Hence the awkward and absurd expedient of defining the term 'Royal Family' so as to exclude the Princess. Blackstone, the famous commentator, then a member of the House of Commons, put the point in a manner which it was difficult to answer, —'The Act of the 24th George the Second, by which the Princess of Wales is named for

The task of reconciling the Lords to the reversal of that important clause which they had introduced, as they had been led to believe at the special instance of the Sovereign, was appropriately confided to the callous effrontery of Sandwich. Their Lordships were, not unreasonably, in much ill-humour at having been so grossly trifled with. When the Duke of Richmond had proposed the assent of the Lords to the amendment introduced by the Commons, Lord Sandwich had got rid of the motion by moving the adjournment. When the Duke taunted him with his inconsistency, he coolly denied that he had been opposed to His Grace's motion, and said that he had moved the adjournment because it was improper that so important a question should be debated without due notice! * And this assertion was made in Parliament, where it was of the most recent notoriety that Sandwich had been a principal contriver of the intrigue, by which both the King and the House of Lords had been betrayed and insulted. But it was the same man who had acted as talebearer to the King; † and, himself an impudent and ribald debauchee, had stood up in his place and called upon the House of Lords to protect public morals against his sometime friend and boon companion Wilkes. Indeed, it is a striking proof of the low and coarse tone of morality in that generation, that it should have been possible for such a man, capable as he undoubtedly was, to have filled the office of Minister of State.

regent, is not yet expired; there is a possibility still of its taking effect, and therefore it seems to me highly improper to exclude her from this. If the Crown should devolve on a minor son of the late Prince of Wales, she would be regent.'— *Speech on Mr. Norton's motion, reported in* GRENVILLE *Correspondence*, vol. iii. p. 30, n.

* Walpole's History, vol. ii. p. 152.

† See ante, p. 153. Letter from Sandwich to the Duke of Bedford, dictated by the King, and informing His Grace that he had been proscribed by Pitt.— Bedford and Chatham Corr.

1765.   GRENVILLE'S INSOLENCE TO THE KING.   173

After the Regency Bill had received the royal assent, the principal business of the session was disposed of, and Grenville came to take His Majesty's pleasure as to the prorogation of Parliament. The King no longer thinking it necessary to preserve appearances with his ministers, coldly answered that he would have Parliament *adjourned* for a fortnight. Grenville did not for a moment affect to misunderstand His Majesty's meaning. Time was required for making the new arrangements which were in process of negotiation. Grenville refused at once to be a party to any such proceeding. He declared, in his usual style, that His Majesty wished him to do what would be disgraceful and dishonourable, in making him instrumental to a change in the Government without his advice or approbation. He went on in the same strain of insolence to tell the King that all the world knew he had empowered the Duke of Cumberland to make offers to everybody from right hand to left; that those offers had been rejected; that there was but one voice on the subject; that all the world saw it was Lord Bute's doing, and contrary to the express declaration made to the Government when they took office, with more to the same purpose. The King, as usual, kept his temper. He merely said that Lord Bute was not concerned in his present purpose of changing the Ministry.*

[Marginal note: The King wishes to dissolve Parliament.]

Both Bedford and Grenville had for some days been aware of what was going on. While the Regency Bill was in the House of Commons, the Duke had taxed His Majesty with the rumours which were afloat relative to his design of changing the Ministry; and the King, by his evasive replies, sufficiently admitted the charge. So closely, indeed, was he watched, that no precaution, nor dissimula-

* Diary.—Grenville Corr. vol. iii. p. 171, almost verbatim.

tion, could elude the suspicious vigilance of his ministers.*

While these intrigues were in progress, the capital was disturbed by one of those tumults which occasionally arise from the pressure of distress upon the labouring classes. In the last year, a parliamentary committee had inquired into the causes of the depression which affected the trade of the silk weavers; and in pursuance of their report, a bill had been introduced into the House of Commons during this session to regulate the trade, but the practical effect of which would have been to apply the vulgar remedy of excluding foreign manufactures. The measure passed through the Commons without discussion, and almost without observation; the interest of the House being wholly absorbed in the more exciting but far less important question of the regency. But when the Silk Bill reached the Lords, the Duke of Bedford, who had the rare accomplishment in those days of being versed at least in the elementary principles of political economy, at once declared against a measure which could only have aggravated the misery it was designed to alleviate. Upon his opposition, the Lords rejected the bill with the same facility with which the other House of Parliament had passed it. But though the Duke of Bedford was the only member of the Government and of the legislature who showed the knowledge of a statesman on this subject, there was little of discretion or kind feeling in his manner of dealing with it. Some portion of the distress in the silk trade was owing to the diminution of the demand

---

* 'Lord Northumberland is known to have been, on Saturday night [May 18th], at Richmond with the King, who waited for him in the garden, and let him in himself.'—GRENVILLE *Papers*. George the Second acted a more straightforward and manly part, at least, when he sent for Lord Waldegrave to deliver him from 'those scoundrels.'

for English manufactures in consequence of the policy which the Government had adopted with regard to the colonies; and it was not unnatural at a time when the laws which regulate commerce were but little understood even by professed politicians and financiers, that the workmen should attribute their privations to a cause so obvious as the competition of the foreigner. A wise and considerate minister, under such circumstances, having at once to oppose popular prejudice, and apparently to deny relief, would have sought to employ a soothing and conciliatory manner in the discharge of a painful duty. But Bedford is said to have adopted a tone of harshness and contempt in moving, as he did, the peremptory rejection of the bill. The disappointment of the weavers was, consequently, aggravated into rage and resentment. A large body of these people made their way to the King's presence, and meeting with a kind reception, quietly dispersed. All their fury was then diverted to the peers, and especially upon the Duke of Bedford. The Lord Chancellor, among other lords, was attacked, and asked, with menaces, if he had been against the bill? He answered boldly in the affirmative; and his fearless bearing, producing the effect which such conduct always does upon the English populace, he passed on unmolested. But the Duke was assailed with violence, and his house threatened with destruction. Much more was made of this affair than its importance demanded, and it was even converted to party purposes. Bedford everywhere asserted that Bute was the instigator of the disturbance; and when Lord Northumberland with his Countess made a visit of condolence at Bedford House, they were treated, both by the Duke and Duchess, with rudeness, almost amounting to insult.*

Riots among the weavers.

---

* Walpole's History, vol. ii.

About this time, the Marquis of Granby had sent in his adhesion to the Ministry; and Halifax, forward and officious as usual, took upon himself to write to the King his advice that Lord Granby should receive the command of the military force intended to suppress the riot. The only notice which His Majesty took of this impertinence, was to offer the command immediately to the Duke of Cumberland. His Royal Highness, in signifying his obedience to the King's pleasure, expressed a wish that His Majesty had no more formidable enemies than these poor people. Order was ultimately restored without military aid; and the weavers were pacified by a promise that the goods which were to be supplied by the foreign manufacturers should be countermanded.

Resignation of the Ministry. In the audience of the 18th of May, when the King intimated to Grenville his wish to have Parliament adjourned while the new arrangements which he contemplated were in progress, Grenville positively refused to move an adjournment which was to facilitate his removal from office, and told His Majesty that he would leave that duty to be discharged by his successor. This was on Sunday; and on the same or the following day, the ministers informed His Majesty that they should resign on the next Tuesday, whether the new Government was formed or not.*

Further negotiations. Meantime, the negotiation which had been set on foot under the auspices of the Duke of Cumberland, proved unsuccessful. The first suggestion which His Royal Highness made was unfortunate. In an interview with Temple, he proposed the Earl of Northumberland as the head of the new administration. Temple at once objected to this appointment, considering this lord to be nothing more nor less than Bute's lieutenant. Lord Albemarle

* Grenville Corr.—Diary, 3rd vol.—Rockingham Memoirs, vol. ii. p. 201.

was sent to Hayes next day, but met with little encouragement. Pitt was not disposed to enter on the subject with a subordinate agent, and said little more than that he would have nothing to do with Northumberland. The Duke's idea, in naming Northumberland, was, of course, to propitiate Bute, whose countenance and support he thought necessary to the permanence of any administration. He probably considered the nominal head of the Government as a matter of small importance; and, under the circumstances, perhaps better suited for an obscure politician than for a statesman of established position; since Pitt must be the real chief of any government of which he was a member. As to Pitt, or any other public man of note, really serving under the Earl of Northumberland, a notion so preposterous never could have occurred to a man of sense and knowledge of affairs.

Albemarle's mission having, after a second visit to Hayes, terminated unsatisfactorily, the Duke himself, by the King's express command, waited on the great statesman; and, in a conversation which lasted five hours, the whole matter was fully discussed. The terms upon which Pitt insisted were principally three :—First, that a counter alliance should be formed to balance that of the house of Bourbon. Secondly, that military, as well as other officers, who had been dismissed for their votes or political connections, should be re-instated. Thirdly, that the illegality of general warrants should be formally declared. Lastly, that Bute should be excluded from power and influence. It is remarkable, that no stipulation was made as to the removal from Court of those persons generally designated as 'King's Friends,' whose machinations are described as counteracting the policy and destroying the credit of the responsible government. Pitt could not have been ignorant of the rumours which attributed to these people an unconstitutional interference with the Executive Government. He certainly, of all ministers, would have been the last to tolerate such interference. But it is equally certain that as long as the courtiers did not meddle with affairs of state, it would be a matter of indifference to him who filled the minor offices in the household. The loftiness of his character, indeed, might have left considerable latitude to low intrigue; but had the 'King's Friends,' as they were called, really possessed the influence which has been attributed to them, certainly by great authorities,* it is difficult to believe

---

* Burke's pamphlet bears on the face of it the marks of oratorical exaggeration. The cooler judgment of Lord John Russell is entitled to greater weight. 'There appears no reason to doubt that, from the commencement of the reign there was a party called "The King's Friends" who attempted to exercise all real power, while the show of it only was left to the responsible minister; that on them all favour was bestowed, and by them the measures of the Court were directed: that while such was their influence, they kept in the background, occupying permanently lucrative subordinate places, and leaving the labour and the risk of political affairs to the ostensible rulers of the country: that at a signal from the Court, any minister was at once removed, and a subservient House of Commons were directed to transfer their votes to some other puppet, destined to hold a rank equally powerless, by a tenure equally precarious'— LORD J. RUSSELL'S *Introduction to Bedford Correspondence*, vol. iii. p. 45.

That the King wished to restore prerogative to some degree, at least, of efficiency, and to break up those party connections by which prerogative had been supplanted, is undeniable. It was quite consistent with this design, that he should not give his confidence to any of the public men whom he was forced to employ in responsible office, because they were, one and all, committed to party engagements. But after the sudden failure of Bute's crude experiment, it took several years to mature the plans of the Court. The negotiation for a change of ministry, in 1765, was conducted, not by a courtier, but by a prince of the blood long estranged from Court, and in close connection with the great party leaders. It had for its object, not the substitution of a puppet ministry, but the formation of a cabinet which should consist of the first men in the country.

Neither does it appear that the court cabal had at this period the means of acting decisively upon Parliament. The case of the Regency Bill is, at least, an instance to the contrary. It was

that Pitt would have been content with the removal of Bute, while the agents of his system were left as before in the full exercise of power.

The narrative of this transaction, drawn up by the Duke of Cumberland himself, and lately published in the 'Memoirs of the Marquis of Rockingham,' is somewhat obscure as to the particular ground upon which the negotiation with Pitt and Temple was finally broken off. The Duke had full authority, and seems to have offered no serious opposition to any of the terms proposed. The only article which seemed to present difficulty was the formation of new foreign alliances; but all that could be required or conceded on this head was that it should be open to the new administration to pursue such a policy. Pitt, in fact, was willing to take office; but Temple had evidently, from the first, determined that the proposed arrangement should not take place: and his influence prevailed with his illustrious kinsman. The explanation of Temple's apparent perverseness is to be found in the significant fact that, two days after the Duke of Cumberland announced to the King the unsuccessful result of his commission, a reconciliation took place between

The negotiation broken off.

the fear of an adverse vote of the House of Commons which induced the King to consent, at the instance of one of his responsible advisers, to a slight being put upon his mother. But if he could have dismissed the ministry at his pleasure, and commanded the acquiescence of the House, he might have spared himself a degree of anxiety and annoyance far greater than any public measure had yet cost him. So far, however, was he from relying on any illegitimate influence with the Commons, that we find him up to the last moment endeavouring to conciliate Grenville, as the only channel through which he could hope to guide that assembly.

The great measure of the peace also had been carried, not by secret influence, but by the well-established means of bribery and corruption, administered through the agency of one of those party chiefs, whom it was the object of the new Court system to discard. The first real trial of this system seems to have been made on the Rockingham administration, and certainly proved very successful. But it was not until after the election of 1768 that it became completely efficient.

Grenville and his elder brother. They both, indeed,
took the pains to inform their respective friends that
this was a family matter, having no connection with
politics. But the event had for some time been in
contemplation on either side; and it had long been
the object of Temple to concentrate political power
in the family of Grenville.

The Duke of Cumberland made one more attempt
to rescue the King from political duress by
offering the government to Lord Lyttelton,
a nobleman known as the early friend and contemporary
of Pitt, and with some pretensions to oratory
and literature. But Lyttelton prudently shrunk from
an eminence to which he was unequal; excusing
himself on the ground of his connection with the
Grenvilles.

Lord Lyttelton sent for.

Thus was the King made to feel the vanity of his
resistance to party, or rather to the great families to
whom political power at this time almost exclusively
belonged. In announcing to Grenville his desire
that the ministers should resume their duties, His
Majesty said that he had not intended to dispense
with *his* services, an assertion which probably obtained
as much credit as it deserved. But though
Grenville's grumbling, jealous, and quarrelsome temper
must have been to the last degree tiresome and
provoking, George the Third respected his character,
and entertained a high opinion of his talents for
administration. Had it not been for his insufferable
temper, the King would have preferred the comparative
mediocrity of Grenville to the domineering
genius of Pitt; and his arrogance, perhaps, was of a
less offensive quality than that of the Temples and the
Bedfords.

On the same day that the reconciliation took place
between Temple and his brother, the
ministers assembled to consider the terms
upon which they should consent to remain in His

New arrangements of the Ministry.

Majesty's service. The conditions were soon agreed upon, and are in remarkable contrast with those which had been named by Pitt, as having none of them any relation to questions of public policy, but bearing in each a personal and vindictive character. The exclusion of Bute from all employment or concern in public affairs was, as usual, the first article of the new treaty. And here, again, it is remarkable that no mention was made of those mysterious men in office, by whose agency at Court, in Parliament, and in society, the Bute system was supposed to have been carried into effect, and the credit of the responsible Government undermined. But it was demanded that Mr. Stuart Mackenzie, a gentleman whose only demerit was his relationship to Lord Bute, should be dismissed from his office of Privy Seal of Scotland. Lord Holland, also, apparently to gratify the old enmity of Grenville, was at length to be removed from his post of Paymaster. The Marquis of Granby was named for the command of the army, an appointment intended at once to reward a new adherent, and to retaliate upon the Duke of Cumberland for the part he had lately taken in negotiating the change of ministry. The last condition was the only one which did not contain a proper name; it required that the Government of Ireland should be placed at the disposal of the Ministry, the object being, for obvious reasons, to deprive the Earl of Northumberland of the Lord-Lieutenancy of that kingdom.

The King, after consideration, assented to three of the stipulations, but objected strongly to the dismissal of Mackenzie, on the ground that he had accepted office on His Majesty's promise that he should not be removed. The answer was, that His Majesty had no right to make such an engagement. The King refused to yield, and Grenville immediately tendered his resignation. His Majesty's reply was full of spirit and good sense. He said that, having recalled the Ministry, he felt bound to comply with their terms. But he desired Grenville distinctly to understand that his royal word had been pledged to Mackenzie, and, if that word was to be broken, the responsibility should rest upon his ministers, and not upon himself. Grenville appears to have been touched with some sense of shame and remorse on this occasion, for he muttered that something might be done for Mr. Mackenzie, upon which the King contemptuously replied that Mackenzie would trouble himself very little about the matter.*

With reference to the proposed change in the command of the army, the King sent for Lord Granby, and appealed to his feelings as a soldier and a gentleman, not to lend himself to a slight intended to be put upon one who was entitled to respect, as an old and meritorious officer, if not as the near kinsman of the Sovereign. In the result, this point was ungraciously, if not indecently, compromised, by giving Granby the reversion of the command-in-chief after the Duke of Cumberland, whose life, it was well known, could hardly be prolonged many months.

<small>Feud between the King and the Ministry.</small>

The King made little or no effort to disguise his repugnance to the ministers who had been forced back upon him. Parliament having been prorogued immediately on their resumption of office, His Majesty had no other opportunity of showing his aversion than by disregarding their recommendation of candidates for preferment. A vacancy in the household of the Queen having been occasioned by the appointment of Lord Weymouth to the Vice-Royalty of Ireland, Grenville was desirous of naming his successor, but Her Majesty bestowed the office on the Duke of Ancaster, without consulting the Government. In like manner, a vacant

---

* From Mackenzie's own narrative, Mitchell MSS., quoted in a note to Chatham Correspondence, vol. ii. p. 312.

regiment was given to General Keppel, in preference
to Lord Waldegrave, the nominee of the minister,
the former being brother to Lord Albemarle, the
intimate friend of the Duke of Cumberland. The
youthful Duke of Devonshire was introduced at
Court by his uncles, and treated with marked distinction, chiefly, as it would seem, for the purpose of
annoying the Government, the House of Cavendish
being in opposition.

Matters could not remain in this state; the First
Lord of the Treasury, indeed, seems at this *Bedford remon-*
period, when he had some tangible ground *strates with the King.*
for complaint, to have laid aside that querulousness
with which it had been his practice to weary and
torment his royal master. But the proud and irritable
spirit of Bedford could not brook the coldness and
reserve with which the King treated his ministers.
On the 12th of June, three weeks after the recon-
struction of the Government, the Duke demanded an
audience,* on the occasion of his leaving London; and

* This famous interview seems to have been much misrepresented. The mendacious exaggerations of Walpole and Junius may be at once rejected. But even Burke, with somewhat of the facile credulity of a vulgar political opponent, alludes to 'the report of a gross and brutal treatment of the——by a minister at the same time odious to the people.' Other well-informed writers have given their countenance to these coloured versions. Lord Mahon, always candid and temperate, censures the Duke of Bedford for having used the word 'favourite' in speaking of Lord Bute, and for charging the King with a breach of his promise.

The application of the term 'favourite' would no doubt have been offensive; but it is assumed that the Duke actually used this word, from the fact of its being found in the private minute which Bedford made of his intended remonstrance. No mention, however, is made of this pointed phrase having been employed, nor of any disrespectful language having been used in the account of the interview given by Sir Gilbert Elliott (probably from the King's own information), nor in the memorandum of the interview in Grenville's diary. The Duke, as a diplomatist and a courtier, was accustomed to measure his words; and therefore was the less likely to be betrayed into a gross impropriety. And as to charging the King with a breach of his promise, that really was the whole gist of the Duke's discourse. Whether it was of an insulting character or not de-in language firm and decisive, but not stronger than it behoved a minister of state to employ, represented to His Majesty the injustice and ill-effects of bestowing his favours upon persons who were opposed to the confidential advisers of the Crown. The King listened with patience, and merely denied, as he had done to similar insinuations from Grenville, that Lord Bute had been consulted in public affairs.*

But objurgation and complaint were in vain employed to win back confidence and esteem. The King, more than ever disgusted, again had recourse to the unsophisticated loyalty, the experience and discretion of that illustrious member of his house, upon whom he had latterly placed all his reliance. The Duke of Cumberland again appealed to the patriotism of that great subject who alone seemed able to rescue his sovereign and his country from the insolence of faction.

Duke of Cumberland consulted.

Pitt, on this occasion, seems to have laid aside the magniloquence which he usually employed, and to have met the overtures of the Duke in a frank and earnest spirit. In two interviews with the King, the policy of a new administration to be formed under his auspices, and the men of whom it was to be composed, were agreed upon. Its foreign policy was to be indicated by a renewal of the Prussian alliance; the colonial measures recently adopted were to be entirely changed. In

Failure of the new scheme.

---

pended entirely on the manner in which it was conveyed. On the whole, though I cannot go as far as Lord John Russell in bestowing unqualified praise upon the Duke's remonstrance, because it was in a great measure rendered unnecessary by the intolerable rigour of the terms which ministers themselves had imposed upon the King; yet, on the other hand, there is no doubt that Bedford firmly believed in the ascendancy of Bute, and considered such conditions indispensable to carry on the Government.

* The King assured Sir Gilbert Elliott that he had not spoken to Lord Bute on politics since he left office in 1763. This was no doubt literally true; but it is also certain that Bute continued his political intrigues long after his resignation.

domestic affairs, general warrants were to be abolished, and the cider-tax was to be repealed. Finally, though not perhaps least in importance, in the King's estimation, Mackenzie was to be restored to the sinecure office of which he had been so harshly deprived. The only real obstacle to an arrangement so promising was to be found in the pride and selfishness of one individual, and that obstacle proved fatal to the whole scheme. Pitt was unfortunately bound to Temple by ties of affinity, of friendship and gratitude, which a less noble nature would not have considered indissoluble. Temple had been designated by his brother-in-law for the office of First Lord of the Treasury. But he peremptorily refused bearing any part, great or small, in the proposed administration. He said that reasons of delicacy prevented him. Every consideration was to be sacrificed to the renewed connection with his brother, and to the arrogant conceit which had sprung from it of forming a family cabinet. He was willing to take the first place, but it must be as the chief of a Grenville administration.*

Deeply mortified at this undeserved and unexpected failure, Pitt seems to have contemplated withdrawing from public life. He sold his favourite villa near London, and retired to an estate in

---

* Pitt seems to have been unprepared for this result. On the 22nd June, he writes to Temple, to inform him of the progress of the negotiation, and of the frankness and cordiality of the King. But while Pitt was making arrangements in the closet, Temple was in close correspondence with his brother, who records, in his diary, that nothing could be more truly affectionate than Lord Temple's conduct towards him in all this transaction.' About this time, Lord Chesterfield writes to his son,—'Mr. Pitt would have accepted, but not without Lord Temple's consent, and Lord Temple positively refused. There was evidently some trick in this, but what, is past my conjecture.' The 'trick,' however, is now plain enough. Lady Hervey, who was well informed, speaks, in the preceding March, of the connection between Temple and Pitt having 'given way.'—*Letters*.

Somersetshire, which had lately been devised to him by Sir William Pynsent, a gentleman who had been personally unknown to him, but one of the many admirers of his genius and patriotism, scattered through the country. In this remote retreat, he expressed his intention of passing for the most part the remainder of his days.

The King sends for Newcastle. The King, determined not to be again remitted to the intolerable yoke of the Bedfords and the Grenvilles, empowered his uncle to open a communication with the old intriguer Newcastle. Eager as ever for patronage and power, the Duke obeyed the summons with alacrity; and as he still retained considerable credit and influence with the Whig party, there was no difficulty in bringing together the principal members of that connection under his auspices. The first question proposed at the meeting which took place, was the expediency of the Whigs coming into office at all under existing circumstances? And this preliminary being decided in the affirmative by the great preponderance of weight as well as numbers, the terms were easily agreed upon. The first article was the one upon which every minister insisted—whether Grenville, Pitt, or Newcastle—as the basis of the arrangement. The Earl of Bute must be removed from Court, and from all interference in affairs of state. But the Whigs went farther. They required that certain particular friends of that nobleman should be removed ' as a proof to the world that the Earl of Bute should not either publicly or privately, directly or indirectly, have any concern or influence in public affairs or in the management or disposition of public employments.'* They would not even allow an exception in the case of Mr. Mackenzie. They made no other terms. They abstained from entering into any parti-

* Paper drawn up by Newcastle.—Rockingham Memoirs, vol. i. p. 218.

culars of their proposed measures, no doubt advisedly, that they might mark, in the most emphatic manner. the paramount importance which they attached to the Sovereign's entire dependence upon, and unqualified support of, his responsible ministers.

The conditions were agreed to without hesitation. If the Whigs were possessed chiefly with the idea of entering upon a stage clear of favouritism, the King, at this time, was intent only on his emancipation from that galling thraldom in which he had been kept ever since his first attempt to set himself free from party connection.

A new administration and its members.

The new administration comprised in its principal departments no individual of any official experience, and hardly one of adequate ability. At its head was placed the Marquis of Rockingham, a young nobleman who had been appointed a lord of the bedchamber at the King's accession, and distinguished himself by a spirited remonstrance, when abruptly dismissed from office, with others, for objecting to the peace.* If a high character, a good understanding, a great estate, and exalted rank, were sufficient qualifications for the first minister of this country, the Marquis of Rockingham was as eligible as any other person in the like predicament. But Rockingham, though well-known as a patron of the turf, was a stranger to the nation in the character of a statesman. He was unfortunate also in not possessing the faculty of recommending himself to public confidence by a display of ability in Parliament. Bute had been exposed to derision by the sententious, unpractised style of his oratory. But Rockingham was incapable of making an exposition of any sort, even upon the plainest subject, in the House of Lords. The consequence was, that in this

The Marquis of Rockingham.

* Ante, p. 125.

country, where public speaking passes for so much more than it is worth, Rockingham failed to obtain credit for the information and good sense which he really possessed.

<small>General Conway.</small> The appointment of the Leader of the House of Commons was one still more unfortunate. General Conway, who had been dismissed from his office in the Household and from his regiment the year before, for voting against the Government on the question of general warrants, was selected for the most important post in the new administration. He was a brave officer and an amiable man, but had hardly any qualification for the management of the House of Commons. It is true that he was not altogether deficient in the power of expressing himself; and in this respect he had the advantage of his coadjutor in the other House of Parliament. But he had to succeed Grenville, who, from long study and experience, was thoroughly acquainted with the House, and was no mean proficient in the art of oratory. He had to fill that position instead of Pitt, by whom the House and the country had hoped and expected that it would have been filled. Conway's intimate friend* has mentioned the repulsive coldness of his manner, and the nice sense of honour, which rendered him unfit for the management of the House of Commons as it was then constituted. So little discrimination was observed in the allotment of places, that it was proposed to make Conway Chancellor of the Exchequer, although he had no knowledge of financial affairs.† He had been reluctant to join an administration in the stability of which he had no confidence; and at length gave a military reason for his acceptance of office—the commands, namely, of His Majesty and the Duke of Cumberland.

<small>* Walpole's History, vol. ii. p. 195.　　† Ibid.</small>

Conway became Secretary of State. The other secretary was the Duke of Grafton. Except in the instance of very rare endowments, it is considered necessary for the efficient ad- ministration of high office that the minister should have acquired experience in subordinate employment. Grafton had never been in office, and did not come within the exception. He afterwards became the head of an administration himself, but he owed this elevation partly to accident, partly to his great rank and fortune, qualifications which have always had too much weight with the Whig party. Unsteady, capricious, and indolent, he had hardly any quality of a statesman; and, like many men who have little of personal merit to stand upon, he was disposed to presume on his accidental advantages. The department of finance was entrusted to Mr. Dowdeswell, a respectable and intelligent county member, but hardly fitted to be Chancellor of the Exchequer at a time when the increase of the public debt, and the signal failure of the fiscal policy, which had been recently attempted, rendered that office one of more than ordinary weight and solicitude. Lord Northington, who had kept very much aloof from the factious counsels of his colleagues in the late Government, retained the great seal; but with this exception, all the official experience of the administration was centred in the Duke of Newcastle. He held the privy seal, to which was attached for his peculiar gratification the church patronage.

Some of the best and foremost Whigs refused to take part in the new Government. Sir George Savile, member for the great county of York, and a man of high standing both in respect of character and ability,* though willing to give the administration his sup-

* He had been designated by Newcastle for Speaker at the commencement of the reign.

port, would not compromise his position by becoming a party to an arrangement so precarious. The rising reputation of Lord Shelburne was not among them. Charles Townshend, though eager for high place, was content to let his brilliant talents remain in the comparative obscurity of the Pay Office, rather than accept a seat in a cabinet so frail.

The earliest acts of the Government showed vacillation, and distrust in their own stability. They sought, at the same time, to cultivate popularity and to conciliate Pitt, by conferring a peerage on Pratt, the Chief Justice of the Common Pleas, who had gained public applause by acquitting Wilkes with some high patriotic sentiments somewhat in the style of his illustrious patron. So much importance had Pitt attached to the elevation of his friend, that he had made it one of the articles in the negotiation with the Duke of Cumberland. Not satisfied with this, they went so far as to appoint one Nuthall Solicitor to the Treasury, for no other apparent reason than that he was the private solicitor of Mr. Pitt. But all this was to little purpose. Pitt smiled at such artless devices; while the King, still wholly intent on breaking up the old historical parties, could never encourage a new combination of great Whig families such as that which had just been formed under the Marquis of Rockingham.

<small>Chief Justice Pratt created Lord Camden.</small>

While they thus failed in acquiring strength and support, the Ministry sustained a heavy, though not unexpected, loss by the death of the Duke of Cumberland. Without any claim to the character of a great man, this prince was distinguished by some noble and commanding qualities. In his profession of arms he shared the personal courage which was common to his race; and though sorely tried in the prime of life by grievous and incurable maladies, his patience

<small>Death of the Duke of Cumberland.</small>

and fortitude never forsook him. His military talents were not above mediocrity. On the only occasion when he held a difficult command, his plans were so unskilfully contrived that they ended in the surrender of his army. His failure on that occasion, having been harshly censured by his father, he bore the rebuke with the silent submission of a soldier and a son, but resigned all his military employments, and, at the age of thirty-seven, retired from the active pursuit of a profession to which he was warmly attached. In the early part of his military career, he had incurred popular odium by the stern severity with which he had put down the Scotch rebellion of 1745. But in his latter years, though without the least effort on his part, he had acquired the esteem and almost the affections of the people. His personal honour was of the purest kind; and he had that high and overruling sense of duty which is one of the most admirable qualities of a public man. A keen and yet disinterested politician; a judicious and consistent supporter of the principles which had placed his family upon the throne; a loyal subject and a faithful friend;—such was the Duke of Cumberland,—who may fairly be pronounced one of the most estimable princes of the House of Hanover.

CHAPTER VII.

DISTURBANCES IN AMERICA—ASSEMBLY OF CONGRESS—IRRESOLUTION OF THE GOVERNMENT—DEBATES IN PARLIAMENT—PITT'S DENIAL OF THE RIGHT OF PARLIAMENT TO TAX THE COLONIES—REMARKS ON THIS SUBJECT—FRANKLIN'S EXAMINATION AT THE BAR OF THE HOUSE OF COMMONS—REPEAL OF THE STAMP ACT—THE DECLARATORY ACT.

Reception of the American Stamp Act.

The Ministry coming into office during the recess of Parliament, had ample time to concert their policy and measures. But the pressure of one important question would have been sufficient to test the energy and skill of the ablest administration. In the summer and autumn, intelligence reached the Government of the spirit of discontent and resistance with which the Stamp Act had been received throughout North America. At Boston, New York, and Philadelphia, the principal cities of the colonial continent, there were riots almost simultaneously. The act was publicly burnt, and the houses of persons connected with the Government were set on fire. The newly-appointed distributors of stamps were compelled to renounce their offices on peril of their lives. And the respectable inhabitants, in coming forward to protect life and property, did so with the more readiness, because these disorders brought discredit on the noble and righteous cause of resistance to tyranny and oppression in which they were engaged. But the sentiments of the people were expressed in the most solemn and authentic form. The great and flourishing province of Virginia, the eldest of the colonies, as well as the one most distinguished for ancient loyalty and attachment to the parent state, protested through her Representative Assembly against the aggression of the British legislature. The Virginia House of Burgesses passed a series of resolutions, asserting, in terms the most unhesitating and distinct, the hereditary right of the colonists to all the immunities and privileges which appertained to the people of Great Britain. They referred to the charters of James the First for an express recognition of that right; and they claimed, in their representative capacity, the first and most important of those privileges—that, namely, of imposing taxes upon their constituents. So entirely were these sentiments in accordance with the opinions of the whole province, that, when the English Governor dissolved the Assembly for the vote which they had passed, all the members who concurred in that vote were re-elected, while its opponents were invariably dismissed.

Similar demonstrations were made by other provinces; and, in order to secure unity of purpose, it was determined that a General Congress of Deputies, from such of the Provincial Assemblies as thought fit to send them, should meet at New York on the ensuing first of October. Thus, without any such extensive design on the part of its original promoters, was laid the foundation of that famous Federal Union which, in a few years, altered the condition of a few scattered and dependent states, vain of the patronage and notice of Great Britain, into a mighty Commonwealth, asserting its undisputed claims to an equality with the proudest sovereignties of the old world.

The Congress, though of course discountenanced by the representatives of the Crown, assembled on the appointed day, at New York, to the number of twenty-seven, delegated by no less than ten of the provincial legislatures. These delegates proceeded to business in due order, observing all the forms of a regularly constituted senate. They soon agreed to a series of resolutions, condemning in strong, but not indecent terms, the recent statutes affecting their trade and commerce, the Stamp Act, and the invasion of the right of jury-trial by giving the Court of Admiralty exclusive jurisdiction in offences against the new laws. They also referred to the well-known principle of the British constitution that taxes were the free gifts of the people, and could be imposed only by their representatives duly elected; and they denied that the House of Commons represented the colonists, or that they had any other representatives than their respective Provincial Assemblies. At the same time they were emphatic, and probably sincere, in their expressions of loyalty to the Crown, and of due deference to the Parliament. Petitions to the same effect, but embodying the arguments upon which they founded their demands, were also prepared for presentation to the King and both Houses of Parliament.

The consequence of these proceedings was, that on the 1st of November, when the Stamp Act was to come into operation, not a sheet of stamped paper was to be had in either of the provinces of New England, New York, New Jersey, Pennsylvania, Virginia, Maryland, and the Carolinas.

Proceedings of the Home Government. The resolutions of the House of Burgesses, in Virginia, which were passed so early as May 29th, constituted the first important movement which came under the consideration of the Home Government. The Board of Trade, to which the matter was, in the first place, referred, considering it a declaration of rebellion against British sovereignty, recommended, in their memorial to the Privy Council, that the execution of the law should be rigorously enforced. But the Government more prudently decided, that the question was of sufficient importance to be submitted to the deliberation of Parliament.

The minute of the Privy Council is dated October the 3rd; and as Parliament, though summoned before Christmas, did not meet for the despatch of business until after the holidays—the usual time for the commencement of the session being November—it is to be inferred either that the Government thought lightly of the disturbances in America, or that they were not disposed to carry out the policy of their predecessors. General Conway's letter to the Governor of Virginia, dated September the 14th, is weak and confused. It expresses a futile hope that the Burgesses would rescind their resolutions when they came to reconsider them in a fuller assembly, and desires the Governor, by every prudent measure in his power, to maintain the just rights of the British Government, and the peace of the province; but declines giving him any instructions on the subject, as the matter was before the Privy Council. The circular dispatch, dated October 24th, and addressed to the governors of the several provinces, is more in the tone becoming a secretary of state; it authorised them to do their duty in repressing disturbances, by military force, if necessary, but was altogether silent on the subject of measures to carry the Stamp Act into execution.

It is evident that the administration felt unequal to the emergency which had arisen; they were afraid of moving in the matter; and instead of assembling Parliament immediately, as they ought to have done, they postponed the session to the latest possible period. The Speech from the Throne merely stated that matters of importance had lately occurred in some of the colonies in America, which would demand their serious attention after the recess,—a strangely guarded phraseology, when it was notorious that there had been riots in almost every part of the American continent, that the

Timidity of the ministry.

authority of Parliament had been denied, that their law had been made a dead letter, and that the Civil Government had been insulted and defied with impunity.

It was hoped by the Ministers that this short preliminary session might have closed without any discussion of colonial policy; but the subject was introduced in both Houses by amendments to the Address, stigmatising the conduct of the Americans as traitorous and rebellious. In the Lords, the only speakers on the part of the Government were the Duke of Grafton and Lord Dartmouth, and they said as little as possible. Lord Shelburne opposed the amendment, and Lord Temple supported it; from which it is plain that he had no longer any concert with Pitt, and that, at least, while this question remained open, they could not act together in administration. The amendment was rejected, on a division. In the Commons, Grenville himself moved the amendment, although the leader of the House, and the principal members of the Government, were necessarily absent at their elections; and he would have proceeded, notwithstanding this circumstance, to take the sense of the House, but was restrained from proceeding to such an extremity by the influence of his friends.

The deliberations of the cabinet on the affairs of the colonies were deferred until the 27th of December. At the meeting of that day, counsels were suggested worthy of the occasion. It was proposed to assert, by a declaratory act, such as was subsequently passed, the unqualified right of the British Parliament to legislate for the colonies. This being done, it was further proposed to modify the Stamp Act, and the other acts relating to trade, which had been found oppressive and objectionable. But timidity and indecision preponderated, and the council broke up without having determined upon

anything but the terms of the King's Speech,* which
was so framed as to cast upon Parliament the whole
responsibility of a question which began to affect the
integrity of the empire.

Parliament re-assembled on the 14th of January,
and the affairs of America became imme-
diately the subject of debate. On that Re-appearance of Pitt in the House.
memorable night, when the fate of an em-
pire was to be decided, Pitt, who had not attended
in Parliament since the great debate of the general
warrants in the preceding year, appeared in his place.
Since his retirement from office, he had rarely borne
a part in the proceedings of the House, or even taken
his seat, except on some important occasion. His
unrivalled fame and eloquence always made his appearance a matter of the highest interest and excitement; but at this time his reputation had risen to a
degree of grandeur and importance which it hardly
ever before attained. The Court, as well as the
country, had long been agreed that he alone was fit
to rule. Cabinets might have been affected more
or less by favouritism and intrigue, but they existed
only by the sufferance of Pitt. The empire, which he
had raised from the prostration to which it had been
reduced by weak and factious government, was again
brought low by rash and selfish counsels. England,
which, under his guidance, had humbled France and
Spain, was set at nought by a distant colony of her
own children. Her commerce, which he had made to
flourish amidst the din of arms, was now threatened
with destruction by the perverse policy of his successors. Her navy, instead of taking treasure-ships
from the enemy, was employed in suppressing the
traffic of her own people. A trade of three million
sterling was all but annihilated. The merchants had
to bear the loss of their commodities, because new

* Adolphus' History of England, vol. i. p. 198. 'From private information and minutes of
the conference.'

laws had disabled their customers from paying for them. The streets of London had been frightened by the desperate tumults of starving artisans, the home victims of this policy. The Government were evidently too feeble and inexperienced to provide a remedy for these disorders; and the people could have no confidence in the wisdom or patriotism of the Parliament. At this crisis, all men were eager to hear the counsels of that illustrious citizen who, from his public spirit and the eminent services he had rendered, alone possessed any influence or authority.

The debate had made considerable progress before Pitt addressed the House. He rose imme-

Burke's maiden speech.

diately after a new member who had spoken for the first time. This was the private secretary to the First Minister, *Edmund Burke*, a man destined, not indeed to emulate the fame of Pitt as a minister or as an orator, but surpassing him in eloquent composition, and in the philosophy of a didactic statesman. The great speeches, or, more properly to describe them, the profound and splendid dissertations, on public questions which Burke delivered before various audiences during a period of thirty years, are, for the most part, happily preserved for the instruction and delight of posterity; but no note of this first speech appears to have been taken. It was distinguished by the praise of Pitt; but this is a compliment which a parliamentary leader would, if possible, bestow upon any new member whom he followed in debate.

The great ruler of debate was himself, on this occasion, equal to his fame. He desired

Speech of Pitt.

that the Speech from the Throne which had already, as usual, been read to the House by the Speaker, and the address which had been put from the chair, should each be read again, in order that his comments upon them might assume a greater weight and emphasis. He was indulged without question in this unprecedented demand. After some fine sarcastic

play upon the present administration—dismissing
their predecessors with an incidental remark that
every capital measure they had undertaken had been
entirely wrong—Pitt censured in terms of noble reprobation, as he had formerly done in his speech on
the general warrants, the illiberal practice of visit-
ing the delinquencies of Bute upon his countrymen.
' When I ceased to serve His Majesty as a minister,'
said he, 'it was not the country of the man by
which I was moved; but the man of that country
wanted wisdom, and held principles incompatible with
freedom.' At the same time, he plainly adverted to
the existence of secret influence. Then, approaching
the great question of the day in those striking terms
which he sometimes employed with such effect, he
said, that if he could have borne to be removed from
his bed, he would have been carried to the floor of
the House, so great had been the agitation of his
mind, when the question of taxing America was first
propounded. Having wound up the House to the
highest pitch of interest by this exordium, he proceeded at once to state his opinion (hitherto carefully
reserved) upon the affairs of the colonies. Laying
aside for the moment the expediency of the Stamp
Act, he told his astonished hearers that Great Britain
had NO RIGHT to lay a tax upon the colonies. He
argued that taxes, being the free gift of the Commons,
could be imposed only by their actual representatives;
that the colonies being directly represented in their
provincial assemblies, they alone had the power of
granting the money of their constituents; but that in
every other matter of legislation, including regulations
and restrictions as to trade, navigation, and manufactures, the Imperial Parliament had supreme power
and authority.

Such was the substance of this remarkable speech,
which, however it might fail to carry conviction to its
hearers, nobody was ready to answer. The leading

minister was therefore compelled to rise; and Conway, whose vague opinions and infirmity of purpose only wanted information and support from the decision and energy of Pitt, was content to express an entire acquiescence in his sentiments. But he positively denied, on behalf of the Government, the existence of that 'overruling influence' to which Pitt had so pointedly alluded.*

Grenville next addressed the House in defence of the colonial policy which he had pursued, and combated the arguments of Pitt on the fundamental question of right with great ability and success. He maintained that taxation was a part of legislation; that Parliament had, without dispute, exercised the right of imposing taxes on bodies which were unrepresented in the same sense that the colonies were unrepresented. He instanced the cases of the East India Company, the merchants of London, the proprietors of stocks, and the great manufacturing towns. The palatinate of Chester and the bishopric

<small>Grenville's reply.</small>

---

* This allusion referred not, as has been supposed, to Bute, but to Newcastle.—LORD CHARLEMONT'S *Letters*.

A little consideration, indeed, will show that Bute could not have been meant. Pitt alone, of all the eminent public men of the day, had never refused to be politically associated with the obnoxious Scotchman. He had been willing to return to office through the mediation of Bute in 1763; the persons whom he proscribed on that occasion were not the 'King's Friends,' but the Bedfords and the Newcastles, who had thwarted his war policy. So in 1765, he was quite willing to restore Stuart Mackenzie to his sinecure, and to let the King's men remain in the enjoyment of their obscure places, but he insisted on the reversal of the policy which had been pursued both at home and abroad since his retirement from power. He had finally broken with Newcastle in the early part of the same year. The Rockingham administration was notoriously formed in opposition to the Bute school of policy, and was composed of those Whig grandees whose yoke the King had once declared he never would endure. It included Newcastle, whose political resurrection was extremely offensive to Pitt: having ever regarded the Duke as the father of jobbery and intrigue, a far more formidable obstacle to good government than the manager of a futile system of prerogative policy.

of Durham had also been taxed before they sent
representatives to Parliament. Having exposed the
fallacy of the distinction between external and internal
taxes, he reminded the House that, in proposing to
extend taxation to the colonies, he had distinctly
raised the question of right, but that no member had
been found to dispute it; and he inveighed against the
ingratitude of the Americans in thus refusing, with
violence and insult, to bear any share of the vast
burdens which England had incurred for their defence
and protection. But he attributed the seditious spirit
of the colonists to the recklessness of faction at home.
Gentlemen were careless of the consequences of what
they said, provided it answered the purposes of opposition, and he concluded with an indignant vindication of his conduct against the charge of hostility
to the trade of America.

Amidst numerous competitors for the Speaker's
eye, when Grenville resumed his seat, it *Pitt called to*
was observed that Pitt seemed disposed to *order.*
rise. His name was eagerly called from all parts of
the House. But when, instead of confining himself
to explanation, as in regularity he ought to have done,
Pitt announced his intention of replying to Grenville
upon every point of his speech, an attempt was made
to stop him on the point of order. The Speaker,
however, decided that he was entitled to be heard.*

Stimulated by the force and cogency of Grenville's
argument, the great orator put forth all his *Pitt replies to*
strength in this reply; and never, certainly, *Grenville.*
had his genius made a more brilliant effort. After
a few words of scornful comment, he burst into a strain
of oratory not unlike, and not inferior to that famous
passage in which Demosthenes justified the Battle of

---

* The rule had been established for more than a century
and a half, of not allowing a member to speak twice to the same
question, when the House was
not in committee.—HATSELL's
Precedents, vol. ii. p. 74.

Chæronea. 'The gentleman tells us,' said he, 'that America is obstinate; America is almost in open rebellion. I REJOICE THAT AMERICA HAS RESISTED. Three millions of people, so dead to all the feelings of liberty, as voluntarily to submit to be slaves, would have been fit instruments to make slaves of the rest.'

The instances cited by Grenville of classes subjected to taxation without being represented, he treated with contempt as the argument of a lawyer. He had not come down 'armed at all points with law cases and acts of Parliament; with the statute-book doubled down in dog's ears to defend the cause of liberty.' Grenville had dwelt much on the benefits which England had lavished upon the colonies; on the favour which had been shown to their trade: on the return she was entitled to expect for the protection which she had extended to them. Pitt's reply was singularly striking and happy. 'The gentleman boasts of his bounties to America. Are not those bounties intended finally for the benefit of this kingdom? If they are not, he has misapplied the national treasures. . . . . The profits to Great Britain from the trade of the colonies, through all its branches, is two millions a year.* This is the fund that carried you triumphantly through the last war. The estates that were rented at two thousand pounds a year, threescore years ago, are at three thousand pounds at present. Those estates sold then from fifteen to eighteen years' purchase; the same may be now sold for thirty. You owe this to America. And shall a miserable financier come with a boast, that he can fetch a peppercorn into the exchequer to the loss of millions to the nation?'†

He then affected to console the fallen minister for the misrepresentations and unpopularity of which he

* They amounted to three millions.
† The estimated produce of the stamp tax was only 100,000*l.* a year.

complained, by telling him that it was a common
misfortune to be abused in the newspapers; and in
allusion to the argument upon which he had laid
much stress, that nobody had contradicted him when
he asserted the right of Parliament to tax America;
Pitt remarked, in a style of more pointed mockery,
that members were modest about contradicting a
minister; and reminded the House that when he had,
session after session, challenged objection to the German war—*his* German war, as they called it—one
gentleman only had the courage to tell him that he
did not like a German war. 'I honoured the man*
for it,' said Pitt, 'and was sorry when he was turned
out of his place.'

His concluding sentences were grand and impressive. 'A great deal has been said without doors of
the power, of the strength of America. It is a topic
that ought to be cautiously meddled with. In a good
cause, on a sound bottom, the force of this country
can crush America to atoms. But in such a case
your success would be hazardous. America, if she fell,
would fall like the strong man. She would embrace
the pillars of the state, and pull down the constitution
along with her. Is this your boasted peace? Not to
sheathe the sword in its scabbard, but to sheathe it
in the bowels of your countrymen?'

His advice was that the Stamp Act should be repealed absolutely and immediately; but
that at the same time the sovereign authority of this country over the colonies should be asserted in as strong terms as could be devised, and be
made to extend to every point of legislation, except
that of taking their money without their consent.

The doctrine advanced by Pitt that Great Britain
had no right to tax the colonies, found little favour at

---

* 'The man' was Sir Francis Dashwood, Bute's Chancellor of
the Exchequer.

the time,* and has ever since been treated as untenable. But the proposition, though too broadly stated, is not destitute of plausibility. The Commons were originally summoned to Parliament solely for the purpose of granting aid; the right of making laws being reserved to the Crown and the greater barons; and though the power of granting money soon proved to be the most important power in the state, and drew towards it every other branch of legislation, it is certain that in the old institution of Parliament, the distinction was recognised between the right of granting money and that of making general laws.† And if in those rude times, when the Commons had hardly ascertained their position as an estate of the realm, it was not attempted to take their money without their consent, it seemed an exorbitant stretch of power now to refuse this right to a people who had been admitted to all the privileges and liberties of Englishmen. As to the colonies being virtually represented in the British Parliament, that was an assertion much too violent. The same might as well have been said of Ireland before the Union. Ireland, like New England, had been planted by British colonists. Ireland and New England had each her own representative assembly; and the Parliament of Great Britain exercised supreme legislative power over both. But it was never pretended that the British Parliament could tax the Irish people without the consent of their own representatives. On the same ground, it might appear that

margin: The right of taxing the colonies.

---

* 'His (Pitt's) opinion about the power of taxing the colonies seems to be peculiar to himself and Lord Camden.'—LADY HARVEY'S *Letters*.

† 'In the reign of Elizabeth, the House of Commons was considered in no other light than as a means of supply; insomuch that the Queen made a merit to her people of seldom summoning a Parliament. No redress of grievances was expected from these assemblies. They were supposed to meet for no other purposes than to impose taxes.'—HUME'S *History*.

Great Britain was not justified in laying taxation
upon the represented colonies of America.

On the other hand, it would have been of dangerous
precedent for the sovereign legislature *Theory of self-taxation.*
either to limit its power, or to lay down
such a position as that which was advanced by Pitt and
afterwards distinctly affirmed by Lord Camden, that
no man could be lawfully deprived of any portion
of his property, except with his consent, signified
personally, or through his representatives. On the
broad basis of such a principle, the theory of the
universal suffrage which has been, for the most part,
rejected by practical statesmen as incompatible with
our mixed constitution, must have securely rested;
since every subject who is not kept on the public
bounty contributes to the public burdens, in con-
suming the merest necessaries of life. It can make
no difference to the argument whether the contribution is levied directly by a poll-tax or indirectly by
a duty on commodities. The very tax which gave
rise to this doctrine was an indirect one. The representative principle was, in fact, very *The representa-*
imperfectly developed in Great Britain *tive principle.*
itself.* The constituency did not comprise a tenth
part of the population. It is indisputable that a
large proportion of the public revenue was derived
from persons who were denied the elective franchise.
If every citizen who is subjected to taxation directly
or indirectly is entitled to the suffrage as of *right*, it
is obvious that no consideration of expediency or good
government can justly avail to withhold it from him.
But this is the question which lies at the root of the
argument. Of what kind is the right asserted? Is it

---

* The Reform Act of 1832 merely advanced the process of development a stage. The estimated male population of England and Wales, according to the Census of 1851, was nearly nine millions (8,863,298)—Census of Great Britain, vol. i. p. 29. The registered voters in that year were, for England and Wales, 918,162.

natural right? The answer is, that natural right is given up on entering into civil society. But every other right is the creature of municipal law, or is natural right modified in accordance with political exigency. Thus the attempt to square political institutions with exact principles must ever be attended with failure. The imperfection of human nature, and the conditions imposed by the Creator himself upon human existence, render it impracticable to observe the laws of perfect justice in political institutions.

The other ground upon which it was sought to found the claim of taxing the colonies, in consideration of the protection afforded them, is equally unwarrantable. Upon this pretence some remarks have been made in a former page; but the short answer given by Pitt is conclusive. England maintained and protected her colonies solely for the sake of commerce, and might as fairly have exacted a contribution from her own merchants and traders, who derived three millions annually from their traffic with the colonies, as have set up a claim for tribute from the colonies on that account.

Pitt's speech decided the wavering policy of the administration. Indeed, it would have been hardly possible to enforce the Stamp Act, after the highest authority in the empire had pronounced it illegal, and the resistance of the Americans righteous and commendable. It was determined, therefore, to pursue the course prescribed by Pitt; to bring forward two bills—one to affirm the supreme legislative authority of Great Britain, the other to repeal the obnoxious impost. But before adopting a measure of such grave importance to the dignity and authority of the empire, as the surrender of a statute which had been advisedly enacted, to the rebellious opposition of those whom it concerned, it was deemed expedient to give time for the expression of public opinion on the subject, and to institute a parliamentary inquiry into the reasons which could be alleged against it.

The disastrous effects of the late commercial policy upon the trade of Great Britain were forcibly represented by petitions from the merchants, showing the losses which they had already sustained by the Americans having been deprived of the means of making good their engagements; and the probability that the trade itself, to which it was the primary purpose of colonies to be subservient, would be altogether annihilated. The Colonial Assemblies, resenting the contemptuous treatment which their petitions had received the preceding year, with one or two exceptions, did not deign to prefer their complaints before the British Parliament; but the grievances which the colonists endured, as well as the measures which they had taken to secure redress, were represented at the bar of the House of Commons with consummate ability and skill by the statesman whom they had sent over for that purpose. The evidence of Franklin, given before the Committee of the whole House, subjected as it was to the jealous scrutiny of Grenville, and other supporters of his colonial measures, must have carried conviction to every candid mind of their impolicy, at least. His testimony went far, also, to prove that they were unjust and impracticable. He showed that there was no necessity for compulsory taxation, as the colonies had always contributed their share, and sometimes more than their share, towards the defence of the empire, when duly called upon by the official requisition of the Home Government; and he stated, in positive terms, that, though his country was willing to pay customs' duties in consideration that England, by her fleets, kept the seas clear for commerce, they never would submit, under any circumstances, to arbitrary internal taxation. He stated, in answer to a question, that the value of the annual imports from Great

Britain to the province of Pennsylvania alone was
computed at half a million sterling, while the exports
of that colony, in return, did not exceed forty
thousand pounds, the differences being remitted in
specie, obtained chiefly from the produce of a traffic
with foreign countries, which the English Government
had lately suppressed as contraband.

Prepared as he was for his examination by the discussions which had already taken place in
Parliament, Franklin displayed, in addition to a thorough knowledge of his subject, that
readiness of reply and dialectic skill which are always
successful in a popular assembly, but have ever enjoyed an immediate triumph in the British House of
Commons. The evidence of Franklin * was a material
support to the Government.

Franklin's dialectic skill.

But, while American grievances were to be redressed, the honour of Parliament was,
at the same time, to be saved by an act
affirmative of its supreme legislative authority over all
the dependencies of the empire.† The more accurate
reading of the constitutional lawyers, by whom the
ministry were advised in framing the Declaratory
Bill, rejected the dangerous distinction between the
power of imposing taxes and that of making other
laws, which Pitt and his disciple, the Chief Justice of
the Common Pleas, sought to introduce. Each of
these eminent persons, therefore, objected to the unqualified language of the resolution upon which the
bill was to be founded; but, as the fate of the more
important measure was involved in the integrity of
this, they abstained from any attempt to modify its
terms. Lord Camden, however, entered into a
lengthened exposition of his views; and, as this was

Declaratory Bill.

---

* His examination is to be
found in the ordinary form of a
parliamentary report in the Parliamentary History, Almon's Papers, Sparks's Life of Franklin,
and many other publications.
† 6 Geo. III. c. 12.

the first occasion upon which he had addressed the House since his recent elevation to the peerage, his speech was listened to with the interest which became the dignity of the question, no less than the reputation and authority of the speaker.

He set out by denying the omnipotence of Parliament, and its right to pass the law which was about to be repealed; illustrating the first position by referring to the incompetency of Parliament to deprive a man of his property without compensation, or to pass a bill of attainder without a hearing. In proof of the limited power of Parliament in the matter of taxation, he quoted several precedents, as the clergy who formerly taxed themselves, likewise the counties palatine, Wales, and Ireland.

Lord Mansfield's argument, in reply, was a masterpiece, full of historical and legal learning, lucid in arrangement, cogent in reasoning; and all these merits were set off by the most exquisite grace of elocution, and the happiest adaptation of style and manner to the fastidious audience which he addressed. *Lord Mansfield's argument.*

The Chief Justice of England maintained that the authority of the British legislature was coextensive with the Empire; that in this respect there was no difference between the parts within and those without the realm; that the colonies, from the circumstances and conditions under which they were established, instead of being entitled to claim independence, were made especially subject to the control of Great Britain. He declared that, after the most diligent research, he had been unable to discover any distinction between the power of levying taxes and making laws. The cases cited by Camden he disposed of very successfully. The clergy, it is true, were at one time exempted from taxation by the laity, but that was a concession to the predominance of the priesthood in a rude and superstitious age. Wales had been specially excepted out of many statutes for imposing taxes, because the people contributed their proportion in the shape of *mises*; but when that tribute was abolished by the acts which incorporated Wales with England, in the reign of Henry the Eighth, the Welsh were taxed like the other inhabitants of the realm. He showed that the counties palatine, and other places which had been named, were bound by the laws of Parliament long before they were represented; and that the right of sending members to Parliament was conferred upon them in consequence of their being bound by its acts. He placed in a striking light the futility of the pretensions of a chartered colony to be independent of Parliament, when its constitution was liable to be dissolved (as that of Massachusetts Bay had been in the time of Charles the Second) in the English courts of justice for a breach of the conditions upon which it was founded; and he concluded with a solemn warning to Parliament not to abandon its functions.

The Declaratory Bill gave rise to much discussion in both Houses; but there was only one division upon it, and that took place in the Lords upon the motion of Camden. A minority of four peers only agreed with him in denying the assertion of the unlimited authority of Parliament.

The Declaratory Bill.

This enactment * accompanying, as it did, another which retracted the practical assertion of the power on the first occasion of its being resisted, was certainly

---

* 'That the said colonies and plantations in America have been, are, and of right ought to be, subordinate unto and dependent upon the Imperial Crown and Parliament of Great Britain; and that the King's Majesty, by and with the advice and consent of the Lords Spiritual and Temporal, and Commons of Great Britain, in Parliament assembled, had, hath, and of right ought to have, full power and authority to make laws and statutes of sufficient force and validity to bind the colonies and people of America, subjects of the Crown of Great Britain, *in all cases whatsoever.*'—6 Geo. III. c. 12, sec. 1.

not a very dignified proceeding. It would have been more becoming the magnanimity of the Imperial Legislature to have simply repealed the Stamp Act, without condescending to an idle vaunt of omnipotence. But the Government probably had no choice in the matter. Many persons even among those who were opposed to Grenville's colonial policy felt incensed at the insolence of the colonists; and more sober men were inclined to think that the dangerous tenet put forth by such an authority as Pitt required an authentic refutation. Both Whigs and Tories were in the main agreed in upholding the ascendancy of Parliament against a democratic theory more formidable than the actual resistance which had been offered to it.

The bill for the repeal of the Stamp Act was then brought forward. It was well known that the act could be put into operation only by force of arms; yet it was for some time doubtful whether the repeal could be carried. The Ministry themselves had no weight or credit to carry this or any other measure. The regular parliamentary opposition, headed by Bedford and Grenville, were vehemently adverse to the abrogation of their own capital policy. The Tories, including many of the subordinate placemen, voted against the minister. Lord Mansfield was of opinion that the repeal of the act would be an imprudent concession to the rebellious spirit of the provinces; but was content that it should be stripped of all its offensive provisions, and in point of fact be reduced to a nullity. Many independent members, who were against enforcing the act, preferred this middle term to the precipitate repeal of a statute passed with the all but unanimous assent of Parliament only the year before. The King also caused it to be made known * that he was

Sidenote: Repeal of the Stamp Act.

---

* Through Lord Strange, one of the Tory placemen. The ministers had intimated that His Majesty approved of their plan;

favourable to the policy of modification. On the other hand, the bill was supported by the influence of Pitt, backed by a strong expression of public opinion, and by the wholesome fears of many who were not prepared to risk the effusion of blood and the integrity of the Empire. The policy of concession prevailed, and the Government were ultimately enabled to carry the bill through both Houses by commanding majorities.

Propriety of the repeal. It will hardly be disputed at the present day that the unconditional repeal of the Stamp Act was the preferable course. A great legislature can afford to admit that it is not infallible, even when it has been most deliberate in its proceedings; and the prompt acknowledgment of error is far more respectable than the attempt to preserve the form while the essential of consistency is abandoned. But in this instance Parliament had, in truth, little or no sacrifice in dignity to make; the Stamp Act had passed almost unnoticed as one of the minor financial projects of the year; and unless the matter had been swollen into importance by perverse pride and party spirit, it would have been easy to repair the inadvertence by withdrawing a measure too insignificant to affect the revenue in any material degree. But there was one conclusive argument for the repeal. After Pitt had openly countenanced and encouraged the resistance of the colonies, British legislation on this head was deprived of all moral

and when Rockingham, who had certainly so understood the King, heard that Strange had been making a contrary statement, he instantly demanded an audience; and, Strange being present at his desire, reminded His Majesty of having sanctioned the measure of repeal. The King, however, asserted that Rockingham omitted a very important qualification, and made a memorandum of what he had said,—'The question asked me by my ministers was, whether I was for enforcing the act by the sword, or for the repeal? *Of the two extremes*, I was for the repeal, but most certainly preferred modification to either.'— WALPOLE's *History*, vol. ii. p. 281.—GRENVILLE's *Diary*.

force, and could be maintained only at the cost of civil war. It is easy to censure Pitt for giving the weight of his great name to open rebellion. Ordinary prudence and loyalty, indeed, can afford no justification for such conduct. But there are times and occasions when a more enlightened discretion sees the path of safety beyond the beaten tracks of precedent and routine. Pitt's daring and decisive opposition prevented England at this time from entering upon a doubtful and disastrous conflict with her colonies: had he taken a different course, and directed it, as he must have done, the same zeal and energy would doubtless have 'crushed America to atoms.' But the dictates of justice, of humanity and sound policy would have been alike violated by such a disastrous triumph.

CHAPTER VIII.

MEASURES OF THE ROCKINGHAM ADMINISTRATION—ITS DISMISSAL—PITT PRIME MINISTER AND EARL OF CHATHAM—HIS SCHEMES—HIS ILLNESS AND SECLUSION—DISTRACTED STATE OF THE CABINET—TOWNSHEND'S RASHNESS AND AMBITION—MINISTERIAL CHANGES—NULLUM TEMPUS BILL.

Conciliatory measures towards the colonies.

THE repeal of the Stamp Duty was followed by another healing measure freeing the commerce of the colonies from many of the vexatious restrictions to which it had been subjected by the former administration. At the same time the trade in bullion and cattle, formerly carried on with the Spanish colonists, and the suppression of which by the custom-house cruisers had been one of the most substantial grievances of which the Americans complained, was restored to them by an act constituting Dominica and Jamaica free ports for live stock and manufactured commodities.

While they pursued this course of just and reasonable conciliation towards the colonies, the Government sought to strengthen themselves at home by other popular measures. The ill-advised Cider Act, the principal financial measure of Bute's administration, *Cider duty rearranged.* was materially altered. The duty of four shillings in the hogshead, which the most ignorant of Chancellors of the Exchequer * had imposed upon the manufacturer, with no other effect, as might have been anticipated, than to check

---

* Sir Francis Dashwood. He had the sense to perceive, and the good humour to acknowledge, his own incapacity. 'People will point at me,' said he, 'and cry,—"There goes the worst Chancellor of the Exchequer that ever lived!"'—WALPOLE'S *History of George the Third*, vol. i. p. 260.

the trade, was transferred with an additional duty of two shillings to the retailer, who was much better fitted to deal with it; and the differential duty of forty shillings upon the foreign article was, by way of compensation, increased to a prohibitory duty of three pounds. Upon the short-sighted principles of political economy which then obtained, an act was passed for the exclusion of foreign-wrought silks, in order that the distress of the weavers might be relieved by forcing the inferior domestic production. This measure was of course received with clamorous joy by the poor people, whose untaught resistance to Parliament the year before thus received the same consideration as the revolt of the injured Americans. The House of Commons also, at the instance of the administration, passed a just though tardy condemnation on the proceeding of arrest by general warrant, and the arbitrary seizure of private papers. The Government are likewise entitled to the praise of having discredited the practice of dismissing military officers for insubordination in their political capacity. The law of England still recognises in the soldier his indelible character of a citizen, impaired though it be for the time by the rigour of military discipline; and though standing armies, in this country at least, are perhaps no longer dangerous to liberty, it must ever be of importance in a free state that the absolute obedience of the soldier should be limited to his military commission. Since this period the distinction between the civil and military character in the same individual has been respected; and General Conway himself was the last officer deprived of professional employment for his vote in Parliament.

But notwithstanding that the Government had succeeded in carrying through all these as well as other useful measures during a single year, they acquired no strength nor stability.

Their short tenure of office was almost from the first but a lingering existence * protracted from day to day, contrary to public expectation. A few noblemen and gentlemen of little or no official experience, of moderate personal ability, hardly known to the public, and with a slender parliamentary connection, had undertaken to carry on the government in opposition to the most powerful section of the Whig party, disparaged by the highest parliamentary authority, and thwarted by the courtiers at every turn. The country had endured, with one brilliant exception, a succession of weak and short-lived administrations during the twelve years which had elapsed since the death of Pelham; but the Rockingham administration was the weakest and most transitory of them all. They had little, indeed, beyond integrity and singleness of purpose to recommend them; and for these qualities they hardly obtained any credit, so little had the nation been accustomed to look for public spirit and disinterestedness in those who directed its affairs.†

Insubordination of state officers. The exact discipline which has been long established throughout the administration, from the highest to the lowest offices, was but

---

* 'The fall of the ministers was so much expected, that it was said, "They were dead and only lying in state, and that Charles Townshend (who never spoke for them) was one of their mutes."'— WALPOLE's *History of George the Third*, vol. ii. p. 283, n. The wit was probably Walpole's own.

The Ministry had been desirous of making the brilliant parliamentary talents of Charles Townshend available for their service. They had offered him the seals of Secretary of State, and a peerage; and when he persisted in refusing to quit the lucrative obscurity of the Pay Office, he was told that his conduct endangered the existence of the Ministry, and was desired to explain what he meant by it. His answer was, 'that he meant to keep his place, and they durst not take it from him if they could, and could not if they durst, which he hoped was sufficiently explicit.' — *Whately to Grenville*, May 23, 1766. — GRENVILLE *Correspondence*, vol. iii. p. 237.

† 'A little dirty low interest seems to guide both the ins and outs. This country has been at its zenith, and is now in its decline.'—LADY HERVEY's *Letters*, March, 1765.

imperfectly exercised during the first century after
the Revolution. The principal ministers frequently
opposed each other in Parliament,* and the inferior
tenants of office followed their example. Sometimes,
indeed, the first minister, enraged at such insolence,
would dismiss all the delinquents, including even
their kinsmen and friends who had given no offence.
Walpole, Fox, and Grenville had each inflicted a cruel
vengeance upon insubordination. But never had this
mutinous spirit reached such a pitch as under Rockingham. Not only did the whole tribe of courtiers,
but several men holding political office go against
him. On one occasion, after he had complained to
the King, and obtained a promise of support, he was
run to a narrow majority of eight in the House of
Commons the same evening, the Tory placemen voting
in a body against the Government; and when he asked
for the dismissal of a junior lord of trade† for the

---

* At this period the regular meetings of the principal members of the administration, for the purpose of deliberating upon important measures of public policy, known in modern times by the name of Cabinet Councils, did not exist. No provision was made for any concert between the ministers; nor was it necessary that the head of a department should communicate to his colleagues, collectively or individually, the measures which he proposed to take. The consequence was, that differences of opinion between the members of the Government, which should have been accommodated in the closet, was first exhibited in the face of Parliament. In the Grenville administration, it was agreed that the principal ministers should dine together once a week, for the purpose of discussing public business. These meetings were confined to the Chancellor, the President of the Council, the First Lord of the Treasury, and the two Secretaries of State. When the Regency Bill was under consideration, Lord Mansfield was present, and on one or two occasions Lord Egmont attended. When Mr. Dowdeswell accepted the office of Chancellor of the Exchequer, which had generally been held by a first-rate minister, it was doubted whether he would be invited to the Cabinet Councils. — *C. Townshend to Dowdeswell, August 6, 1765.—*CAVENDISH *Debates.*

† Dyson. This man had been kept in office, when the Rockingham administration was formed, at the express instance of the King, who answered for his fidelity and subordination. Yet he had the presumption to move an amendment upon one of Con-

sake of example, he was met with a refusal. The
King had not been so forbearing on the question of
the Peace and of the General Warrants. On those
occasions, the division lists had been closely scanned,
and every placeholder who hesitated to approve of
either of those measures was immediately expelled.

Overtures made to Pitt. — The Ministry were conscious that their only chance of maintaining their position was by an alliance with that great man who alone
possessed public confidence, and could bend both
Courts and Parliaments to his will. Many overtures
accordingly had been made to Pitt; his wishes had
been consulted by the Ministry, on the most important measures of public policy, and even in the
dispensation of official patronage. But all in vain.
Pitt admitted that their characters were 'fair,' that
he had never been 'betrayed' by any of them, that
they had sometimes been guided by his 'poor opinion,'
—but still he could not give them his 'confidence.'

Partial resignation of the Ministry. — It was far from the wish of Rockingham and his colleagues to cling tenaciously to office; and so disheartened were they by the difficulties which gathered around them,
and the want of support from every quarter, that
they meditated resignation, even before the all-important measures for tranquillising the colonies had
been presented to Parliament. And this intention
would have been carried into effect, if Bedford and
Grenville had succeeded in an attempt, which they
made about the same time, to form a coalition with
Bute and the Tories.* The Duke of Grafton indeed,

---

way's resolutions upon American affairs; and actually divided
the House upon a proposition of
the minister to make the usual
provision for one of the Princesses, when about to marry.
He voted against the Government upon almost every occasion.

* Bedford and Grenville were
induced by Lord Eglinton to
meet Bute at his house. Bute
however, disappointed at not
finding them accompanied, as he
had expected, by Temple, seems,
according to Walpole's and even
Grenville's own account, to have

unwilling to be involved in the fate which inevitably awaited the Ministry, withdrew, not very handsomely, in the middle of the session, and the Duke of Richmond succeeded him as Secretary of State. At length, the Lord Chancellor Northington seized the opportunity of a difference of opinion with the other members of the Cabinet, on the subject of a bill for the government of Canada, to tell them plainly that he should not again sit in council with them ; and, proceeding from the cabinet to the royal closet, informed His Majesty that the Government could go on no longer, and tendered his resignation of the Great Seal. Northington, who had courted the King's favour both in the present and in the former Ministry, knew that this intelligence would be very graciously received, and, for purposes of his own, was willing to be employed as the mediator of a new administration.

Pitt was, of course, to have the refusal of office ; and Northington was desired to communicate with him on the subject. At the same time, the King informed the Ministry of the step which he had taken. Rockingham received the intimation with silent acquiescence; but Conway, sensible of his incompetency for the office which he had reluctantly undertaken, and of Pitt's paramount qualifications, expressed his unfeigned satisfaction at the intelligence. *Pitt forms a new administration.*

Pitt was at his house in Somersetshire when he received the King's commands. His answer to Northington's letter was in that florid style which he affected on such occasions, and which in any other man would have been fulsome and ridiculous.* This was the third time within a period of *Pitt's florid style.*

---

treated the ex-ministers rather cavalierly, and affected to inquire what was their business with him?—WALPOLE's *History.* —GRENVILLE's *Diary.*

* 'Penetrated with the deepest sense of your Majesty's boundless goodness to me, and with a heart overflowing with duty, and zeal for the honour

five years that the administration had been formally offered to this eminent person; and now, under circumstances the least auspicious, he was induced to accept the charge. His constitution, which had been for some time past sinking under the increase of years, and the repeated ravages of that disease which had embittered his whole existence, now exhibited a new form of disorder. The gout had disappeared, and a low fever, freer from anguish, indeed, but more depressing than acute pain, had taken possession of him. The excitement of a sudden summons and a hasty journey to London aggravated his malady. The climate of Richmond, where he had to attend the King, was too mild for his feverish frame; and every day, after the audience, he retired to the cooler air of Hampstead. The progress of the arrangement of the new Ministry was not such as to allay his irritation. His unhappy connection with Temple proved, on this occasion, as it had formerly, the source of difficulty and disappointment. That proud and ill-conditioned peer, who derived all his political importance from Pitt, thought himself entitled to exercise an influence over his illustrious kinsman, to which he had little or no title in respect of ability and good sense. The year before, he had defeated the opportunity of forming an efficient administration under Pitt, because he had determined that the country should be governed exclusively by the family of Grenville. The same arrogant and silly project was again pressed upon Pitt. Temple had,

Interference of Temple.

and happiness of the most gracious and benign Sovereign, I shall hasten to London as fast as I possibly can, wishing that I could change infirmity into wings of expedition, the sooner to be permitted the high honour to lay at your Majesty's feet the poor but sincere offerings of my little services.' Yet the man who could use language more fitting an eastern vizier than an English statesman of the highest rank and authority, addressing a sovereign for whom he had no great respect, was really as haughty and dictatorial in the closet as he was in the cabinet, or in the great council of the nation.

indeed, just discretion enough to see that his brother
George, at that moment the most unpopular man in
England, was not quite eligible as a minister. He
engaged, therefore, that Grenville should support the
Ministry without office, intending no doubt to admit
him into the Government at a future day. Pitt's treatment
Pitt, however, determined on this occasion of him.
to deal with his brother-in-law on the same footing
as any public man, charged by his Sovereign with the
construction of a ministry, would deal with any other
public man whom he wished to include in his arrangements. He offered him office—the office of
First Commissioner of the Treasury*—which included a seat in the Cabinet, together with the nomination of his colleagues at the Board, including the
Chancellor of the Exchequer; but this did not satisfy
the overbearing temper of the chief of the Grenvilles.
If all political power could not be concentrated in
his family, he required at least that he should be
associated with Pitt in an equality of power and
patronage. Such a plan as that of two joint first
ministers was unprecedented and absurd; and Pitt,
of all men, was the last to endure the trial of such an
experiment in his person. He placed before Temple
the names of the persons whom he had designated
for the different offices in the administration, informing him, at the same time, perhaps in the peremptory style which belonged to him, that the list
could not be altered. Temple, in his audience of
the King, which had preceded his interview with
Pitt, insisted on the removal of the whole Rockingham connection, while Pitt proposed to retain a large
proportion, including some of the principal of them,
such as Conway and the Duke of Grafton. Temple
then offered to nominate two of his friends, the Lords
Gower and Lyttelton, for high places in the Govern-

* This office, since the time of Lord North, has been in-variably held by the first mi-nister.

ment; but even this being refused, he took his leave with strong expressions of resentment. Thus was severed, at the same time, the political connection and the private friendship of these kinsmen.

Relieved from a captious and impracticable colleague, Pitt was enabled, without difficulty, to complete his administration. Grafton, who had declared himself ready to serve under Pitt in the humblest capacity, and had refused to continue in office without him, was placed at the head of the Treasury. Camden, his able and devoted follower, received the Great Seal. Conway retained his office of Secretary of State with the lead of the House of Commons. Northington was transferred to the dignified post of President of the Council, receiving at the same time some substantial compensation* for the emoluments of Chancellor, the duties of which his infirmities rendered him unable any longer to discharge. Charles Townshend became Chancellor of the Exchequer; Shelburne was the other Secretary of State. Pitt himself was contented with the Privy Seal; and at the same time it was announced to the astonished and indignant nation, who seemed willing to claim him ever as their own, that their Great Commoner had merged in the EARL OF CHATHAM. I need not here repeat the observations in a former page upon the shallow and vulgar quality of the censure which is often lavished upon eminent statesmen who accept honours and emoluments from the Crown. That those favours have been often unworthily conferred is no reason why they should

Composition of the new Ministry.

Pitt created Earl of Chatham.

---

* While Northington, Camden, and others were securing reversions, sinecures, and pensions, the old Duke of Newcastle, who now finally took his leave, or rather was thrust out, of public life (in which, as I have before mentioned, his fortune had been greatly impaired), refused a pension of 4,000*l.* a year which was offered him.—*Wm. Gerard Hamilton to Temple, August 3, 1766.*— GRENVILLE *Correspondence*, vol. iii. p. 294.

always diminish the credit and character of great men. The first Chatham peerage and pension had indeed too much the appearance of compensation for the loss of place and power; and the abject language and demeanour to which Pitt descended on that occasion in the presence of his Sovereign, while it favoured the malice of his enemies, and caused his friends to grieve that he should so misrepresent himself, was in truth only an exhibition of that exaggerated and affected style which pervaded all his public conduct, and marred, as far as it could, his real greatness. To the liberal mind, a title may appear a thing of little or no value; it can neither give real elevation to meanness, nor enhance true dignity; but the bulk of mankind do not refine so curiously. A title by them is taken for what it professes to be—a badge of honour—and is perhaps by none valued higher than by those whom envy prompts to employ the cant of philosophy in its disparagement. If ever there was a title fairly won, and well bestowed, it was the Earldom of Chatham. For thirty years had Pitt been a member of the House of Commons; and now the state of his health even more than his years, disqualified him from sustaining an active part in that assembly. He was first minister; and in that capacity he could not continue in the House of Commons without assuming the lead and management. To retire from Parliament, disdaining a seat in the Upper House, the comparative tranquillity of which was suitable to his years and infirmities, might have obtained a certain kind of popular applause, but must have ended in his retirement from public life. Pitt took a wiser and more dignified course. He relied upon his fame; upon the authority derived from past success; and upon the generous confidence of the people, who had once before called him to power, and whom he had ever nobly served.

The Chatham administration has been criticised, as if, from its very construction, it must necessarily have fallen to pieces.* But upon examination, without reference to the event, there appears to be no reason why it should not have worked well. The materials of which it was composed were, upon the whole, better than those of its predecessors in the existing reign. The experience and ability of Northington were retained, though in another department. Camden, Shelburne, and Townshend were all men of ability superior to the Egremonts, the Halifaxes and the Grenvilles. Grafton, though he had only a few months' experience of office, was a good speaker and a man of acknowledged promise. These with Chatham himself formed the Cabinet. They were all of the Whig connection. In the inferior offices there were Lord North, a rising statesman, and destined shortly to be the chief of an administration; Barré, a partisan of Shelburne, and one of the most effective speakers in Parliament, and James Grenville, a brother of Lord Temple, but a staunch adherent of Pitt. A large proportion of the Rockingham party continued in office with the consent of their chief.† The Court also seemed favour-

* 'He made an administration so checkered and speckled; he put together a piece of joinery, so crossly indented and whimsically dovetailed; a cabinet so variously inlaid; such a piece of diversified mosaic; such a tesselated pavement without cement; —here a bit of black stone, and there a bit of white; patriots and courtiers, King's friends and republicans,—Whigs and Tories, —treacherous friends and open enemies;—that it was indeed a very curious show, but utterly unsafe to touch and unsure to stand on.'—BURKE's *Speech on American Taxation.*

† 'As Lord Chatham professed to be actuated by the same political principles as the late Government, Lord Rockingham desired such of his followers as the new premier did not remove to remain at their posts. Accordingly, the Duke of Portland continued Lord Chamberlain; the Earl of Bessborough, one of the joint Paymasters-General; the Earl of Scarborough, Cofferer; Lord Monson, Chief Justice in Eyre; while Sir Charles Saunders. Sir William Meredith, and Admiral Keppel, remained at the Admiralty.'— ROCKINGHAM *Memoirs,* vol. ii. p. 12.

able to the new Government. The King* significantly expressed his belief that 'the Earl of Chatham would zealously give his aid towards destroying all party distinctions.'† Some of the 'King's men' were retained; others were provided for in the new distribution of offices; and Bute was propitiated by the restoration of his brother Mackenzie to the Privy Seal of Scotland.

It was said then, and has been repeated since, that the Government was founded on no principle. But this is merely verbal objection. The enunciation of a particular principle upon which a government is to be conducted is only called for when the principle is ripe for application. Thus, in Pitt's former administration, the chastisement of the house of Bourbon was the object. To quell the evil spirit of a democracy which threatened universal despotism was in like manner the mission of Pitt's illustrious son. Again, in 1830, Peace, Retrenchment, and Reform were the intelligible aims of Lord Grey's administration. But to lay down a principle without any definite purpose savours too much of empiricism; and must either have a mischievous effect in stirring questions prematurely, or end in exposing the projector to just derision. It would be easy to draw up a catalogue of measures which were wanted in 1766. The representative system, for example, was more depraved, and Parliament itself far less entitled to public confidence and respect in that year than in 1832. But

margin: Objections to Chatham's Ministry.

---

* George the Third was sincere in his support of Chatham. The Duke of Grafton states, that when His Majesty read Sir Andrew Mitchell's despatch relative to his interview with Frederick on the subject of the Northern Alliance, on coming to the passage in which the Prussian monarch remarked on the frequent changes in the British administration, the King started, and with great earnestness exclaimed, 'God forbid that there should be any more!'—*Grafton to Chatham, September 26, 1766.*—CHATHAM *Correspondence.*

* Letter from the King to Pitt, July 29.—Ibid.

the reform of Parliament would nevertheless at that time have proved a hopeless attempt. Religious liberty, education, and commerce were each in a deplorable state for want of wholesome laws; but a minister would in vain have called upon public opinion for support in legislating upon such matters. Pitt had in his earlier years descended to the arts of popularity; but now in the fulness of his age and fame, it was surely not for him to concern himself about the mere pedantry of principles. His very name was a principle. All men understood that an administration of which Pitt was the ruling genius, meant terror to the enemies of England, conciliation to her dependencies, the discouragement of factions at home, and the cause of honest government. The unfortunate fate of this Ministry is not, therefore, to be attributed either to its heterogeneous composition, or to its want of fixed principles. Chatham alone destroyed his own work. His situation at this time was very different to what it had been when he entered upon his first administration. In 1757, the patience of the nation had been worn out by misgovernment; the country was literally, and not, as in the declamation of disappointed politicians, on the brink of ruin. Since the reign of Charles the Second, when a foreign fleet were at London Bridge, England was never in such danger of insult. It was notorious that Pitt was the last and only public hope. Fox, the only man of parliamentary standing or ability who could pretend to be his rival, was known in public life to be utterly heartless, profligate, and unprincipled. Pitt, as he justly boasted, was called to power by the voice of the people; and faction, for a time awed and intimidated, shrank into insignificance. There was no man, no party, which could stand against him, flushed as he was by unexampled success and urged on by the enthusiastic plaudits of

Pitt's principles of action.

a grateful and admiring people. Times had since
changed. A new reign, the revival of the
Tory party together with the old maxims *Change of political circumstances.*
of loyalty and submission, and the in-
creased energy of the Whigs to counteract this
doctrine, had brought forward in public life many
individuals of considerable weight from their rank
and talents, who had hitherto remained in comparative obscurity and inaction. Chatham, though still
high above all other men in the public favour, had
no longer that commanding popularity which enabled
him nine years before to overbear the cabals of
jealousy and faction; and his elevation to the peerage, in the estimation of the people, whom experience had made suspicious of all pretensions to
public spirit, reduced him to a level with the corrupt
herd of politicians. Conscious of surpassing ability,
and looking down from a moral eminence still more
exalted upon the sordid intrigues and low ambition
of other men, Chatham had been long inured to a
style of haughty contempt towards his opponents;
and, towards his colleagues in administration, of reserve and dictation almost imperial. The generation
of statesmen which had succeeded the Newcastles
and the Legges, were not disposed to submit to such
treatment. Rockingham, himself a proud and high-
minded man, keenly resented the contumelious re-
pulse with which his advances had been met; and
even Conway, the mildest of men, and the least
assuming of ministers, could not help exclaiming
that such language as Lord Chatham's had not been
heard west of Constantinople.

The first grand object of Chatham's policy was now,
as it had ever been since his fall from *Proposed alliances.*
power, to secure to the country the due
result of those great and successful exertions which,
under his direction, she had made in the last war.
Had he returned to power at an earlier period, it is

probable that he would have broken the peace, so hastily, and, in his opinion, so shamefully, concluded. But now he was content* to effect his favourite object by negotiation. The Northern Powers were to be united with Great Britain in a league to circumscribe the ambition of the house of Bourbon; and this extensive confederation, including Denmark, Sweden, and the States General, was to be based on the triple alliance of Russia, Prussia, and Great Britain. Nor does it appear that Chatham exaggerated the importance of this policy. The Cabinet of St. James's had long been possessed of information † that the French Government contemplated a descent upon the English coast, and that they meant to do so without a declaration of war, by way of reprisal for the seizure of the French ships in 1756.‡ But, even in the absence of any such advice, the English ministry were not justified in waiting supinely for some movement from the parties to the Family Compact, before taking any measure of precaution.

Foreign affairs being thus uppermost in his mind,§ a very few days only elapsed after his resumption of office, before Lord Chatham took measures to carry into effect his great scheme of

Negotiations commenced.

---

* In a conversation with the Duke of Bedford, at Bath, in October (after the failure of the treaty with Frederick), Chatham expressed himself favourable to the peace of Europe, that he would neither subsidise nor court foreign alliances, but that there was *a great cloud of power in the north*, which should not be neglected.—*Private Journal of the Duke of Bedford, December 3, 1763.*

† There is a long memorial drawn up by Egmont, then at the head of the Admiralty, and addressed to Granville, relative to French designs of invasion, and recommending an increase in the Navy Estimates. — Grenville *Correspondence,* vol. ii. p. 175.

‡ Military report by a French officer to the Minister (1767), found among Lord Chatham's papers.

§ 'France is still the object of my mind, whenever thought calls me back to a public world, infatuated, bewitched.' — *Pitt to Countess Stanhope, June 20, 1766.* —*Appendix to* Lord Mahon's *History,* vol. v. p. 6. This was a month before his return to power.

a European alliance. Hans Stanley, the able diplomatist, whom he had formerly employed in the negotiation at Paris, and who had thus become intimately conversant with his views, was appointed to an embassy to St. Petersburg, with instructions to stop at Berlin on his way.* Chatham seems to have assumed that Frederick would be favourable to his views. Whatever cause of complaint the Prussian monarch might have against England, it was well known to him that Chatham had been the vehement opponent of the policy which disappointed his ambitious designs. All Europe knew that he had made a sacrifice of power rather than consent to the peace. But when the matter was first broached to Frederick by Sir Andrew Mitchell, the able and experienced resident at the Court of Berlin, it met with a very cold reception. The King put it off with many excuses, and when Mitchell pressed His Majesty for his real reasons, he alleged the instability of English counsels, owing to the frequent changes of administration. He had confidence in Lord Chatham; but how was he to be assured that Chatham would remain in power, or that his policy would be pursued by his successors? It was not easy to answer this objection; Mitchell could only say that Chatham was high in favour both with the King and the people. The King, better informed, expressed his doubts even on those points.* But Frederick had other reasons which he could not avow. Gratitude had no place in the morals of this great sovereign, and he scoffed at creeds. The subjugation of Great Britain, and the ascendancy of Romish doctrine, would have been matters of indifference to him unless they affected his own political position. But though insensible to gratitude, he could cherish resentment; and so far from being indifferent to the

* 'I fear,' said he to Mitchell, 'my friend has hurt himself by accepting a peerage.'

fate of England, he would have rejoiced at her adversity, or even downfall, because she had refused any longer to minister to his wanton passion for war. Moreover, he was at this time, in conjunction with the Czarina, meditating that act of perfidious and cruel rapacity which was afterwards so ably and shamefully carried into effect by those worthy allies. A participation in the spoil of Poland was a far more attractive scheme to the invader of Silesia, than an alliance with Great Britain for the defence of religion and liberty against the Family Compact.

The reports of the ambassador at Berlin having made it clear that Frederick was impracticable on the subject of the proposed alliance, the mission to St. Petersburg was abandoned; and thus the leading object of Chatham's policy for the last ten years was entirely defeated. A similar disappointment forty years after broke the heart of the younger Pitt; and it is certain that this sudden and unexpected extinction of his long-cherished hopes must have had a sensible effect on the declining years and failing health of Chatham. His private letters, at this time, exhibit the irritation of his mind; and his natural infirmity of arrogance was aggravated to a degree which became intolerable. Soon afterwards that great mind was, for a time at least, obscured.

Chatham's projects defeated.

If there was any avowed principle upon which Lord Chatham formed his administration, it was that of breaking up party connection. The King believed, or affected to believe, that he had at last got a minister who was willing to carry out his favourite idea. But the King and his minister attached different ideas to the terms which they employed. His Majesty meant to exalt prerogative on the ruins of party; Chatham meant that his own will should not again be thwarted by the factions to which he had before fallen a sacrifice. The meaning which the country attached to

Imperious proceedings of Chatham.

the phrase was the ascendancy of the Scottish junto;
yet, under happier circumstances, Chatham would no
doubt have been supported by the people, as far as
they were able to support him, in his hostility to
those combinations of public men, of which none
either possessed or deserved, in the least degree, the
respect or confidence of the country. But his acceptance of a peerage was considered as a desertion of
the people for the Court; and when he talked of
breaking up party, he was told that he had sold himself to the Earl of Bute. To destroy existing party
divisions, and to have consolidated the great party of
the Revolution upon a wide and solid basis, would
have been a design worthy of Chatham; but the
course which he pursued was to affront the Rockinghams, the most respectable of the Whig connection,
for the sole purpose, as it appeared, of bringing in
the Bedfords, who were insatiable of office. The
mode of procedure also resembled the mean and
shifty tactics of Newcastle rather than the lofty style
of Pitt. An inferior place was wanted in furtherance
of the scheme for conciliating the friends of the Duke
of Bedford; and Grafton, whom Pitt employed on
these occasions, wrote to Lord Monson intimating
that his resignation would be acceptable, and offering
him a step in the peerage as a recompense. Monson
drily declined the proffered earldom, and took no
notice of the broad hint to resign. But Chatham
was not to be turned from his purpose; and wishing
to gratify an adherent of Bute's, he fixed upon the
office of Treasurer of the Household, which was filled
by Lord Edgecumbe, who received a peremptory dismissal.* Upon this, the whole of the Rockingham

* 'When Conway ventured to remonstrate against this arbitrary proceeding, and proposed an arrangement by which his object should be answered without offending an adherent, Chatham's answer was, that the honour of the King was engaged, and that he himself had always determined to break up all parties.'
—ROCKINGHAM Memoirs, vol. ii. p. 19.

connection, to avoid the indignity of being turned out, resigned in a body.

Vacillating conduct towards Lord Gower.

Having thus broken with the Rockingham party for no other reason, as it would seem, than that he would not have the freedom of his administration hampered by a powerful connection in office;—so ill were his plans matured, or so little did he act upon any plan in the prosecution of his design, that Chatham had no other resource than to repeat his application to that rival party which had already rejected his advances. But on this occasion, instead of employing the Duke of Grafton, he sent for Lord Gower himself, and placed certain offices * at the disposal of that lord and his friends. Gower immediately communicated the offer to the head of his party; and Bedford, who was at his seat of Woburn, came to London that he might treat in person with the minister upon a matter of so much importance. But in the interim, Chatham had seen the King, who expressed himself strongly averse to the proposed alliance with the Bedford party, both on the general ground of hostility to *all connections*, and on account of his personal dislike to the Duke. In deference to His Majesty's wishes, if not in obedience to his express commands, the

---

* For himself, that of Master of the Horse; for Lord Weymouth, of Joint Postmaster; for Rigby, a political agent of the Duke of Bedford, of Cofferer. Adolphus does not relate this transaction with his usual accuracy. He represents Lord Chatham as having offered Lord Gower the first place at the Board of Admiralty, and of having filled it up before he could get Gower's answer. He also states that no places whatever were reserved for the Bedford party.—*History of England*, vol. i. p. 292. Third edit. 1840.

But there is no foundation for representing Chatham as having trifled with the Duke in this manner. Bedford himself, in a letter to the Duke of Marlborough, mentions the offer of the above-named appointments through Gower, and Rigby told Grenville that, in the interview which took place between Chatham and the Duke, the offer was limited to these three officers.—BEDFORD *Correspondence*, vol. iii. p. 355.—GRENVILLE's *Diary*, vol. iii. p. 392.

Board of Admiralty and other vacancies, except those which had been named to Gower, were immediately filled up, so as to preclude the possibility of making a more extensive provision for the admission of the Bedford party than that which had been already offered and could not be withdrawn. But the dignity or rapacity of the House of Russell was not to be satisfied without a large concession of power and place. Chatham appears to have met the Duke's demands with all the arrogance and contempt with which his royal master could wish his chosen minister to treat the leader of a great party. The negotiation was broken off with high words on both sides; and the interview closed with an offer to call up the heir of the house of Russell to the Lords. This proposal was, of course, rejected, and the Duke retired to hide his chagrin and indignation at Woburn.

The distinguished admiral, Hawke, was placed at the head of the Admiralty; but, with that exception, all the vacancies were filled up by Tories and courtiers. Chatham proved very unfortunate in his dispensation of places; a department, which in his better days he had left to the more expert and congenial management of Newcastle. Whether it be possible to carry on parliamentary government without party is a problem which remains to be solved; but Chatham can hardly be said to have given a fair trial to the experiment. He merely alienated the great Whig families, without attaching any other party, or even any men of promise or influence, to the support of his ministry. His haughty and contemptuous bearing [*] was ill calculated to make friends; and though he bestowed a large number of offices on persons who were supposed to act under the influence of Lord Bute, he gained

---

[*] 'The new peer treats them all as Lord Peter does Jack and Martin.'—*Lord Hardwicke to Hon. C. Yorke, November 28, 1706.*

nothing in stability or influence to compensate for the public odium which attended such patronage.* The party of Lord Bute, if, indeed, any such party can be said to have existed, was founded on a principle hostile to the influence of every minister, because it placed the minister in subordination to the executive instead of the legislative power. It was in vain, therefore, that Bute's brother, Mackenzie, was restored to his place; that his kinsman, Northumberland, obtained the dukedom which he solicited; that his private secretary and confidential agent,† Jenkinson, was preferred to the Board of Admiralty; that many other of his friends and connections were provided for. The Court were rewarded for their perseverance. After undermining and subverting one administration after another, they had at length succeeded in ruining the only man in England who could have destroyed their system. Chatham had been led to believe that, in affronting the Whigs, he freed himself from the control of faction; and that, in sacrificing his popularity to a connection with the courtiers, he asserted his independence. The result was that, within six months after his return to power, his administration was falling to pieces, and he himself was the weakest minister that had held office since Wilmington.

But while Chatham erred so fatally as a tactician,
Indian policy. his measures of public policy were marked by the same commanding genius which had planned the pacification of the Highlands, and the conquest of Canada. His Northern Alliance, though disappointed by the malice of Frederick, was

---

* Newcastle writes at this time—'He (Chatham) tried the Bedfords. He bid, I dare say, high for them; and, when he found he could not buy them, he determined to defy the world, and openly take my Lord Bute by the hand at once.'

† Jenkinson accepted office by desire of Bute and the Princess Dowager. This Lord Harcourt told Grenville.—*Diary*, vol. iii. p. 395.

still a noble scheme. He contemplated that great
Asiatic empire,* formed within these few years by
adventurous valour and commercial policy, and which
had as yet hardly obtained the attention of any
British statesman, in a spirit worthy of its paramount
importance. Before he could carry his plan into
detail, he was afflicted by the malady which for a
time obscured his faculties and terminated his connection with the Government; but the leading idea
was the assumption of sovereign power over these
new conquests by the Imperial Government, and the
restriction of the Company to their proper province
of mercantile monopoly.

He had also turned his attention to the state of
Ireland, that country so rich in natural
resources, and so closely connected by State of Ireland.
geographical position with this island, though as
much neglected as if it had been a distant and worthless province. Misrule and corruption in the capital;
agrarian outrage amounting to servile war, complicated with a savage animosity of religion and race—
such, for more than a century, had been the condition of this, the fairest part of the Empire. A nobler
field for the genius of a master-statesman could
hardly be provided; and Chatham, in the vigour of
his intellect and will, might have accomplished what
has baffled the ingenuity of all his successors. He
had already intended, by way of beginning, to assi-
milate the Irish, in duration at least, to the British
Parliament; and to bring the local administration
into closer correspondence with the Home Government.

Thus we see that, even out of office, the authority
of Pitt had saved the colonial empire; that in office,

* In arranging the business for the ensuing session, he speaks of 'East India affairs — the greatest of all subjects, accord-ing to my sense of great.'— *Chatham to Grafton, August 23, 1766.*

he had proposed a scheme to secure the safety of Great Britain, and the peace of Europe; that he had intended to provide for the Government of India; and that he would have attempted at least to remove that grievous blot upon English policy, the misrule of Ireland.

Exportation of corn restricted.

But all these great designs were to be disappointed; and the principal, if not the only, measure adopted by the administration which bore the name of Chatham, was one of an occasional character. The failure of the harvest, in consequence of the extreme wetness of the season, having caused a great rise in the price of corn, the sufferings of the people, as usual under such circumstances, were made known by riots and disturbances. Until a very recent period the country had exported grain to a considerable extent; but the great discoveries in manufactures within the past few years had given such an impulse to the population that England had latterly rather inclined to import than to export corn;* and, as the same causes which had caused a scarcity in these islands, also prevailed on the continent of Europe, apprehensions of famine were entertained, if the foreign trade in corn were allowed to proceed. But the price of wheat in the home market not having reached the limit (53s. 4d.) at which exportation would cease by law, it was for the Executive Government to consider, in the recess of Parliament, whether an emergency existed sufficient to warrant the interposition of that power beyond the law, which, as an immediate resource, must exist in every polity. The Ministry, with the approval, if not at the suggestion, of their chief, determined to exercise the power; and, after issuing a proclamation to enforce the old obsolete laws against forestalling and regrating, or the prohibition of the internal trade in

---

* M'Culloch's Comm. Dict., Art. Corn Laws.

corn by means of dealers and factors, they took the
more effectual measure of an Order in Council laying
an embargo on exportation. This was done on the
24th of September, and in strict propriety Parliament should have been assembled as soon afterwards as the law would permit; but, as Parliament
stood prorogued until the 11th of November, it was
not thought worth while to alter the arrangement
by anticipating the session a few days, for the sake
of a constitutional punctilio.

This proceeding, of itself, would hardly have afforded any ground for opposition. A le- <small>The question in
gislature cannot provide against every the Lords.</small>
accident; and the safety of the people, which is the
supreme law, may occasionally render it the duty of
the executive to dispense, for the moment, with the
municipal law. No candid disputant would think of
comparing such an act as this with the assertion of a
dispensing power; nor could Parliament, if promptly
appealed to, hesitate to grant indemnity, even though
they might be of opinion that the Government had
been precipitate, or had failed to exercise a wise discretion in the particular instance. Chatham brought
the matter forward in the House of Lords with the
moderation and diffidence which became a first appearance in that august assembly, and the nature of
the topic which it was his fortune to introduce. He
made no pretence of defending the embargo on any
other ground than that of necessity; and endeavoured
only to show that an adequate case of necessity
existed. But his supporters, both in this and in the
other House of Parliament, were not so discreet.
The two law lords, Northington and Camden, went
out of their way to exhibit ignorance of constitutional
principle. The former, with a coarse sneer at popular doctrines, maintained that the Order in Council
was not only justifiable, but legal; and Camden,
with that violence of assertion which he had displayed

the year before, so little to the advancement of his reputation for good sense, on the question of colonial taxation, now hurried into the opposite extreme, and asserted that the necessity of a measure was sufficient to render it legal; and he made use of a pointed expression, which was remembered to his disadvantage long after the occasion which gave rise to it was forgotten. He said that 'the Crown was entitled to do whatever the safety of the nation may require during the recess of Parliament, *which is at most but a forty days' tyranny!*' So guarded should statesmen be in the use of epigrams!

Lord Mansfield rebuked these extravagant doctrines, so entirely contrary to the principles of the Revolution, with his usual felicity; and, as he had formerly upheld the authority of Parliament against the too forward advocate of liberty, so he now denied a claim no less dangerous to constitutional government, preferred by the same inconsiderate zeal on behalf of prerogative.

The question in the Commons. In the Commons, the same doctrines were urged to absurdity by Alderman Beckford, whose opinions derived importance from his connection with Chatham. The idle language of this headstrong citizen was taken down on the motion of Grenville,[*] who compelled him ultimately to retract

---

[*] Grenville, conceiving that he could make use of the embargo as a formidable weapon of attack against the Ministry, had consulted Mansfield on the subject before the meeting of Parliament; but the great lawyer gave him no encouragement.—*Mansfield to Grenville, November 10, 1766.*—GRENVILLE *Corr.* vol. ii. p. 337. In this letter he says that the term is well known, and the practice well established, among maritime nations; that it is adapted to sudden emergencies such as war, or the apprehension of war, *or of famine;* and that to the executive the exercise of this extraordinary power properly belonged. But Lord Mansfield never thought of saying that the power was legal.

Lord Campbell endeavours to excuse his favourite Chancellor by suggesting that Northington's doctrine took him by surprise, and that he felt bound to support his colleague. But Northington spoke on the Address,

it. The necessity of the embargo being admitted, it is probable that Parliament would have taken no further notice of the matter; but, in consequence of the strange unconstitutional doctrines which had been advanced by the great legal authorities of the Government, it was considered right to mark the exceptional character of the proceeding by an Act of Indemnity, in which those who advised, as well as those who had enforced, the Order in Council were included.

The first business of importance brought before Parliament, after the question relative to the Order in Council had been disposed of, was the affairs of the East India Company. *East India Company.*
The great idea which occupied the mind of Chatham was to place the territorial revenues arising from the British conquests in India on a different footing from the mercantile profits of the Company; and probably to provide for the entire separation of functions so essentially distinct as those of Government and commerce. But before any definite measure could be proposed, it was necessary to obtain that authentic information which the Company alone could supply. Within a month after his assumption of office, Chatham had advertised the Court of Directors of his intention in the ensuing session to institute a parliamentary inquiry into the state of their affairs. Accordingly, on the thirteenth day of the session, the subject was brought before the House of Commons by Alderman Beckford on a motion for papers.

---

and never ventured to maintain the opinion which he then expressed, after the correction which it immediately received from the Chief Justice. The Chancellor spoke on the same occasion, and is reported to have adopted in the extreme the doctrine of his predecessor; but the language which drew down upon him so much obloquy was contained in his speech on the second reading of the Indemnity Bill, and must therefore have been used advisedly. — CAMPBELL'S *Lives of the Chancellors* —*Life of Lord Camden.*—ADOLPHUS's *History*, vol. i. p. 286.

That a question of such importance should have been introduced by a private member with the sanction of the minister, after an intimation to the Company that the Government meant to take it up, was a very strange proceeding. Questions of political interest upon which it is not intended to legislate, but merely to obtain an expression of the sense of Parliament, have sometimes been brought forward by independent members in concert with the administration; but I am not aware of any great measure of public policy having been founded on an inquiry originated by a private member of Parliament on behalf of the Ministry. Beckford, a City alderman and a West Indian proprietor, a man remarkably deficient in information and judgment, had no vocation to lead the House of Commons in an inquiry into the affairs of the East India Company, and the whole state of the revenues and government of India. But it was notorious that he was put forward as the agent and mouthpiece of Chatham. It would seem incredible that a first minister, however immeasurable his superiority, should so insult his colleagues charged with the public business in the House of Commons as to depute a gentleman unconnected with the Government to open a cabinet question. But just at this time the rupture between Chatham and the Rockingham party had taken place; and Conway deeply resented the treatment which his friends had experienced. As for Charles Townshend, Chatham appears to have always disliked and slighted him, and it was with difficulty that he consented at the last hour to his being appointed Chancellor of the Exchequer, and admitted to a seat in the Cabinet. Conway was silent on Beckford's motion; and Townshend, without actually opposing, said what he could to discredit it.*

Breach of parliamentary etiquette

---

* A letter from Lord Chatham to the Duke of Grafton, pub-

But though the principal measure of the session was brought forward in this strange and irregular manner; though it was assailed by the Opposition as a breach of faith, and a violation of charters; and damaged still more by the silence or cold and qualified support of the ministers in the House of Commons, the ascendancy of Chatham, upheld by the vote and influence of the Court, obtained a large majority. The Company also, knowing whom they had to deal with, were anxious to come to terms. Chatham himself, rendered more haughty and resolute by the opposition which he encountered, went down to the House of Lords before the close of the session, and took occasion to tell the Peers that he defied their combinations. But the domineering style and manner with which he had been accustomed to rule the Commons was not to succeed in a more decorous and select assembly. The great orator was told at once that the old nobility of England would not submit to insolence. Chatham attempted to vindicate himself, but was conscious of failure; and he

Chatham's measure passed.

lished by Lord Mahon, in the Appendix to the fifth volume of his History, makes it clear (if there could be any doubt) that Beckford acted by his instructions. He threatens to dismiss Townshend, and declares, that if Beckford's motion for inquiry is not carried, he will 'wash his hands of the whole business.'—*Earl of Chatham to the Duke of Grafton, December 8, 1766*. Walpole, who was in daily and confidential intercourse with Conway, speaks of his deep disgust at the treatment which the Rockingham party had lately received at the hands of Chatham. 'The wound rankled so deep in Mr. Conway's bosom, that he dropped all intercourse with Lord Chatham; and though he continued to conduct the King's business in the House of Commons, he would neither receive nor pay any deference to the minister's orders, acting for or against, as he approved or disliked his measures.'—WALPOLE's *History of George the Third*, vol. ii. p. 385. Conway and Townshend declared they thought the East India Company had a right to their conquests.—*Ibid*, p. 627. And on the subsequent motion of Beckford's for printing the papers of the East India Company, Townshend absented himself, saying he must have voted with the Opposition, if he had stayed.—GRENVILLE's *Diary*.

did not attend the House again while he continued minister.

During the recess, he returned to Bath. Parliament was to reassemble the middle of January. On the tenth of that month the Duke of Grafton, the colleague with whom he chiefly corresponded, received a letter from Chatham announcing his intention of being in London in a day or two. But a whole month passed, and he was still at Bath, detained by illness and unable to attend to business. Another letter indeed came, expressing in general terms disapprobation of the proceedings of the East India Company, but refusing to disclose to his own cabinet any intimation of his particular views and opinions on the subject. He should reserve himself for Parliament. In vain did the Duke ask permission to wait upon him—for an interview even of a few minutes; his visits were positively declined; and Chatham would neither give any directions himself, nor authorise the cabinet to exercise their own discretion.

The Government was in a state of anarchy. Those members who might have been able to take a leading part were unwilling to assume responsibility. Those who were willing, were incompetent to rule. The Lord President, from his age and experience; the Lord Chancellor, from his high reputation and close alliance with Chatham, might in his absence have taken the helm. Once, indeed, Northington did attend the Council, and his presence and authority are gratefully commemorated by a colleague* as having for the moment restored order and even unity to the distracted cabinet. Camden, though not wanting in ambition or energy, was perhaps deterred by the fear of displeasing his capricious and despotic patron. The leader of the

* Grafton to Chatham, Feb. 15, 1767.—Chatham Corr. vol. iii. p. 204.

House of Commons had quarrelled with his chief, and was moreover the most irresolute of mankind. Townshend, unrivalled in eloquence, but from his levity and rashness utterly unfit to take a leading part, showed an eagerness, but not the courage, to seize the vacant helm.

Parliament, on reassembling, found the country without a government. The East India question had increased in magnitude and difficulty. *Disorder of parliament.* The Company, in the absence of Chatham whom alone they feared, amused the administration with impracticable propositions, or affected to treat with them on the footing of an independent power. The House of Commons, no longer under management, became unruly; violent attacks were made upon the absent minister, and not a voice was raised in his defence. Conway sat in sullen silence. Townshend, either from malice or folly, or a mixture of both, did all the mischief in his power. He openly encouraged the East India Company in their opposition to his chief. And just as the dangerous rupture with the colonies was healing after the bold and skilful treatment of Chatham, the giddy rashness of his Chancellor of the Exchequer reopened that wound which was never again to be closed. A few days after the meeting of Parliament, Grenville moved that the colonies should be made to support a military establishment, and Townshend, in opposing the motion, commended the Stamp Act, ridiculed the colonial theory of the distinction between external and internal taxation, and to the astonishment and dismay of his colleagues, undertook to raise a revenue from America which should be nearly adequate to the object proposed. Lord George Sackville, a strenuous supporter of American taxation, took advantage of these idle words—for such they probably were—to pledge the administration upon the question. The pledge was given, and from that night the American revolution may be dated.

Revenue from America.
The fatal scheme of raising a revenue in America was not, however, taken until after the failure of Townshend's first experiment in finance, the increase of the land-tax to 4s. in the pound. On the motion of Mr. Dowdeswell, his predecessor in office, 3s. was substituted for 4s. by a majority of 206 against 188. This result, it is true, was in a great measure attributable to the combination of the country gentlemen, whose interests were particularly affected by an increase of this impost; but no Government had met with such a reverse since the Revolution as to have a part of its Ways and Means for the year refused by the House of Commons. Townshend, as a Chancellor of the Exchequer, was held in less esteem even than Sir Francis Dashwood.*

Chatham taken ill.
Lord Chatham arrived in London two days after this event, and immediately applied for, and obtained, the King's permission to appoint another minister of finance. But Lord North, to whom the office was first offered, having declined it, Townshend remained undisturbed; for before Chatham could make any other arrangement, he was afflicted with that grievous distemper both of mind and body, which totally disabled him from attending to business during the remainder of the time that he continued nominally a member of the administration.

Chatham refuses to consult his colleagues.
The principal ministers had eagerly and anxiously looked forward to Chatham's arrival in London, to relieve them from all their perplexities. He arrived on the afternoon of the 1st of March; and instead of sending for

---

* Earl of Shelburne to Earl of Chatham, Feb. 1, 1767.— Chatham Corr. vol. iii. p. 186.— Grenville's Diary, G. P. vol. iv. p. 211.

either of his colleagues—the Duke of Grafton or Lord Shelburne, who had done all they could, during his absence, to consult his pleasure, and to carry on the government upon his principles—the only person he would see was Lord Bristol, the viceroy of Ireland. The East India question, to which he attached so much importance, had been postponed from week to week, in order that Beckford, or the ministers, might receive his instructions. Disorders which called for immediate redress had appeared in two of the principal colonies of America. The state of the finances was critical. Upon neither of these matters could Bristol have afforded any useful information or advice. He was not even a member of the cabinet. Yet the Lord Lieutenant appears to have been the only minister with whom Chatham held any communication.* He continued in London a few weeks, and then retired to Hampstead, where he remained in strict seclusion, still refusing to see any of his colleagues, or even to receive any communication relative to public business.

At length, by the intercession of the King, Grafton obtained an interview with the Prime Minister. Nearly six months had elapsed since their last meeting before the Christmas recess, yet the Duke was deeply affected at witnessing the change which disease had wrought in the mind no less than in the person of his revered friend and chief. The proud imperial spirit was bowed down, and the clear intellect had lost its discernment. It was to little purpose that Grafton poured forth his accumulation of cares, doubts, and anxieties. No instruction, no advice was to be obtained. He was desired to remain in office, to keep Northington and

Grafton obtains an interview.

* Townshend describes him 'in the morning, not up; at noon, taking the air; in the evening, reposing, and not to be fatigued; in fact, nobody is supposed to see him now, except Lord Bristol.' — GRENVILLE's *Diary, March* 27, 1767.

Camden, and to recruit the administration by new connections.

There was but little encouragement to be drawn from this visit; but the very sight of the venerable statesman whom he had been accustomed to regard with entire confidence and devotion, revived, for the moment at least, the sinking courage of Grafton. He relinquished his purpose of resigning office altogether; and in the hope that Chatham might still be able to resume the lead, was content to undertake the vicarious responsibility of Prime Minister.

Movements of the Opposition. Meanwhile the Opposition were making every effort to profit by the weak and distracted state of the ministry. Early in the session, the Duke of Bedford, being then in communication with Lord Chatham, had separated himself from Grenville, and given a general support to the Government; but when he found that Chatham had espoused the principle of the new reign, and was determined to resist the combination of the great Whig houses, the Duke, who was equally firm in his adherence to political connection, renewed his correspondence with the Grenvilles, and, though indifferent to office himself, did not disdain the arts of faction for the purpose of restoring his party to power. The conduct of the Marquis of Rockingham was very different. No man had been so ill-used by Chatham as Lord Rockingham. When at the express desire of his sovereign, without any intrigue or solicitation on his part, he had assumed the government, after it had been refused by the very man who now denounced all connections, because he could not obtain the support of his own particular connection, Rockingham had frankly and at once acknowledged the paramount importance of Pitt's services. But all his efforts, which were pushed to the verge which self-respect could allow, to obtain the co-operation of that states-

man, had been met with sneers and contempt. Yet
when he had been compelled, partly by this wanton
insolence, to abandon his ungrateful office, Rockingham, though he personally marked his indignation at
the treatment which he had experienced at the hands
of Chatham, did not suffer resentment in any way to
affect his public conduct. He advised his friends to
remain in office; and even when that respectable
band had been forced, by repeated insult, to retire,
Lord Rockingham still maintained the same dignified
moderation, and scorned to avenge his private
wrongs, by any conduct which in his capacity as a
public man he could not entirely justify. At the
commencement of 1767 there seemed to be a favourable opportunity of putting an end to the administration. Chatham, by his elevation to the peerage,
had forfeited the popularity which formerly attended
him; while his arrogance had revolted all the great
political families. He had been signally defeated in
the principal measure which he had as yet attempted,
the revival of that system of foreign policy which
had been so triumphant in his former administration.
And now bodily affliction had obliged the most reserved and dictatorial of ministers to leave the
management of affairs to colleagues who were either
disaffected towards his person, or incapable of com-
prehending his policy.

Under these circumstances, it was proposed to the
Marquis of Rockingham, through the
medium of Lord Lyttelton, to unite with Lyttelton's proposals to Rockingham.
the Grenvilles in forming an administra-
tion on the basis of conciliation with, or, as it was
termed, *management* of Bute. The reply was
prompt and manly. 'I told him,' said Rockingham,
'that making Mr. Grenville minister would be the
most inconsistent act for us that could be thought of;
and that, of course, we who were determined to act
consistently would never join in such a plan; that

our credit had risen with the public in opposing Mr.
Grenville's measures when he was minister, and that
we had confirmed our credit by reversing his measures
when we were in administration.'* The refusal of
Rockingham to lend himself to any scheme for supplanting the ministers merely to occupy their places,
enabled them to carry through the necessary business
of the session.

Lord Chatham had intended to deal with the
Indian question on a scale commensurate
with its greatness; but as he had not in
any degree developed his plan, the ministers prudently abstained from making an attempt at new
and extensive legislation on this subject, which the
weight and authority of a powerful minister could
alone sustain. They therefore contented themselves
with a provisional measure which should postpone
the great question until a more convenient time. A
farther lease for two years of the government and
commerce of India was granted to the Company in
consideration of a fine or premium of four hundred
thousand pounds.† By another act, the company
were restrained for the present from increasing their
dividend.‡ But there was another matter of much
delicacy and importance, upon which the
ministers could not altogether evade responsibility. The irritation which had been caused by
the attempt to impose taxes on America had not subsided with the reversal of that policy. The British
Government had thought that concession should not
be altogether unconditional; and though they resisted an attempt to mar the grace of the act repealing the stamp duty by the introduction of a clause
compelling the American Assemblies to provide for
the compensation of the persons whose property had

* Lord Rockingham to Mr.   Debates.
Dowdeswell.—Rockingham Me- † 7 Geo. III. c. 57.
moirs, vol. ii. p. 32.—Cavendish ‡ 7 Geo. III. c. 49.

been injured during the riots, the House of Commons, by resolution, expressed a strong opinion on this subject; and the Secretary of State, in a circular letter to the governors of the different provinces, instructed them to lay the resolutions of the House before the Assemblies, and to recommend the question of compensation in the strongest terms to their consideration. These injunctions were obeyed, though reluctantly, by each of the Assemblies; but that of Massachusetts Bay* thought fit to insert in their bill a clause of amnesty in favour of the rioters. This being a direct encroachment upon the royal prerogative, the bill was, of course, annulled by the Privy Council. It was impossible for the Government, without a dereliction of their duty, to have pursued any other course. In the matter, which was one of mere law, they acted under the advice of the law officers of the Crown. Yet upon ground so strong as this, they narrowly escaped a defeat in the Upper House, where a motion was made by Lord Gower to declare the indemnity clause absolutely null and void. Upon this, the Duke of Grafton moved the previous question, and Gower's motion was negatived only by a majority of three. The legislature of the state of New York displayed a similar spirit of resistance to the authority of Great Britain. They deliberately refused obedience to an

---

* 'The House of Assembly was offended at the term "requisition," which the Governor had used in referring to this subject. This word was what lawyers call a "term of art," and was equivalent to a King's message, asking the House of Commons for a supply. The Colonial Assemblies had been accustomed to vote war supplies upon the "requisition" of a secretary of state's letter; and the Assembly of Massachusetts complained that the governor had taken upon him to use a phrase of peculiar significancy, which was not employed in the resolutions of the House of Commons or in the letter of the Secretary of State. Whether or not the Governor used the word advisedly, the circumstance shows how extremely sensitive the Assembly was upon this subject.'— ALMON's *Papers*.

enactment of the Imperial Parliament. The Mutiny Act of the last session had required the Colonies to provide certain necessaries for the troops quartered upon them. The New York Assembly considered, or affected to consider, this as an attempt to enforce the principle of the Stamp Act. They argued, and not without reason, that if the Parliament were to pass laws obliging the provincial assemblies to make provision for troops quartered upon them by the authority of the Crown, it was equivalent to taxing the people of the Colonies without their consent. Accordingly, in framing an act to provide for the accommodation of a certain number of troops in the barracks, they studiously omitted those articles* which, by the Mutiny Act of the last session, they were required to furnish. When this omission was brought to the notice of the home Government, Lord Shelburne, as Secretary of State, wrote to the Governor of New York, acquainting him that the Assembly was expected to comply with the terms of the Act of Parliament. This letter was formally communicated to the House by the Governor, with an earnest exhortation to obedience. The Assembly, however, unanimously resolved they could not, consistently with their duty to their constituents, comply with the requisition contained in the Governor's message.

The Government had, therefore, to decide whether they should yield to the Assembly or enforce its obedience. It was impossible to take the former course after the declaratory act of the last session. It would have been wise, considering the sensitive jealousy of the Americans at that time, to have overlooked the matter; but having noticed it, there was no alternative but to call upon Parliament to vindicate its authority. The British legislature, on their part, were in no temper

Suspension of the New York Assembly.

* Salt, vinegar, cider, and beer.

to indulge the license of the Colonies; and an act for which its authors claimed the praise of mildness and moderation,* but which really was one of a very stringent character, easily passed both Houses. The Assembly of New York was suspended until it should have made provision in exact conformity with the Mutiny Act. Many members were for still more coercive measures, nor did the bill pass through its stages, without many expressions, calculated to aggravate the ill-feeling of the Colonies to which recent legislation had given birth.

It only required the rash measure of the Chancellor of the Exchequer to reopen with increased malignity those wounds which the wise and generous patriotism of Chatham had closed in the preceding year. Consistent in nothing else, Townshend was steadfast to the fatal policy of extracting a revenue from the colonies; and, being now freed from the control of his great chief, he took an early opportunity, as we have seen, of committing himself to the delusive project of American taxation. The House of Commons, who had yielded to the importunity of the merchants and the authority of Pitt in repealing the Stamp Act, were nevertheless extremely averse to the doctrine of independent right, which had been claimed and asserted on behalf of these provinces in matters of fiscal legislation; and the intimation made by Townshend had, therefore, as he himself boasted, been very favourably received.† It was urged by the apologists of the scheme that the taxes proposed would yield but a trifling revenue; but this fact seemed to favour the argument, that it

Townshend's rash measures.

---

* Duke of Grafton's MS. Memoirs.
† On this question, Townshend differed from his colleagues, who were all faithful to the policy of Chatham. It is lamented by the Duke of Grafton that none of the ministry had sufficient authority to procure the dismissal of Townshend.—*MS. Memoirs quoted in Appendix to* LORD MAHON's *History*, vol. v.

was intended to lay a foundation for a renewal of the financial system which the late administration had reversed. On the other hand, it was maintained that import duties on such articles as tea, glass, and paper, which were all that the Chancellor of the Exchequer proposed, were included in the category of external taxes, to which it was understood the Colonies made no objection. The produce was estimated under £40,000. These money bills passed without opposition.

After the session was closed, the King, at the pressing instance of his ministers, again called upon their chief to arouse himself from his lethargy, and to resume the direction of affairs, or at least to afford some aid and counsel to his bewildered colleagues for the conduct of the Government. But this remonstrance, though couched in the most emphatic language, produced only an effusion of anguish and imbecility—so deep was the prostration of that lofty spirit!

Physical prostration of Chatham.

Chatham still retained the seal of his office, but his administration was now virtually at an end. The King had supported him from first to last with a sincerity which none of his former ministers, with the exception of Bute, had ever experienced. His Majesty had, in fact, supported both on the self-same principle of restoring the independence of the Crown, which domineering factions conspired to destroy. George the Third had, from the commencement of his reign, been intent upon this one object of breaking up and dispersing those connections of the Whig aristocracy, which had for all practical purposes usurped the prerogative, and monopolised the government of the country. In the pursuit of this object, he had made many mistakes, sustained many reverses and much personal insult; but now, after an incessant warfare of six years, it seemed that his perseverance was likely to achieve the success which usually attends that invincible virtue. The sovereign had succeeded in en-

The King's confidence in Chatham.

gaging his greatest subject in his design of emancipating himself from the duress of party. Chatham had every qualification for so difficult an undertaking, and, supported by the public confidence, it is more than probable that he would have succeeded in crushing cabals which were hardly less odious to the nation than irksome to the Crown.

The effect of Chatham's retirement, when it became certain, was immediately felt. The Duke of Grafton, unable to continue the government without an accession of strength, was forced at once to abandon the system which his great master had commenced, but which he alone could carry on. Grafton was obliged again to have recourse to the Whig connection; and, after an ineffectual attempt to accommodate the several pretensions of the parties which respectively acknowledged the Duke of Bedford and the Marquis of Rockingham as their chiefs, the alliance of the latter was abandoned, and the three principal members of the Bedford faction, the Lords Gower, Weymouth, and Sandwich joined the administration in the offices of President of the Council, Secretary of State, and Joint Postmaster-General. Lord Northington and General Conway retired.

Effect of Chatham's retirement.

An important change in the administration was also effected by the hand of death. In the recess of Parliament, Charles Townshend, in the vigour of his age and the fulness of his reputation, was cut off while engaged, as it was supposed, in framing a plan for a new administration of which himself should be the chief. The most competent critics among his contemporaries concur in representing Townshend as the most accomplished orator of his day.* But this gift, unaccompanied as it

Death of Townshend.

---

* Walpole, jealous of merit of any kind, speaks of his eloquence in the highest terms. Lord Charlemont says, 'he alone is the orator, the rest are only speakers.' Burke's splendid panegyric is well known.

was by principle, judgment, or stability, only served to render his defects more glaring. Townshend, like every other effective speaker, found little difficulty in obtaining office; but though he was in Parliament for twenty years, and had the advantage of social position, it was only in the last year of his life that he was promoted to the cabinet. His conduct as Chancellor of the Exchequer showed him utterly unfitted for such an office. Not content with making rhetorical exhibitions in the House of Commons for no other purpose than the display of his versatile powers, he openly thwarted the measures of his chief, reviled his policy, and finally, to gratify his own absurd vanity, revived the grievance of American taxation. Townshend was only forty-two years of age when a fever suddenly terminated his career. His loss as a public man was not deplored. His brilliant talents had been useless, and even mischievous to his country; and such was his fickleness, that no party could depend upon his support, or feel secure from his sudden freaks of enmity.

Lord North who had refused the office of Chancellor of the Exchequer when Chatham had been desirous to prefer him to Townshend, was induced to accept the office when vacated by the death of his predecessor. The Earl of Hillsborough, a Tory nobleman of some promise who had served in subordinate office, was appointed a third Secretary of State, to have charge of the colonial department. These arrangements were concluded shortly after the commencement of the autumnal session. But as Parliament had now nearly completed the legal term of its existence, routine business only was transacted preparatory to the dissolution.

CHAPTER IX.

GENERAL ELECTION—STATE OF THE CONSTITUENCY—WILKES RETURNED TO THE NEW PARLIAMENT—DISTURBED STATE OF THE COUNTRY—RESIGNATION OF CHATHAM—EXPULSIONS OF WILKES—LETTERS OF JUNIUS.

THE general election took place early in the spring of 1768. This which should be one of the most imposing events in the history of a free people had in fact become a periodical exposure of foulness and disease in the body politic. A great number of seats in the House of Commons were the property of individuals who, in returning their nominees, had only to observe the legal forms of popular election. Many of these nominations belonged to party leaders, and were made use of for party purposes;* others were sold for what they would fetch; and now that the payment of members for their votes in ready money was commuted for the more decent but more expensive bribery by official

---

* Lord Chatham's infatuation in dismissing Lord Edgecumbe, a borough proprietor, just on the eve of an election, was strongly reprobated at the time.—WALPOLE's *History*.

'Elections have been carried to a degree of frenzy hitherto unheard of; that for the town of Northampton has cost the contending parties at least 30,000*l*. *a side*, and —— has sold the borough to two members for 9,000*l*.'—CHESTERFIELD *to his Son, April* 12, 1768.

'I spoke to a borough jobber, and offered him five and twenty hundred pounds for a secure seat in Parliament; but he laughed at my offer, and said that there was no such thing as a borough to be had now; for that the rich East and West Indians had secured them all, at the rate of three thousand pounds at least, but many at four thousand, and two or three that he knew at five thousand.'—CHESTERFIELD *to his Son, December* 19, 1767.

patronage, the value of these seats had been much enhanced.* The competition of the East Indian interest, which at this time wanted representatives in parliament, likewise raised the market. The average price was 4,000*l*. Boroughs which were so fortunate as to be free from the domination of proprietors, for the most part sold their votes to the best bidder; and these transactions, not being attended with the order and punctuality which were always observed in the hire of a seat for a close borough, were not nearly such eligible adventures. The candidate, having to satisfy the cupidity of many instead of one, incurred a much larger outlay; nor was he certain that success would reward his lavish expenditure. Again, if he won the battle at the poll, he might

* There is no trace of this practice after the Grenville administration. Up to that period, money was received and expected by members from the minister whose measure they supported, apparently without any consciousness of infamy, very much in the same manner as the voters in certain boroughs at the present day receive head money from the candidate as a matter of right and custom. There is an amusing letter in the 'Grenville Correspondence,' which shows that the Lords also condescended to partake of these *gratifications*, as the bribes were termed.

'*London, Nov.* 26, 1763.

'Honoured Sir,—I am very much obliged to you for that freedom of converse you this morning indulged me in, which I prize more than the lucrative advantage I then received. To show the sincerity of my words (pardon, sir, the perhaps overniceness of my disposition) I return enclosed the bill for 300*l*. you favoured me with, as good manners would not permit my refusal of it, when tendered by you.

'Your most obliged and most obedient servant,

'SAY AND SELE.

'As a free horse wants no spur, so I stand in need of no inducement or douceur to lend my small assistance to the King or his friends in the present administration.'—*Lord Say and Sele to Grenville.*

I fear it is more probable that the noble lord thought he could make more than 300*l*. of his services, than that he was actuated by the motive which induced Judas to return the thirty pieces of silver. The most exquisite satire could not be more felicitous than the care which this nobleman takes to guard his conduct from the imputation of fastidiousness, or the notion of good breeding conveyed in not immediately refusing a bribe when offered.

have to fight it over again in the House, where election petitions, instead of being referred to judicial investigation, were favourite subjects for the trial of party strength. So notorious was this traffic in seats, that the Mayor and Corporation of Oxford, in whom the right of electing the members for that important city was exclusively vested, offered to re-elect the sitting members for the sum of 7,500*l.*, which they meant to apply, not to their private purposes, but to the discharge of a corporate debt. The members having thought fit to lay the letter containing this offer before the House, the Mayor and Aldermen were committed to Newgate; and after remaining imprisoned some days were brought to the bar of the House, and discharged with a lecture from the Speaker, who gravely told them that their crime was one, the enormity of which could not be exceeded. The Mayor and Aldermen listened to this edifying harangue with due humility; and rising from their knees at its conclusion, disposed of the seats to the Duke of Marlborough and Lord Abingdon.

In a population of eight millions, there were no more than one hundred and sixty thousand electors. The representation of the people was merely a phrase. The people of England had, for the most part, no more voice in the election of the House of Commons than the people of Canada. The counties were in the hands of the great landowners, who mostly settled the representation by previous concert. When they could not agree, or when there was a rivalry between two great families or parties, the contest which in former ages would have been decided in the field, was fought at the hustings; and at least as many ancient houses have been ruined in modern times by these conflicts, as were formerly destroyed by private war. The great feud between the houses of Lascelles and Wentworth, when they disputed the county of York for fourteen days, cost according to a credible statement three hundred thousand pounds. Sums as large as this, and proportionally as large, have frequently been lavished at elections. The contest for the borough of Northampton in 1768 is said to have been the most costly in the annals of English elections. The poll was kept open for three months. The contending parties were the Earl of Halifax, the Earl of Northampton, and the Earl Spencer. The struggle resulted in the ruin of the first nobleman. Lord Northampton was, in consequence of it, forced to break up his establishment, and live abroad for the remainder of his days. Lord Spencer's great estates were not relieved from the burden thus imposed upon them until sixty years had passed away. The Duke of Portland won the small county of Westmoreland from the Lowthers at a cost of forty thousand pounds. The latter family afterwards recovered the undisputed possession of this as well as the adjoining county of Cumberland. Upwards of fifty villages and hamlets were each entitled to return two members to Parliament. Many of these boroughs had no constituencies, but such as were created for the purpose of an election. Some of them had no existence. Many of the small towns which could furnish a few electors were entirely under the influence of some one or two of their great neighbours, who named the members commonly without question. A gentleman would no more think of contesting Launceston or Calne, than Gatton or Old Sarum. Of the few populous towns that possessed the elective franchise, in the greater proportion, it was confined exclusively to the municipal body. And in those places where freedom of election was possible, in consequence of the qualification being almost nominal, venality in its grossest form, accompanied by brutal debauchery, were for the most part exhibited. On the whole, it would perhaps be an exaggeration to say that the fifth part of the

House of Commons was elected upon a fair application of the representative principle. It is a remarkable instance of the tenacity of life which belongs to established abuses, however glaring and enormous, that such a system as this should have lasted nearly a century and a half, and have at last only yielded within these few years to a national struggle which before it could succeed was pushed close upon the verge of revolutionary violence.

The immediate effects of this system were for a long time but little understood. The rigour with which Parliament interdicted the publication of its debates; the want of a daily press; the tardy and imperfect means of communication between different parts of the kingdom; the scanty diffusion of knowledge among the middle classes and even the inferior order of the rural gentry, and the dense ignorance of the mass of the people; all these circumstances saved the mean and selfish factions which infested the legislature, from exposure to public hatred and contempt. In the dearth of authentic intelligence and rational opinions of public affairs, lies and libels of the grossest character were eagerly devoured. But the nation, however ill informed upon public transactions, were well aware that the conflict between the Court and the Whig oligarchy was merely a struggle for power, in which their interests were but a secondary consideration. Burke, writing in 1770, laments 'the indifference to the constitution which had been for some time growing among the gentry.' But this very indifference, to which, in a great measure, he justly ascribes the predominance of the Court faction, was itself produced chiefly by the mean and selfish politics of the party to which the Revolution had given the undisputed ascendancy. The gentlemen of England beheld the Crown, which had ever been the object of their reverence and affection, stripped of its ancient prerogatives and transferred to a foreign race. They saw the Crown degraded, and all real authority centred in a Parliament. But instead of that august assembly which had once reigned in England, and knew how to restrain as well as vindicate the liberties of the people, they beheld a body of sordid wretches, the spurious offspring of a representative system which was itself a mockery and a fraud. The party which had the control of this vile senate, and therefore the government of the country, in their hands were the degenerate heirs of the Revolution, men who abused the power which they had derived from statesmen and patriots to the purposes of shameless and reckless faction. It was impossible that the independent gentry should view with any other feeling than that of disgust the interests of the country sacrificed or neglected amidst a constant succession of intrigues for place and power;* or that they should fail to be indifferent, if they were not hostile, to a constitution which had been attended with such results. The middle classes, almost excluded from political influence, yet rapidly growing in wealth and intelligence, joined with the populace

---

* Whig writers, even of the present day, are fond of imputing the weakness of the national councils and the disasters which befell the Empire to the effect of Court intrigues. But in 1756, some years before the Court system came into operation, the country was reduced to the lowest ebb by the long prevalence of Whig jealousies and cabals, and was rescued from that prostrate condition by the minister 'whom the people gave to the King.' That minister was subsequently set aside in the midst of his glory, not by Court influence alone, but by Court influence in connection with Whig discontent. It was the Bedfords, the Newcastles, and the Foxes, quite as much as the Mansfields and the Butes, who prevailed against Pitt. It was not without the utmost vigilance and exertion that the energy and sagacity of Walpole could uphold the Protestant succession against the coalition of Jacobites, Tories, and Malcontent Whigs. After the clamour of the patriots and the partisans of the Stuarts had driven the great statesman of the Revolution from the helm, the country was saved, under Providence, only by the infatuation and folly of the Pretender himself from a new Restoration.

whenever an opportunity offered of expressing contempt and hatred of the Government. And so alarming had the manifestation of these sentiments become, that many persons of high station and authority openly expressed their apprehensions that the political fabric was in imminent danger.*

But happily a free constitution found in its own resources a remedy for the disease. It was not necessary that the country should perish through this internecine war between the Crown and the aristocracy. A third party at this time began to rise, equally hostile to both the cabals which distracted the State,† and more powerful than either. The people had happily begun to find out that they had an interest in these matters, and that they possessed the ability, if they chose to exert it, to save the institutions, which had been intended for better things, from becoming a prey to the wrangles and intrigues of courts and factions. It was not the least of the splendid services which consecrate the name of Pitt, that he resigned the government of the country when he 'could no longer administer it upon a full and entire responsibility to the people by whom it had been committed to his charge.' Those memorable words which sounded strange and uncouth in the ears of courtiers and privy councillors, sunk deep into the heart of the nation. If it was true that this incomparable statesman had been called to power by the public voice, then had the country been saved through the interposition of the people; and though they might not always find a Pitt to whom they could abandon their entire confidence and affection, it was much that they had been taught to rely upon themselves, and to assert their right of independent action.

* Lord Mansfield among others.
† Butler's Reminiscences, vol. i.

Popularity is a word of wide import. On the one
Political hand, there is nothing more noble and
popularity. affecting than the spontaneous effusion of
public gratitude and esteem for a benefactor of his
country. On the other, there is hardly anything
more painful to witness than the same meed of approbation lavished upon a vile impostor. It is this
unhappy want of discrimination which the people
too often manifest in bestowing their favour, that
causes real merit to turn aside with indifference, if
not disgust, from popular applause. The popularity
of Pitt, solicited only by public virtue and great
deeds, was an example of the better kind; that of
Wilkes must always be quoted by those who would
represent the favour of the multitude as despicable
and degrading. But the people, though often lament-
ably mistaken, have this advantage over Courts and
Parliaments, that they are always sincere in their
manifestations, whether of hatred or affection; and
the rise and influence of a popular minion is commonly but the malignant sign of some distemper in
the State.

Wilkes, with the keen perception of a demagogue,
Wilkes saw in the public discontent a chance of
reappears. renewing his traffic in popularity. Five
years had nearly elapsed since this man had been
selected as the vile subject for an experiment upon
the liberty of the press and of the person. Wilkes
had aggravated his grievances for the sake of lucre
in the same way as a beggar makes a living by his
sores. Having obtained all the money that his wrongs
would yield in the shape of actions for damages,
having exhausted the liberality of Lord Temple, and
other factious patrons of sedition, and endeavoured
in vain to raise a public subscription, he retired to
France, where he remained until the general election of this year afforded him the opportunity of
making a new adventure. He had previously ap-

plied in vain, under the Rockingham administration, for a remission of the sentence under which he lay; and had subsequently besought the Duke of Grafton, with no better success, to intercede for him with the King. To return to England under these circumstances, for the purpose of obtaining a seat in Parliament, was the act of a bold and desperate man. The outlawry to which he had been prosecuted not only disqualified him from obtaining any civil right whatever, but rendered his person liable to immediate arrest. To avert a calamity which might have been fatal to his plans, he wrote to the Solicitor of the Treasury, pledging himself to appear in the Court of Queen's Bench on the first day of the ensuing term; and having thus secured his liberty for a few weeks, he proceeded to make the most of his short respite. The City was astounded by an announcement that Wilkes was a candidate for its representation. On the hustings he was elected by a great majority of the show of hands; but this decision was reversed on an appeal to the poll. Rendered only more resolute by disappointment, and indeed encouraged by the evident revival of his former popularity, the energetic adventurer, on addressing the people at the close of the poll, having attributed his failure, after the manner of defeated candidates, to the lateness of his application, to bribery and influence, concluded, amidst the loudest acclamations, by declaring himself a candidate for that support from the freeholders of Middlesex, which he had failed to obtain from the livery of London.

On the day of the county election, Wilkes was attended to the hustings of Brentford by an immense multitude, who took possession of all the roads, and compelled every person to declare for their candidate. Contrary to all expectation, a large majority of the electors ratified the popular choice. The sudden triumph of the people

Wilkes elected for Middlesex.

overflowed all bounds. They compelled London to
illuminate for two nights successively in honour of
the member for Middlesex who had been rejected by
the City a few days before. Not content, however,
with such harmless demonstrations, they proceeded
to attack the houses and persons of those who refused
to join in their exultation. The windows of Lord
Bute's house were demolished, and the Mansion
House was attacked, the Lord Mayor Harley being
a notorious partisan of the Court, and the same
person who as Sheriff had received the thanks of the
House of Commons in 1763, for his firmness in su-
perintending the ceremony of burning No. 45 of the
'North Briton.'

The Ministry regarded these proceedings with astonishment and dismay. Recent experience had taught them the prudence of
avoiding, if possible, a conflict with this
audacious demagogue. They might, by merely letting the law take its course, have shut him up in a
prison, as soon as he landed in England; but they
were willing to hope that his popularity had eva-
porated, or at least that it was confined to the refuse
of the populace. They were, therefore, content to
let him remain at large until the ensuing term,
when he had undertaken to appear to the process
which had issued against him at the suit of the
Crown in the two charges of libel. But his tumultuous return to Parliament for the metropolitan
county forced the Government to determine whether
they would acquiesce in the choice of the freeholders
of Middlesex, or, by annulling it, provoke a new
collision between the House of Commons and the
people. Had the Ministry been left to their own
discretion, it is probable that they would have declined the conflict. Sound policy advised that Wilkes
should be allowed to take his seat, and sink into
insignificance. Justice even might have admitted a

Embarrassment of the Government.

virtual banishment of four years as an expiation of his offences. The submission also of Wilkes himself, contained in a letter which he addressed to the King immediately on his return to England, might have been accepted as a final atonement. But the resentment of George the Third could not be appeased by anything short of the ruin of an enemy whom he thought he had in his power.*

On the first day of Easter term, Wilkes, according to his engagement, presented himself in the Court of King's Bench; and the Attorney-General moved that he should be taken into custody. But the Court refusing to interfere, except on regular process, a writ of Capias utlagatum was issued, upon which Wilkes was arrested. But the populace interposed to prevent his being carried to prison; and had it not been for the prudence or humanity of Wilkes in eluding the vigilance of his excited partisans and rendering himself to safe custody, his incarceration would not have been effected without bloodshed. The raging multitude, baffled for an instant, appeared the next day before the King's Bench prison where Wilkes was lodged. They tore down the railings which enclosed the jail, kindled a bonfire, compelled the neighbourhood to illuminate, and were at last only dispersed by a military force. This tumultuous excitement continued from the 27th of April when Wilkes was

marginalia: Wilkes imprisoned. Riots of his partisans.

---

* Walpole's History, vol. iii. p. 200. In a note, the editor, Sir Denis le Marchant, confirms the accuracy of Lord Orford's statement, that the King directed and urged on the proceedings against Wilkes; and, as a proof, quotes a passage from the correspondence between the King and Lord North, in the possession of Lady Charlotte Lindsay. In a letter to Lord North, of April 25, a few weeks after the Middlesex election, His Majesty says, 'though entirely relying on your attachment to my person, as well as in your hatred of any lawless proceeding, yet I think it highly expedient to apprise you that the expulsion of Mr. Wilkes appears to be very essential, and must be effected.'

arrested, until the 10th of May, the day fixed for the meeting of Parliament. In the morning, vast crowds assembled before the prison, expecting and demanding that the member for Middlesex should be liberated for the purpose of taking his seat in the House of Commons. The magistrates, accompanied by the military, made their appearance, and the reading of the Riot Act furnished the occasion for the first act of violence which had been committed during these disorders. The magistrates and soldiers were assailed by a shower of stones and brick-bats. A man, mistaken in the confusion for a rioter, was shot dead by a soldier before orders had been given to fire. The fury of the populace could then be repressed only by more bloodshed; and the troops being ordered to fire, about twenty persons were killed and wounded.

The coroner's inquest which sat upon the body of the man who had first fallen, sympathising, as usual on such occasions, with popular prejudice, returned a verdict of wilful murder against the soldier whose hand had fired the fatal shot, and against the commanding officer and another soldier as accessories. An indictment for murder was also preferred against Mr. Gillam, the magistrate who had given the order to fire. These persons were all properly acquitted. But the conduct of the Government in this transaction was at once impolitic and indecent. Not satisfied with throwing the whole weight of the Crown into the defence of the accused, by instructing the law officers to appear on their behalf, they anticipated the verdict of the jury by conveying to the commanding officer the royal approbation for his firmness and prudence. The private whose breach of discipline and precipitation in firing without orders had caused the death of an innocent man, was publicly presented with a purse of money by his colonel. Gratuities were also given to the soldiers who had been hurt in the conflict with the populace. This unconstitutional interference with the course of justice — these extraordinary rewards bestowed upon soldiers for the discharge of an odious duty, while they exasperated the public discontent, gave just cause of offence to many persons who would be little moved by popular clamour. The employment also of a Scottish regiment* was regarded in the inflamed state of the public mind as a significant proof that the Court were actuated not merely by the desire of maintaining order, but by bitter resentment of the contumely which had been heaped upon a particular faction.

Popular discontent increases.

The riotous spirit of the populace did not, therefore, on this occasion, as usual, succumb in the presence of a military force. The tumults increased daily, and assumed a more alarming character. The general spirit of sedition was aggravated by the particular grievances of certain classes, who availed themselves of that opportunity, when law and order seemed tending towards dissolution, to seek redress by force. The seamen, insisting upon an increase of wages, would not suffer the outward bound ships to leave the river, nor those which were entered inwards to unload their cargoes. This led to a collision with the coal-whippers, in which several lives were lost. On another occasion, a body of tailors surrounded the House of Commons, and almost interrupted its deliberations with their clamour. Nor were these disorders confined to the metropolis. It was stated by a minister in his place in Parliament that there was 'either actual or impending riot in every part of the country. From the tinners of Cornwall to the colliers of Newcastle, the spirit of insubordination prevailed.'†

Universal insubordination.

---

* The third regiment of guards, now called the Scots Fusilier Guards. There is good reason to believe that the selection of this regiment was advised, and not accidental.

† Lord Barrington's speech in the House of Commons, on introducing a Militia Bill.—*Cavendish Debates*, i. 21.

Parliament was prorogued until the autumn, without any attempt having been made to redress these disorders; the remedies for which, in truth, lay far beyond either the capacity or courage of ministers, who were fit for nothing more than the ordinary routine of office.

The name of Chatham had as yet sustained the credit and hopes of the administration; but a few days before the reassembling of Parliament this support was withdrawn. In the summer, the Earl had been relieved by an attack of gout, and the first use which he made of his partially restored faculties, was formally to separate himself from the administration originally formed under his auspices, but which no longer retained any trace of his policy. The King, as well as the Duke of Grafton, used every effort to dissuade Lord Chatham from his purpose; but he remained inflexible. The infirmity of his health would have been a sufficient excuse for declining to resume the cares of office; and it was not to be expected that he should lend his great name to a policy which he could not dictate and control. But the particular reasons which he assigned for quitting the administration were referable to that arrogant and intolerant temper which had always rendered him impracticable as a colleague.

Chatham withdraws from the Government.

Sir Jeffrey Amherst, the Commander-in-Chief of the forces in America during the late war, had been rewarded for his services by the government of Virginia; but, according to the lax practice of those times, he had enjoyed the emoluments of the office without having ever proceeded to the seat of his government. The Assembly of Virginia, in their ill-humour with the mother-country, enumerated among their grievances, the absence of this great officer, whose salary they voted from the resources of the colony. A complaint, which

Circumstances of his withdrawal.

was merely reasonable, would perhaps have obtained
no redress under ordinary circumstances; and it is
probable, indeed, that the opportunity of providing
for a needy partisan was more regarded by an administration of the period than the just remonstrance of
a great and aggrieved dependency. However that
might have been, Amherst was informed by the Secretary of State of the determination of the Cabinet
that the Governor of Virginia should be resident;
but as the office had been given to him as a reward
for past services, rather than one of active duty, he
was offered an equivalent, in the shape of a pension,
in case he should be disinclined to proceed to his
government. This alternative was rejected by Amherst on grounds as frivolous and unworthy as the
proposition in itself was just and reasonable. He
was unwilling to go to America at all; he objected
to serve under General Gage, where he had himself
commanded in chief; he considered a pension derogatory. Lord Hillsborough, while he yielded to the
General's objection to assume the active duties of his
government, pointed out to him that there was no
loss of dignity in becoming a civil governor in a province, where he had once exercised military command;
and reminded him that neither Lord Chatham nor
Sir Edward Hawke had thought it derogatory to
accept an acknowledgment for past services in the
shape of a pension. The truth was, that Amherst,
like other public men, only aimed at making terms
with the Government. He now stipulated for a peerage and a grant of lands in America, as well as a
pension; and this attempt to overreach his position
resulted both in the loss of his office and of the pension by which it was to have been compensated.*

* It was stated at the time, by Junius, and it has lately been stated by Lord Mahon, on the authority of that writer, that the Cabinet were in such haste to provide for a courtier, that Amherst's government was given to his successor, Lord Botletort,

The Duke of Grafton took pains to explain to the Countess of Chatham, through whom he communicated with her lord, the circumstances attending the removal of Amherst; his grace at the same time intimated the probability of Lord Shelburne's retirement from office, in consequence of irreconcilable differences between that minister and himself. To his surprise and dismay, the Duke received, two days after, a letter from Chatham, desiring that his resignation should be laid before the King, alleging generally his broken health, but censuring in significant and pointed terms the dismissal of Amherst, and the contemplated breach with Shelburne. It was in vain that Grafton remonstrated against this decision; in vain did the King himself address a letter to his haughty minister claiming his services as a right. Chatham remained inflexible; and thus, because the insolence of one adherent was not to receive unbounded license, and the unreasonable demands of another were refused, the first minister did not hesitate, at a moment when the integrity of the Empire was at stake, to withdraw from the Government not only the moral weight and influence of his name which had hitherto sustained it, but those counsels of which his country had never stood in greater need.

Anxiety of the Ministry to retain Chatham.

---

before the former had time to make his election. But Knox, who had his information direct from Lord Hillsborough, and Whately, who was singularly well informed in the political transactions and intrigues of the period, give a different version of the affair in their letters to Grenville.—*Correspondence*, vol. iv. According to those gentlemen, who would not misrepresent the matter in favour of the Ministry, Amherst, in his interview with Lord Hillsborough, positively declined to go to America, and only bargained about the terms on which he should give up his office. The *next day*, Lord Botetort was appointed. The exigency was pressing, Virginia having all but disclaimed the authority of the mother-country. Neither was the appointment by any means an improper one; Botetort, though a courtier, was a man of energy and talent, with persuasive and engaging manners.

At the same time, Shelburne quitted the Government with every mark of contempt.* The Lord Chancellor, while he expressed similar sentiments towards his colleagues, nevertheless consented, by the express desire of his great patron, to retain for a while the Great Seal.† At the instance of Camden, the Privy Seal was given to Lord Bristol, who was distinguished by the especial confidence of his predecessor in that office.

An administration thus constituted preferring no other claim to public confidence than that which belonged to the great name of its founder, could hardly last long even in times when public opinion was but imperfectly developed, and when the House of Commons was a pliant tool in the hands of any Government. But the support of the Crown, together with the disorganised state of the Opposition, again split up into self-seeking factions, kept even the listless and reluctant Grafton in power: and having no policy of his own, he accepted that which was dictated by the pride and passion of the King. *[marginal: Internal weakness of the Government.]*

Besides his fixed idea of destroying party, George the Third was now intent upon two particular objects to which he seemed to attach equal importance. The one was the suppression of the American revolt; the other was the destruction of Wilkes. *[marginal: Determination of the King.]*

Modern experience has ascertained that the best mode of quenching a political firebrand is to put him into Parliament. The fame and popularity which have been acquired on the hustings or the platform, fade away beneath the fatal contempt or neglect of the House of Commons; and the patriot sinks into insignificance, *[marginal: Popular orators lost in Parliament.]*

---

* Whately to Grenville, Oct. 27.—Corr. vol. iv.
† Chatham Corr. vol. iii.
p. 345.—Diary, Grenville Papers, vol. iv. p. 402-6.

unless he should be qualified to aim at a higher object of political ambition. Had Wilkes been allowed to take his seat for Middlesex, the prosecution against him being at the same time terminated by requiring him to enter into his recognisance to come up for judgment when called upon, it is certain that his vocation as a demagogue would have been terminated at once, and for ever. But the King and his Parliament combining to effect the same object by forcible means, were baffled at every turn.

In the spring of this year a vacancy had been caused in the representation of Middlesex by the death of Mr. Cooke. On that occasion, Sir William Proctor, the defeated candidate at the general election, was again put forward by the Government; but Sergeant Glynn, the nominee of Wilkes, obtained an easy victory. This election, like its immediate predecessor, was attended with riot and bloodshed. Two men, partisans of the unsuccessful candidate, were tried for murder and convicted; yet the Government not only granted a free pardon to these persons, but conferred a pension upon one of them. As there appeared to be no sufficient ground for interfering with the course of justice in either of the cases, certainly none for rewarding the principals in the fatal affray, these proceedings revived and aggravated the resentment which had been excited by the largesses given to the soldiers, who were charged with murder in firing on the populace during the riots in St. George's Fields.

Glynn elected for Middlesex.

At the meeting of Parliament in November, Wilkes preferred a petition enumerating the wrongs which he had endured at the hands of the Government during the last five years. His complaints, however, were pronounced frivolous; and the House of Commons, in return, proceeded to bring a charge against their petitioner.

Wilkes petitions.

Lord Weymouth, as Secretary of State, had addressed a letter to the magistrates of Surrey, instructing them to resort promptly to military aid in the repression of tumults within their jurisdiction. This imprudent measure having been immediately followed by the collision between the military and the populace in St. George's Fields, Wilkes seized an opportunity so favourable to his purpose, and published the official letter, accompanied with comments of the most inflammatory and insulting character. His object was probably to provoke a new prosecution against himself, as well as to exasperate the people. The publication was, no doubt, a seditious libel, and if noticed at all, should have been made the subject of an information by the Attorney-General. But instead of taking this, the fair and legitimate course, the Government, either fearful of not getting a verdict, or determined to make sure of a pretext for the expulsion of their formidable foe, brought the matter forward as a breach of privilege. It is plain, however, that Wilkes's publication applied to Lord Weymouth in his ministerial conduct, and did not in any wise affect him in his capacity as a member of Parliament. But there was another difficulty. The privilege alleged to be violated, was the privilege of the House of Lords; and as it was the settled law of Parliament that each branch of the legislature was solely competent to judge and to punish any breach of its privileges, it followed that neither House could visit upon one of its own members, or any person, a breach of the privileges of the other. Wilkes must accordingly be dispunishable in the Commons for a breach of the privileges of the Lords. Upon a conference between the two Houses, therefore, the charge, as it affected the privileges of the Lords, was dropped; and the Commons proceeded to take the matter into their own hands.

Nothing could be more arbitrary and absurd than

their mode of dealing with it. To pronounce an offence against a peer of Parliament a breach of the privileges of the House of Commons would have been too violent. But they proceeded to *try* Wilkes as for a libel. And, instead of requiring him to attend in his place, or to withdraw, according to the practice of the House when the conduct of one of its members is to be impugned, they had him brought to the *bar* in custody, and there required him to answer to a charge of libel, in support of which, they had without a shadow of authority, and by usurping the functions of a court of law, already taken evidence.

Wilkes might, of course, have declined such an unconstitutional and illegal authority. But it suited his purpose to accept the issue now ripe for trial between the House and the Constituency. When put to his defence, therefore, he at once avowed the publication of the libel; and, with the cool effrontery which belonged to him, added the expression of his regret, not for having written it, but for the mildness of the language in which it was couched.

The expulsion of Wilkes was, therefore, moved by Lord Barrington, the Secretary-at-War and a leading member of the King's party.* The grounds stated were not merely the seditious libel which he had just avowed, but the libels for which he had already suffered the penalty of expulsion in former Parliaments. A proceeding so repugnant to the principles of national justice, as to inflict the same punishment twice for one offence, could not pass altogether unquestioned in an assembly, of which some of the members were men of integrity and independence. But the motion was carried by a large majority.

A new writ for Middlesex was accordingly ordered. Wilkes was again put in nomination, and re-

* He had been a partisan of Bute's.

turned almost unanimously; his opponent, Serjeant Whitaker, a respectable member of the bar, obtaining only five votes.

The House of Commons was determined to persevere. On the day following the return of the writ, they resolved, by an increased majority, 'That having been expelled, Mr. Wilkes was incapable of serving in that Parliament.' The election was, therefore, declared void, and another writ was issued.

House of Commons determined to persevere.

To return Wilkes again in the face of this resolution was to treat the House with open defiance and contempt. But the freeholders of the metropolitan county did not for a moment hesitate to take this course. Many persons of weight and character, who had hitherto taken no part in the quarrel, now came forward and made common cause with the electors of Middlesex in defence of the violated rights of the Constituency. Money was subscribed, not merely to defray the expenses of the Middlesex elections, but to liquidate the private debts of the candidate who was the champion of the people; and an association was formed, under the title of the 'Supporters of the Bill of Rights.'

Under these circumstances, no man of character could be found to undertake the hopeless and invidious task of becoming the Court and House of Commons' candidate at the new election. One Dingley, indeed, a broken speculator, who had made a ridiculous attempt to procure an address to the King from a public meeting in the City, appeared on the hustings at Brentford; but as he could not induce any person to put him in nomination, Wilkes was declared duly elected.

Wilkes elected for Middlesex.

The House of Commons had hitherto been content with annulling the choice of the electors. The Government were now prepared to go a step farther, and, by means of their servile

Colonel Luttrell.

T 2

majority, to seat a man whom the electors had rejected. Colonel Luttrell, a young officer of the Guards, without any pretension to the representation of Middlesex, was the individual fixed upon to be the sitting member; and as if to make their settled purpose more apparent, Luttrell already possessed a seat in Parliament which he was obliged to vacate on becoming a candidate for the representation of another constituency.

The influence of the Court obtained 296 votes for their candidate, against 1143 freely and eagerly recorded for Wilkes. The latter was, of course, declared duly elected.

<small>Col. Luttrell declared member.</small>

On the return of the writ, a motion was made to erase the name of Wilkes, and substitute that of Luttrell. But the House hesitated to go the length of bestowing the seat upon a candidate whom the Constituency had refused. After a warm debate, the Government prevailed only by a small majority.

<small>Motion to erase the name of Wilkes.</small>

There was no reasonable ground, however, for this squeamishness. The House of Commons has the right of expulsion over its own members, and though the infliction of this extreme penalty on the mere allegation of an offence against the law of the land was a stretch of power, still the House must, in every instance, be guided by its own discretion in the exercise of a privilege which is neither defined nor limited by any general law. The House was, therefore, justified according to strict parliamentary law, in the first expulsion of Wilkes. But the act of expulsion purged his offence, as far as guilt attached to him in his capacity as a member of Parliament. Even a convicted felon, after he has suffered the punishment awarded by the law, is restored to his civil rights. Again, every man, subject to certain qualifications and disqualifications by statute law, is eligible to serve in Par-

<small>Right of the Commons to expel a member.</small>

liament as a representative of the people. Wilkes laboured under none of the incapacities so ascertained. It is plain, therefore, that when the House of Commons avoided his re-election, on the ground that he was disqualified by their resolution, they assumed nothing less than a dispensing power. The violation of the law of the realm, and of the essential rights of the electoral body, was complete when they voted that a knight of the shire duly elected was not duly elected; and the instalment of a candidate who had not been chosen, in the place of the rightful and legal representative, was but the logical consequence of the act which they had already committed.

These scandalous proceedings were reprobated by almost every man of mark and station in the House of Commons. Grenville, *Grenville's remonstrances.* surpassed by none in his knowledge of parliamentary law, in his tenacity of privilege, and in his assertion of the power and authority of the House of Commons, denounced these unconstitutional and lawless votes with the combined weight of argument and authority. As he had been prepared to vindicate the just claims of Parliament even, if necessary, by force of arms, so did he now, from the same upright motive, resist an aggression which neither law nor precedent could justify. If the House of Commons had been swayed by any consideration of public spirit, the integrity, the knowledge and experience of Grenville must, on such a question as this at least, have gone far to influence its deliberations. But in vain were the high constitutional arguments of an English statesman addressed to an assembly which represented, not English interests or feelings, but the crooked policy and petty vindictiveness of the Court.

Whenever the people had an opportunity, directly or indirectly, of expressing their sentiments, in

regard to the conduct of the Court and Parliament,
Public indignation excited. they were those of indignation and contempt. An attempt made by the obscure adventurer Dingley to get up a loyal address to the King during the Middlesex elections resulted in some excesses on the part of the populace. The rioters were prosecuted; but the grand jury of Middlesex ignored the bills. Wilkes himself, as a martyr in the cause of liberty, received not only every mark of public sympathy and respect, but also honours and rewards of which he was personally unworthy. His action against the Secretary of State for seizing his papers by a general warrant, after having been delayed by every species of chicanery on the part of the defendant, came on for trial in the midst of this agitation, and resulted in a verdict with damages of four thousand pounds. A vacancy occurring about the same time in one of the City wards, Wilkes was elected an alderman almost by acclamation. His debts were paid, and a competency for life was provided for him by public subscription.

Nor were there wanting demonstrations of a still *The county of Middlesex petition the Crown.* more grave and ominous character. The metropolitan county, not satisfied with the reiterated expression of its opinion at the poll, drew up a manifesto of grievances in the form of a petition to the throne. The language of this paper was more libellous and seditious, inasmuch as it was more vigorous and pointed, than any for which Wilkes had been pursued with such infatuated pertinacity. But the Court were content to receive this insult in sullen silence. The city of Westminster petitioned expressly for a change of administration and a dissolution of Parliament. The county of York, under the guidance of the Marquis of Rockingham,* took the milder course of thanking their

* Burke's Correspondence, vol. i. p. 186.—Though the great orator urges more vigorous counsels on the weak and fastidious

representatives for their votes in favour of the freedom of election. Other counties, however, less under the influence of the Whig aristocracy, followed the example of the metropolitan province, and addressed their bold remonstrances to the Crown itself, the fountain and origin of all these evils.

The popular cause also received powerful and unexpected aid from an ally which had hitherto been of small account in the political system. The present age, accustomed to the freedom, information and ability with which affairs of state are discussed in the public journals, can hardly understand the sensation produced by a series of letters which, at this time, appeared in the principal daily newspaper published in London. The writings which obtained so much celebrity under the signature of 'Junius,' were, however, compositions of extraordinary merit. Disdaining blanks, hints, and innuendoes, and all the shabby devices by which meaner libellers had been wont to evade the terrors of the law, this undaunted champion, in the face of day, rushed

[margin: Power of the press.—Letters of Junius.]
[margin: Rancour of Junius.]

Rockingham, he is himself enervated by the jealousy and hesitation which pervaded the whole Whig party. Lord Temple's earnest and wise proposal for an oblivion of past animosities and a union of all parties against the Court, he met with coldness and reserve.—*Correspondence*, vol. I. p. 218. And then he complains 'of the coldness and dilatoriness of many of our friends in their manner of acting,' and laments that 'bold men take the lead to which others are entitled.' The truth is, that while the Whigs were frittering away the great question at issue between the Crown and the people in frivolous discussions about the mode of proceeding, a democratic party had sprung up, rude indeed, and perhaps violent in conduct, but with an energy and zeal which gave a practical direction to their views. The old legitimate party of the Revolution were so distracted by divisions as to be incapable of leading any great popular movement; and liberal opinions demanded a more broad and vigorous expression than the Whigs were either able or willing to give it. The society of 'Supporters of the Bill of Rights' were the germ of that great popular party which, if it has not yet superseded the old aristocratic connection, has at least dictated its tone and policy.

upon his victim, and laid him prostrate in the dust. Disdaining, too, inferior prey, he singled out those of the highest mark for the subjects of his prowess. The Duke of Grafton and the Duke of Bedford, the Earl of Mansfield and Sir William Blackstone, were each assailed with the utmost fury; nor was it long before his audacity reached the Crown itself. The greater part of these libels were false, or had only colourable truth; and they were, in some cases, imbued with a rancour which seemed to spring from feelings of the bitterest hatred and revenge.

The extraordinary fame which these compositions have acquired is owing less to their intrinsic merit, considerable as that may be, than to more vulgar qualities. The mystery which surrounded the writer, and the intense personality of his style, were calculated to excite popular interest in the highest degree. No dissertation, however eloquent, upon any public question however momentous, has been read and discussed with the eagerness which attended a series of brilliant libels, dictated by an unknown hand, upon the greatest and foremost men of the age. The pamphlets of Burke are as superior to the letters of Junius as the French Revolution was a theme of greater magnitude than the Middlesex election; but the invective against regicide never agitated the public mind so much as the abuse of the King or the Duke of Grafton. Junius excelled in the least worthy part of political warfare. The subject of his satire is generally represented in terms as the vilest of mankind; yet when the imputations are examined, they turn out, for the most part, to be frivolous or absurd. In the numerous letters addressed to the Duke of Grafton, forming the principal portion of the writings to which the signature of Junius is attached, the grounds upon which the Duke is held up to odium

Mysterious authorship of Junius.

Unfounded charges of Junius.

are chiefly his illegitimate descent from Charles the
Second; his marriage with a cousin of the man who
had debauched his first wife; the mature age and
faded charms of his mistress. The charges against
the Duke in his political character are less prominently put forward, and are equally futile. Among
other things, he is censured for preferring a claim as
hereditary ranger to the timber in the royal forest
of Whittlebury—a mere question of law. He is
repeatedly charged with gross corruption in the sale
of a patent for the purpose of gratifying General
Burgoyne, whereas this matter, which is made of so
much importance, proved to be the ordinary case of
a minister bestowing a small place at the recommendation of a political adherent.* The odium
attendant upon the pardon of M'Quirk,† the man
who had been convicted of murder at one of the
Middlesex elections, was especially fixed upon Grafton; though it is probable that the First Lord of the
Treasury had little or nothing to say to an act for
which Lord Rochford, as the Secretary of State who
signed the order, was officially, and the House of
Commons was really, responsible. Finally, he is
held up as the successor of Bute and the leader of
the King's party; though almost in the same para-
graph, he is described in a style of puerile antithesis
as 'a minister by accident, adopted without choice,
trusted without confidence, and continued without
favour.'

* Whately to Grenville.— Corr. vol. iv. p. 493.

† The House of Commons by a unanimous vote desired that the prisoner should be pardoned. The Government, however, very properly referred the question as to the cause of the deceased man's death to the Surgeons' Company; and ten gentlemen of this body reported that the blow for which M'Quirk was respon- sible had not been the cause of death. Yet Junius, with these facts before him, writing on the 18th of March, represents the par- don of M'Quirk as an undue in- terference of the Crown with the course of justice, and attributes it to the advice of the Duke of Grafton.

Again, the Chief Justice was to be blackened. As a statesman, none presented a fairer mark for political satire than the Earl of Mansfield; but as a judge, he had attained unrivalled excellence. Yet Junius, passing lightly over the glaring faults of the politician, chooses to attack Lord Mansfield in his judicial character. The pusillanimity, the duplicity, the remarkable selfishness of Mansfield are barely alluded to; but the Chief Justice happened to belong to a Scottish family of rank which had adhered to the fortunes of the Stuarts; and now in his advanced age, and a quarter of a century after the cause of the Pretender had been extinct, this great magistrate was to be discredited by a story of his having, in early youth, drunk the Pretender's health upon his knees! One of the highest merits of this pre-eminent judge was the introduction of a principle of Equity, that is to say, of common sense and substantial justice, into the harsh and narrow doctrines of the Common Law. For this innovation, he is reviled by Junius in the very spirit of a special pleader. But when the Chief Justice, on the trial of Junius's printer for libel, directed the jury that the fact of publication, and the quality of the publication were different questions—that the one was for the determination of the Court and the other for the verdict of the country—then the judge was assailed with still greater virulence for adhering to the well-established rule.*

But the slanders of Junius were perhaps carried to their extreme point in the case of the Duke of Bedford. By a sudden stroke of Providence, that nobleman had been deprived of his only son, a young man of superior

---

* The law of libel remained in this state until 1792, when it was altered in favour of the liberty of the press, by Mr. Fox's celebrated act, which empowered the jury, in prosecutions for libel, to return a general verdict.

character and promise. A circumstance which would
have disarmed the hostility of an ordinary foe was
made use of by this writer for his purpose of holding
up the Duke to public detestation. Because the
bereaved parent had not allowed his affliction to
interrupt his public duties, he was charged with insensibility to the loss of a son with whom, as must
have been known to a person so well informed as
Junius, he had lived on terms of the most affectionate
and unreserved intercourse. Upon the same painful
subject, the writer could not refrain from adding an
anecdote, more like the tattle of a disappointed valet,
than one to which the malice of a man of liberal
attainments could descend. The great faults of the
Duke were that he abused the advantages of a commanding position to factious ends, and that he preferred the petty interests of his particular party to
consideration of the public service. To expose with
the utmost severity of censure a policy so injurious
to parliamentary government would have been just
and useful; but Junius thinks it more damaging to
relate a pitiful story of the Duke's having been as-
saulted by some ruffian at a race-course. Even the
famous letter to the King which was elaborated with
the greatest pains, has hardly an allusion to the point
on which His Majesty's conduct was most reprehen-
sible. The design of exalting the power of the Crown
beyond the limits assigned to it by that settlement
which placed the house of Hanover on the throne;
the unconstitutional and unworthy system of discre-
diting the responsible ministers by means of agents
instructed to baffle their policy and to supplant them
whenever it suited his purpose to do so :—these grave
offences are passed over. The dismissal of the great
administration which the King found in power at his
accession was attributed, not to the design long since
matured at Leicester House of carrying on the Government by means of the King's creatures, but to

an occasional pique and resentment. Legge, the Chancellor of the Exchequer, had refused to recommend the nominee of Bute at an election; therefore he and his colleagues were turned out. George the Third is reproached, after the fashion of the vulgar libellers of the day, for employing Scotchmen, because they had been the last to give up the cause of their ancient kings. The only happy stroke in this, the most ambitious and the least successful of all his libels, was, that the destruction of one man had for years been the sole object of the King's government.

It may be consistent with the vile policy of libel
Politics of Junius. to address itself to the coarsest intelligence, and to make use of vulgar delusion and prejudice; but when we find Junius, for a moment, treating public questions apart from personality, his views are narrow, and his expressions trite. The first letter which bears his signature, and which, fortunately for his fame, provoked the hostility of Sir William Draper, is a dissertation upon political affairs and public men, little, if at all, above the level of other articles on the same subject in the public prints. On the American question, his opinions were those of Grenville; on the question of parliamentary reform, then just in its dawn, he denies the right of the legislature to disfranchise the rotten boroughs, and he is so ill read in the elements of constitutional law as to style the elective franchise the birthright and the freehold of its possessor. He asserts with equal ignorance, that the reform in the representation of the people is a matter exclusively for the House of Commons, like a money bill. Even upon the exciting topics of the day, he contributed little in the way of argument or felicity of exposition. He showed a remarkable want of discrimination also in assigning its due importance to every subject;—an essential qualification

for a public writer. The question upon which he seems to have bestowed the greatest pains, was one of mere technical law; his aim being to show that Lord Mansfield illegally, and therefore corruptly, held a man to bail whom he ought to have committed;—a matter in which the public took little or no interest, and upon which they were not qualified to judge. And as there was no slander to which he would not stoop for the purpose of wreaking his malice (as in the instance of the Duke of Bedford); in like manner he would descend to the grossest arts of the political incendiary. A regiment of guards, for example, had incurred odium for acting against the populace in Wilkes's riot. Every man of sense and candour knew that the soldiers had done no more than their duty; but the people were to be flattered at any price; the animosity against the Household troops was therefore to be inflamed; while invidious comparisons were made between this corps and the infantry of the line.

The writings of Junius, rescued from the perishable columns of a newspaper, have long since been transferred to the library, and the libeller is elevated into an English classic. Swift, indeed, a genius of the first order, had previously occupied the same place, but with a title far higher and more secure. Setting aside the two matchless apologues which immortalize Swift, Junius can even then stand no comparison with the Dean of St. Patrick. Even in rancour, the anonymous libeller is excelled by the Irish satirist, almost as much as in wit. Both were animated with strong personal malice; but the intensity of scorn and hatred with which the lampoons of Swift are often charged, imparts to them something of the sublime; while the malignity of Junius, though sometimes almost appalling, is too much mingled with the vanity of literary display.

Junius become a classic writer.

Junius compared to Swift.

Of humour, in which Swift excels every English author, Junius had but a small share; nor is his invective ever poured out in that torrent of derision with which the Dean overwhelms his victims. Nothing, again, can be more in contrast than the respective styles of these great masters of libel. That of Swift is the perfection of homely simplicity; while the periods of Junius are of the most artificial construction, and polished with the greatest labour. The Irish writer, full of meaning, and intent only on being understood, makes use of common words and short sentences. The point is in the meaning, not in the expression. The contrary may be said of Junius, who affects only scholastic terms, and that balanced antithetical style which denotes poverty of genius. The best of his performances are his letters to Sir William Draper. Free from the virulence which deforms most of his compositions, these letters are models of cool contemptuous ridicule. The quality of his antagonist was not such as to put a strain upon his powers, and he obtains an easy victory. Scattered up and down his works there are some fine passages and striking expressions; but on the whole, they are inflated, exaggerated, and tiresome.

Supposed authorship of the letters of Junius. The authorship of these celebrated letters has been the subject of more extensive and ingenious speculation than any other question of historical curiosity. They have been ascribed to almost every leading member of the Opposition; to Lord Temple, to Lord George Sackville, Burke, Gerard Hamilton, Wilkes, Glover, and many others of less note. It is not my intention either to examine the pretensions of these several claimants, or to contribute any new theory on the question. The evidence which connects Sir Philip Francis with these publications is perhaps the strongest, though it is not so completely satisfactory to my mind as it has appeared to more competent judges.*

* The proofs against, or in favour of Francis, have been lately summed up by Lord Stanhope, and corroborated by the high authority of Lord Macaulay.

1. A similarity is traced between the handwriting of Junius and that of Sir Philip Francis. Now, it is agreed by all persons who have had experience in trials at *Nisi Prius*, that there are few questions of fact so perplexing as the identity of handwriting. Witnesses of intelligence and integrity constantly differ in opinion as to whether a particular paper is written by a person with whose handwriting they are familiar from habits of correspondence, or from having seen him write. But comparison of handwriting—that is, the collation of one paper with another for the purpose of proving that both are in the same handwriting, is a test so fallacious that it is utterly rejected by the English law of evidence. Yet this is one of the proofs relied upon by the supporters of what is called the Franciscan theory of Junius.

2. The speeches and writings of Francis resemble the compositions of Junius in point of style. But the best evidence of this description is loose and unsatisfactory. Nothing is so easy to imitate as style. The history of literature abundantly proves that fact. Pope, Johnson, Scott, Byron, and many other great authors, have had numerous imitators, more or less successful. Junius had many copyists both in Parliament and in the press. There is a letter in the 'Gentleman's Magazine,' of 1770, which might be read for one by Junius. 'The Vindication of Natural Society by a late Noble Lord' was, by many good judges, believed to have been the production of Bolingbroke, until the ingenious deception was avowed by Burke. With regard to the immediate question, as it is a matter of opinion, I may be permitted to say, that I can discover no remarkable similarity between the acknowledged productions of Francis and those of Junius. Some superficial resemblance there is, indeed, in the style and sentiments, such as any writer might acquire with a little trouble; but I can detect little of the terseness and point of the anonymous writer in the orations of the Indian Councillor.

3. The circumstantial evidence to my mind is not more weighty. It is said that Junius spared Lord Holland. But why should a public writer, in the newspapers of 1769-72, attack Lord Holland? That nobleman had retired from public life many years. He might as well have attacked the Duke of Newcastle, or the memory of the Earl of Orford. Besides, there were many public men whom Junius abstained from attacking as well as Lord Holland. One would infer, from this argument, that Junius had run a-muck against every public character in the country. But he did nothing of the kind.

Again, it is said, that twenty years after it was delivered, Francis supplied Almon with notes of a speech of Chatham's

In the midst of the conflict between the House of Commons and the electors of Middlesex, a message from the Crown was brought down by Lord North, announcing that the Civil List was

Deficiency to the Civil List.

in 1770; and a close similarity in sentiment and expression is pointed out between several passages of that speech and several passages of Junius. The legitimate conclusion would be that Chatham himself was Junius; but as he certainly was not, it is suggested, why or wherefore I am unable to discover, that Francis himself must have been the man. Many persons besides Francis attended the galleries of both Houses, and it is possible, in those days, when the debates were not published, that some persons besides Francis might have thought it worth while to take notes of a speech of Chatham's. It has been well observed, also, by the editor of the 'Grenville Papers,' who has bestowed much pains on the investigation of this curious question, that no speech in writing of Francis, *previous* to the publication of Junius, has been produced; therefore, the similarity of Francis's speeches and writings (if any) proves only that he was, like others, infected by the style of Junius.

But the conclusive proof, it seems, is the mistake which Junius made about Sir William Draper's half-pay. When Lord Macaulay expresses so strong an opinion that such a mistake could have been made only by a person familiar with the business of the War Office (in which Francis was chief clerk), and that good judges of evidence agreed with him in that opinion, I must differ from it with great hesitation. But I am bound to say, that I do not feel the force of this evidence, or except, indeed, for the ingenious turn given to it, that it is any evidence at all. The fallacy seems to lie in the assumption, that nobody but a clerk in the War Office was likely to know the forms required to be observed in drawing half-pay. But every recipient of half-pay was himself acquainted with those forms; many clergymen and magistrates before whom the requisite declaration is commonly taken must have known them. So that, as far as this proof is concerned, Junius might have been any half-pay officer, any minister of a parish, any justice of the peace.

Some of the circumstances, however, have a more pointed application. Francis left the War Office in the spring of 1772, because another man was promoted over his head; and this promotion is the subject of numerous letters by Junius, though under a disguised hand, written in a strain of passion, which, the comparatively insignificant nature of the subject considered, seemed to betoken a personal interest. The cessation of the Junius' letters coinciding with the departure of Francis for India is also a significant fact; and, if the other evidence had been equally cogent, would have gone far to complete the chain of testimony. As it is, however, I

in debt to an amount exceeding half a million, and requiring the House to make good the deficiency. This large excess upon an annual income of 800,000*l.* within eight years was attributed by the minister to various causes; such as, the expenses of the late King's funeral, of the present King's marriage, and of his coronation; to the re-purchase of the Crown jewels from the Duke of Cumberland, to whom they had been bequeathed by his father; and the high price of provisions. But Grenville, fully master of the details of finance, and armed with official experience, soon disposed of these excuses, and demanded that inquiry should precede supply. Dowdeswell, the Chancellor of the Exchequer under the Rockingham administration, spoke to the same effect. 'Nobody,' said Sir George Savile, 'refuses to vote the payment of the debt; what we want is to know how it has been contracted.' Several of the popular members said, that they had been instructed by their constituents not to vote supply without inquiry. But this demand, however reasonable, was opposed by the Government. They said that it was contrary to precedent; that the preparation of the accounts would take a long time; that the King's necessities were urgent; * that it would be indecent to inquire into his Majesty's private expenses. Rigby, the Paymaster, better known as the parliamentary agent of the Duke of Bedford, had the assurance to claim

must venture to doubt whether Lord Macaulay would have hanged a man upon such evidence. If denial is to go for anything, it is certain that Francis denied the authorship of these productions in the most positive and indignant terms that could be employed. In fact, no *man* dared hint such a thing to him.

The interest in this question has hardly yet abated; for, while I write, a new pretender has been set up in the person of 'the wicked' Lord Lyttelton, whose claims are supported with as much plausibility as those of any other candidate for the honour.—*Quarterly Review*, 185.

* Two members who spoke in the debate said that the wages of the King's menial servants were unpaid.—*Cavendish Debates*, p. 285.

credit to the King for having applied the proceeds of the ceded islands and prizes during the war to the public service; as if there was any pretence for saying that these funds were vested in the Crown otherwise than as a trustee for the nation by whose blood and treasure they had been gained. None of his colleagues ventured to support this argument; nor did any member of the Opposition think it worthy of an answer. Both Grenville and Dowdeswell, who had been Treasury ministers, stated that the accounts could be produced without delay; and as to the impropriety of examining the accounts of the Civil List, Grenville replied that, so long as it defrayed its expenditure, Parliament had no right to inquire; but when the Crown came to Parliament to pay the debts of the Civil List, it then became their duty to do so. As to the assertion that the grant of an extraordinary supply before inquiry was in accordance with precedent, its absurdity was exposed by several speakers. 'To what purpose,' asked Burke, 'do we determine to take His Majesty's gracious message into consideration, if there is nothing to consider? Why deliberate, if we are to be denied any materials for deliberation?' 'Suppose,' said Grenville, 'the King were to ask a grant for some purpose which he did not disclose, were we to comply?' 'What would be thought of a steward,' said Savile, 'who paid the bill first, and examined the account afterwards? The House of Commons does not always go through the form of inquiry before granting an extraordinary supply, because there are occasions on which inquiry would be needless or mischievous to the public service; but to infer that the House of Commons had therefore relinquished the right of inquiry, was a departure from that great principle of appropriation by which the convention Parliament had sought to provide for ever against the abuse of the public money.' The Court, however, carried its point by large majorities.

The public discontent was, as might have been expected, greatly aggravated by this transaction. To withhold accounts in commercial or even private affairs is always regarded as a badge of fraud; and the reason applies to public expenditure. There was, no doubt, good ground for the suspicions that were entertained. Even supposing that the large annuity granted to the Crown was only adequate to the ordinary charges of the Civil List, still the extraordinary expenses mentioned by Lord North could hardly amount to half a million of money, in addition to nearly two hundred thousand pounds left by His Majesty's predecessor. A portion of this money must have been spent in a manner which would not bear public investigation. The universal belief of bribery and corruption could not be altogether unfounded. It is certain that great sums had been lavished by Lord Holland in purchasing a majority for the peace; and it is equally certain that the secret service fund was inadequate to meet such a heavy requisition. If the Court had really nothing to conceal, their infatuation in refusing inquiry was marvellous indeed.

Aggravation of public discontent.

While the Court and the House of Commons were bringing the Government, and even the Constitution itself into disrepute by invading the highest privilege of the people, and tampering with the public money, the colonial policy of administration was rapidly dissolving the bonds of allegiance and affection between the American provinces and the parent state. In the last session* Parliament had imposed some small import duties on certain articles of consumption to be levied in the colonies and to be paid into the Imperial treasury. This measure, as might have been foreseen, and as they were assured by the best authority,† revived all

Disastrous colonial policy.

---
* 7 Geo. III. c. 46.
† Pownall, who had been Governor of Massachusetts, in a remarkable speech on the Bill

the irritation which the prompt repeal of the Stamp
Act had been calculated to allay. The Assembly of
Massachusetts Bay, which had from the first taken
the lead with that of Virginia in vindicating the cause
of colonial freedom, took the most vigorous measures
of resistance to the new colonial acts, and formally
invited the co-operation of the other provincial assemblies.
They addressed a manifesto to their agent
in England, Mr. de Berdt, which they desired him to
communicate to His Majesty's ministers. This was
followed up by a petition to the King himself; by a
letter to Lord Shelburne and Mr. Conway respectively,
then Secretaries of State; and by letters to
Lord Rockingham, Lord Camden and Lord Chatham.
These papers were all to the same effect; and
were couched in decent, though firm and pointed
terms. To the grievances which were familiar to
Parliament and the country, the writers added the
legislation of the session of 1767,—the suspension
especially of the Assembly of New York, which they
treated, not without reason, as an alarming restriction
on the freedom and independence of legislative
bodies. Bernard, the governor of the colony, instead
of observing that policy of conciliation and forbearance
which the circumstances required, was intent
only on upholding his authority. Always at variance
with the House of Assembly, his official messages to
that body and their answers were a series of unseemly
altercations. He laid before them letters
from the Secretary of State, censuring their conduct,
and commending him. They retorted by accusing
him of misrepresenting them to the Government. At
length he had the folly to communicate to the House

---

for the Suppression of the Assembly of New York, had emphatically said, 'That the people of America, universally, unitedly, and unalterably, are resolved not to submit to any internal tax imposed upon them by any legislature, in which they have not a share by representatives of their own election.'—*Speech in the House of Commons*, 1767.

an article in a Boston newspaper, commenting severely upon his conduct,* and required them to take it into their serious consideration. The House, with cool derision, referred the governor to the law for redress, and declined to take any notice of the matter. Upon this, Bernard, with many bitter reproaches, immediately prorogued them; and wrote home a strong complaint of the conduct of the House of Assembly in sending a circular to the other colonial assemblies in reference to the acts of Parliament of the last session. Lord Hillsborough, the Secretary of State, emulating the intemperance of Bernard, instructed him to demand of the House that they should rescind the resolution upon which the obnoxious circular had been founded; and in their default he directed that the Assembly should be forthwith dissolved. Though it was in strict analogy with that constitutional usage to which the Americans loved to appeal, that the Executive should have a discretion in remitting the representative body to its constituents, there was no precedent in the history of the British Parliament, since the reign of Charles the First, of the Crown having dictated to the House of Commons a certain line of conduct under pain of immediate dissolution. The Assembly, on this trying occasion, were studious that their conduct should be deliberate and advised. They asked for a prorogation, in order that they might consult with their constituents; but this being peremptorily refused, they determined by a large majority in a full House† to refuse compliance with the arbitrary demand of the Government. The next day they were dissolved.

But even supposing these extreme measures justifiable, writs should have been immediately issued

---

* This paper was written by Otis, an impetuous orator in the Assembly.

† The division was 92 to 17. The House consisted of 110 members. June 30, 1768.

for the election of another Assembly. The suspension of the legislature of New York in the
preceding year was a strong measure; but
it was a measure taken by the British
Parliament, that supreme authority which can be
restrained only by its own sense of justice and expediency from any stretch of power. But for the
Crown to assume the right of suspending a representative body, was to take a course which could be
warranted only by precedents drawn from the most
ominous period of the monarchy. The Government,
however, signified no intention of restoring to the
people of the province the legitimate organ for the
expression of their wishes; and from a passage in
Lord Hillsborough's despatch communicated to the
House of Assembly before their dissolution, some
design appeared to be entertained of providing for
the future government of the colony in a manner inconsistent with their charter.

Views of Go-
vernment as to
America.

While this disastrous quarrel between the Imperial
Government and the legislature of one of
its most powerful and extensive colonies
was advancing towards a crisis, it was inflamed by
events which showed too plainly the arbitrary and
oppressive spirit of administration. An English regiment had been quartered in the town, and a frigate,
with some smaller vessels of war, were stationed in
the harbour for the purpose of overawing the inhabitants, or affording protection to the authorities.
Commissioners of Customs were appointed to reside
at Boston for the purpose of carrying into effect the
revenue laws, and especially the late act for imposing
import duties. These persons appear to have discharged their odious functions in the most offensive
manner.* Early in May, a trading sloop, called the

Disputes with
the colonies.

---

* Governor of New Hampshire to Lord Rockingham.—Lord Albemarle's Memoirs of Rocking-
ham, vol. ii. p. 88. Mr. John

'Liberty,' belonging to Mr. Hancock, a merchant of Boston, and a prominent member of the Opposition in the Assembly, entered the harbour laden with a cargo. She was immediately boarded by an officer of the Customs; but the master, resisting his authority, locked him in the cabin, landed the goods, and made a return at the Custom House. The Commissioners, thereupon, confiscated the sloop, and affecting to be apprehensive of a rescue, ordered her to be towed under the guns of the frigate. This harsh and unnecessary proceeding provoked a disturbance. The windows of the Commissioners' houses were broken, and some of the Custom House officers were used with violence. Upon this, the Commissioners, with the exception of Temple, who had the good sense and the good temper to treat the matter lightly, declared the King's authority violated, and abandoning their duties, retreated, first to the frigate, and afterwards to the fort. Bernard called upon the Council for aid in asserting the authority of the Government, but though he had hitherto found this body ready to support him against the aggression of the Assembly, they showed no disposition to countenance the proceedings of the Custom House. What the Commissioners had styled 'an insurrection rather than a riot,' the Council pronounced to have been only 'a small disturbance;' and that 'the disorders which happened were occasioned by the violent and unprecedented manner in which the sloop "Liberty" had been seized by the officers of the Customs.'

Notwithstanding that Lord Hillsborough had addressed letters to the governors of the different colonies, denouncing in the severest terms the circular of the Massa-

Attempt to prohibit importation from England.

Temple (one of the Commissioners of Customs) to Grenville, Nov. 7, 1768.—Grenville Corr. vol. iv. p. 356.

chusetts Assembly, four of those colonies to whom the circular had been sent, namely, Virginia, New Jersey, Connecticut, and Maryland, sent favourable answers, through their respective Speakers. The people of Boston did not, however, succeed in obtaining the concurrence of the other States to a proposal for putting a stop to the importation of goods from Great Britain. This failure elated the Government, and encouraged them to persevere in coercive measures. Lord Hillsborough instructed Bernard to inquire if any persons had committed acts which under the authority of a statute of Henry the Eighth for the trial in this country of treasons committed without the realm, might justify their being brought to England to be tried in the King's Bench.* This suggestion for depriving the colonists of trial by jury belongs, I regret to add, to a great Whig chief, John, Duke of Bedford.

Public excitement at Boston. The excitement at Boston was undoubtedly raised to a dangerous pitch, when it became known, in the autumn of 1768, that two regiments were on their way from Halifax to that city. The leaders of the old Assembly met together,

---

* This statute (35 Hen. VIII. c. 2) was intended for the relief of English subjects who committed treason in foreign parts, and to afford them the benefit of the trial by jury, and of the laws which defined and regulated the trial of this offence. Yet, notwithstanding the plain language of the statute, which mentioned treasons, &c., committed out of the King's realm of England and *others His Grace's dominions*, the Crown lawyers maintained that it was applicable to the case of subjects, inhabitants of a colony, part of the King's dominions, and having tribunals competent to take cognizance of the crime. If this act was, as the Solicitor-General, Dunning, maintained, in favour of the subject, it would have been a singular perversion of it to transfer the venue for the purpose of securing a conviction. As to a fair trial, a Boston man would have had little chance of obtaining one in England at that time. The people did not understand the colonial question; they thought the colonists were resisting the mother-country, because they wished to avoid bearing their share of taxation. The attempt, however, was not made.

and having instituted themselves a select committee, proceeded to pass several resolutions. They began by affirming, as usual, the exclusive right of self-taxation. Their next resolution was more significant. They reminded their countrymen that as there was an apprehension of *a war with France*, each inhabitant should observe the law by which he was required to provide himself with arms. And lastly, as the Governor refused to call an assembly they determined to call a convention. Letters were accordingly despatched to the ninety-six towns which returned representatives to the Assembly, inviting them to send deputies to Boston. All these constituencies, with one exception, obeyed the summons. But the members of the convention, when they met, seemed alarmed at the boldness of the step which had been taken, and were very guarded in their proceedings. They disclaimed at the outset any executive or legislative authority, and appointed a deputation to wait upon the Governor, for the purpose of representing their grievances and their desire to be relieved by a general assembly. The Governor, though he declined to receive these gentlemen as a committee of the convention, addressed a letter to the delegates, warning them of the danger they incurred, and earnestly admonishing them to separate before they incurred penal consequences by presuming to transact business. The convention took this advice, and having drawn up a petition to the Crown, dissolved themselves after a session of a week.

This pretence of calling a convention was certainly ill-advised, and in no wise warranted by those English precedents to which the Boston patriots loved to appeal. The two convention Parliaments of England had assembled under very different circumstances. They owed their existence to that supreme necessity which is above the law. They met of their own accord, because the Crown was in abeyance. And the purpose of these great assemblies was, in the first instance, to restore legitimate monarchy; and on the second occasion, to provide for the vacancy of the throne. The people of Massachusetts were under no such pressure of necessity. The Government was not dissolved; nor could it be said that the Executive had violated the constitution. It was true, that the Governor had arbitrarily dissolved the Assembly, and refused to call a new one. But the charter had not limited his discretion in using the power which it conferred upon him of dissolving the legislative body; and the period prescribed for summoning a new Parliament had not yet arrived. A convention under such circumstances was, to say the least, premature; and to summon one merely for the purpose of petitioning the Crown was ridiculous.

But the single indiscretion of the patriots was far exceeded by the rash and domineering conduct of the Government. On the last day of the convention, a fleet, consisting of several frigates and sloops, together with transports, containing two regiments and a detachment of artillery, entered the harbour of Boston. The men-of-war took up a position to command the town, and anchored, with springs on their cables, as if they were about to attack an enemy's port. The troops and artillery were then landed; and the soldiers, amounting to seven hundred men, marched into the town, with loaded muskets and fixed bayonets. No provision had been made for the accommodation of these unwelcome visitors. The self-constituted committee, called 'the Selected Men,' who had no official capacity whatsoever, were absurdly required to find quarters for the troops. They of course refused any assistance. The Council were then applied to; but they referred the authorities to Castle William for barrack room. An attempt was made to seize private property for the purpose of sheltering the troops; but this, being resisted as illegal, was relinquished. At length some houses were hired; but in the meantime the people beheld with indignation the Chamber of the Assembly, the Court House, Faneuil Hall, the places appropriated to legislation, law, commerce and public business, occupied by a military force brought there to insult and overawe them.

General Gage, the commander-in-chief on the North American station, shortly afterwards arrived with reinforcements which had been sent from Ireland; and before Christmas, Boston was garrisoned by an army of four thousand men. These formidable demonstrations produced for the moment the desired effect. Neither was the time ripe for action, nor had the colony any means of entering upon a conflict with the military power of Great Britain. Many of the firmest friends of colonial freedom thought the Boston people had gone too far; that their advice to their countrymen to take up arms was rash and unjustifiable; and that the shallow pretence under which that advice had been given was unworthy of their cause.* Even the leading agitators, suppressing for a time their chagrin, evinced a disposition to conciliate the naval and military authorities who might soon be their masters. The Commissioners of Customs, protected from personal violence by the bayonets of the soldiery, and enabled to discharge their hateful duties under the guns of the men-of-war, quitted the fortress of

margin: General Gage garrisons Boston.

margin: The colonists intimidated.

---

* Graham's History of North America, vol. iv. p. 274 n.

Castle William and returned to the town. Not a word of complaint was heard, and, to outward appearance, order was restored.

Opening of Parliament.— King's speech.

The disturbances in North America were referred to in several angry paragraphs of the King's speech at the opening of the session of Parliament in the ensuing autumn. The House of Lords immediately entered on the consideration of this momentous subject, and agreed to a series of resolutions condemnatory of the late proceedings of the Assembly and people of Massachusetts Bay. The Duke of Bedford, as has been mentioned, carried an address to the Crown for a special commission to try the popular leaders in that province under the provisions of the statute of Henry the Eighth. Some faint disapprobation of these arbitrary counsels was expressed by Lord Shelburne and the Duke of Richmond; but the American patriots met with little sympathy in the Upper House of Parliament. In the Commons, the address was ably opposed, chiefly by Grenville and the Rockingham party, but was carried by a large majority.

State of opinion in Massachusetts.

It is not probable that the American colonies, especially Massachusetts, entertained a sanguine expectation, or perhaps wish, that the British Government and Parliament would make any important concession to their demands. But they were not prepared for the wanton outrage on their liberties contained in that address to the Crown which had been adopted at the instance of the Duke of Bedford. This design of ousting the jurisdiction of their own courts of justice in charges of a treasonable character, plainly showed the intention of the Government to wrest the law itself to their purpose of suppressing colonial liberty. A deep resentment prevailed throughout all the states, and many persons who had been hitherto inclined to moderate counsels, from this time began to appre-

hend that the quarrel between America and the
mother-country would become irreconcilable.

The General Assembly of Massachusetts was convened, as usual, in May 1769. Before
proceeding to business, they voted an
address to the Governor, complaining of
the presence of naval and military forces, and requiring him to give orders for their removal from
the harbour and city during the session. The Governor replied that he had no power to remove them.
The House then passed resolutions condemning the
introduction of a military power, independent of the
Governor, for the purpose of enforcing the execution
of the laws. They came to votes also declaratory of
the right of the colonial subject to be tried by a jury
of the vicinage in all indictments for treason; and
condemnatory of the conduct of the Governor, against
whom they preferred charges, which their agent in
London was instructed to lay before the Privy
Council. And as they resolutely refused to proceed
to any other business while their deliberations were
overawed by an armed force not under the control
of the local authority, they were prorogued.

The legislative assemblies of Virginia, and several
other leading States, passed resolutions
similar to those of Massachusetts, relative
to trials for treason, and in some instances
made use of such strong language that they were
visited with the penalty of dissolution. Compacts of
abstinence from British merchandise, which the inhabitants of Boston had in vain proposed the year
before, were now readily entered into, and means
were taken to enforce obedience to these engagements
by publishing the names of persons who infringed
them as the enemies of their country.

Before intelligence of this determined spirit of resistance on the part of the colonies could reach England, the affairs of America had become the subject of serious deliberation in the British Cabinet. There was one course which, if promptly taken, might have had the effect of stopping the alarming spread of disaffection towards the mother-country. By the total and immediate repeal of Townshend's Act, Great Britain would practically relinquish the assertion of her right to tax her colonies. This course was earnestly recommended by the Lord Chancellor Camden, by General Conway, and by the Duke of Grafton himself. Hillsborough and Rochford, with the Duke of Bedford's nominees, Gower and Weymouth, were for repealing all the duties imposed by the Act of 1767, *except the duty on tea.* It only remained for Lord North's opinion to decide the action of the Council. There is reason to believe that, if left to himself, he would readily have assented to the wiser and more generous policy advocated by the chief minister; but in deference to the King,[*] who maintained that 'there must always be one tax to keep up the right,' and, against his better nature, he gave his voice for the miserable and fatal compromise upon which the Bedford party insisted.

Change of tone in the Government.

Upon every other point, the Government changed their tone, and began to pursue a policy of conciliation. Their denunciation of the conduct of the people of Massachusetts had only proved that discontent was not confined to that colony. Their authoritative exhortation to the several provincial legislatures to treat the circular letter of the Boston Assembly with 'the contempt it deserved,' was, in most instances, itself treated with the utmost contempt and indignation. The funds had fallen three per cent. when the intelligence of these formidable discontents arrived in London. The merchants, regarding the colonies only as a market for their commerce, made urgent remonstrances to

[*] The King to Lord North. Communicated to Mr. Bancroft by Lady Charlotte Lindsay.—*Bancroft's History.*

the Government against a system of coercion which
seemed likely to interfere with trade. The Government,
therefore, made an effort to compose these
unhappy differences. The Secretary of State sent a
circular letter to the American States, announcing
that no more taxes would be imposed upon the
colonies, and that the duties on all the articles enumerated
in the Act of 1767, with the exception of
tea, would be taken off. The governors of the different
provinces were instructed to lower their tone,
as well as to soothe and flatter the popular leaders.
Virginia, which had not been visited by its Governor
during the present generation, was now to welcome
a representative of their Sovereign in the person of
Lord Bottetort, an English nobleman of spirit and
address, who entered upon his high office with the
splendour which became its dignity and importance.
Even Boston itself, which was to have been made a
signal example by insulted power, was to experience
favour and indulgence. The design of prosecuting
the Sons of Liberty (as the chief malcontents styled
themselves), under the statute of Henry the Eighth,
was silently abandoned. General Gage, the commander-in-chief,
was ordered to send back the two
regiments which had been brought from Halifax in
the preceding autumn to intimidate the town. The
scheme of altering the charter was likewise dropped,
and Bernard, the obnoxious governor, was recalled.

The circular of the Secretary of State, which it
was hoped would propitiate the colonies, *Circular of the Government.*
was published at Boston, on the 27th of
July. The merchants immediately assembled, and
declared it unsatisfactory, the duty on tea being retained
for the purpose of asserting the right of Great
Britain to tax the colonies. This was, in fact,
the whole of their grievance; neither the amount
nor the character of the duties had ever been considered.
It was the principle only which caused all the

discontent. Townshend's Act was a repetition of the Stamp Act in another form, and was so understood by the whole of the colonies.* The people of Virginia, pleased and flattered as they were by the magnificence of their new governor, by his hospitality and urbanity, were never for a moment seduced from the assertion of those principles of colonial independence which they had been the first to vindicate. Their Assembly was still led by the fervid eloquence of Henry, and had lately acquired two illustrious members, in the persons of Washington † and Jefferson. The Governor came down in regal state to open the session; his coach drawn by eight cream-coloured horses, after the fashion of the princes of the house of Hanover, when they open the Parliament of Great Britain. He addressed them in a gracious speech. But all this did not prevent their passing stringent resolutions, asserting the privilege of self-taxation, and the right of concerting with other colonies measures for defending the liberties of all. They also protested against the application to America of the law of Henry the Eighth. For these proceedings, they were immediately dissolved.

At the close of the year 1769, the question which united all men throughout the continent of America was the entire repeal of Townshend's Act; even Boston, for the sake of harmony, was content to recede from its more advanced pretensions, and to make its acceptance of English imports conditional only on the repeal of that obnoxious statute.

This, then, was the crisis of the quarrel. As a financial measure, the Act of 1767 had been passed by the Chancellor of the Exchequer of that day. As a financial

Crisis of the dispute with the colonies.

---

* Sparks's Life of Washington.

† Washington already saw the tendency of affairs. At this time he writes to Mason, that he should have no hesitation in taking up arms in defence of their liberties, if other resources should fail. — *April*, 1769. — SPARKS's *Life of Washington*.

measure, it had wholly failed. There was really, therefore, no pretence for retaining it. The dispute between Great Britain and her colonies, touching the right of taxation, had been settled by the legislation of the preceding year. The resistance of the colonies prevailed. The Stamp Act was unconditionally repealed; and the Declaratory Act was passed to save the honour and dignity of the Imperial Government. It had been the fine policy of Chatham to consign this imperial right of taxation to that limbo of theory with other constitutional claims, the practical assertion of which could not be made without imminent danger. The rash and short-sighted folly of his successors, by meddling with a weapon which they did not understand, dismembered the Empire, and, for a time, imperilled its existence.

CHAPTER X.

REMNANT OF THE CHATHAM ADMINISTRATION—THE OPPOSITION—RE-UNION OF THE GRENVILLE CONNECTION—HORNED CATTLE SESSION—CHATHAM'S REAPPEARANCE IN PARLIAMENT—DISMISSAL OF LORD CAMDEN—SUDDEN DEATH OF HIS SUCCESSOR YORKE—DUKE OF GRAFTON'S RESIGNATION—LORD NORTH PRIME MINISTER.

THE worst government which this country had experienced since the Revolution was the rump administration of Lord Chatham.

Rump administration of Lord Chatham.

While that great man continued at the head of affairs and kept possession of his faculties, it mattered little that the other members of his cabinet were of slender capacity and experience. One commanding genius is enough for any government; and when such exists, it may be well, perhaps, that the other ministers should be content with the discharge of departmental duties. Chatham had sketched the plan of a great administration, which his colleagues, deprived of his direction, were utterly unable to fulfil. For the perverse and calamitous measures which superseded the policy of Chatham, it would be a hard measure of justice to load the memory of his successor. The Duke of Grafton has been termed a minister by accident; and it is certain that no man was more anxious to shrink from a responsibility to which he felt himself incompetent. To be a devoted follower of Chatham was the limit of his ambition; and nothing but the positive injunction of his revered chief induced him for a time to occupy a place which he earnestly hoped that his chief might soon be able to resume.

How came it to pass, then, that a minister who professed himself to be a devoted disciple of Chatham should, in three short years, *Reasons for his conduct.* have departed so widely from the footsteps of his master? How came it that an accidental, a reluctant, an irresolute minister pursued a system which revolted the colonies, alienated the affections of the people of England from the Government, and brought the institutions of the country into contempt? How came it that a man who had no vocation for government, and no desire to rule, was the only minister during this reign who voluntarily relinquished the cares of office? The explanation is easy. When the King and his greatest subject combined for the purpose of breaking up party connections, there is little doubt that they would have accomplished this object; or, at least, that Chatham would have continued in power as long as he had the support of the Crown. Grafton, unconnected with faction, and professing allegiance to Chatham alone, became, as chief minister, a passive instrument in the hands of a determined will, in the furtherance of a definite policy. It was the King who insisted on the prosecution of Wilkes; and it was the King who urged measures of coercion towards the refractory colonies. The remnant of Chatham's administration, originally framed without much regard to the strength of its component parts, and recruited only by the nominees of the Duke of Bedford, whose party was the weakest in Parliament, as well as the most unpopular in the country, could not have existed for a session without the support of that party which, though without palpable existence, could make and unmake administrations. It was the King's party, organised and disciplined to implicit obedience, which kept Grafton and his successor in power, during a long series of years, notwithstanding the most powerful opposition which a minister ever encountered in Parliament—

notwithstanding a disastrous war, and the loss of thirteen colonies.

But circumstances, rather than inclination had made the Duke of Grafton an instrument in the hands of the Court. He had been pained and alarmed at the growing discontent of the colonies, and was anxious to abandon altogether that unfortunate fiscal policy which, after having been relinquished under the advice of Chatham, was renewed by the rashness and presumption of Townshend. The determination of the Cabinet Council, against his opinion, to adhere to the duty on tea for the sake merely of asserting the imperial right of taxation had caused him much disappointment; and from that time he felt a strong desire to be relieved from the responsibility of office.

Duke of Grafton alarmed.

Another event which took place shortly after the eventful deliberation of the Cabinet on American affairs, hastened the determination of Grafton to resign his office. This was nothing less than the reappearance of Lord Chatham in public after his long illness. In the month of July, he was well enough to pay his respects at Court. After the levee, he had an audience of the King, by whom he was received with the most marked expressions of favour. But His Majesty had little encouragement, from this interview, to hope that his system of government would receive the sanction or support of his great subject. Chatham spoke of the measures which had been adopted, especially of the proceedings against Wilkes, with disapprobation, and plainly intimated his purpose of opposing the Government.

Reappearance of Lord Chatham.

Grafton he treated with coldness and neglect. The Duke, who still desired to consider himself responsible to Chatham for his public conduct, had hoped and expected to have been admitted to his presence as soon as he was prepared to resume the consideration of public affairs.

Coolness of Chatham to Grafton.

But Lord Granby was the first to be favoured with an interview, and by that lord the minister was informed that the Earl intended to reserve his sentiments until he should communicate them to the King.* They met at the levee. Lord Chatham treated the Duke with distant courtesy; Grafton, who fairly thought that he had claims to something more, if it were only in consideration of his having taken office at Chatham's earnest desire, was so much hurt and mortified by this unkind and ungracious treatment that he made no further effort to conciliate the goodwill of the wayward and haughty statesman, who had so long been the chief object of his veneration and regard.

During the recess of Parliament, some attempts were made to reconcile the parties in opposition, for the purpose of putting an end to the administration. No material difference of principle separated the two great sections into which the Whig interest was divided. The Marquis of Rockingham had indeed repealed the capital measure of Mr. Grenville; but the latter no longer insisted on renewing the experiment of American taxation. Lord Temple had ceased to have any correspondence with Wilkes, and therefore could no longer shock the head of the house of Wentworth by his patronage of vulgar liberalism. The reunited family of Grenville, with Chatham at their head, were desirous of an alliance with the Rockingham party. Chatham himself declared for an administration in which the people might have confidence. He said that it should be formed on Whig principles; and that the Rockinghams and Cavendishes with the old Whig families should be its leading members.†

_{Attempts at accommodation.}

* Earl Temple to Countess of Chatham.—Grafton's MS. Memoirs, July 1769. Corr. vol. iii. p. 356. App. to vol. v. of Lord Stanhope's History.
† Burke to Marquis of Rockingham, Nov. 14, 1769.—Corr. vol. i. p. 215.

Temple was equally frank and candid. He deprecated any allusion to past differences. 'We have done each other,' said he in an interview with Burke, 'a thousand acts of unkindness; let us make amends by a thousand acts of friendship.' These overtures were received with coldness and reserve on the part of Burke, who was in close correspondence with Lord Rockingham. Alarm at the ascendancy of the Grenvilles in the proposed coalition; jealousy of his own plans and policy; together with a lingering resentment against Chatham for the contempt with which he had treated his administration,—all concurred in keeping back the proud Whig nobleman. The autumn passed away, and no progress had been made towards an allied opposition.

Meanwhile, Chatham and the Grenvilles were busied in detaching their own immediate connections from administration. The Lord Chancellor and the Commander-in-Chief, the two ministers who alone enjoyed any share of popularity, were urged to resign. The former, as will be seen, was advised or thought proper to go into opposition, retaining the Great Seal, and thus forcing upon the Government the odium of his dismissal. Granby took the more fair and manly course of resigning his office before he turned round upon his colleagues. The session of Parliament commenced on the 9th of January. It was a momentous period. A spirit of discontent more wide and deep than had been known since the last reign of the Stuarts, pervaded England. The most sacred rights of the people had been violated by Parliament; and the treachery of their representatives had been abetted by the Crown. The colonies were all but in arms in vindication of their privileges which had been wantonly invaded; and the commerce of the mother-country was deranged by the disturbance of those relations with the colonies, on the stability of which it mainly depended. Lastly, war itself was menaced by the common enemy, restored to vigour by a sufficient interval of peace, and burning for revenge.

In addition to these many and various grievances, there was one calamity of a purely domestic character.* A murrain prevailed among the bullocks; and many thousands of these useful animals had perished. This was a circumstance, no doubt, to be deplored, but hardly one of sufficient dignity and importance, even in the dearth of other matter, to be noticed in that State paper in which the Sovereign inaugurates the annual labours of his Parliament. Yet, while the minds of all men were full of such matters as the quarrel between Parliament and the people; the differences between England and her vast dependencies in America; and an impending war with France and Spain, His Majesty was advised to make the disease among the horned cattle the burden of his speech. The possibility of war was afterwards referred to in ambiguous terms; the distractions in America were slightly mentioned. The discontents at home were wholly omitted. Whether ignorance or insolence possessed the framers of this document may be doubtful; but never was a King's speech received with such an ebullition of ridicule and contempt.

The royal speech.

But the absurdity of the royal speech was for the moment cast into the shade by the interest which the reappearance of Lord Chatham excited in Parliament and throughout the nation. On the first day of the session, and on the usual motion for the address, he moved an amendment, the purport of which was to censure the conduct of the House of Commons in the affair of Wilkes, and to assert the right of the constituency

Reappearance and speech of Chatham.

---

* The distemper among horned cattle was nothing new. Acts of Parliament had been passed in 1747 and 1757 to provide against it.

to make a free choice of their representatives. But though his motion was confined to one particular subject, his censures glanced over the whole field of foreign, colonial and domestic policy.* The grievance of which for nine years he had never failed to explain, that, namely, of a glorious war closed by a peace which secured to this country few of the benefits she was entitled to derive from great exertions and unexampled success, was again forcibly urged. 'If war is unavoidable,' said he, 'you will enter into it without a single ally, while the whole house of Bourbon was united within itself, and supported by the closest connections with the principal powers in Europe.' He then passed 'to the distractions and divisions which prevailed in every part of the Empire.' He objected to the term 'unwarrantable' as applied in the speech to the proceedings of the Americans. Their combinations to exclude English manufactures were indeed dangerous to the commercial interests of this country; but they were, in no wise, illegal. As to the conduct of the Americans in other respects, he would reserve his opinion until authentic information should be laid before Parliament. For the present, he would only say that we should be cautious how we invaded the liberties of any part of our fellow-subjects, however remote in situation, or unable to make resistance. The Americans had purchased their liberty at a dear rate, since they had quitted their native country and gone in search of freedom to a desert. But it was on the proceedings in the Middlesex elections, that he laid the heaviest weight of censure; and never in the days of his greatest vigour did he use more daring and emphatic language. The allusion to the King, in a passage which he quoted from Robertson's His-

---

* This speech is reported by Sir Philip Francis, the reputed author of Junius.—*Note to Chatham Corr.* vol. iii. p. 369.

tory of Charles the Fifth, then recently published, was far more pointed and severe, as well as more apposite, than anything contained in the sharp scurrility of Wilkes, or the classic libel of Junius. 'The peers of Castile,' said he, 'were so far cajoled and seduced by Charles the Fifth (a great, ambitious, wicked man), as to join him in overturning that part of the Cortes which represented the people. They were weak enough to adopt, and base enough to be flattered with an expectation, that by assisting their master in this iniquitous purpose, they should increase their own strength and importance. What was the consequence? They exchanged the constitutional authority of peers for the titular vanity of grandees. They were no longer a part of a Parliament, for *that* they had destroyed; and when they pretended to have an opinion as grandees, he told them he did not understand it; and naturally enough, when they had surrendered their authority, treated their advice with contempt. The consequences did not stop here. He made use of the people whom he had enslaved to enslave others, and employed the strength of the Castilians to destroy the rights of their free neighbours of Aragon.'

When Lord Chatham had concluded, the Chancellor rose, but not to defend that administration of which he was the ablest member. *Speech of Lord Camden.* He rose to support Chatham; and he did so with equal energy, with equal virulence, and hardly with inferior eloquence and effect. He had beheld, he said, with silent indignation the arbitrary measures that were pursued by the Ministry. He had often hung down his head in council, and disapproved by his looks of those steps which he knew his avowed opposition could not prevent. He denounced the vote of the House of Commons by which Wilkes had been incapacitated. It was a direct attack upon the first principles of the constitution. Still he was prudent enough to confine his animadversion to the House of Commons and the Ministry.

Conduct of Lord Camden. These sentiments, however just, reflected more discredit on the speaker himself than on the objects of his censure. Why did Lord Camden behold with *silent* indignation the measures of a ministry in which he occupied the most prominent position? Why did he sanction, by his presence and the authority of his great name, measures which he did not approve? The Lord Chancellor seemed to think it a triumph to provoke his expulsion from office, by holding up to public scorn and detestation those colleagues with whom he had chosen to associate himself in confidential counsel, and from whom he could separate whenever he thought fit. There might have been policy in this position; but certainly it was very different from the conduct of that great man whom he affected to call 'his pole star,' when he was placed in a similar position. Pitt would not remain in office a moment after the Government, of which he was a leading member, determined on a course of policy contrary to his opinion and advice.

Anomalous position of Lord Camden. Lord Camden, notwithstanding his denunciation of the policy of the Government, continued to keep possession of the Great Seal. But his conduct in this particular, though it had the sanction of his friends, seems to have been still more unworthy than his retention of office during the past year. The policy of the Opposition in forcing the Government to deprive Lord Camden of his office, was to make it appear that an upright judge had been dismissed for declaring the law; an independent member of Parliament, for pronouncing his opinion. Nothing could be more false and uncandid. It was not for anything done in his judicial capacity that Lord Camden was to be dismissed. When Chief Justice, he had gained great applause by vindicating, with more than judicial emphasis,* the rights of the people against the proceedings of the Government. The law which had passed at the commencement of the reign protected him from being deprived of his office, but could not have prevented his advancement being barred by this fearless discharge of his duty. Yet so far from feeling the displeasure of the Crown, the bold and independent judge was soon afterwards promoted to the highest dignity of his profession. The position of the Lord Chancellor is a peculiar one. While every other judge of the land is confined exclusively to judicial duties, the Chancellor alone has a two-fold capacity—that of judge and that of minister of state. A judge of the land can be removed by the Crown only upon a joint address of both Houses of Parliament. The Chancellor, who has no commission, but is appointed solely by the delivery of the Great Seal into his possession, is expected to surrender that symbol of his rank as a privy councillor, as well as of his judicial authority, when he ceases to be a political adviser of the Crown. Neither could there be any pretence for comparing the case of Camden to that of a military or other officer not immediately connected with administration, dismissed from his employment for a vote in Parliament. Such a stretch of power is unconstitutional and unnecessary. But when a cabinet minister differs from his colleagues upon an important question of policy, he should either acquiesce in the decision of the majority, or relieve himself from responsibility by resignation. He has no right to appeal from the Council to the Parliament; and he

<small>*Camden's want of delicate feeling.*</small>

---

* 'Upon the maturest consideration, I am bold to say, this warrant is illegal. . . . If a superior jurisdiction should declare my opinion erroneous, I submit, as will become me, and kiss the rod; but I must say, I shall always consider it as a rod of iron for the chastisement of the people of Great Britain.'—*Charge to the Jury by* PRATT, C. J., *Money v. Leach.*

deserts his duty as a confidential adviser of the Crown, if he absents himself from the deliberations of the Cabinet, and reserves his opinion for the House of Lords. Moreover, there is something of treachery in holding office as the Chancellor did, in concert with the Opposition, and in subservience to their party objects. It would be impossible for any confidence to exist among public men, or for the Sovereign to have the least reliance upon his ministers, if Lord Camden's conduct is to be justified.

Lord Mansfield also took a part in this remarkable debate; but, with his usual caution, studiously forbore expressing an opinion as to the legality of the proceedings of the House of Commons with reference to the Middlesex elections. He treated the question as one of privilege; and consequently as one the Lords were precluded from entertaining by constitutional etiquette. Arguing upon this narrow ground, he deprecated the amendment which Chatham had moved, as calculated only to produce a collision between the two Houses.

<small>Lord Mansfield's speech.</small>

Chatham felt the force of this reasoning, and made a laboured reply. But instead of putting the question on its proper footing, namely, that the Commons, under the pretext of privilege, had interfered with the law of the land, which defined capacity and incapacity to sit in Parliament, the great orator went off into a declamation about liberty, which, however eloquent and impressive, did not meet the plausible objection which Mansfield had stated with his usual perspicuity and reasoning power.

The address was carried by a large majority. Immediately after the division, Lord Rockingham gave notice of a motion to inquire into the state of the nation for the morrow, upon which Lord Pomfret moved an adjournment for a week. Temple said the purpose for which the

<small>Motion for adjournment.</small>

adjournment was required was obvious; it was to settle the disordered state of the administration; and, particularly, to dismiss the virtuous and independent lord who sat on the woolsack, and supply his place with some obsequious lawyer who would do as he was commanded. Lord Shelburne used still stronger language. 'The Great Seal,' he said, 'would go a begging; but he hoped there would not be found in the kingdom a wretch so base and mean-spirited as to accept of it on the conditions on which it must be offered.'

It seemed that Shelburne's hope was likely to be realised. A week elapsed before any appointment was made. It was known that neither of the Chief Justices would take it. The Solicitor-General, Dunning, whose distinguished merit would have added lustre to the Great Seal, retired with his friend Lord Camden, at whose instance alone he had retained office after the resignation of Chatham. At length it was offered to Yorke, the son of the great Lord Chancellor Hardwicke. No man was better fitted for such preferment. He was a ripe lawyer, and still in the vigour of his age. He had been appointed Solicitor-General so far back as the year 1757, on the occasion of Mansfield's elevation to the bench. He had twice filled the office of Attorney-General; the last time, in the administration of Rockingham. The Great Seal had ever been the object of his ambition; and was one to which he might fairly look, from his professional standing, the high legal offices which he had filled, his acknowledged merit, and even the very name he bore. One reason only has been suggested why Yorke should have refused the splendid offer of the Duke of Grafton; and that was, that his acceptance of it would be a violation of those party engagements, from which no public man can honourably set himself free for the purpose of his own benefit and advancement. But in reality, it appears that no such obstacle existed. Yorke had been in office under Newcastle, under Bute, and under Rockingham. He resigned with the Marquis, not from political attachment, but from private pique and resentment, because the King, after having promised him the Great Seal, had refused him the Chief Justiceship *with a peerage.** For the same reason he abstained from giving his opinion in Parliament on the Middlesex election, although he approved of the course which the House of Commons had taken under the direction of the Court. 'I cannot do it,' said he, when pressed by his brother, Lord Hardwicke, to deliver his sentiments, 'because if I go with the Court, they will betray me, or give me up as they did before; and if with the Opposition, it will be against my convictions.' † He expressed himself in this manner when the Yorke family were assembled at Wimpole in the Christmas of 1769 to consider the line they should follow in the approaching parliamentary session. On that occasion, Lord Hardwicke warns his brother to be cautious in not committing himself to the Rockingham party. It is true that he consulted Lord Rockingham as well as his brother upon the Duke of Grafton's offer of the Great Seal; and that they both advised him to decline it, not because his acceptance of it would be a breach of any party engagement; but on the ground that it was intended only to make use of him as a prop to a government which could not stand.‡ Convinced by this reasoning, he determined to decline the offer. All this time his mind,

* From his own MS. Journal, printed by Mr. Harris in his lately published Life of Lord Hardwicke, vol. iii.

† Lord Hardwicke's MS. Journal. Harris's Life, vol. iii.

‡ Lord Chatham also viewed the matter in the same light. 'Mr. Yorke's refusal is of moment; and I can readily believe it, from my opinion of his prudence and discernment. No man with a grain of either would embark in a rotten vessel, in the middle of a tempest, to go he knows not whither.'—*Correspondence*, vol. iii. p. 398.

relaxed perhaps by bodily ailment, was in a state of
perturbation, distracted between the fear of being
outwitted by the Court and of losing the opportunity
of ambition. Next day, accordingly, he wavered.
In the afternoon he saw the King, fancied that he
was coldly received, declined the Seal, and authorised
his brother to announce that such was his final determination. After passing a restless night, he
attended the levee on the following morning. The
King called him into the closet, and there, <small>He accepts
the Seals.</small>
by dint of importunity, and even menace,
so wrought upon his infirm resolution, that he at
length retracted his refusal, and obeyed His Majesty's
commands. He went immediately to acquaint his
brother with what had taken place. Lord Hardwicke and Lord Rockingham, who happened to be in
the room, expressed their astonishment at this intelligence; and Hardwicke seems to have given utterance to some indignation, as well he might, at the
way in which his brother had trifled with him.
They both urged Yorke to entreat the King to put
the Great Seal in commission, or at least to allow
him until next morning to give his final answer.
But Yorke said it was too late; his word was pledged,
as he had kissed hands. In the evening he went
again to his brother's house, bringing with him the
Great Seal, which the King had just delivered to him.
By this time, Lord Hardwicke's irritation had disappeared; the brothers discussed the matter calmly,
and parted on the most friendly terms. Yorke, as
his brother affectionately remarks, seemed 'composed
but unhappy.'*

Three days after, the Lord Chancellor was no
more. It was reported that he had committed sui-

---

* My account of this melancholy transaction is taken from a
private memorial by the second
Earl of Hardwicke, and printed
in Harris's Life of Lord Hardwicke, from the MSS. at Wimpole.

cide. By another account, which is not improbable,
he had ruptured a blood vessel. But
whether he died by his own hand, or from
natural causes, there is every reason to believe that
his death was precipitated by mental excitement.
The conduct of Yorke, throughout this sad affair,
was certainly not dignified; but his memory must be
freed from the imputation of treachery and breach of
faith which has been rashly cast upon it.*

Sidenote: Death of Yorke.

Lord Granby, one of the most amiable and popular
men in England, was more fortunate. On
the first night of the session, he had expressed his contrition for the vote which he gave
on the Middlesex election; but, notwithstanding the
utterance of a sentiment so much opposed to the
favourite policy of the Court, both the King and the
Duke of Grafton were extremely reluctant to lose an
adherent whose gallantry and good nature had en-
deared him to the nation. They entreated him not
to resign;† and, when he was firm upon that point,
the Duke thought it something gained, that he should
yield so far as to defer his purpose for twenty-four
hours.‡ Lord Chatham was impatient that he should
have made even this trifling concession. Several
other resignations by noblemen and gentlemen of inferior note took place about the same time. Among
these were James Grenville, a brother of Lord
Temple's, and Dunning, the Solicitor-General.

Sidenote: Resignation of Lord Granby.

The Ministry, thus broken and discredited, had to
meet the party movement of the Opposition, which was to take effect in the Lords,
after the adjournment. Rockingham's resolution was,

Sidenote: Rockingham's motion.

---

* A touching anecdote is related of his last moments. When
he was asked whether the Great
Seal should be put to the patent
for his barony of Morden,—'I
had hoped,' he said, 'it was no
longer in my possession.'—LORD
HARDWICKE's *Narrative*.

† Earl Temple to the Earl of
Chatham.—Chatham Corr. vol.
iii. p. 391.

‡ Calcraft to the Earl of Chatham, p. 393.

that the House would take into consideration the
state of the nation on an early day. This was for
the purpose of introducing a speech in which he
censured every act of the Government. He dated
the present discontents from the King's accession,
ascribing them to the change which had been introduced into the system of Government, and the
prevalence of the maxim that the royal prerogative
alone was sufficient to support Government, to whatever hands it might be committed. The Duke of
Grafton assented to the motion, professing himself
ready and willing to enter into the whole question
whenever it should be brought forward; and, in the
meantime, vindicated some of the measures of his
administration. Chatham followed in another great
oration similar to that which he had made on the
first day of the session, and going over the same
ground. He stated, moreover, that a reform in the
constitution of the House of Commons was a necessary remedy for the corruption and abuses which
impeded the wholesome action of the Government.
His plan of parliamentary reform, however, was far
more limited than that which a later generation has
thought adequate to the exigencies of the case. He
was content to retain the rotten boroughs, although
he believed that they were the source from which
the evil mainly flowed; and the principal change
which he proposed was to add one representative to
each of the counties, for the purpose of increasing
the weight and influence of the independent gentry.
He concluded by emphatically asserting the existence
of a cordial union between himself and the noble
mover; and announced that Rockingham and his
friends were united with him and his adherents on a
principle which he trusted would make their union
indissoluble. It was not to possess or divide the
emoluments of office that the coalition had been
made, but, if possible, to save the State.

VOL. I.   Y

The Government had little to fear from an Opposition founded on such a principle as that enunciated by Lord Chatham; indeed, no Opposition could be held together upon such terms. Public spirit may be a sufficient bond of union among a few generous and independent men; but the staff, as well as the rank and file of a party, must always be actuated at least in an equal degree by motives of a more gross and selfish character.

The day for the renewal of the debate was fixed for the 2nd of February. But three days previously, the Duke of Grafton resigned his office.

Resignation of Grafton.

This resignation appears to have been as unexpected, and to have caused as much surprise, as that of Lord Bute, in 1762. But if the retreat of the latter was capable of rational explanation, that of Grafton seems to be still more intelligible. Advanced to the post of principal responsibility by an unforeseen event, he had always been an unwilling minister, conscious of his own incapacity. Every day, after the loss of that leader, whom it had been his pride to follow, Grafton found himself borne away, by an overruling will, farther and farther from the policy of Chatham. He had been forced into connections alike hostile to that policy and to its author. On a question of the greatest moment, and upon which he entertained a profound conviction, he had been outvoted in his cabinet. And, lastly, he was deserted by that eminent colleague,*—the

---

* Lord Camden had expressed the strongest disapprobation of the course which the Cabinet resolved to pursue with regard to the Middlesex election and the American colonies. He had even addressed a formal letter of remonstrance to Grafton on both those questions. Finding his opinion overruled, he had ceased, for more than a year, to attend the Cabinet councils, with the exception of that one memorable meeting at which the Duke proposed the repeal of Townshend's Act. The King had urged Grafton to dismiss the Chancellor before the meeting of Parliament

chosen friend and follower of Chatham, the constitutional judge,—whose presence in the Government afforded the angry nation some hope that it was not altogether ruined and betrayed. Far from wondering at Grafton's resignation, the difficulty is to discover any motive which could induce him to remain.

The Government was now a mere wreck. The Duke of Bedford's nominees still adhered to it,—Weymouth, Gower, and Rigby. There were also Lord Rochford, and the colonial minister, who had almost lost the colonies. The only man of mark who remained was Lord North, the Chancellor of the Exchequer.

But the King was determined not to yield. He told General Conway he would rather abdicate, or appeal to the sword.* And, as Lord North was the only one of his adherents who could pretend to reconstruct the Government, he laid his commands upon that nobleman to undertake the task.

Lord North constructs a new Cabinet.

If it had been the intention of the Court to insult and defy public opinion, a more appropriate selection of a minister could not have been made. Lord North had recently, when speaking in his character of leader of the House of Commons, gone out of his way to remind the House that he had opposed every popular measure for the last seven years. He had supported the cider-tax, and afterwards opposed its repeal. He had voted for the American Stamp Act. He had been against the reduction of the land-tax. He moved the first expulsion of Wilkes, and supported every subsequent proceeding against that champion of

in 1773. But this the Duke had positively declined doing.—LORD CAMPBELL'S *Lives of the Chancellors*, vol. v. p. 284.

Grafton, so far from having wilfully deserted Chatham, afterwards deplored his resignation and consequent absence on that occasion, as the cause of all the misfortunes that ensued.—*MS. Memoirs.*

* Lord Albemarle's Memoirs of Rockingham, vol. ii. p. 179.

popular rights. He had even refused his assent to
the recognition by Parliament of the plain law of
the land with respect to General Warrants.
Nor would he agree to a statute of limi-
tation upon dormant claims of the Crown. But the
truth is, the appointment of North was a matter of
the last necessity. There was no other man capable
of conducting the public business through Parliament
who would undertake the office. Even Conway,
though he no longer belonged to the Rockingham
party, refused to remain in the Cabinet. There was
no doubt about the stability of a Court administration; for the Court could command a parliamentary
majority. The difficulty was to find any public man
of character who could accept office on the King's
terms; the first condition upon which every minister
had hitherto insisted being the expulsion of the
King's friends. Lord North was probably the only
man of parliamentary reputation who would have
forborne to press this essential article. But no creep-
ing ambition actuated his conduct. When he enumerated his unpopular votes as a proof that he was not
ambitious, he spoke with perfect sincerity; although
it so happened that the very course which seemed to
him to lead in an opposite direction, was the one
which conducted him to power. He had never been
in connection with either of the great Whig parties;
he knew, as every man knew, their pride, their
jealousy, their selfishness, their want of public spirit.
Though himself of a gentle temper and an easy disposition, Lord North's political tendencies were all
in favour of power and authority. He
supported the King against the aristocracy, the Parliament against the people; and the
nation against the colonies. His loyalty at this
critical period postponed for many years the progress
of good government, and involved the nation in great
calamity. Had Lord North shrunk from the post of

danger, it is not likely that any other man could have been found to occupy it. The King must have given way. Chatham and his friends, Temple and the Grenvilles, Rockingham and his followers, much grown in public importance since their short tenure of office, would have come into power, if not with acclamation, at least with more general assent and confidence than had attended the advent to office of any previous administration. The same causes which had so long prevented the union of these parties might, indeed, have soon again dissolved the auspicious coalition. But, in all probability, great results would have been first obtained. The dissolution of Parliament, followed, perhaps, by the amendment of its constitution, and the settlement of the American question, would probably have resulted from the new administration. And, if nothing else had been accomplished, the monarchy might, by these means, have escaped an agitation which, twenty years afterwards, imperilled its existence; the country would have been spared the ignominious loss of thirteen colonies; the burden of an enormous debt, and those unfriendly feelings on the part of our emancipated dependencies, the most dire effects of the quarrel, which it may take more than a century to allay.

CHAPTER XI.

DISUNION OF THE OPPOSITION—GRENVILLE'S BILL ON CONTROVERTED ELECTIONS—CITY ADDRESS AND REMONSTRANCE—DISPLEASURE OF THE COURT—RENEWAL OF PETITIONS—THE TEA DUTY RESISTED IN AMERICA—BLOODSHED AT BOSTON—THE IRISH PARLIAMENT.

Success of Lord North.

THE resolution and promptitude of the King had the effect which those qualities usually command. The appointment of Lord North, without hesitation or delay, to the head of the Government baffled the tardy and ill-concerted schemes of a half-united Opposition. While the King was wholly intent on securing his only chance of success, the Opposition, with a great game in their hands, played it so badly that they were beaten without difficulty. It was of moment that they should act in unison in both Houses. But on the first day of the session there was a difference of opinion between Chatham and Grenville, as to the course to be taken in Parliament. Thus, while Chatham moved an amendment to the address, it was allowed to pass in the Commons without opposition.* In the crisis of the Ministry, some stiff and formal notes were passing between the two great lords of Opposition relative to a motion in the Upper House. Rockingham kept haughtily aloof from Chatham's city friends, who, of course, took umbrage at such treatment.† The Society for the Support of the Bill of Rights was the vigorous offspring of the popular agitation on the Middlesex elections. Its leading members were

* Chatham Corr. vol. iii. p. 389.   † Chatham Corr. vol. iii. p. 436.

merchants, lawyers, and other persons of substance and respectability. They were earnest men brought together by a deep resentment against injustice and oppression. Some of their notions were crude, some wild and impracticable. Their language was not always measured, though hardly so strong as that which Chatham was in the habit of using, with the approbation of Rockingham. But what was commendable in the House of Lords, was intolerable at Mile End. The Whigs accordingly denounced the Bill of Rights men, who, in their turn, declared open war against the Whigs. Chatham justly despised this squeamishness * which would risk the loss of a great cause, rather than accept the aid of sincere though, perhaps, rude and coarse allies. The Court regarded these differences with much complacency, and saw in them the most favourable prospect for their system.* The Opposition, nevertheless, was carried on with great vigour in the House of Commons. The violated rights of the constituency gave occasion for various modes of attack. On bringing up the report of the address, Sir George Savile, the member for the county of York, a person of great weight, endeavoured to provoke a quarrel by language of insult and contumely. 'I look on this House,' said he, 'as sitting illegally, after their illegal act.† They have betrayed their trust. I will not add epithets, because epithets only weaken; therefore I will not say that they have betrayed their trust corruptly, flagitiously and scandalously; but I do

---

* 'I was in town on Wednesday last; saw Lord Rockingham, and learned nothing more than what I knew before; namely, that the Marquis is an honest and honourable man, but that "moderation, moderation" is the burden of the song among the body. For myself, I am resolved to be in earnest for the public, and shall be *a scarecrow of violence* to the gentle warblers of the grove, the moderate Whigs and temperate statesmen.' — *Chatham to Calcraft.* — *Correspondence*, vol. iii. p. 469.

† In seating Luttrell.

say they have betrayed their country. And I stand here to receive the punishment for having said so.' A young member uttered a faint threat of committal to the Tower, and Conway opened a door for retreat by suggesting that the words were spoken in heat. Savile disclaimed the excuse; but Lord North, who was very successful in meeting the violence of opposition with a passive good humour, treated the matter lightly, and it was suffered to drop. Serjeant Glynn, the new member for Middlesex, tried to revive the old practice of withholding supply until grievances should be redressed, and there ensued a very disorderly debate, in which the authority of the new Speaker * was wholly set at nought. Lord North took this opportunity to speak of the petitions, which had been presented to Parliament on the subject of the Middlesex election, with the greatest contempt. He denied the existence of any grievance which required redress. Ignorant mechanics and rustics had been treated with beer, and had broken windows. Was the annual supply to be withheld, every function of Government suspended, the public creditors unpaid, and the army and navy want clothes and bread, because the drunken and the ignorant had been made dupes to the crafty and the factious, signed papers they had not read, and determined questions they could not understand?

Such language could be held with impunity in a House of Commons, which neither represented the people, nor showed any regard to English liberty. It was safe, also, from the indignation of the people themselves, who were kept in ignorance of what passed within the walls of Parliament. No constitutional minister would have spoken in this insolent manner of the right of petitioning, which is as ancient as Parliament, or the Crown itself. It would be easy

* Sir Fletcher Norton, who had been elected on the resignation of Sir John Cust.

to fritter away the character of any petition by scanning the motives and competency of the several persons by whom it was signed. And if ever there was a plain question which ignorance itself might comprehend, it was this. The House of Commons had taken upon itself to refuse the man whom the electors had chosen, and to admit another whom they had rejected.

A motion of a more precise and pertinent character was brought forward by Mr. Dowdeswell. It was this :—' That, in judging of elections, the House ought to be regulated by the law of the land, and the known and established law and custom of Parliament, which made a part thereof.' This was a proposition which could not be disputed; and could only be opposed as being an unnecessary statement of an abstract truth, or as introductory to some particular application which was not equally admissible. Lord North, choosing to recognise its real import, and to qualify its effect, moved, by way of addition,—' And that the judgment of the House, on the Middlesex election, is conformable to law and the usage of Parliament.' This distinct and deliberate affirmation of a vote passed the year before, in the heat of the conflict with the Middlesex electors, was well calculated to prove the extent of the influence which the Government, when supported by the Crown, could exercise over the House of Commons. The resolution which seated Luttrell, instead of Wilkes, was carried by a diminished majority of fifty-four. But Lord North's amendment to Mr. Dowdeswell's motion prevailed only by forty-two, in the fullest House which had divided for many years.*

A motion of much more importance, as regarded

* The numbers were 224 to 182. The King, in a letter to Lord North, declares himself satisfied with the division. Well he might be; for, if the Court could carry such a proposition as Lord North's, they could carry anything.

its practical bearing, was also made by Dowdeswell.

Dowdeswell's motion to disfranchise revenue officers.
The great and growing increase in the customs and excise since the late war had enlisted in the service of the Government numerous persons, engaged in the collection and supervision of this extensive revenue. These men were necessarily spread over the country, and most of them had votes for members of Parliament. Holding their offices at pleasure, their votes were of course at the command of the Government, and the memorable example of 1762, when the vengeance of the minister for parliamentary insubordination was visited upon every public servant, from Lords-Lieutenant and great officers of State, down to the humblest individual, who ate his daily bread at the pleasure of the Crown, was doubtless still regarded as the leading rule and precedent. Dowdeswell moved for leave to bring in a bill to disfranchise these revenue officers; and considering that they mainly influenced the elections in nearly seventy boroughs, and numbered nearly twelve thousand votes in other places,* it is not surprising that the Government made a strenuous effort to defeat a measure which, if carried, might have gone far to destroy their influence in the House of Commons. The Treasury members affected to be shocked at this attempted confiscation of the franchise; and were apprehensive that men would not be found to sacrifice their votes for appointments as revenue officers. But it was not to argument that they trusted for the defeat of such a formidable motion. A House still more numerous than that which had affirmed the vote of the preceding year, on the Middlesex election, now assembled to protect the menaced rights of electors. The motion was rejected by a majority of seventy-five, in a division of four hundred and fifty-one members.

* Such was the uncontradicted statement of Lord Rockingham, when he introduced and carried a similar bill in 1782.

There was, however, one measure relating to the constitution of the House of Commons proposed by a high authority, and which, notwithstanding the opposition of the ministers, obtained its assent. This was Grenville's justly-celebrated bill for the trial of controverted elections. The House, indeed, must have been lost to all sense of decency, if they had rejected a proposal to redress a most flagrant scandal touching the administration of justice. The Commons had always been extremely jealous of their exclusive jurisdiction in questions relating to the due election of their own members. In the earlier times, these questions were sometimes referred to committees of their own body, especially chosen for the purpose, but more commonly to the committee for privileges, which was appointed at the commencement of each session, and consisted chiefly of eminent lawyers. The report of the committee was always adopted by the House. During the civil troubles of 1640, the committee for privileges was increased to a hundred members, and in 1672 its members swelled to two hundred and forty. So large an assemblage being found quite unfit to transact business of a judicial character, it was thought preferable, for the sake of order and solemnity, that election petitions should be tried at the bar of the whole House; this practice was adopted at the accession of the house of Hanover, and had been continued ever since; but the result, as might have been expected, was that the judicial character of the proceeding was quite lost sight of, and an election petition came to be treated as a party question. The vote which ultimately decided the fate of Sir Robert Walpole's administration was taken on a petition complaining of an undue return for the borough of Chippenham; and Lord Rockingham himself, when lately in office, complained of being outvoted by the King's friends on a similar question.

The operation of this system was detailed in striking terms by the distinguished mover, who spoke from a parliamentary experience of thirty years. 'When petitions, complaining of undue returns, are presented, what is the practice? Every gentleman knows what it is, though perhaps it has not till now been publicly stated. The petitioner applies to all his private friends. When that is done, his next care is to apply to one of the two parties, to the Court or the Opposition. The next step is, "Pray hear my case; pray attend for me." A meeting is appointed; fourteen or fifteen gentlemen, all judges, are to meet, to settle the proceedings of the case, which they are to judge upon, on the hearing of one party only. When they come into the House, as might be expected from such judges, they become managers on one side or the other, like advocates at the bar. The next thing is, "How are we to vote? It is almost dinner-time. I am for A.; you are for B. Let us be off."' Other members corroborated this statement.[*] Dunning, just on the point of leaving the office of Solicitor-General, which he retained until the appointment of his successor, bore testimony to the 'strange decisions of the House upon cases heard at the bar. Decisions in Turkey would, in his opinion, be far preferable.'

The main provision of Grenville's bill withdrew the trial of election petitions from the body of the House, and transferred it to a committee of thirteen sworn members, chosen on the principle of a special jury; though in the numbers, and in the mode of deciding by a majority, it resembled the grand inquest. This clear and simple plan seemed to be open to no material objection; for, while it retained the trial of controverted elections in the hands of the House, it took care that justice

[*] Among the influences employed, Grenville mentioned that 'strings of ladies were brought down to muster the troops.'

should be done, by conducting the trial in accordance with the practice of the regular tribunals. Experience, however, has proved that the analogy of a jury does not exactly apply to this case. A jury, taken from the body of the people, is likely to be indifferent between the parties; but a select committee of thirteen members, drawn from the body of the House, could hardly enter with impartial minds upon an inquiry, in the result of which each member of the committee, as a party man, was immediately interested. This natural bias insensibly sways even the most upright and honourable minds; and its tendency is necessarily increased in times of severe party conflict. The only way in which it can be diminished is, by diminishing the number of triers, and thus augmenting the sense of individual responsibility. The election committee has recently been reduced to five members, and might, perhaps, be farther reduced to three, with advantage to the dispensation of justice.

Rigby and Dyson were the ministerial members appropriately put forward to disparage a measure which had for its object the removal of an abuse in parliamentary elections. But even these shameless abettors of corruption did not attempt to gainsay the facts. They took higher ground. The measure, they said, was a surrender of the constitutional rights of the House by delegating its functions to a small body of its members, without revision or appeal. This argument, however, was too gross. The bill was suffered to pass into committee, where Lord North did his best to obstruct its progress; and failing there, he opposed the third reading. The country gentlemen, however, who usually supported the King's Government, gave an independent vote upon this occasion, and the bill passed its final stage in the Commons by a considerable majority. In the Lords it encountered but little opposition. Lord Mansfield, in a matter which concerned the administration of justice, laid aside his usual cautious reserve, and gave the bill a cordial reception. Chatham took the opportunity of paying a graceful and well-merited compliment to his old antagonist.

While an able and vigorous Opposition were harassing administration in both Houses, they were aided, or perhaps damaged, by a daring and violent proceeding on the part of the City of London. This great corporation had for centuries been distinguished for its love of liberty and its bold assertion of popular rights. It was the only corporation in England, the members of which were elected by popular suffrage. It was the most dignified, the most powerful, the wealthiest of all the municipal bodies. Its origin, like that of many other corporations, was lost in prescription; but its privileges were recognised or extended by no less than one hundred and twenty charters, beginning with the reign of William the Conqueror, and ending with that of His Majesty's immediate predecessor.* The constitution and privileges of this famous body are, indeed, a remarkable proof of what the bold and independent spirit of the people could effect even in the earliest times. They erected a Government side by side with that of the Sovereign in his capital city; imitating, if not emulating, the great institutions of the realm. This Government had its Chief Magistrate, its Court of Eldermen, its Common Council, analogous to King, Lords and Commons. It was in some respects an *imperium in imperio* affecting independent rights, and almost equal degree. The City of London to this day closes its gates on certain occasions at the approach of royalty, or the representatives of the Crown. By a particular exception in the annual

* Report of the Commissioners appointed to inquire into the state of the Corporation of the City of London, p. 15 (1854).

Mutiny Act, soldiers are not to be billeted within its domain. In all acts of Parliament touching municipal rights, the privilege of the City is expressly excepted. When the Corporation address the Crown, the Lord Mayor and principal officers insist upon being received in state by the King on the throne. If they approach the House of Commons, their petition is not presented in the ordinary way by one of their representatives, but is delivered at the bar by their Sheriffs in full dress.

On the 9th of November in every year, the new Lord Mayor is presented to the Judges of the land sitting in banco in their respective courts. On that occasion, their lordships appear in their robes of state, but the great magistrate stands covered, while the Recorder claims respect for the ancient rights and privileges of the City of London. Every event of great national importance, the demise of the Crown, or a declaration of war, is immediately communicated to the Lord Mayor by one of the principal Secretaries of State. But it would be tedious to enumerate in all its particulars the grandeur of this mighty corporation; which if it has sometimes assumed the air of sovereignty, equals many sovereign states in the extent of its revenue and the value of its domains. But though declined from the eminence which it maintained for centuries, the Corporation of London will claim a more prominent place in history than many petty states whose existence has not been illustrated by any great or useful actions. The liberties of England are indebted to the City of London. Many a time has it been a safe refuge from tyranny, and at all times the steady and potent ally of national freedom. Not to go back to ruder periods, it was in the City that the five members found a secure retreat from the vengeance of Charles Stuart. When the quarrel between the King and the Parliament came

to an issue of arms, the City was the first to declare
for the Parliament, and to place its vast resources at
their command. Again, when the royal army approached the capital, the City turned the scale in
favour of the Parliament by placing its trained bands,
a corps of high military reputation, under the orders
of the parliamentary general. And as they had been
foremost in vindicating the cause of the nation against
the violence of the Crown, so when the Parliament
had dwindled away under military violence, the City
were equally prompt and decided in declaring for
a free Parliament. It was probably, indeed, the
firmness of the City which determined the indecision of Monk, and gave one more trial to legitimate
monarchy.

The last memorable occasion on which the great
Corporation had interposed between the
Crown and the people, was when they demanded a Parliament in 1680, to protect religious
liberty, then supposed to be endangered by Popish
machinations. They now stood forward to vindicate
the rights of the people in the choice of their representatives. In the former year, they had presented
an address to the Crown on the subject of the Middlesex election, to which no answer had been vouchsafed.
It was determined to repeat this proceeding, but in
a more solemn and emphatic manner. A common
hall having been convened in pursuance of a requisition, was attended by nearly three thousand of the
livery. The Lord Mayor, Beckford, addressed this
large assembly in a speech which would have been
inflammatory but for the already heated temperature
of public feeling. A paper was eagerly signed containing language such as had never before been addressed by a subject to a sovereign. After complaining of the contempt with which the petitions of the
people had been treated, it referred to 'the secret
malignant influence,' which through each successive

administration had defeated every good and suggested every bad measure, and had at last procured the majority of the House of Commons to deprive the people of their dearest rights. The petitioners, or rather the *remonstrants*, for so they styled themselves, affirmed that the House of Commons had no longer any validity, and intimated to His Majesty in significant terms that in tampering with the constitution of Parliament, he was pursuing a course similar to that which lost James the Second his crown. And they assured him that if the substance of liberty had been violated, it would make no difference that its forms had been respected. 'The misdeeds of your ministers in violating the freedom of election, and depraving the noble constitution of Parliament, are notorious, as well as subversive of the fundamental laws and liberties of the realm; and since your Majesty is both in honour and justice, obliged inviolably to preserve them according to the oath made to God and your subjects at your coronation, we, your remonstrants, assure ourselves that your Majesty will restore the constitutional government and quiet of your people, by dissolving this Parliament, and removing those evil ministers for ever from your councils.'

This paper, which was entitled 'An Address, Remonstrance and Petition,' they determined to present, according to the privilege of the City, to the King on his throne. A copy having been previously sent to the Secretary of State in the usual manner, it was debated at Court whether an address worded and entitled in such an extraordinary manner should be received. The Attorney-General was indeed consulted whether such an address would not be impeachable, but it seems that learned functionary declined giving an answer to a question so absurd. Lord Weymouth wrote an impertinent letter to the Sheriffs of London, inquiring what was

Address and remonstrance of the City.

the nature of the meeting at which the address had been voted, and how the document was authenticated? promising that when these queries were answered, His Majesty's pleasure would be signified. The Sheriffs informed the Secretary of State, that their answers to his questions would be delivered to the King in person, and they demanded an audience for that purpose. The claim was allowed, and the Sheriffs having formally satisfied His Majesty of the authenticity of the address, a day was named for its being presented. The Lord Mayor, accompanied by some of the Aldermen and a numerous body of the Common Council and Livery, accordingly attended at St. James's. The Recorder, whose duty it was to read the address, had excused himself; the Common Serjeant, the law officer of the Corporation next in rank, undertook the task, but was so confounded at the audacity of the language, that, after reading a few sentences, he refused, or was unable to proceed. The Town Clerk then took the paper, and succeeded in getting through it.

The King's answer, which was said to have been revised by Lord Mansfield, administered a severe rebuke to the citizens. He pronounced their remonstrance disrespectful to himself, injurious to his Parliament, and irreconcilable to the principles of the constitution. Taking the remonstrance as a charge against himself rather than his ministers, he denied that he had ever invaded any of those powers which the constitution had placed in other hands; and concluded by avowing his belief that the conduct which he had pursued was such as to entitle him to the steady and affectionate support of his people.

It was observed,* that since the Revolution there

---

* Wedderburn. Debate in the House of Commons on motion for a copy of the Remonstrance and the Answer. — Cavendish Debates.

had not been an instance of an answer from the throne carrying with it a degree of censure. But it may be also said, that since the Revolution such an address had never been carried up to the throne. There are many who think that the throne should never be approached but with the choicest expressions of duty and loyalty. To such persons the tone and language of the City remonstrance must appear altogether unjustifiable. But it would be difficult to show, that it is inconsistent with a due respect for monarchy—for a constitutional and limited monarchy at least—that a free people should sometimes address their complaints to the Sovereign in plain and simple language. The City address was, no doubt, exaggerated in its terms, and not altogether accurate in its assertions. Still it was far from being that mere ebullition of civic insolence which courtiers and flatterers would fain have made it out. The City had received provocation. Their first petition, which was not so strongly worded as many other petitions emanating from less important bodies, had not received the common courtesy of an answer. In complaining of undue irresponsible influence under the direction of the Crown, the Corporation did no more than had been done by every minister who had served the Crown since the accession of His Majesty. In saying that the House of Commons was corrupt, and that its proceedings had been illegal, they merely repeated what had been said by men of the highest mark in their places in Parliament; by Lord Chatham in one House, and by Sir George Savile in the other. The question was, whether the country should be governed by a free Parliament, acting under the guidance of known responsible ministers, or by a packed Parliament under the direction of a secret irresponsible cabal. If such is a true statement of the issue between the Crown and the country, then surely it became a body of Englishmen to lay aside courtly

The City's address censured by the Crown.

phrases, and to tell the Sovereign the truth in plain terms. But if there was no corruption in the House of Commons, and no intrigue in the Court, then, indeed, the language of the remonstrance was to the last degree insolent and seditious.

The anger of the Court was extreme; and finding that the movers of the City agitation were not accessible by the ordinary process of the law, they tried to engage Parliament in their design of inflicting vengeance on the petitioners. But even if the Court had been content to let the matter rest, the House of Commons could hardly have passed over imputations of the grossest kind upon their character and title, contained in a paper which had been laid at the foot of the throne. Sir Thomas Clavering, a country gentleman, moved for a copy of the remonstrance; and such was the temper of the majority that some violent proceeding would have been adopted, had it not been for the prudence of Lord North as well as the firmness of the City representatives.*

The anger of the Court.

The principal members of the Corporation were members of the House of Commons. Lord Mayor Beckford and Alderman Trecothick immediately stood up, justified what had been done, and challenged the censure of the House. The Sheriffs, Townshend and Sawbridge, followed to the same purpose. Lord North then interposed, and seeing the danger of provoking a collision with the City, and thus reviving the agitation of the preceding

Angry feelings of the Crown.— Firmness of the City members.

---

* 'Let it be sufficient, when I tell you that I have been menaced with impeachment, sequestration of my estates and banishment; but I was supported by a worthy colleague, one of your representatives, and your two worthy Sheriffs; and I verily believe that without such support, something very hostile and disagreeable to me, your Lord Mayor, would have been the consequence.'— BECKFORD's *Speech to the Livery on announcing the King's Answer to the Address and Remonstrance.* —*Gentleman's Magazine,* vol. xL p. 100.

year, aimed at imparting a calmer tone to the debate.
Contenting himself with a simple denial of parliamentary corruption, he addressed his argument to
that part of the City manifesto which was the least
defensible. To contend that the House of Commons
had ceased *legally* to represent the people, because
they had committed one questionable or even illegal
act, was utterly extravagant. The bonds of law and
order might constantly be in danger of dissolution, if
such a doctrine were to obtain; since the House of
Commons is the last resort of that supreme power
which must exist in every polity. Such vast responsibility can rest only on the ample faith and
dutiful obedience of the great body of the people.
To censure the conduct of the House, even to dispute
the validity of its acts, as was done in the case of the
Middlesex election, was one thing; but to deny the
title of the House of Commons is to deny the title of
Parliament, since the other branches of the legislature
have no power to make binding laws without the
concurrence of the representative body.*

Lord North attacked this point, upon which he
could obtain an easy victory, as if it had been the material point in the remonstrance. He would no doubt have got rid of Clavering's motion, had he been a free agent; but, urged on by the Court, he assented to it, the less reluctantly, perhaps, because he knew it could end in nothing. Wedderburn, in an excellent speech, showed the House that the remonstrance was protected by the express terms of the Bill of Rights; and asked the Government whether they proposed to proceed

<small>Lord North's conduct.—Wedderburn's speech.</small>

---

* Upon this view, that the House of Commons, by their vote on the Middlesex election, had ceased to become a legal assembly, Sheriff Townsend refused to pay the land-tax; and being distrained upon, brought an action of trespass against the bailiff. Lord Mansfield, who tried the cause, told the jury that the only question was, whether there was any government in the country? Yet the verdict was for the defendant.

against the Corporation by quo warranto, after the
precedent of 1679, or whether they meant to bring
in a bill of pains and penalties?

The issue of the debate was for some time doubtful.
If the Opposition had been firm and united, it is said
they might have prevailed;[a] but 'the moderate
Whigs and temperate statesmen' of the Rockingham
school, who regarded the City movement with great
aversion, either stayed away or voted with the Court.
The motion was carried by a large majority. The
debate was renewed when the papers came regularly
before the House, but the matter ended in an empty
resolution.

If the Court were indignant at the City address, the
Westminster re- people of London and its neighbourhood
monstrance. were not less exasperated at the unprecedented style of the royal answer. The City of Westminster immediately sent up a petition, or remonstrance, after the pattern of London. The counties
of Middlesex and Kent did the like. Lord Chatham
Popular move- gave his sanction and support to these
ments sanc- popular movements. He had announced
tioned by Lord his intention of attending at the West-
Chatham. minster meeting, but was prevented by illness. Lord
Rockingham, at his instance, was present at a great
political dinner, given by the Lord Mayor to the
members of the Opposition in both Houses, on the
very day that the resolution of the Commons on the
City remonstrance was sent up to the Lords for their
concurrence.

A few weeks afterwards, Chatham brought in a
Chatham's con- bill, condemnatory of the resolutions of
demnatory bill. the Lower House with respect to the
Middlesex election. The enacting clause was in the
following extraordinary terms:—'That all the adjudications contained in the above-mentioned re-

---

[a] Calcraft to Chatham, March 13.—Chatham Corr.

solutions are arbitrary and illegal, and the same are
and shall be hereby reversed, annulled, *Chatham's*
and made void to all intents and purposes *speech.*
whatsoever.' To suppose that the House of Commons
which had passed the several resolutions recited in
this bill by large majorities only a year previously,
could concur in such an enactment, was to expect a
marvel. Nor could a House of Commons of any
spirit have suffered the hereditary branch of the
legislature to originate a bill which dealt with the
right of election. But the bill was of course introduced only for the purpose of keeping up the
agitation against the Government. Chatham's speech
on the occasion was, according to his practice in opposition, highly aggressive and inflammatory. He accused the King, almost in plain terms, as the author
of the proceedings which he asked the House to pronounce 'arbitrary and illegal.' He was called to
order, but he refused either to retract his words or to
explain away their meaning. Lord Mansfield, without venturing expressly to defend the *Mansfield's*
doctrine of the Lower House, opposed the *speech.*
bill on the ground that it professed to interfere in a
matter which belonged exclusively to the Commons.
They are the only judges of questions arising out of
contested elections, and from their judgments there
was no appeal. This called up his rival, Camden,
who supported his friend and patron, Chatham, in a
speech more declamatory than argumentative. He
also alluded in a significant manner to *Camden's*
the 'secret influence' which had decided *speech.*
that 'Wilkes should not sit,' and repeated the ominous
allusions to Charles the First and Hampden, which
formed part of every speech and paper on this subject.
After the bill had been rejected, Lord
Chatham desired that the House might *Chatham pro-
poses a vote of*
be summoned for the following day, when *censure.*
he intended to submit a motion of great importance.

This was a vote of censure on the King's answer to the City remonstrance, by way of retaliation for the censure which Parliament had passed on the remonstrance itself, at the instance of the Court. Chatham, as had been his practice this session, used language of the most provoking and insulting character; but the ministers, relying on their secure majority, prudently avoided the hazardous ground of debate. The veteran leader of Opposition, not checked by these repeated failures, nor by the still more disheartening coldness and reserve on the part of his Whig allies, persevered in bringing forward motion after motion. A few days after his last discomfiture, and in spite of the contrary opinion of Lord Rockingham, he moved an address to the Crown for a dissolution of Parliament. In order to frustrate the object of these motions, which was to keep up the excitement of the public mind, the Government rigidly enforced the standing order for the exclusion of strangers on the day when Chatham's motion was to be debated. The motion was negatived without a division.

Chatham moves an address to the Crown.

While the Court, the Parliament, and the country, were engaged in these angry discussions about the Middlesex election, a far more momentous subject was comparatively neglected. The persecution of Wilkes was an unworthy condescension on the part of the Sovereign; the substitution of Luttrell for Wilkes was a violent and unlawful act on the part of the House of Commons. But, after all, the constitution was really in no great danger by these proceedings. The time had gone by when a King of England could ruin an obnoxious subject. The oppression of Wilkes, so far from ruining that worthless adventurer, had made his fortune. The House of Commons had no plan of usurping the elective franchise. Their corruption, indeed, had a tendency to subvert the institution of

Neglect of the American question.

Parliament; but even this was a remote danger. The real, the pressing danger, which menaced the integrity of the Empire, its wealth, prosperity, and power, was the wide-spreading disaffection of its American provinces. But though no English statesman took so wise and liberal a view of the Colonial question as Chatham, American independence was the last word to answer the purpose of party opposition. The people of this country believed that the colonists were their inferiors, and were content that the Government should use measures of coercion to bring them to submission.*

Upon this point, the King and the people were of one mind. There was hardly any public man of credit who did not agree in the expediency of discontinuing American taxation. Substantially, this was done by the proposal to repeal the whole of Townshend's Act, with the exception of the tea duty, which, valueless to the revenue, was retained only, as we have seen, at the instance of the King, for the purpose of taking away the whole virtue, as well as grace, of the concession. Nevertheless, it is probable that Parliament would for once have taken a wise and independent course by repealing the act entirely, had not Lord North assured the House of Commons, on the authority of some letters which he read, that the colonists were about to give way, and to abandon their non-importation agreements.†

Proposed repeal of Townshend's Act.

This unfortunate assertion was more likely to have had weight with the House than the argument by which it was followed. 'To what purpose,' said the minister, 'should we repeal this statute while we

---

* I may be reminded that the Assembly of North Carolina sent 1500*l.* to the Society for the Support of the Bill of Rights. But the democratic doctrines of that Society met with little support.

† Sir Denis le Marchant's note to Walpole's History, vol. iv. p. 96.

retain the Declaratory Act? The colonies would continue discontented as long as this country asserted the right of imposing taxation upon them.' But what had been the consequence of the repeal of the Stamp Act? The agitation of the colony immediately subsided. Nor did it make the least difference that the removal of the substantial grievance was accompanied by an empty affirmation of the right to inflict it. The Kings of England, for centuries after they had lost their French possessions, continued to style themselves Kings of France; but this vain title was never for a moment regarded by the French people, than whom none are more distinguished by high spirit and jealousy of their national honour. So the Americans did not consider the Declaratory Act to have been passed wih a view to future aggression upon themselves, but simply to gratify the pride of the mother-country; and as such, they treated it with indifference. But the tea duty was regarded by the people of Boston in the same light as the tax of twenty shillings upon Hampden was regarded by the people of England.

Notwithstanding Lord North's endeavour to reduce the question to one of merely commercial expediency, there was a visible inclination to support the amendment for including tea among the articles to be exempted from duty, and thus repealing Townshend's Act altogether. Grenville justified the policy which it had been his ill-fortune to originate, but declined to vote on the question before the House. Lord Barrington, the Secretary-at-War, and a staunch adherent of the King's party, also declined to vote. The amendment was lost; but a minority of 142 out of 346 was sufficient to show that the sense of the House was opposed to the policy of the Government. It is worthy of remark, that this question, though at length fully recognised, in political society at least,

as one of the gravest importance, did not attract
nearly so large a concourse of members as any of the
matters of party interest which had been agitated
during the session. Whenever a vote was taken
which involved the fate of the Government, more
than four hundred members had divided. The
largest House which had been collected this Parliament was on Dowdeswell's motion to disfranchise the
revenue officers, when four hundred and fifty-one
members voted. Of so much more consequence did
it seem, that the influence of the Crown over the
House of Commons should be maintained and increased, than that the integrity of the Empire should
be preserved.

The same day on which this discussion took place
—nay, at the very hour when the House
was assembled, and while Lord North was *The Revolution breaks out in Boston.*
persuading them that America was about
to give way, the first blood of the Revolution was
flowing in the streets of Boston. The
bitterest animosity had, from the first, ex- *Affray between the soldiers and the citizens.*
isted between the people of Boston and
the two regiments quartered there, for the purpose
of overawing them. The soldiers treated the inhabitants as rebels, and were in their turn regarded
as the hateful instruments of tyranny and oppression.
Nor was this feeling confined to the lower sort. The
traders, merchants, and even the magistrates, who
were drawn from those classes, were ever ready to
show their dislike to the soldiers, and to punish them
with rigour for every act of license or infringement of
the law which they might commit.* The populace

---

* Colonel Mackay, who spoke from personal knowledge, derived from recent military service in the colony, stated in the House of Commons, that the clamour against the troops was confined to a few individuals of no great importance. And as a proof that they were not unpopular, he mentioned that 60,000*l.* had been spent in the town in consequence of their being quartered in town.

insulted them whenever they appeared in the streets; and nothing but the patience and forbearance enjoined and taught by military discipline prevented a bloody quarrel. Frequent affrays, indeed, had taken place, but none of these had resulted in bloodshed. At length, on the evening of the 5th of March, upon one of the numerous causes of provocation which had been daily occurring, a conflict took place between some soldiers and some townspeople. The latter raised an alarm, crowds rushed into the streets calling upon the inhabitants to defend their houses. The officer on duty having reason to apprehend that the Custom House was to be attacked, called out a serjeant's party, and accompanied them himself to the scene of tumult. Captain Preston seems to have behaved with the temper and self-possession which a British officer usually displays in scenes of civil commotion: but the soldiers, exasperated at the ill-usage which they had received, fired, as they will sometimes do on such occasions, without the orders of their commanding officer. The result was that four persons were killed, and a few others wounded. The populace fled; but shortly afterwards reassembled in still greater numbers; and the troops would again have fired, had they not been restrained by the positive orders of Preston. The governor and the colonel commanding the regiment were shortly on the spot; and, the men being dismissed to their quarters, the people were induced to disperse.

The malcontent party, as was to be expected, made the most of this unfortunate affair. A meeting of

The farmers and tradesmen could now get a good price and ready money for their produce and goods; therefore, so far from being discontented at the presence of the military, they were delighted to have them. There always are an abundance of 'respectable' people, as the gallant Colonel termed them, ready, under any circumstances, to welcome soldiers or any other class of persons who circulate money. The English farmer, for example, is generally an advocate for war, because it brings high prices.

the inhabitants was held at the Town Hall, and language of the most exciting description was uttered. A deputation waited on the Lieutenant-Governor Hutchinson, demanding that the troops should be removed out of the town; and this the Governor, with the unanimous advice of the Council, consented to do. The two regiments were sent to Fort William; and the soldiers who had fired the fatal shots, together with the commanding officer Preston, were committed to take their trial for murder. It was generally believed that the fate of these unhappy men was prejudged; and that nothing but the prerogative of the Crown could save them either from a judicial sentence, or from popular fury. It was doubted even whether a counsel could be found to undertake the odious task of conducting their defence. But none of these anticipations were verified. The accused found an advocate in one of the popular leaders. It was John Adams, the future President of that great Republic which his patriotism and ability did much to create, who at the call of professional duty, never for a moment hesitated to hazard his political prospects by defending the men who were charged with having shed the blood of his fellow-citizens. The Boston jury also, to their honour be it recorded, acquitted all the prisoners on the capital charge, convicting only two of them of the minor offence of manslaughter. And the people quietly acquiesced in the decision. Very different from this was the conduct of the people, both high and low, who took part in the proceedings against the Scotch soldiers charged with murder in one of the riots arising out of the Middlesex election. Not only were the men convicted by a harsh sentence, but the court of justice was disgraced by the savage clamour of the exulting populace. And the Government, as if emulating the prejudice and passion of the mob, were not content with giving the criminals a free

Immediate results of the tumult.

pardon to which they were perhaps entitled, but must confer upon them honours and rewards to which they certainly had no claim.

But though the people of Boston allowed public justice to take its even course, the angry excitement did not subside, and the unhappy affair of the 5th of March was designated as a 'massacre.' Still, even Massachusetts, though the principal seat of agitation, seemed far from a rupture with the mother-country. The non-importation compact had been reluctantly entered into by several of the states; and after some months' experience of the privation inflicted by the suspension of commercial intercourse with Great Britain, many were disposed to abandon the league. Rhode Island had already withdrawn, and the more important colony of New York was about to do the like. The arrival of the Act of Repeal was only wanted to sever the last tie which held the confederacy together. A trade worth five millions annually seemed too great a price to pay for political principle; and had it not been for the firmness of one province, the day of American independence might have been long postponed. The people of Massachusetts adhered to their determination of offering an uncompromising opposition to British policy; and these sentiments prevailed not merely in Boston, but throughout the whole province.* The non-importation compact was enforced with as much rigour as if it had been law. They would suffer none to infringe it; ships containing what they called contraband goods, that is, all imports from Great Britain, except certain enumerated goods, were sent back without being permitted to land their cargoes. The importers remonstrated that they should be ruined; the answer was that a ship which brought the plague would be excluded; much more one which brought British

* Lieutenant-Governor Hutchinson to Lord Hillsborough, April 27. 1770.

goods. The revenue officers in vain endeavoured to
enforce the laws. A tide-waiter having, in the discharge of his duty, seized a small coasting-vessel,
containing a few casks of sugar, was seized, stripped,
tarred, and feathered, and in this state paraded
through the town for several hours. The magistrates
never interfered to suppress these disorders. Some
of them were kept back by sympathy; others were
deterred by fear. Even the Council, which had
hitherto always supported the Government against
the Assembly, now refused their sanction to any
measures for the restoration and maintenance of its
authority. It had been hoped that the removal of
Bernard, the obnoxious governor, and the appointment of Hutchinson, a native of the province and a
man of ability, in his room, might have mitigated
discontent. But it was evident that no secondary
measure of conciliation could be of any avail. There
remained but one alternative to England; that of
giving up the claim to tax the colonies, or giving up
the colonies themselves.

A few days before the prorogation the affairs of
Ireland were brought under the consideration of the House of Commons. It so *Affairs of Ireland.*
happened that, at this time, a dispute had arisen between the Parliament of Ireland and the Government,
very similar to that which had almost ended in a
rupture between the colonial assemblies of legislature
and the same supreme authority. The Irish legislature had been originally constituted in the reign of
Henry the Seventh, on the same model as the English Parliament, with this difference, that, instead of
originating measures of legislation, they could only
entertain those projects of law which had been approved of by the King in council and certified under
the Great Seal.* This rule was so far relaxed by an
act of Philip and Mary, that, instead of waiting

---

* The practice of the House of Commons, of which the earliest record is the 22nd of March, 1603, to commence the business of the

until all the measures for the session were prepared, the Parliament were permitted to commence business as soon as the draft of a single bill had been certified. This bill was usually a money bill, and in time came to be considered a mere matter of form; but in the first Parliament holden in Ireland after the Revolution, two money bills having been presented in the usual manner, under the Great Seal, the House of Commons took that opportunity so favourable to such pretensions, to assert their right of originating all bills *of supply*. One of the bills, which was for an additional excise, they allowed to be read, in consideration of the pressing exigencies of the public service; but they desired that it should not be drawn into a precedent. The other bill they rejected, on the ground that it had not originated with themselves; and they caused a resolution to be inserted in their journals to that effect. This pretension was, however, severely censured by the viceroy, and condemned by the judges both of England and Ireland. The Parliament was prorogued and never suffered to meet again. Its successor was more submissive, and affirmed an entry in the journals of the date of 1614 by which the right of the English Government to initiate their legislation was expressly recognized. The right, though often questioned, was not again practically resisted until 1764, when a motion for expunging from the journals the entry of 1614 was made and carried; but the influence of the Government, which, in Ireland at least, was that of the grossest corruption, caused this vote to be rescinded.

Duration of the Irish Parliament.

session by reading a bill, is supposed by Hatsell to be a claim of right on the part of the Commons to proceed in the first place upon any matter which they think material, without being limited to give a preference to the subjects contained in the King's Speech.

—HATSELL, *Precedents*, vol. ii. p. 58.—' Before Her Majesty's Speech is reported, some bill is read a first time *pro formâ*.'— *Rules, Orders and Proceedings of the House of Commons*, Rule 34. —1854.

Efforts, also, were made to promote the independence of Parliament by fixing the period of its duration, the Irish Parliament being indissoluble save by the demise or pleasure of the Crown. At length, after frequent miscarriages, a bill was carried in 1767 for terminating its existence at the octennial period. In the ensuing session, the claim to originate money bills was revived; a bill of this description coming down as usual from the Executive Government, was rejected on the ground of privilege; but, instead of bringing the question to an issue in a parliamentary way, by withholding supply altogether, the Irish Commons, with characteristic improvidence, voted, of their own free will, a supply for two years, being just the amount which would enable the Government to dispense with their attendance until the regular time for their being reassembled. And this was the course which the Government pursued. Accepting the money voted, the Lord-Lieutenant severely reprimanded the Parliament for the violation of the law in rejecting the bill sent down by the Privy Council; and, having ordered his protest to that effect to be entered on the journals, he immediately prorogued them.

This arbitrary measure, although in accordance with precedent, caused much excitement in Ireland, and was the subject of a party motion in the English House of Commons. The debate was remarkable for the absence of sympathy with the real grievance of the Irish legislature. Not a word appears to have been said with respect to the denial of that first and essential privilege of a representative body, the entire and exclusive right, namely, of taxation. But the Government was denounced by the Opposition for having *prorogued*, when they ought to have *dissolved*, a Parliament which had a great amount of important business before it. They were, no doubt, censurable for having taken a course which postponed the whole legislation of the country; but this consideration was insignificant, in comparison with the paramount importance of the principle at issue between the Irish Parliament and the Crown. The House of Commons at Westminster, however, regarded the House of Commons at Dublin in the same light as the House of Burgesses at Virginia, or the Assembly at Boston. The provincial character was common to all; nor could the Irish Assembly be permitted to advance pretensions inconsistent with due subordination to the Imperial legislature. Walsingham's motion, though supported by Grenville and Burke, excited little interest; and was negatived by a large majority in a thin House.

CHAPTER XII.

DISUNION OF THE OPPOSITION—ANOTHER CITY ADDRESS—DEATH AND CHARACTER OF GRENVILLE—OF LORD GRANBY—OF THE DUKE OF BEDFORD—THE FALKLAND ISLANDS—PROSECUTION OF THE PRINTERS—QUARREL BETWEEN THE TWO HOUSES—SHOREHAM ELECTION.

THE session of Parliament closed on the 19th of May, leaving the Government uninjured by the vigorous efforts of the Opposition in both Houses, as well as out of doors. Nor is this result by any means unaccountable. There was no frank or cordial intercourse between the leaders of the parties in alliance against the Court. Rockingham, proud of his position as chief of the Whigs and bigoted to the tradition of Government by the great Revolution-families, was jealous of the predominance of Chatham. Himself a rigid Whig, he probably regarded Chatham as unsound in doctrine, and in some measure as an upstart who ought not to take too great a lead in affairs which appertained to hereditary statesmen. Rockingham was certainly much scandalised by the irregular connection which his brilliant ally had formed. He had no toleration for persons who formed associations and presumed to deal with grievances independently of Whig direction and control.* Chatham, on the other hand,

Mutual dissensions of the Opposition.

---

* Burke, in his letters to Lord Rockingham—and he writes, too, evidently to please his patron—rails at the 'Bill of Rights people,' their violence, rashness, and wickedness, calls them villains, traitors, and so forth. Yet these people had said no more than great Whigs had said, and had done no more than had been done with the approbation of the Whig party. But it was one

did not dissemble his contempt for the narrow views and decorous moderation of the Whig aristocracy; while the arrogant and dictatorial tone which he affected, had always proved peculiarly offensive to, and throughout his political life had gone far to alienate from him, that proud and exclusive race. Again, the Rockingham party bore no good will to the Grenvilles. We have seen how coldly the earnest overtures of Lord Temple had been received by the agent of that party the year before. A political connection which consisted of a single family, and that too of recent origin, had no right to set itself up, and court alliances on a footing of equality with the great houses. Neither were the Opposition in any harmony with regard to the great political questions of the day. On the Middlesex election, the Whigs would not be led by Chatham; and the Grenvilles seemed to have troubled themselves very little about that matter. On the Colonial question, Grenville was of one opinion, Chatham of another, and Rockingham of a third.

The Government, on the other hand, possessed the great advantage which is derived from unity and decision of purpose. The King was, as ever, determined to resist the domineering rule of the Whig lords; to maintain the present Parliament; to uphold the decision of the Commons in the Middlesex election; and to chastise American revolt. He found a minister with no fixed opinions on any of these subjects, but faithful to his service, and possessed of tact and ability to carry on his business. The fate of the administration was for some time doubtful; but the patience and courage of the minister, his good humour and address, backed

Determination of the King.

thing, it seemed, for the county of York to petition under the auspices of the Marquis of Rockingham, and another for the county of Middlesex to petition under the direction of Alderman Sawbridge or Serjeant Glynn.

by the hearty support of the Crown, at length prevailed. The time-servers who decide the fate of so many Cabinets, at length gave in their adhesion; and at the end of its first session, Lord North's government showed signs of that longevity which, unhappily for the Empire, it was destined to attain.

A few days after the prorogation, the City, unwilling to submit patiently to the rebuke which they had received from the mouth of the Sovereign, resolved to go up with another address, expressive of their discontent. And the Lord Mayor, in anticipation of the answer which he would probably receive, prepared himself with a reply. The address, though resolute in its tone, was worded in decent, and even courtly terms. The King replied briefly that he had done no more than his duty in censuring the remonstrance. And here properly the audience should have terminated. The Lord Mayor, as the chief of the Corporation, had presented the address which they had voted. Having done so, he had fulfilled his duty; and his authority, in that particular, was at an end. According to ancient precedent, he had demanded and obtained, as of right, the privilege of presenting the City address to the King on the throne. But he had no right to add anything to that address. He had come determined, however, to reply upon the King. No sooner therefore had His Majesty spoken, than Beckford asked permission to say something more, and at once proceeded in a set speech * to entreat a

---

* It was written by Horne Tooke. Adolphus's History, vol. i. p. 438. 'Mr. Maltby says that Horne Tooke told him, that he with others was waiting at the Mansion House when Beckford returned from St. James's—that he was asked what he had said? and his answer was that he was so flurried, that he could not remember any part of it. "But," said Horne Tooke, "it is necessary that a speech should be given to the public," and accordingly he went into a room and wrote the one which was attributed to Beckford. Mr. Maltby said that Horne Tooke invariably men-

more favourable answer; and to denounce as a violator of the public peace and a traitor to the constitution, any person who should attempt by false insinuations to alienate His Majesty's affections from his subjects in general, and from the City of London in particular.

The King took no notice of this extraordinary address; and the Lord Mayor with the other members of the deputation were allowed, as usual, to kiss hands and withdraw.

Death of Beckford. This incident was for the time a subject of much discussion. Courtiers could only regard the conduct of the Mayor as a shocking breach of etiquette. The Whigs did not approve of it. The more uncompromising asserters of popular rights, with Chatham at their head, were loud in their applause. Beckford, dying a few weeks afterwards, the Corporation caused his statue to be erected in the Guildhall, with his speech to the King engraven in letters of gold on the pedestal.

Death of Grenville. His character. Other men of greater note also died in the course of this year. Grenville, whose health had been failing for many months, expired on the same day that Parliament reassembled for the usual autumnal session. His vacant seat must have given rise to some emotion in that House, of which he had been a constant attendant for thirty years, and one of its most important members during the greater part of that time. He left behind him some men his superiors in eloquence and address, but none who equalled him in knowledge of parliamentary law and public business. These are qualities more highly valued in the House of Commons than the most brilliant talents without such attainments.

---

tioned the speech as his composition; and that some years since he [Maltby] had a request from the Corporation of the City to give them some information on the point.'—*Note, Correspondence of Gray and Mason.*

Charles Townshend could always carry away the applause and admiration of the House; but Grenville was looked up to as its leader. Indeed, of all the public men who filled the office of chief minister in the House of Commons during his time, there was none—Pitt of course being out of question—who obtained so great a share of influence as Grenville. Nor did he owe this influence to any great superiority of talents or accomplishments. In the important art of secret management, he was far excelled both by Pelham and Fox; in amenity of manners by Conway; in debating power by Lord North. Even in respect of connection he was weaker than any of his competitors. Pelham was backed by the unparalleled parliamentary interest of his brother, the Duke of Newcastle. Fox and North were supported by the Court, and Conway by the great Rockingham party; whilst Grenville during the greater part of the time that he filled the most prominent place in the administration, was at variance with his family, and was opposed by the Court. But his unremitting application to public business, the fulness and accuracy of information with which he spoke; and, it must be added, the honest and consistent course which he pursued, gave a stability to his character, which that of no other contemporary statesman can be said to have possessed.

His mind was of the common capacity. He had no idea of public opinion, save as expressed by its legitimate organ, the House of Commons.* His notions of public policy were strictly regulated by law and precedent. Hence it was, that finding the taxation of the colonies by the parent state was neither contrary to their charter nor to parliamentary precedent, he submitted

Grenville of no extraordinary ability.

---

* 'Sir, the Parliament of England is in all cases supreme; I know no other law; I know no other rule.'—*Speech on Repeal of Townshend's Act, March 5, 1770.*—CAVENDISH *Debates.*

his measure of colonial taxation to the House of
Commons, and, having obtained its sanction, he never
was able to understand how there could be another
side to the question. In like manner, he prosecuted
Wilkes as he would have prosecuted any other seditious libeller; and, afterwards, was the most strenuous as well as the ablest, defender of Wilkes's seat,
when the House exceeded their privilege and tres-
passed on the domain of positive law. In either case,
he was guided by a strict sense of right and justice,
regardless alike of popular clamour or applause. At
the commencement of the reign he supported the
policy of peace, because he thought, with the leaders
of the Whig party, that the war had accomplished its
objects; and on that important point he did not
hesitate to relinquish the powerful political connection of his kinsman Temple, and Pitt. On the other
hand, he submitted to be displaced rather than lend
himself to the foolish precipitation of Bute in concluding a treaty, and was prepared to give up office
altogether rather than be a party to a peace which
did not secure to his country the benefits and advantages she had a right to expect from her arduous
and triumphant struggle. A man of high spirit
would not, indeed, have submitted to the indignity
of being set aside for a rival, who was thought more
fitted for a particular service than himself. But
Grenville was measured and limited in his sense of
self-respect, as well as in every other part of his conduct; and he thought he had made a sufficient sacrifice to his independence by quitting his place in the
Cabinet for a place of subordinate importance. The
same decent consistency is maintained throughout
his character. Essentially an honest man, he had no
conception of the exalted probity of Pitt, and, though
incorrupt himself, was not too nice to dabble in
that foul channel of corruption on which public
business had been borne during his experience of

Parliament; one of his grounds of quarrel with Bute being that he had not been permitted that peculiar confidential intercourse with members which was then considered necessary by a leader of the House of Commons.* For the rest, he was a frugal manager of the public revenues; nor would he consent to what he considered any, the smallest, misappropriation of the public funds, whether for the gratification of the Sovereign,† or the meanest of his servants. Grenville's private life was regulated with the same method as his public conduct. Respectable in all his domestic relations, he had from his youth been remarkable, in a dissolute age, for the decorum of his manners. In one respect, at least, his practice is deserving of imitation by public men. He made it his rule, whether in or out of office, to live within a private fortune by no means ample; and thus he was enabled to preserve that independence so valuable to a man embarked in public life, but which can be maintained only by a due regard to private economy. Grenville was only fifty-eight years of age at his decease.

About the same time, the hand of death fell upon another person of less political note, but of wider fame, the brave and generous Granby. Born in the highest rank, and heir to great estates, this amiable nobleman was doomed to experience, during many years of a life which terminated in middle age, the bitter effects of

---

* Diary, Grenville Papers, vol. i. There is no ground for supposing that he ever descended to the grossness of direct money bribes. What he meant was, that he desired to have the dispensation of patronage; but as Grenville was not privy to the Court plan of secret influence, the disposal of places and of the secret service fund could not be entrusted to his hands.

† I have already mentioned his refusal of the King's request to purchase a plot of ground overlooking the gardens of Buckingham House, and which might have been obtained for 20,000*l.* Grosvenor Place is now built upon this site. He was equally strict with regard to petty peculation, or waste and extravagance in expenditure.

early profusion and improvidence. Having adopted the profession of arms, he distinguished himself in the German war; and especially at the great battle of Minden, being the second in command of the British cavalry, he had, by his promptitude, endeavoured to retrieve the opportunity which was almost lost by the cowardice or hesitation of his superior officer, Lord George Sackvile, the general officer in chief command. Towards the close of the war, he held the chief command of the British forces in Germany, but without an opportunity of rendering any extraordinary service. He was the idol of the army, with whom he always shared the dangers of the field and the privations of the camp. On one occasion, when they were in bad quarters, he provided for the soldiers at his own cost, and kept an open table for his officers. By these means, as well as by a too lavish and indiscriminate bounty, and not through selfish indulgence, he became involved in pecuniary embarrassment. His qualities were such, indeed, as in his station render a man beloved rather than respected. Easiness of access, open-handed charity, facility of disposition, may, when carried to an extreme, cease to be virtues, but they will always obtain the love and admiration of the common people. Granby was long remembered as the model of a brave soldier, and a kind English nobleman. And, to this day, many a village sign-board exhibits that open countenance and bald head which were well known in every parish nearly a hundred years ago. As a politician, he had no weight but what he derived from his high rank, his military reputation, and his extensive popularity. Chatham, however, knew the value of such a partisan; and when desirous of breaking up the Grafton administration, there was no man, not even Camden himself, whom he showed so much anxiety to detach from the Government as the Marquis of Granby.

Of a very opposite character was John, Duke of Bedford, who also paid the debt of nature about this time. If Granby was the most popular man in England, Bedford may be described as the public man of all others most odious to the people. Bute, during his short career, was reviled by the populace; Grenville, and other statesmen, had experienced their displeasure; but none of these had been pursued with the enduring obloquy which through life assailed the great Whig peer. When the Duke returned from Paris, after concluding the treaty of peace, he was charged, in conjunction with Bute, with having sold the country.* Two years later, he was accused of insulting the distress of the silk-weavers, and his house in London would have been torn down, had it not been guarded by a strong military force. At a subsequent period, he narrowly escaped with his life when he went down into Devonshire, where he had great estates, to dissuade that county from joining in the petitions to the Crown on the subject of the Middlesex election. Popularity is hardly any criterion of a statesman's merit; and it is not to be supposed that Bedford was justly obnoxious to all this odium. Nevertheless, it was not altogether without cause that hatred and contempt had sullied the once dear and honoured name of Russell. The Duke of Bedford, as Secretary of State, had dictated the pusillanimous treaty of Aix la Chapelle, or had assented to it as dictated by the enemy. The war, it is true, had been foolishly commenced, but that was no reason why it should be brought to an ignominious conclusion. It might not have been practicable to obtain the entire renunci-

Death of the Duke of Bedford.

---

* Prior to the Duke of Bedford's departure for his embassy he was hooted by the mob, and as he was getting into the boat at Brighton that was to carry him to the packet, some one in the crowd called out, 'It is not the first time he has turned his back on old England.'—ROCKINGHAM *Memoirs*, vol. i. p. 30.

ation of the Right of Search, which was often exercised in a manner so vexatious to British commerce; but hardly an attempt was made to procure a modification of its rigour, or a limit to its exercise. The island of Cape Breton, which had become a conquest of the British arms, and was an important acquisition to the British possessions in North America, was unconditionally restored to France. Nay, so unnecessarily anxious had Bedford been to conciliate the belligerents, that he withdrew two frigates which had been sent on a voyage of discovery into the South American waters, because the jealousy of the Spanish minister was alarmed lest Great Britain should establish some settlement in those seas. The same spirit was displayed in the subsequent negotiation of the treaty of Paris, which the Duke of Bedford conducted in person. He had been so eager to conclude the peace that even Bute had checked his ignoble ardour; and he suffered his parasite, Rigby, to write him letters, expressing hopes that some disaster might befall the British arms. When he was conducting the negotiations at Paris as Plenipotentiary for Great Britain, Egremont, the Secretary of State, frequently expressed his disapprobation of the unworthy tone of his diplomacy, and at length the King himself thought it necessary to lay his express commands upon the ambassador to demand some terms in consideration of the Havannah, a most important conquest, and one which had tasked the military skill and energy employed more than any other service during the war. The Duke of Bedford showed the wisdom and forethought of a statesman in opposing the ignorant clamour of the silk-weavers for protective laws; but he showed, at the same time, a cruel insensibility to the sufferings of those poor people. On the question of the Middlesex election, he deserted the Whig party and Whig doctrine, and joined the Court in assailing the fundamental principles of constitutional law. The same arbitrary temper directed the whole of his public conduct. Nothing daunted by the detestation in which he was held by his own countrymen, he seemed to court the resentment of the colonial people likewise. The revenue laws, the Declaratory Act, the suspension of the legislation of New York, were all acts of power; but they were acts passed in the face of the world, and of which the Imperial Parliament assumed the full responsibility. But it was to Bedford's malignant research that the Government were indebted for the discovery of an act passed by the timid and obsequious Parliament of Henry the Eighth, to serve his tyrannical purpose; and it was this obsolete statute, long since forgotten in the prevalence of better maxims of Government, that the Duke of Bedford sought to turn against the rising liberties of the American people. He would have deprived the colonists of that cherished maxim of English freedom, that every man shall be tried by his peers and fellow countrymen. It is true that this scheme, though adopted, was never put in force: but the attempt, or the threat of employing it, did more to alienate the colonies than any stretch of power by which they had hitherto suffered; for it showed that the parent state could be vindictive as well as oppressive, and that they could no longer feel any security against a fresh attempt upon their privileges, whenever an opportunity should occur.

The memory of the Duke of Bedford has derived some benefit from the reaction produced by the foul slanders of Junius; but he will ultimately be written in the page of history as a man who exercised an evil influence on the fortunes of his country. If an individual in a private station, who squanders the gifts of providence in mere selfish gratification, is to be held responsible to society, how much more so must that man be, who, placed in a great and commanding position, regards nothing but his own wilful pride, and the personal aggrandisement of his retainers! Yet such was the case with the Duke of Bedford. The measures of public policy which he advanced may have been matters on which a fair difference of opinion could exist; but he was a great English noble, the possessor of a historic name, the head of a powerful party in the State. He found the Crown openly avowing an intention, and actively organising a system of governing independently of political parties, and in a manner hardly consistent with the principles of the Revolution. The Duke of Bedford might have frustrated this design. Had he come forward at the time when there was a disposition on the part of other eminent men to dismiss the petty jealousies by which they had for so many years been divided, he might have been a principal agent in consolidating a great national party which would have revived public spirit, and spared the nation many calamities which she afterwards endured. But instead of taking a course worthy of his name and his ability, the head of the house of Russell was intent only on securing the preponderance of his own weight in the Government. What that Government should be was a secondary object. His first desire was, that it should be constituted principally of his nominees. The Court might take what line of policy they pleased, the Whigs might be a scattered and disbanded corps, the Duke of Bedford would not take the responsibility of office upon himself, but must have his Gowers, his Weymouths, and his Rigbys in administration. Those men, whom his interest had placed in their offices, retained them afterwards against his will; and the Duke, before his death, found himself deserted by the party, for whose sake he had abandoned the higher duties of his position.

Since the conclusion of the treaty of Paris, it was generally believed that the 'Family Alliance'

were only waiting for a convenient opportunity to
avenge their disgrace by provoking a new
war. Every movement of France and
Spain was, therefore, jealously watched in this country. In 1768, the French, partly by intrigue and
partly by gold, had obtained possession of Corsica, a
dependency of the Genoese republic; an acquisition
of no real value, and which did not affect, in the
least degree, the European balance of power. The
island itself, as it could not maintain its independence, was better off under the protection of a powerful and generous monarchy, than under the dominion
of a petty Italian state. The English ambassador at
Paris was, however, instructed to make a strong remonstrance against this addition to the French territory; and Choiseul, not being prepared for war, it is
thought, would have abandoned the project rather
than hazard a rupture with England. But Lord
Mansfield, who was then at Paris, having spoken with
ridicule of his country going to war on such a frivolous pretence, the representations of the British
minister were disregarded; and Corsica, after a spirited
resistance by a band of patriots in arms, was annexed
to the French Empire.

But an event of a more serious character took
place in the following year. It is said,
that the treaty of Paris was accompanied
by a secret article between France and Spain, in which
it was agreed that, at some future period, the war
should be renewed by an attack on the Falkland
Islands. Why such an intention should have been
entertained, or, if entertained, why it should have
been the subject of a secret article, does not very
clearly appear; since the Falkland Islands were not,
at that time, occupied by the English, or by any
other Power; nor was there any reason to suppose
that their occupation by France or Spain would have
been considered by England as a matter in which she

was much concerned. These dreary, inhospitable islands had been visited at different periods by the English, Dutch, and French; each of whom claimed them to the extent of giving them a name; but neither nation had taken any further step to confirm its possession of such barren and useless territory. The English Government, in 1748, had sent out an exploring squadron, with instructions to visit the Falkland Islands; but on some objection being raised by Spain, the expedition was withdrawn. At length, in 1764, one of these islands was occupied in the name of the King of France, but immediately afterwards ceded to Spain, to which, if it was to be occupied at all, it was of more importance, as being near the Strait of Magellan and the Spanish provinces in South America. But it happened, that later in the same year the British Government sent out an expedition under Captain Byron, who took possession of an adjacent island forming part of the same group, in the name of his Sovereign; and this officer having carried home an exaggerated account of the value of the acquisition, a small fort was built, and a garrison was established there.

An encounter soon took place between the settlers from the two nations. The Spanish governor affected to be ignorant of the pretensions of Great Britain; while the English captain, on the other hand, required the Spaniard to evacuate territory which belonged to His Britannic Majesty. After a great deal of recrimination, the dispute ended in the expulsion of the British by a superior Spanish force.

For this insult and aggression, as it was termed, though in point of fact England was the aggressor, the British Government peremptorily demanded redress from the Catholic King. A correspondence was commenced both at London and Madrid, and extended, as usual, to a great length. The English and French Govern-

Satisfaction demanded by England.

ments made active preparations for hostilities; but it proved that Spain was in no condition for war. Her finances were unable to support a war establishment; and her regular military force was only sufficient to maintain internal order in that distracted and decaying empire.* Choiseul, indeed, was still as ever intent on a warlike policy; but Louis the Fifteenth, sunk in debauchery, was averse to a policy which might disturb his voluptuous repose. A change also, of more importance than that of a minister, took place about this time at the Court of Versailles. A new mistress came into power. Pompadour, who had been the immediate instigator of the Seven Years' War, was dead; and Du Barri had succeeded to her place. This lady was a friend of England. She was even connected by marriage with an Irish nobleman.† Still these might not have been sufficient inducements for her interference to prevent a war, had not the Duke de Choiseul, too confident in his power, committed a mistake similar to that which Frederick the Great had made with regard to Madame du Barri's predecessor. He treated the mistress with contempt instead of conciliating her favour. The consequence was, that the long administration of Choiseul was terminated by a *lettre de cachet*; and the Court of Madrid, finding all hope of support from France at an end, immediately terminated the negotiation with the English Government by agreeing to the terms which the latter had prescribed. The act of the Spanish commandant who had expelled the British was disavowed, and the Falkland Islands were ceded to Great Britain. The Government of Spain, to save their credit and the

---

* Despatches of Mr. Harris, the English minister at Madrid. Malmesbury Corr. vol. i.

† It was required by the rigour of Court etiquette, that the French mistress should be a married woman. A husband was therefore found for the new favourite (who happened to be a common courtesan) in the person of the Count du Barri, who claimed relationship with Lord Barrymore.

pride of the nation, gave out that they had received a verbal assurance from England that she would evacuate the Falkland Islands in two months. But though Lord Weymouth, who was not a very skilful diplomatist,* was not unlikely to have intimated something to this effect in his conversation with Masserano, the ambassador at London, there certainly was not, as the Opposition maintained, any secret article of such an import.

While the negotiations relative to this affair were in progress, loud clamours were raised against the Ministry as if they had compromised the national honour by failing to resort to immediate hostilities. The people were in that temper that they were ready to put the worst construction on every act of Government; and as self-interest and corruption seemed to govern the conduct of each individual engaged in public affairs, the vilest motives were assigned to almost every doubtful or disastrous act of policy which had been adopted during later years. The Government were not in this instance, however, worthy of blame. They were bound to demand reparation for the insult offered to the British flag, but there was no case of war until the Catholic King had avowed and adopted the act of his officer. The people showed a bad spirit on this occasion. The Government having put several ships in commission with a view to war, the seamen, though willing to serve, were dissuaded from coming forward by representations that they had been ill-used in the distribution of the Havannah prize-money in the late war; and they were persuaded to resort to the practice much in fashion, though very foreign to the habits of their calling. They presented a

Popular discontent.

---

* Choiseul said to Walpole, the Secretary of the English embassy at Paris, 'Your minister does not want to make war, and does not know how to make peace.'—WALPOLE'S *History of George the Third*, vol. iv.

learned argument to the throne in the shape of a petition against the legality and justice of recruiting the navy by means of impressment. The City of London also, no longer under the influence of Beckford, who himself acted under the guidance of Chatham, took a foolish and factious course. The magistrates at first refused to back the press-warrants. Meetings were held under the superintendence of Wilkes, who was again at liberty to bring discredit on the cause which he affected to espouse. One meeting resolved that Lord North should be impeached. Another voted a fresh remonstrance to the King, praying him not only to dismiss his ministers, but also to remove Lord Mansfield from his councils, and not to admit a *Scotchman* into the administration. Such pitiful impertinence was calculated to disgust all men of reflection, and to alienate its best supporters from the popular cause. Chatham, who never for a moment suffered any consideration of party interest to weigh in the scale against the dictates of a high public spirit, rebuked the conduct of the City in attempting to obstruct the recruiting of the navy at the moment of impending war.*

Parliament assembled for the autumnal session as usual in November. The royal speech dwelt chiefly on the quarrel with Spain, which at that time had a doubtful aspect; and invited the counsel and aid of Parliament in determining this important affair. The Opposition did not require

---

* 'There is also, I perceive, reason to fear a race of frivolous and ill-placed popularity about press-warrants. I am determined to resist this ill-judged attempt to shake the public safety. ... As to what the City now intends to do, I wish to hear nothing of it; resolved to applaud and defend what I think right, and to disapprove what shall appear to me wrong and untenable. All the rest is to me nothing.'—*Correspondence*, vol. iii. p. 485.—He spoke to the same effect in the Lords on the first day of the session.

this suggestion to enter upon a topic so attractive. The Middlesex election had been exhausted by repeated debates during two sessions; and a new question was required for party purposes. The conduct of the Ministry in the transaction with Spain was assailed in both Houses with great eloquence, but with little reason and small effect. The debate in the Commons was remarkable only for a ridiculous blunder by Lord Barrington, the Secretary-at-War. The Government had been censured, among other things, for omitting to fill up the office of Commander-in-Chief, which had been left open since the resignation of the Marquis of Granby. The Secretary's excuse was that he knew not whom to appoint, and challenged the House to name a proper person. He intimated, moreover, that there was no necessity for a Commander-in-Chief at all; and that he himself, with the assistance of the Adjutant-General, was perfectly competent to the management of the army. Barrington had been a placeman since the commencement of the reign, and had even filled some important offices, though never with any degree of credit. He had succeeded the able and experienced financier, Legge, as Chancellor of the Exchequer; but fulfilled the duties of that arduous office in such a manner that even Sir Francis Dashwood was considered an improvement upon him. As Secretary-at-War, he had incurred odium and contempt by issuing the General Order, thanking the soldiers employed to clear the streets in the riots of St. George's Fields, and who, in the discharge of that disagreeable duty, had been so unfortunate as to kill an innocent man.

Barrington's indiscretion. Shortly afterwards he took upon himself, without consulting his colleagues, to move the House of Commons for leave to bring in a bill to enable the King, on certain emergencies, to embody the militia without the previous notice required by the Militia Acts. This motion, meeting with no

favour, and being disavowed by Lord North, who
conducted the business of the Government, the Secretary-at-War withdrew it in some confusion. He
put himself forward to move the expulsion of Wilkes,
and when Lord North proposed the partial repeal of
Townshend's Act for taxing the colonies, the whole
House, with the exceptions of Barrington and Wel-
bore Ellis, another partisan of the Court, agreed to
a measure intended to heal dissensions which every
man of moderation and good sense considered dangerous to the integrity of the Empire.

But his flippant and presumptuous answer to the
question put to him in the House of Commons, relative to the appointment of a Commander-in-Chief—a
question of some pertinence when the country was
supposed to be on the eve of war—was only wanting
to cover this lord with derision and contempt. The
general officers, indeed, resented it as an insult to
their order, and considering that there were such
men as Conway, Waldegrave, Albemarle, Amherst
and Monckton, either of whom had professional pretensions equal at least to those of Granby, it is hardly
credible any man who had been thought fit to fill an
office of responsibility could be guilty of such stupid
impertinence.

Lord Waldegrave and General Monckton took the
matter up with a high hand, supported by the indignation of the whole service; and Barrington, over-
whelmed with confusion, made an awkward apology.*
Barrington, however, is responsible only for his awk-
wardness. He did not intend to put an *Hissubserviency
to the King.*
affront upon any of the distinguished
generals who were eligible for the chief command.
The real difficulty was supposed to exist in the highest quarter. The King was unwilling to give up the
immediate control of the army. It has been said,

* Lord Barrington to Earl Waldegrave.—Rockingham Corr.
vol. ii.

and the statement is not improbable, that he contemplated the possibility of resorting to military force in defence of his prerogative. He had told Conway that he would draw the sword or abdicate, rather than yield to the petitions for a dissolution of Parliament. Barrington, who had no will but that of his Sovereign,* would hardly have thought it his duty to recommend any person for the office of Commander-in-Chief, if it was His Majesty's pleasure that it should remain vacant.

The other business transacted in both Houses during the remainder of this short session, was for the most part of a very unprofitable nature. The printers and publishers of Junius's letter to the King had been prosecuted for libel. These indictments were tried before Lord Mansfield in the usual course. In the case against the printer of the newspaper in which the libel first appeared, he directed the jury to confine their inquiry to the fact of publication and the truth of the innuendoes, that is, the suggestions in the indictment putting a libellous construction upon the several passages of the letter, and applying them to the King. The jury, however, determined not to give a triumph to the Court, returned their verdict 'Guilty of publishing *only*,' thereby implying that the paper was not a libel; and as it was doubtful

---

* Lord Barrington was merely the mouth-piece of the King. 'The King has long known,' said he, 'that I am entirely devoted to him, having no political connection with any man, being determined never to form one, and conceiving that, in this age, the country and its constitution are best served by an unbiassed attachment to the Crown.'

In thanking the soldiers who dispersed the rioters in St. George's Fields, in moving the Militia Bill, in moving the expulsion of Wilkes, in opposing Lord North's concessions to the colonies, in keeping open the office of Commander-in-Chief, Lord Barrington, there is every reason to believe, acted under the King's express instructions. His whole official life, in fact—which was nearly his political life—was a mere reflection of the royal will and pleasure. It is only on this account that it is worth while to commemorate his conduct and opinions.

how judgment should be recorded on such a finding, the Court of King's Bench ordered a new trial. But as the Crown lawyers had little hope of getting a better verdict against the publisher of Junius, the prosecution was suffered to drop. Miller, a printer who had re-issued the letter to the King, and in point of law had incurred the same guilt as the original publisher, was acquitted.

The only conviction obtained, was in the case of Almon, a bookseller who had sold the libel in the way of his trade. It so happened that the particular paper which was the subject of the indictment had been purchased not from the hands of the defendant himself, but from those of his shopman; and a question was therefore made, whether a man could be criminally liable for the act of his servant. The rule of law certainly is, that no person can be responsible for a crime committed through the free agency of another. But this rule was never without exception. For example, a man is in many cases liable for an offence committed by the hands of his wife; and the woman is acquitted on the presumption that she acted under her husband's influence and authority. If the general rule were to be applied to the charge of publication in the case of a libel, it is obvious that every printed libel might be circulated with impunity; but the judges never allowed the law to be reduced to a practical absurdity; and long before the case of the King and Almon, it had been ruled * that when a libel is sold in a bookseller's shop, the bookseller shall be responsible, unless he can prove that it was sold without his knowledge or authority. Lord Mansfield, therefore, acted in accordance with precedent as well as common sense in directing the jury that there was sufficient evidence to convict the defendant; and the Court of King's Bench confirmed

* Bacon's Abridgment, Libel B. 2.

the law as laid down by the Chief Justice. Yet the
Interference of Parliament. conduct of Lord Mansfield in respect to these trials, or more correctly the decision
of the Court of King's Bench—for the ruling at
Nisi Prius was merged in the adjudication in banc—
became a subject of question in both Houses of Parliament; and lawyers of eminence were found not
only to dispute the judgments of the King's Bench
delivered after solemn argument, but to enter into
the discussion, as if the law laid down on one side of
Westminster Hall was a fit subject for review on the
Independence of the Judges. other. It can hardly need demonstration,
however, that such a practice is not only
most inconvenient, but incompatible with that independence on the part of the judges which it had
been the wise and patriotic object of recent legislation to secure. The statutes of William and of His
present Majesty had indeed deprived the Crown of
all control over the judges, but had virtually transferred that control to the Parliament, since on the joint
address of both Houses a judge was still removable.
And if judicial decisions were to be subjected to
the censure of Parliament, then were the judges
still dependent; only they were to be intimidated by
faction, instead of being intimidated by the Court.
Such certainly was not the spirit or intention of those
righteous laws. If a judge is partial or corrupt, it
is right that there should be a power of dismissing
Responsibility of the Judges. him; and that power is properly reserved
to the Crown at the instance of the responsible council of the nation. But the power so
vested should be exercised with the utmost caution,
and it is abused whenever Parliament takes upon
itself to discuss the conduct of a judge upon any
other pretence than that of a motion for his dismissal.
If they except to the law as laid down by a judge
or a court of justice, they have the remedy in their
own hands; they can alter or declare the law; but

they can have no right to attempt that object by the intimidation of its sworn ministers.

Chatham, who was never more scrupulous than other leaders of Opposition in the choice of his offensive weapons, took the occasion of a motion on the Middlesex election which he had himself introduced, to comment with his usual force of language on what he had been instructed to call the modern doctrine laid down by the Chief Justice. But the eloquence and authority of Chatham, without knowledge of the subject on which he declaimed, could avail little in that assembly in which Mansfield spoke with equal eloquence, equal authority and consummate learning. The great Chief Justice replied with a well-sustained assumption of superiority. He respected the abilities of his accuser, he said, in other matters; but on this point he was entirely destitute of information; so much so indeed, that, were it not for misconstruction, it would hardly be worth while to distinguish his statement by a reply. He proceeded to show that the directions lately given to juries were the same that they had ever been—the same that he had himself given during the fourteen years that he had held the first place in the administration of the common law. He then went into the particulars of the case, and quoted the authorities and arguments bearing upon it, a detail not out of place in the House of Lords, accustomed, as the court of appeal in the last resort, to the highest order of legal argumentation. After having thus completely disposed of the charge which had been so rashly made against him, he concluded by rallying his old antagonist on an assertion, which, in his ignorance of the elementary principles of the common law, he had ventured —that an action would lie *against the House of Commons* for expelling Wilkes.

Lord Camden was never scrupulous in hazarding assertion for the momentary purpose of debate;

still it was hardly to be expected that a law lord would have the audacity to rise in his place, and defend the nonsensical opinion which Chatham, either in loose declamation, or arguing from the bare theory of the law, that there is no right without a remedy, had hastily thrown out. Yet this great legal dignity, who had himself been a Chief Justice, ventured to tell the House of Lords that there was no such ignorance in maintaining 'that an action for damages would lie against the House of Commons for disfranchising the county of Middlesex.' He did not, indeed, venture to maintain such a position in terms; but he reasoned upon it as if he thought it was not altogether untenable. To refute Lord Mansfield's elaborate vindication of his judgment in the case of the printers, was not so easy, and he therefore reserved his opinion upon that head, until an authentic version of the judgment, if such was to be obtained, should be laid before the House. The charge of the Chief Justice and the whole of the proceedings could easily have been obtained, if Lord Camden had thought proper to move for them. This motion he omitted to make.

Lord Camden.

Lord Mansfield, however, took the hint, and left a copy of the judgment with the Clerk of the House. This was a very irregular and not a very dignified proceeding. If the Chief Justice thought it worth his while to make a more formal vindication of his conduct, he should himself have challenged inquiry by moving for a copy of the judgment. It would have been more becoming his dignity and reputation, however, to have let the matter pass. The course which he took showed a want of moral courage, and gave an advantage to his disingenuous opponent, who did not fail to profit by it. Lord Camden, having taken a day to examine the paper, boldly contradicted the law which it laid down, and came down with a series of questions

Unworthy proceeding in the Lords.

artfully prepared for the purpose of confounding the
Chief Justice. He partly succeeded in this unworthy
object. Mansfield being assailed at once, and with
very little fairness or decency, by Camden, Chatham,
and other members of the Opposition, faltered, contradicted himself, and sat down in evident distress.
It was a scene which did no credit to any of the
parties concerned.

The Commons entered into long debates on the same
subject. Serjeant Glynn, the popular
member for Middlesex, moved for a committee of inquiry into the administration of justice
in Westminster Hall, especially with reference to the
liberty of the press. The House of Commons, that
evening, resembled a court of common law in term,
when a rule for a new trial is argued by two or three
counsel on either side. Dunning and Wedderburn
supported the motion with great ability indeed, but
which would have found a more appropriate theatre
for its display on the other side of Westminster Hall.
The Attorney and Solicitor-General, on the other
hand, supported the doctrine of the judges, and clearly
showed that this doctrine was no innovation, but
founded on a series of precedents from the earliest
times. Dunning contended that these precedents
originated in arbitrary and corrupt times—with
Queen Elizabeth's judges, with Scroggs and Jeffreys;
and that the sages of the law were not then unanimous upon the subject. After citing and discussing
cases at great length, he proceeded to insinuate a
graver charge against the great judge who presided
at Almon's trial. He said that the defendant had
been prepared to rebut the *primâ facie* proof of
notice established by the fact that the alleged libel
was sold from his shop, but that some intimation
from the bench having given the counsel to understand that there was no evidence against their client,
they had thought it needless to call his witnesses;

upon which Lord Mansfield told the jury that, as the
defendant had not contradicted the presumptive case
made out on the part of the Crown, it must be taken
as conclusive. If it had been true that Lord Mansfield obtained the verdict by such a trick, the strong
language of Dunning would have been amply deserved. 'His management,' said Dunning, 'was
much superior to that of the judges he had cited
(Scroggs and Jeffreys, among others of the same
class); whatever their doctrines were, they declared
them from the beginning, and throughout the trial;
they did not, by skulking and concealment, filch a
conviction from the jury, but committed a bold rob-
bery on justice, looking in the faces of the laws and
the defendant.' * But Dunning's statement is neither
borne out by the report of the trial, nor was it corroborated by Glynn, who defended Almon, or by any
other lawyer who took part in the debate. Counsel,
who have exercised a mistaken discretion in the
conduct of their case, especially with reference to
the perplexing question of calling or omitting to call
evidence, are sometimes apt to believe, or to persuade their clients, that they have been misled by
the presiding judge. Even supposing Mansfield to
have been capable of such iniquity as he is here
charged with, he would hardly have ventured upon a
trick as palpable as it would have been infamous.
But Dunning was not incapable, for party purposes,
of making a scandalous assertion upon light and insufficient grounds. He was the intimate friend of
Camden, whose party spirit and personal animosity
against Mansfield had always been allowed too much
license. He had lately been flattered by Chatham,
who previously had taken no notice of him. It must
be remembered, moreover, that Dunning, who now
so loudly denounced precedents drawn from arbitrary

* Parliamentary History, vol. xvi.

times, had himself a few months before, being the
Solicitor-General, defended the arbitrary proposal of
the Duke of Bedford to revive a statute of Henry the
Eighth, for the purpose of depriving the colonists of
trial by jury.

Wedderburn, who followed Dunning, was much
more measured in his language. He spoke
of Mansfield with respect, and gave up the *Speech of Wedderburn.*
whole question by admitting that the judges had
acted in accordance with the weight of precedent.
He only maintained that, in a criminal prosecution
for libel, the jury should return a general verdict of
guilty or not guilty, and not be restricted in their
inquiry merely to the fact of publication. To this
every friend of liberty and constitutional right readily
assented; and such is now happily, by an act of the
legislature, the state of the law.* Burke and other
eminent laymen took a part in this debate, but as
they could not speak with any authority upon a
question which was properly one of mere law, it
dwindled in their hands into an ordinary party
motion. And such, in reality, it was.† The motion

---

* The Libel Act, 32 Geo. III. c. 60.

† The Rockingham party abstained from any participation in these attacks upon the independence of the judges. Lord Rockingham writes thus to Mr. Dowdeswell on the subject,—'I early thought that the mode of proceeding in the House of Lords by debates, queries, questions, &c., between Lord Camden and Lord Mansfield, would ultimately end in nothing advantageous to the public.

. . . . 'However disagreeable these doctrines may be, yet if it must be acknowledged that they can be defended by the opinions of the generality of the present judges, upon the old authorities from good constitutional lawyers, I cannot think that it would be honourable or just to suffer ourselves to be led away in order to gratify personal animosities, instead of doing what may effectually secure the public from receiving in future great injury from the impressions the doctrines may make.' — *Rockingham to Dowdeswell,* 11*th Feb.* 1771.— ROCKINGHAM *Correspondence,* vol. ii. p. 260.

The popular clamour was referred to by Dunning as an apology for bringing it before the House of Commons. Lord Mansfield was stigmatised as a Scroggs or a Jeffreys. One story was,

was negatived by a large majority; as was, also, one made on a previous day by Mr. Constantine Phipps for depriving the Attorney-General of the power of exhibiting informations *ex-officio* in the Court of King's Bench.

The Government cared little for these attacks on the administration of justice; they refrained as much as possible from stirring the old grievance of the Middlesex election, and were content to leave the defence of the judges in the competent hands of Lord Mansfield and the other law officers of the Crown. They saw that Lord Chatham was supported in these violent proceedings only by his own immediate friends, and the clamours of the Middlesex and City parties out of doors; and to encounter these, they could rely with certainty on a large majority in Parliament. But the energetic efforts of the Opposition on the subject of the war which was then supposed to be inevitable, were regarded by the Ministry with serious alarm. On this question every section of the Opposition was united. The orthodox Whigs, of whom the Marquis of Rock-

---

that after the trial of Woodfall, the Chief Justice had taken the jury home with him, and treated them, for the purpose of inducing them to return a corrupt verdict; the fact being, that Lord Mansfield, finding the jury were not agreed, adjourned the court to his house, in the usual way, to afford them time to deliberate. Nothing but the grossest ignorance and prejudice could have put such a construction upon so notorious a practice. Yet the posthumous malignity of Walpole has sought to perpetuate this idle and scandalous fiction.—*History of George the Third*, vol. iv. p. 159.

With regard to the charge of disingenuousness or treachery on the part of Mansfield in the trial of Almon, there was clearly no foundation for it. The counsel for the defendant could easily have ascertained the opinion of the court by submitting, at the close of the case for the prosecution, that there was no evidence to go to the jury. And if the judge had ruled that there was evidence, the counsel would have at once understood that he had to dispose at least of a *primâ facie* case. But Serjeant Glynn wanted the Chief Justice to advise him as to the expediency of calling witnesses, which, of course, Lord Mansfield declined doing. —See Report of the Trial; Howell's *State Trials*.

ingham was now the acknowledged chief, were as earnest as the 'Bill of Rights men;' and neither could for a moment dispute the undoubted right of Chatham to take the lead when the honour of England was to be vindicated. It was certain, that if England was again to declare war against the allied house of Bourbon, the minister of 1756 must have the direction of that war. No Court intrigue, no secret influence, no amount of parliamentary corruption, could in that event avert the ascendancy of Chatham. His very name in the Ministry would prevent a war,* or, if war was inevitable, would secure a successful and a glorious result.

The dispute with Spain had already been twice the subject of debate during this short session in either House of Parliament. Chatham, on those occasions, had exhorted the Government, in his most solemn tones, to prepare for war,† and, casting aside with contempt 'the petty policy of concealment,' had, with a knowledge and an authority which belonged only to himself, exposed the defenceless position and the vulnerable parts of the Empire. Both Houses appear, however, to have treated the matter with apathy until a few days before the Christmas recess, when, upon a motion of the Duke of Manchester for accelerating the preparations for war, an extraordinary scene took place. While the Duke was in the middle of his speech, censuring the inactivity of the administration, Lord Gower, the President of the Council, interrupted

Extraordinary scene in the Lords.

---

* Gerard Hamilton (Single-Speech), one of the most acute observers of the time, and no partisan of Chatham's, thus writes to Calcraft:—'The best solution for all this difficulty will be to send for Lord Chatham. I look upon myself to be a moderate man; and yet there is nothing of which I am persuaded more, than that his very name in the Ministry would bring Spain to what is required, and, if well managed, would prevent a war.'—CHATHAM *Correspondence*, vol. iv. p. 26.

† Chatham Corr. vol. iv. p. 1. Speech in the House of Lords.

him with a motion that the standing order for the exclusion of strangers should be read. A shout of 'Clear the House!' was immediately raised; two Court lords, Marchmont and Denbigh, being conspicuous in their vociferations. Chatham, having in vain endeavoured to obtain a hearing, withdrew in high indignation, accompanied by eighteen other peers, sixteen of whom subsequently recorded a protest, in which, after describing the proceeding as a 'tumult in which every idea of parliamentary dignity, the right of free debate, and all pretence to reason and argument were lost and annihilated,' they went so far as to assert that it was 'premeditated and prepared for no other purpose than to preclude inquiry on the part of the Lords; and, under colour of concealing secrets of State, to hide from the public eye the unjustifiable and criminal neglects of the Ministry, in not making sufficient and timely provision for the public honour and security.'

In consequence of Gower's motion, the members of the House of Commons who were present were required to withdraw, and some lords actually went to the bar for the purpose of enforcing this order. In vain did some of the members represent that they were there in the discharge of their duty, being charged to carry up a bill. They were turned out with the rest; readmitted to go through the form of delivering the bill, and, having performed that ceremony, were actually hooted out of the House. The members returned to their own House, boiling with indignation, and complained of the insult which they had received. The Commons, in a fury, immediately retaliated by forcing their own order against strangers; and it happened, ridiculously, that the first persons turned out were the sixteen peers, with the Duke of Manchester and the Marquis of Rockingham at their head, who, a few minutes before, had quitted their own chamber, to mark their disapprobation of the proceeding. The Commons, laying aside all other business, could talk of nothing but avenging the insult they had received. Several motions were made. Speeches, incoherent with rage, were uttered. Colonel Barré gave a ludicrous account of the scene in the Lords, and even held up the personal peculiarities of Marchmont and Denbigh, the chief actors in it, to the derision of his excited audience. One member reflected in contemptuous terms on the low and corrupt origin of many of the peers. Others used still coarser terms of abuse. The equanimity of the chair even was disturbed. The Speaker having occasion, in one of the debates, to rebuke the impatience of the House, reproached them with being as unmannerly and disorderly *as the House of Lords!* The more moderate members, who preserved a command of their tempers, were nevertheless sufficiently pointed in their remarks. Sir Gilbert Elliott observed, that if the Lords could not conduct themselves like gentlemen, the Commons should show them a better example. And Lord North, whose good humour was seldom ruffled, though he tried to allay the irritation, was evidently vexed at the petulant folly which had provoked such a conflict. Mr. Jeremiah Dyson, the busy and servile agent of the Court, and well known to be such, did what he could to aggravate the quarrel, by defending the conduct of the Lords. The only redeeming incident of this wretched affair was, that it afforded occasion to one man of genius to pay a graceful and noble compliment to another. Burke, among others, expressed his indignation at being excluded from the Upper House; but his regret, he said, was chiefly because he was thus deprived of the instruction which he derived from the wisdom and eloquence of Chatham. 'I desire,' said he, 'to learn the opinions of that great person who, at a moment of national humiliation when the

country lay prostrate, was considered by great and
by small to have some political knowledge. Though
not a member of the Cabinet, he seems to have the
key of it, and to possess the capacity of informing
and instructing us in all things.'* The compliment
was the more happy, as there had never been any
personal cordiality between Chatham and Burke.

The Commons, when the first heat had subsided,
relaxed their order against the admission of strangers;
but the Lords were so ill-advised as to persevere,
and their doors remained closed during the whole
session. The *immediate* consequence was, that the
usual interchange of courtesy between the two Houses
was suspended. The Lords treated the members of
the Lower House when they came up on business
with no more respect than ordinary messengers; and
the Commons, when they brought up bills, instead
of making the usual obeisances, walked erect up to
the bar, and having delivered their bills, with a single
bow to the lord who came from the woolsack to receive them, retired, with the same omission of ceremony. The *ultimate* result of this quarrel was, as
we shall presently see, the most important political
event that had taken place since the Revolution—
the regular publication, namely, of the debates and
proceedings of Parliament.

Before this short session closed, a flagrant case
of electoral corruption was brought under
the notice of the House of Commons. A
petition was presented complaining of an
undue return for the borough of Shoreham. The
returning officer, encouraged, probably, by the example of the House of Commons itself, had taken
upon him to set aside the candidate who polled the
large majority of votes, and to declare duly elected the
candidate who had obtained less than half as many.

Electoral corruption at Shoreham.

* Cavendish Debates, vol. ii.

The former petitioned; and, upon the inquiry, it came out that the election for Shoreham was managed by an association called the Christian Club, which, under the pretext of being concerned in works of charity, had organised a system of bribery, and regularly sold the borough to the highest bidder. The members of this association were bound by an oath of secrecy, and by bond in the penalty of 500*l.* to adhere to their corrupt combination. A committee of management negotiated with the candidate, and whenever business was to be transacted which required the presence of the whole body, they were convened by a signal. The returning officer had at one time been a member of this society, but, influenced by some qualms of conscience, or by apprehension of danger from such proceedings, had requested leave to secede, and, long before he became returning officer, had ceased to attend its meetings. These facts were proved before the election committee, and were afterwards stated at the bar of the House by the officer in extenuation of his conduct; his reason for passing over Rumbold, the candidate highest on the poll, was that he had been informed on affidavit, of the truth of which he was assured from his own knowledge of the Christian Club, that Rumbold had purchased his votes for 35*l.* each. The officer had, no doubt, exceeded his duty in trying the question of bribery, but as he appeared to have acted without a corrupt motive, he was dismissed with a reprimand.

The Shoreham election was the first case tried by a committee constituted under Grenville's Act of the former session. The Treasury and Court agents, wishing to discredit a measure calculated to interfere so materially with their secret management of elections, had sought, in this instance, to impede its operation, and to secure the seat which by decision of the returning officer was

_{Operation of Grenville's Act.}

held by their nominee. The act seemed to provide only for *two* parties to an election petition—the sitting member and the defeated candidate. Dyson, the agent of the Court, with the skill of the pettifogger, caused a petition to be presented on behalf of a third candidate who (being probably the honest and independent candidate) only polled four votes. Thus there were *three* parties before the committee; it was objected, consequently, that they had no jurisdiction under Grenville's Act. And as that act had abolished the jurisdiction of the House in such matters, the result was that the sitting member must be declared duly elected.* This ingenious argument having been overruled, the sitting member made no attempt to impugn Rumbold's claim on the ground of bribery, but at once retired.

* Gerard Hamilton to Calcraft.—Chatham Corr. vol. iv. p. 59, nota.

CHAPTER XIII.

PARTIES—THE CONSTITUTION, ITS THEORY AND PRACTICE—LOYALTY—POLITICAL ADVENTURERS—NEWSPAPERS AND PAMPHLETS—PARLIAMENTARY ELOQUENCE—MANNERS OF THE HOUSE OF COMMONS—DECAY OF PARTY.

I PROPOSE in this chapter to attempt a sketch of the different political parties and their auxiliaries, and of the Parliament in which their conflicts were carried on, during the period to which the earlier part of this history refers. *Sketch of parties.*

The generic divisions of Whig and Tory had undergone a great change since the commencement of the century. The distinction between Whigs and Patriots—that is, Whigs in office and Whigs in opposition—no longer existed. But the party was still disunited, not by any principle of policy, but by a low and sordid rivalry for office, emoluments, and patronage. The Tories were freed from the Jacobite heresy which had so long reduced their distinctive doctrine to a mere speculative tenet. The anomalous faction of the heir-apparent was extinct. It was the fashion at Court, during the earlier years of the reign of George the Third, to say that the distinctions of party had vanished, and that Whig and Tory were obsolete terms. It is true, that many men of moderate opinions approximated so closely, though starting perhaps from opposite points, that there was no essential difference between them. But men of this mild political temperament have always been numerous, though they necessarily occupy a less prominent place in history than those who mingle in the bitter strife of faction. Still such politicians have occasionally been forced by circumstances into a conspicuous position. Falkland and Temple, Halifax and Nottingham, Walpole and Waldegrave, were statesmen who modified their opinions according to the exigencies of the times. They thought that political principles were not like the laws of an exact science, fixed and invariable; but that they were affected by the unceasing revolution of human affairs, and by accidents, against which no human prescience could provide. Such men, who prefer expediency to principle, are commonly described as trimmers and traitors by those who extol consistency as the greatest of political virtues. But, in truth, this anomalous class of politicians, which it is the policy of party to denounce, comprises almost every statesman whose genius or virtue has conferred permanent benefits on mankind. The bigot who sacrifices everything to his tenet; the faithful disciple of traditionary dogmas; the sordid camp-follower of party—may vaunt their mean and shallow consistency; but in many more instances has it happened that great states have been ruined by an infatuated adherence to obsolete maxims and mischievous prejudices, than by rash innovations or premature changes in policy.

The manners of the present age, humanised by knowledge and by the increased facilities of social intercourse, are obviously favourable to the mitigation of political asperity; but this very age, in which party is said to be extinct, has witnessed the most cruel struggles in which parties have ever been engaged. The great conflict of religious freedom; the still sharper contest for electoral rights, were transactions in which the leading statesmen of to-day took a prominent part; while the greatest war of all, the war between the commercial and the territorial powers,

Extinction of party.

1828-32

in which Catholic principles fought with ancient privileges, has only just been terminated. Peace may continue for a time, but no great political discernment is required to point out many questions which may yet give rise to conflicts as furious as any that have hitherto raged between the party of progress and the party of conservation.

The distinction between Whig and Tory was not more sharply defined during the greater part of the eighteenth century than it is at present. So early as the reign of George the First, two classes of Whigs were recognised, the Court Whigs and the Country Whigs;* and little or no difference could be discovered between the latter and those Tories who cordially assented to the settlement of 1688. The Tory who admitted the validity of a parliamentary title to the Crown went nearly the whole length of Whig doctrine in 1710. His loyalty perhaps was of a purer and warmer character than that of the Whig; and his reverence for the Church was certainly greater. But both Whig and Tory were agreed in the main principle of upholding monarchical and episcopal government. Both assented to the important doctrine that the ministers of the Crown were responsible to Parliament; but the one held that the Sovereign had the right to choose his own confidential advisers; while the other thought they should be nominated by the Whig aristocracy. The moderate Tory was a friend to toleration; but he could not go the length of believing that the concession of political power to the Dissenters would be compatible with the due ascendancy of the Church. These seem to have been really the degrees of difference between the two parties; the other differences which, from time to

* Lady M. Wortley Montagu's Correspondence, vol. i. p. 96, Lord Wharncliffe's edition.

time, arose, being merely occasional, or invented for party purposes.

<small>Disadvantages and dangers of party.</small> Philosophers and statesmen, contrasting the turbulence and distraction of popular councils with the domestic tranquillity and the unity of action which belonged to absolute government, have sometimes been disposed to give a preference to the latter. Without touching upon an argument so extensive as this, it must be admitted that party spirit, which is peculiar to free institutions, has too often a tendency not only to impair the vigour of Government, but to bring those institutions themselves into disrepute. So long as the conflict of party is about great principles, the political atmosphere is purified, and public opinion undergoes a wholesome ventilation by the storm. But when important questions are settled, or cease to be contested, parties are then apt to dwindle into factions, intent only upon selfish and sordid objects. This is the time of peril for free institutions. The people, either themselves infected by the corruption of their rulers, or disgusted by it, hardly think their liberties worth a struggle, or perhaps willingly submit to the authority of an ambitious prince, or even a daring adventurer. History can show examples, both from ancient and modern times, of nations which have lost their liberties, when party, its public spirit evaporated, had sunk to the dregs of faction; and this would seem to be the danger with which free constitutions are menaced at the time, when every vexed question being settled, tranquillity and concord prevail throughout the legislature and the Government.

<small>Party appeals to the constitution.</small> The constitution has been always appealed to by the orators and writers of party in support of their particular tenets and opinions; and it is a common practice, at this day, to speak of a thing as constitutional or otherwise, as if there were an expressed law by which the point could be deter-

mined. But, in truth, it seldom happens that there is any such law; and, even in respect of certain cardinal maxims which are supposed to be well defined, doubts and difficulties have arisen. I need mention only one, the very elementary principle of the constitution, that the people cannot be taxed but by the consent of their representatives in Parliament. During ten years of the reign of George the Third, that question was debated with reference to the claims of one class of the subjects of the realm, and was at last decided by an appeal to arms. The trial by jury, the Habeas Corpus, the act which provides for the regular session of Parliament, the exclusive power of the Commons in the matter of supply, the Appropriation Acts, the annual Mutiny Bill—these, indeed, constitute a complete system of liberty, but leave ample room for difference of opinion upon minor points of great importance. The theory and practice of the constitution, again, are essentially at variance with each other; if the theory were carried out, the Government of this nation, instead of being the purest and best, would become one of the most corrupt and degrading tyrannies by which the world has ever been oppressed. For what is the strict law of our boasted constitution? The Sovereign can do no wrong; he is absolute, irresponsible; he can make war and peace of his own will; he can appoint and dismiss all his principal ministers, both civil and military, together with most of the subordinate public servants, at his pleasure. He can impose an absolute veto upon any law which the other two branches of the legislature have passed never so often. He can dissolve Parliament when he will. He can at any time command a majority in one House of Parliament by the creation of legislators, either for life or with hereditary succession. He has the direct nomination of one class, the lords spiritual of that assembly. These are the unquestioned privileges and prerogatives of the Crown, and make the Sovereign of Great Britain, on paper at least, equal in power with the most absolute monarch in Europe.

The House of Lords ranks next in dignity as well as in authority to the Crown. But the peers of England, in Parliament assembled, are responsible neither to the Crown nor to the people. They sit, for the most part, by hereditary right; they constitute not only an independent branch of the legislature, but the supreme court of justice in the kingdom. A peer of the realm, therefore, is competent, without the least knowledge, or with no more than bare understanding, both to make laws and to interpret existing laws on appeal from all the judges of England.

Privileges of the peers.

When we come to the House of Commons, they appear to be the weakest and most dependent in authority, as well as the lowest in order. They must accommodate their measures to the taste and interest of the aristocracy as well as the Crown. They act under the constant apprehension of giving offence to the Sovereign, and consequently of being harassed and impoverished by frequent remissions to their constituents. Obnoxious candidates are met at the hustings by the nominees of the Court, armed with all the advantages which the influence and protection of the Court alone can confer. A large proportion of seats must necessarily be under the immediate control of the territorial aristocracy. The people themselves have numerically but a small share in the choice of their representatives. Under such conditions, it would seem hardly possible that there could be much independence or vigour in the House of Commons.

The House of Commons.

Such, then, is the theory of the constitution. But what is the practice? Nearly the reverse of this speculation. The House of Commons, instead of being the weakest estate, is by far

Power of the Commons.

the most powerful, after making every abatement for the foreign influences by which its purely democratic character is modified and corrupted. The popular branch of the legislature being then supreme, it necessarily follows that the powers and privileges which the constitution assigns to the other great estates of the realm can practically exist only so far as they are compatible with the sovereign authority of the third estate. Thus it is that the veto has become a dead letter; and the legislative power of the Crown is reduced to a mere formality. Nor is its executive power much more substantial. The King can, indeed, declare war; but he can do no more, while the Commons retain the exclusive control of the means by which war is carried on. He can create peers and turn the scale of the House of Lords, but this dangerous prerogative has been exercised but once since the Revolution; and was almost forgotten, when the people, enraged at the contumacy of the peers in 1832, called for its revival. He may still dissolve the Parliament at his pleasure, but only for the purpose of ascertaining the sense of the nation; any attempt to use this prerogative vexatiously would be attended with serious consequences. The nomination of the great ministers of State rests with the Crown, but is practically subject to the approval of the House of Commons; and the appointment to minor offices rests with those ministers. The King, however, is irresponsible; according to the decent maxim of the constitution, he can do no wrong: but he purchases this immunity by the sacrifice almost of the power to offend.

A peer of the realm is, in fact, more removed from responsibility than the Sovereign. He can speak and vote in Parliament without any fear for his peerage; and his conduct as a public man is regulated only by his own sense of what is right, and his regard for public opinion. Yet what a single peer is comparatively free to do, the body of the peerage dare not attempt. If they were really irresponsible and independent, all the other orders must be dependent on them, and the Government would thus become an aristocracy. But the fact again is, in opposition to the theory, that the House of Lords is a far less independent body than that great co-ordinate legislature which owes an immediate responsibility to its constituents. Some portion of the veto which the Crown has lost has devolved upon the second estate; thus the province of the Lords is rather to revise the legislation of the Commons than itself to initiate laws. And, in so doing, they fulfil not the least important and honourable office in the constitution. In their judicial capacity, they command the confidence of the people, because their decisions are pronounced exclusively by the sages of the law, of whom the most eminent are usually raised to the peerage.

Former character of the Commons.

It must not be supposed, however, that this is a correct sketch of the constitution a century ago; and if the capacity of George the Third had been equal to his resolution, such might not be the state of the constitution now. We have seen a House of Commons nominated partly by the aristocracy, partly composed of the proprietors of close boroughs, or the representatives of these proprietors; but comprising very few members elected by independent suffrage. We have consequently seen the nation and the Parliament opposed to each other; the people regarding with hatred and contempt a body which usurped their name and betrayed their interests; the House of Commons seeking the favour of the Crown, the minister, or a patron, and reciprocating the scorn of the people. We have seen the Crown, after long subservience, struggling for mastery with the great nobles, and obtaining an advantage. We have seen that proud nobility, in its turn, subservient to the Crown. But it does not fall

within the compass of this narrative to describe that
happy development of the constitution, in which
Queen, Lords and Commons can each find an honourable place, and, by their harmonious union, so administer the government of this country, that the
wisdom and patriotism of future generations will be
tasked only to maintain it unimpaired.

The settlement which circumscribed the power of
the Crown, extended that of the Parliament in the same proportion; what was
taken from the one was transferred to the
other. The Parliament, again, was for a long period
almost entirely in the hands of the great landowners;
of whom the Whig families, which supported the
Protestant succession, obtained the predominance;
and the Government, for more than seventy years,
was, in substance, an aristocracy. The
tendency of modern times has been to
transfer the balance of power to the third estate.
But for a long period after the Revolution, the people
had very little influence in the Government, and took
only an occasional interest in public affairs. Loyalty
much more than liberty was for many centuries the
ruling principle of the English people. The man
who cried 'God save the Queen!' immediately after
he had undergone the cruel punishment of mutilation
for presuming to censure the proposed marriage of
Elizabeth with a popish prince, was hardly an uncommon instance of the devotion and obedience of
the Commons. Nor could the misrule or personal
worthlessness of the Sovereign do more than suspend
this feeling. Charles the First endeavoured to subvert the ancient institutions of the country, to govern
without law, and to take the money of his subjects
without their consent. The people rose against the
man, for there was nothing of oriental servility in
the generous sentiment which they professed; but
they never for a moment transferred their allegiance

either to that Imperial Parliament which had effected their deliverance, or to the great Dictator, who for a time ruled over them with so much wisdom and moderation. No event in the history of the English nation ever gave rise to such widespread and heartfelt joy as the return of their fugitive prince to the throne of his ancestors. Nor could the unparalleled scandal of his government, the shame which it brought upon the English name, nor the personal delinquencies of Charles himself prevail so far as to alienate the affections of the people from their rightful princes. The first of this race of kings had been a driveller; the second a false and lawless tyrant; the third a mean and selfish profligate who had sold his country for the sake of harlots and buffoons. His successor had once been declared by a vote of the House of Commons unfit to reign because of his adhesion to the hated superstition of Rome. But the people, anxious to find some justification of the loyalty to which they clung, discovered in him a virtue hitherto unknown to the house of Stuart. The Duke of York, it seemed, was a man of his word; and the accession of James the Second was greeted with approbation less passionate, indeed, but more deliberate than that which had hailed the restoration of his line.

Acceptability of William the Third.

It has been asserted by high authority, that the dynasty of 1688 was acceptable to the great majority of the nation. The majority of the nation probably acquiesced in the new settlement rather than surrender their religion and laws; but we may look in vain among the scanty records of the public opinion of those times for any decided manifestation of public approval of the change; or for the least degree of that enthusiastic assent which attended the Restoration. Certainly not a particle of that loyal attachment which had hitherto constituted the main support of the monarchy was transferred to the able and politic prince who had been elected to the vacant throne. Such was the insecurity of his reign that wary and self-seeking politicians thought it prudent to keep a communication open with the exiled court at St. Germains. This correspondence was continued during the reign of Anne, at whose decease the return of the heir of James was thought highly probable, if not desirable. The adventures of 1715 and 1745 were regarded with indifference, if not with sympathy. Nor was it until the accession of George the Third, that the old English loyalty, after a suspension of more than seventy years, was partially revived.

During this interval, the government of the country was the government of party through the medium of the Parliament. The people seldom interposed, and when they did so, it was for the most part to show their ignorance and folly. The Whigs in the reign of Anne thought it desirable that a solemn exposition of the doctrine of the Revolution should be put forth; and they made an opportunity by prosecuting a parson who preached a sermon inculcating the old church tenets of divine right and obedience. The first manifestation of public feeling which had taken place for many years, was exhibited on this occasion. Sacheverell, the accused clergyman (who afterwards proved to be an agent of the Pretender), was immediately elevated to the height of popularity. The statesmen and lawyers who conducted the impeachment, some of whom had taken a prominent part in the great business of 1688, were assailed with popular fury. A few years after, Walpole was forced by popular clamour to abandon a well-considered scheme of finance; and popular clamour afterwards compelled him into one of the most foolish and unjust of the many wars which this country has needlessly undertaken.*

Government by party.

* I refer to the war with Spain in 1739; which was termed the War of Jenkins's Ear.

The people knew no better. Education, as yet, had hardly penetrated beyond the upper layer of society. There was little communication between the capital and the provinces. The few newspapers that existed, seldom contained either political information or discussion. The proceedings in Parliament were kept a profound secret. Under such circumstances, it is not surprising that public credulity was easily imposed upon by the grossest fictions, and that public opinion was for the most part a mass of stupid and absurd prejudices.

It was the aim of faction during the half century after the regeneration of the monarchy, *Party squabbles.* to turn this ignorance and credulity to account. The coalition of disappointed Whig place-seekers, of Tories, Jacobites, and Prince's-men, which banded together for the purpose of overwhelming the administration of Walpole, unable to agree on any point of practical policy, betook themselves to vague declamation on liberty, and loose invective against corruption and arrogance of power. This style, wrought up to a pitch equal to the cold enthusiasm of the French devotees of speculative tyrannicide and classic patriotism in that age of corruption which preceded the downfall of the French monarchy, produced a great effect on the unsophisticated people. They believed in the high-sounding professions of the orators. They believed in the Roman virtue of Pulteney and Wyndham; they believed that Walpole had planned and was effecting his nefarious designs for the ruin of the Commonwealth.

The people had but little voice in the constitution *The people unrepresented.* of the House of Commons. The electors for counties were almost entirely under the control of the landowners. A large proportion of the close boroughs belonged likewise to the aristocracy. Many seats might almost be considered hereditary, having been occupied for successive generations by members of the same family. In other places, the interest was divided among two or more proprietors who, if they could not concur in the nomination of a member, contested the place often at a ruinous expense. Frequently the owner of a borough let the seat either by the Parliament, or the session, at an exorbitant rent. This kind of property could always be realized in the public market; and was worth from twenty to twenty-five years' purchase. It was made the subject of wills and family settlements. Many independent corporations also, having the exclusive right of the elective franchise for the towns which they governed, invariably let the seats to hire, and passed the receipts to the corporate fund. The general election in 1761 was remarked for the appearance of a new class of candidates for Parliament.* West Indians, nabobs, commissaries, stock-jobbers, Scotch and Irish adventurers, successful gamblers are mentioned as infesting every borough, and invading old family interests. The number of new members who took their seats in this Parliament more than doubled the usual return; and the expenditure at this election was beyond all former precedent. These men, unconnected with either of the great parties in the State, independent also of the Crown, constituted a new element in the composition of the House of Commons. And they may be said to have represented the principle of electoral venality, which their ambition had organised into a regular system. The political opinions of this class of members were vague and undetermined. Having no party attachments, no connection with each other, and owing nothing beyond a pecuniary responsibility to their constituents,

---

* They were, however, not altogether new. Davenant, so early as 1700, mentions stock-jobbers and East India proprietors as going about corrupting boroughs. A similar complaint is made in the 'Gentleman's Magazine' and other contemporary publications of the general election in 1741.

they were free to vote as they pleased. But their objects were almost uniformly of a personal character. One was content to have purchased the social position of a member of Parliament. Another, perhaps, wanted to be made a baronet, or an Irish peer. A third would look to a more substantial return for the capital which he had invested in bribery. The natural tendency of this class, therefore, was to support administration.

Members by purchase. Nothing could more happily coincide with the views of the Court at the accession of George the Third than the sudden rise of this new order of men. Each could give exactly what the other wanted. The King, though steadily supported by that party whose leading tenet was loyal submission to the will of the Sovereign, could hardly have prevailed without further aid against factions, which, however jealous of each other, were always united on the one point of resisting his attempt to govern independently of their dictation and control. He found the aid which he required in the class of adventurers who had lately obtained a footing in the House of Commons. These men, untrammelled by engagements, and indifferent to creeds, were generally ready to vote as the private agents of the Court directed. This system, of course, required time to bring to maturity. It was first brought into operation against the Rockingham ministry; and became fully efficient when the King found in Lord North a minister both able and willing to serve his purpose.

Jealousy of the country party. The country gentlemen and the old historical parties regarded these upstarts with extreme jealousy and disgust. The possibility of expelling the intruders seems at one time to have been in contemplation. After the general election of 1768 a great number of petitions complaining of undue elections on the ground of bribery

were presented; and several strong opinions were
expressed against the propriety of admitting adventurers who went about canvassing from borough
to borough with no other recommendation than
pockets full of money. But though it was agreed
that there might be good reason for opposing the
admission of such persons, yet, if bribery could not
be proved against them, it would be difficult to
question their right to be the sitting members.*

The King himself was active and vigilant as a
party leader; surpassing even the Duke of Newcastle
in attention to the minute details of party management. He daily scrutinised the votes of the House
of Commons, rewarding and punishing the members
according to their deserts. The patronage of the
Government was dispensed under his immediate direction; and he frequently interfered in the disposal
of the inferior offices. The pension list became a
potent engine of corruption; and by an ingenious
evasion of the law which disqualifies pensioners from
sitting in the House of Commons, members were
bribed by offices tenable with their seats, but having
a salary or gratuity annexed to them, revocable at
pleasure.† In this manner every member of Parliament who wanted a place or a pension was taught to
understand that his success depended not so much
on the favour of the minister as on that of the King.

Such, then, was the condition of Parliament and
of parties when George the Third began *Power of the*
his reign. The territorial aristocracy pos- *aristocracy.*
sessed almost the whole of the county representation
as they always had done, and as they do at the present day. They had also a considerable number of
boroughs in which the form of an election alone re-

---

* Cavendish Debates.
† This was so stated by Mr.
Cornwall, without contradiction,
in the debate on Mr. Dowdeswell's bill for disfranchising revenue officers.—Cavendish Debates.

mained. Some of these belonged to the King; and some to the Government.* A few of them had been secured by the new party of political adventurers, though these latter sprung mostly from the corruption of the open constituencies. 'Thus,' said the son of Chatham a few years later, 'this House is not the representative of the people of Great Britain. It is the representative of nominal boroughs; of ruined and exterminated towns; of noble families; of wealthy individuals, of foreign potentates.'†

Party policy. Each petty chief of party had his staff of spies, agents and go-betweens. The business of the Court was principally managed by Jenkinson and Dyson. The former had been employed by Lord Bute at the commencement of the reign; the latter was a political adventurer of the lowest grade.‡

Whately and Lloyd, the one Secretary to the Treasury, and the other a clerk in that department, when Grenville was at its head, were ever afterwards his faithful adherents. Lloyd, under Grenville's direction, drew up a pamphlet on the state of the nation, intended to justify his administration, and which drew forth Burke's more celebrated reply. Whately was indefatigable in collecting political intelligence for his patron, and his letters to Grenville throw great light on the movements and intrigues of parties. The Duke of Bedford's man was the notorious Rigby, a model of the hardened partisan, and parliamentary bully of that generation. The Marquis of Rockingham had a more distinguished, but not less devoted follower in Edmund Burke. Lord Chatham, in his earlier days, despised

* Bubb Dodington's Diary, Feb. 2, 1761.

† In allusion to the Indian princes, the Rajah of Tanjore and the Nabob of Arcot. The latter potentate had at one time eight nominees in the House of Commons. — Speech on Reform of Parliament, 1783.

‡ See an account of him in Lord Albemarle's Memoirs of Rockingham.

and neglected the arts of political management and
intrigue; but he always made use of the services of
Beckford to keep up his interest in the City; and
latterly, Calcraft, a rich contractor and borough proprietor, acted as his political agent. These men, by
their flattery and tale-bearing, contributed much to
maintain the jealousies and divisions between their
respective patrons and parties which ultimately secured the triumphs of the Court. The Bedford party,
indeed, was broken up some time before the death
of their chief. The Duke, though he renounced
office for himself, insisted on being amply represented
in any administration to which he gave his support;
and though he desired to withdraw his nominees when
the Duke of Grafton resigned, the Gowers, the Weymouths, the Sandwiches, and the Rigbys preferred
their places to the obligations of party allegiance.

Besides the more important manifestoes occasionally put forth under the immediate direc-
tions of the leaders of parties, a regular Employment of political partisans.
staff of hackney writers was kept in pay
both by the Court and the Opposition. At the commencement of the century, the political press was
illustrated by writers who will ever be the purest
models of the English language. But after Swift,
Addison, and Bolingbroke, party literature degenerated, all at once, from the classic standard, and fell
into the vilest hands. Walpole, himself no scholar,
and almost devoid of elegance and taste, cared little
about the quality of the pamphlets and essays which
were written in support of the Protestant succession;
trusting more perhaps to those grosser means from
which he was accustomed to see an immediate and
practical result. From that time to a period far
within living memory, party writing had been the
meanest walk of letters; and its adepts had ranked,
for the most part, among the most degraded of
mankind. It is only within later years that political

literature has been restored to eminence by a periodical press, the creation of public patronage, and the faithful exponent of public opinion.

The hired political writings of these times were much on a level with similar performances both before and since. What they wanted in argument and wit, they made up in scurrility. Dull abuse of the Opposition was encountered by dull abuse of the Court. Bute was designated as Sejanus; and a dreary parallel was drawn out between persons and circumstances so unlike, as the Cæsar, accomplished in policy as well as in vice, and a parasite of congenial qualities, with a respectable English king and his shallow Scotch governor. On the other side, the servility of Pitt in fomenting German wars, merely to gratify the prejudices and predilections of a weak sovereign, and the waste of British blood and treasure on such unworthy objects, were held up to public execration and contempt. Such was the burden respectively of two periodical papers, 'The Monitor' and 'The Briton,' the one written in the interest of liberty, the other in the interest of the Court. There were other papers manufactured in a similar style, and which appeared daily, or at more distant intervals, during the early years of this reign. The best of them, indeed the only one which had any merit, was 'The North Briton,' the celebrated sheet set up and written by Wilkes, in conjunction with Churchill. 'The North Briton' has shared the fate of far greater literary compositions, the Whig 'Examiner,' 'The Craftsman,' and others, and is perhaps hardly known at all in the present generation, except to those who have been engaged in literary or historical research. 'The North Briton,' however, is a very clever series of libels on the Court and the Scotch nation, written in a style far superior to the 'Britons,' the 'Auditors' and 'Patriots' of the day. The author plainly took

Swift for his model, and imitated the manner of that great master and inventor of irony with considerable success. Number 2, for example, is a remarkably happy specimen of the illiberal satire on the Scotch nation which was then so much in vogue. The 13th number, on the other hand, is an invective against the Scotch, which, for degrading images and filthy abuse, may be compared with the foulest and most ferocious ribaldry of Swift. In another number, a parallel is drawn between Bute and Mortimer, for the purpose of conveying the grossest insinuations against the Princess Dowager. This paper was written with a view to prosecution, and so to political martyrdom, one of the last resources of a desperate adventurer. Wilkes was, however, disappointed; no more notice being taken of this than of the many other libels of the same kind, which had been published since the commencement of the reign. Determined not to be baffled, Wilkes at length proceeded, in the celebrated forty-fifth number, to attack the King himself; and this paper, though as inferior in audacity and virulence as in literary merit to the equally celebrated letter of Junius, was completely successful. The fortunate author was prosecuted, imprisoned, half-killed,* expelled from Parliament; banished, prosecuted, imprisoned, and expelled again; the upshot being, that his debts were paid, and that a handsome provision was made for the remainder of his life.

The principal writer in the pay of the Court was Dr. Shebbeare, whom Bute took out of Newgate for the purpose of employing his pen. This man had been in prison for libelling the late King and his predecessors, but would more justly have been there for certain fraudulent practices in which he had been engaged at Oxford. Shebbeare wrote one of the

---

* In a duel by Martin, Secretary to the Treasury.

Court papers called 'The Monitor,' under the immediate direction of the Solicitor to the Treasury,[a] and applied himself for some time to the defamation of Lord Camden, then Chief Justice of the Common Pleas, who had given great offence by the energy with which he had reprobated the illegal resort to general warrants. Shebbeare was rewarded for his services with a pension of 200*l.* a year. Another periodical organ of the Government, called 'The Auditor,' was written by Murphy, a man of considerable literary talent, although it does not appear in his paper. He was a writer for the theatres; two of his plays, 'The Way to Keep Him,' and 'All in the Wrong,' have survived to the present time, and are still performed with approbation. The 'Briton,' which probably suggested the title of Wilkes's famous publication, was established also under the auspices of Bute, and conducted by Smollett. But no trace of the genius which produced 'Roderick Random,' and 'Humphrey Clinker,' is to be found in this production. Like his continuation of the History of England, a vapid chronicle, put together by contract with the booksellers, these political essays, written for the wages of a minister, were among the dullest productions of their kind.

Some of the pamphlets written in behalf of the Court were, however, of a high order of merit. 'The Consideration of the German War,' was a very able depreciation of the war policy of Pitt. I have nowhere else seen the argument against that policy stated with so much breadth and plausibility. The author was Israel Mauduit, a Jew, and a colonial agent; he received a pension for this service. During Bute's administration and for some time afterwards, the exaltation of the royal prerogative was a prominent topic in most of these pieces. One of them is worthy

[a] Walpole's History of Geo. III.

of notice; it is entitled 'Prerogative Droit de Roy; or a Digest of the Rights and Prerogatives of the Imperial Crown of Great Britain.' It is, in fact, an elaborate vindication of the prerogative as it existed in the times of the Tudors. The single authority of the Crown is distinctly asserted; and the modern idea of a mixed monarchy is refuted with an abundance of obsolete learning. The legislative authority of the Houses of Parliament is shown to be an usurpation of the Crown; their proper province being the 'rogation,' not the enactment of laws; they are merely 'consultative and preparative; but the making of laws, being part of the sovereign power, necessarily belongs to the Crown, the privilege of which is peculiar and incommunicable.' The writer then proceeds to enumerate the constituent parts of the prerogative in thirty-four divisions, the sum of which leaves little or no power to the other members of the constitution. This tract would have been very appropriate in 1686 when the last of the Stuarts was seeking to set up the dispensing power; but in the seventy-fourth year of the constitutional era, it was a curiosity, revealing the visionary speculations of the school of Bolingbroke, which had been indulged in the sequestered recesses of Leicester House.

But the most powerful of the pensioned writers for the Court was Samuel Johnson. The dogmatic assertion, the strong sense and impressive style of this great English classic, were all brought to bear upon a subject, respecting which he entertained decided opinions. The 'False Alarm' is, perhaps, the most arrogant political pamphlet that ever was written, and probably did more harm than good to the cause which it sought to recommend. Nothing can exceed the dictatorial and offensive language directed against all who disapproved of the proceedings in the Middlesex elections. The public discontent is compared to the Jacquerie.

The Opposition, which comprehended the most distinguished members of the Whig party, and many persons of station and respectability who took no part in ordinary political conflict, was stigmatised in the mass as 'a despicable faction, distinguished by plebeian grossness and savage indecency.' It is not surprising that the son of a huckster should rail at 'low-born railers,' and compare the popular leaders to Tiler and Ket. The man who could find nothing in the character of William the Third but 'gloomy sullenness' was likely to eulogise George the Third 'as the only king who for *almost* a century [a *whole* century would have included his favourite King Charles the Second] has much appeared to desire, or much endeavoured to deserve the affections of the people.' But he proceeds farther, and in a passage as false as it is illiberal, seeks to avenge the injuries which political as well as religious despotism had received at the hands of the great Puritan party. 'None,' he says, 'can wonder that these disturbances have been fomented by the *sectaries*, the natural fomenters of sedition and confederates of the rabble, of whose religion little now remains but hatred of establishments.' And this, with much more in the same strain, was written by a man of genius, a scholar, and a moralist, who was the contemporary of Wesley and Whitfield.*

The stage a political instrument.
The stage even was made instrumental to the policy of the Court. Not only was the censorship vigilantly exercised in the suppression of every passage the recital of which might bear an application to popular topics, but plays were written and licensed for the purpose of holding up the new system of government to public admiration and applause. For instance, the tragedy 'Electra,' by W. Shirley, founded on the fable

* Review of Lord Bute's administration.

of Sophocles, was stopped in rehearsal; while, at the same time, a wretched piece called 'Elvira,' a translation from an old French drama, which had for its theme the exaltation of sovereign authority and the panegyric of a minister who had been the preceptor of his royal master, was allowed to be performed. This task was written—probably, to order—by Mallet, a well-known hackney author of that day.*

The satiric muse was engaged with much more effect on the popular side. Churchill— *Satirists employed.* on whom a perverse fate had imposed the orders of the priesthood—the able coadjutor of Wilkes in libelling the Court, the brilliant companion of his convivial hours, produced a satire called the 'Prophecy of Famine.' He had already achieved a great reputation in this thorny walk of literature, by 'The Rosciad,' which so incensed the players that they threatened personal vengeance on the author, who defied their professional denunciations. The 'Prophecy of Famine' was a still more successful effort. Professing to be a political satire, it was a coarse but powerful invective against the poverty of the Scottish people—almost the only form, at that time, in which English wit and humour were developed and appreciated. This lampoon was eagerly bought up, became the talk of every coffee-house, and was supposed to have hastened Bute's retreat from power.

An intelligent and well-informed contemporary, who has himself preserved some lively *Parliamentary* sketches of the parliamentary eloquence *eloquence.* and manners with which he was conversant, describes the administration of Lord North as an era in the

---

* Mallet edited a posthumous work of Bolingbroke's, of an infidel character. The reader will recollect Johnson's witty remark on this subject, 'a coward who loaded a pistol against Christianity, and left half a crown to a beggarly Scotchman to pull the trigger after his death.'—Boswell's *Life of Johnson.*

history of British eloquence; and, writing half a century after that period, applies to it the observation of Velleius Paterculus with reference to Cicero, that 'no member of either House of the British Parliament will be ranked among the orators of this country whom Lord North did not see, or who did not see Lord North.' *

A contemporary of Lord North's might perhaps have said the same of Sir Robert Walpole.

Present degeneracy of Parliament. Such a man, if he had listened to Wyndham, or Yonge, or Pulteney, or Pitt, or Walpole himself, or Carteret, or Chesterfield, even if he had not been so fortunate as to hear a speech of St. John's,† could not have failed to vindicate the claims of those famous orators to rank second only, if not equal to the Burkes, the Foxes and the Pitts of George the Third. Even in these days, it is believed that Parliament has degenerated not in eloquence alone, but in capacity, in learning, in good breeding and in taste.

As to eloquence, we may perhaps yield the superiority to generations which have passed

Decay of eloquence. away; though perhaps much of the rhetoric which is taken into account by the eulogist of a former age is such as would be rejected by the fuller information and more practical intelligence of the present time. Splendid declamations about liberty, terrible invectives against corrupt and too powerful ministers, would be merely ridiculous in an age when liberty is perfectly secure, and when ministers have long ceased to be formidable or depraved. But though the study of eloquence may be carried too far, when the qualities of a statesman are measured chiefly by oratorical power, it is certain that a sovereign legislature is strengthened as well as adorned

---

* Butler's Reminiscences vol. i. p. 139.
† Mr. Pitt used to say that he would rather recover a speech of Bolingbroke's than any of the lost works of antiquity.

by a due cultivation of that noble art. The eloquence indeed, peculiarly adapted to the parliament of a free and prosperous people, is of the very highest order. It is that which draws its inspiration from reason, and is only illustrated by fancy. It is the eloquence in which the Grecian orator excelled, which it behoves the orator of the House of Commons exclusively to regard. 'Could it be copied,' says a critic of the most penetrating genius, 'its success would be infallible over a modern assembly. It is rapid harmony, exactly adjusted to the sense. It is vehement reasoning without any appearance of art. It is disdain, anger, boldness, freedom, *involved in a continued stream of argument.*' * It is curious to observe, that in the very essay from which the above extract is taken, Hume remarks upon, and endeavours to account for, the dearth of eloquence in the British Parliament. He says, there were about half a dozen speakers in both Houses who had attained nearly the same pitch of eloquence, and that neither of them was entitled to any preference above the rest; 'a sure proof,' he adds, 'that none had reached beyond mediocrity in their art, and that their aim was such as could be reached by ordinary talents and slight application.' Yet at the period when he thus wrote, the administration of Walpole was sinking fast under the attacks of the patriots, whose incessant oratory had brought over not only the Parliament, but the nation which had little sympathy with the Parliament, to their side. The great historian could have given little attention to contemporary events, or must have fallen into the common error of a philosophic mind, that of referring everything to a general truth, when he inferred from the equal excellence of some half dozen speakers that none of them could have attained a high degree of art. We know a good deal about Pulteney, Walpole

* Hume.—Essay on Eloquence.

and Pitt; we have a tradition of Bolingbroke hardly
equalled by the fame of any oratory which has come
down to us. Assuredly, the speeches of these men
were not the easy efforts of ordinary minds; and if
any other speakers could come up to them, the earlier
Parliaments of George the Second were distinguished
by eloquence of the highest order.

The opinion of Hume, however, that the style of
Demosthenes is the most fit for an English
orator is confirmed by the most competent
judges. Knowledge, good sense and reasoning, are the leading principles of this school; and,
while the example of its founder proves that these
simple elements may be wrought to the highest perfection of art, they obtain credit and consideration,
even when exhibited in their rudest form. Yet for
one plain orator of this simple school, we have a dozen
or more of fluent florid declaimers. And no wonder;
for the imagination is a much more precocious faculty
than the understanding; and whenever the one is
unable to exercise its authority, the other, having
no power of self-restraint, indulges in undue license.
Rhetoric, therefore, is common and real eloquence is
rare, because imagination is abundant, while good
sense and the power of reasoning are perhaps the rarest
gifts of Providence.

Lord Chesterfield, a man of the most exquisite
discernment, and far beyond his age in
refinement of taste, has described parliamentary eloquence, of which he was himself a master, in terms which are quite as accurate
now as they were a century ago. 'The vulgar, who
are always mistaken, look upon a speaker and a
comet, with the same astonishment and admiration,
taking them both for preternatural phenomena....
But let you and I analyse and simplify this good
speaker; let us strip him of those adventitious plumes
with which his own pride and the ignorance of others

have decked him, and we shall find the true definition of him to be no more than this:—A man of good common sense who reasons justly, and expresses himself elegantly on that subject on which he speaks. A man of sense, without a superior and astonishing degree of parts, will not talk nonsense on any subject; nor will he, if he has the least taste or application, talk negligently. . . . . The man who speaks in the House of Commons, speaks in that House and to four hundred people, that opinion upon a given subject, which he would make no difficulty of speaking in any house in England round the fire or table to any fourteen people whatsoever; better judges, perhaps, and severer critics of what he says than any fourteen gentlemen of the House of Commons.'*

The Athenian democracy was not more severe in its oratorical taste than the British House of Commons. Spurious eloquence, when subject to the test of that audience, is immediately detected, and perishes in its birth. The orator, flushed with the triumphs of the platform, enters the House of Commons with no credentials. He will have a fair hearing, but no favour; and if he cannot vindicate his pretensions, it is probable that he will not be heard again. Thus, many a reputation, which might have flourished for ever in the hotbeds of public halls and lecture-rooms, is killed at once by the atmosphere of the House of Commons. A man of any information or sense, however dull, prolix or ungainly, will be listened to with respect; a timid or unpractised speaker, if he has anything to say, or comes recommended by any substantial claims to attention, will be met not only with patience, but with generous encouragement; while the mere rhetorician or impudent pretender, will be encountered

Parliamentary nothingness of rant.

---

* Chesterfield to his Son.

with derision or silent contempt. The justice of the
House of Commons is indisputable; its manly spirit
is such as becomes the representatives of the people
of the United Kingdom; its fine taste properly belongs
to an assembly in which scholars and gentlemen
predominate.

But though the character of its eloquence, and the
other peculiar features of Parliament, re-
Improvement in parliamentary departments. main the same as they were in the age of
Chesterfield, its manners as well as those
of the various classes of society from which it is
selected, have been improved. A style of personal
invective, frequently degenerating into rudeness, a
disregard of order and of the authority of the chair,
which would not be tolerated in these days, prevailed
during the reign of George the Second, and the earlier
Parliaments, at least, of George the Third. The
language which Pulteney and Walpole habitually
used towards each other was of the most contumelious
character. Carteret and Chesterfield, the most accomplished
scholars and the finest gentlemen of their
day, indulged in similar license. Chatham himself
not only used the most insulting and contemptuous
terms towards his opponents, but frequently resorted
to bye phrases and gestures still more offensive. In
the debate on the war, for instance, in 1761, he sneered
at Rigby and Sir Francis Delaval, two members of
some note, in this style:—' He would not disappoint
the gentlemen so far as to take no notice of them;
he confessed he did see the person of the latter
standing up, and recollected to have heard him—
that was sufficient.' * Once, when Grenville was defending
the cider tax, and asking, with some emphasis,
where the Government was to find a substitute,
Pitt merely hummed the burden of a popular air,
' Gentle shepherd, tell me where.' This, we are told,

* Milbanke to Rockingham.—Correspondence.

was a great hit. The House was convulsed with
laughter, and the minister was covered with confusion. There is certainly nothing very witty or refined
in this repartee, which would seem adapted for an
audience very inferior to the House of Commons.
Manner, indeed, can do wonders, and no orator,
perhaps, ever had such a manner as Pitt. Nevertheless, I doubt whether any member, however great
his ascendancy in Parliament, will again venture to
take such liberties with the House. Burke, on one
occasion, alluded to Lord North in such terms as
these,—'The noble lord who spoke last, after extending his right leg a full yard before his left, rolling
his flaming eyes, and moving his ponderous frame,
has at length opened his mouth.' Language like
this is to be attributed chiefly to the want of taste
and good breeding in the man who uses it; but such
vulgar impertinence, would not, I believe, have been
tolerated for a moment in any House of Commons
which has sat during the present century. Trans-
gressions, however, of this kind were very rare.
Colonel Barré, when the Commons were turned out
of the House of Lords in the session of 1770, gave
a ludicrous description of two noble lords who had
made themselves conspicuous in clearing the House.
But he was rebuked by Sir Gilbert Elliot. 'Personal
allusions,' said that polite courtier, 'though occasionally met with in books, were not frequent in the
debates of that House.' One of the most distinguished
members of Lord North's administration gives rather
too favourable an account of the parliamentary decorum of his day. 'What passed in the Roman senate
for polished raillery,' said Wedderburn, 'would in
this House be deemed a gross affront, and be perhaps
attended with bloodshed. What Roman virtue called
Attic eloquence, modern honour would construe rude
Billingsgate. The most famous harangues of Cicero

and Demosthenes would, with us, be termed infamous libels.'*

Former rudeness in Parliament

A remarkable proof of the rude and disorderly character of the House of Commons, in the last century, is the want of respect for the chair. The records of the debates, scanty as they are, abound in passages of violence and tumult which the Speaker failed, or did not attempt, to repress. Sometimes he was personally attacked while presiding over the debates. In 1762, for instance, during the trial of an election petition, Rigby interrupted the counsel who was speaking at the bar, to address the Speaker in the following terms:—' Sir, I am very sorry to address you in this manner, and put you in mind of your duty, which you should know much better than I: give me leave to tell you that you are seated in that chair to enforce the orders and support the dignity of this House, and not to suffer our order to be transgressed by that long-winded pleader: permit me to say you are but young in that chair; I wish to see you many years in it, but I have been long enough in the House to know what is, and what is not, obedience to orders.' The Speaker, Sir John Cust, who had been elected in this Parliament, answered mildly, that he endeavoured to do his duty, and that, if he failed, he hoped it would be imputed to the cause which the honourable gentleman had mentioned—his being young in the chair; but, on this occasion, he maintained that the learned counsel had not transgressed the order of the House.

Present authority of the Speaker.

The narrator of this scene,† himself a member of the House, describes it as nothing extraordinary, nor does the House appear to have felt itself called upon to interpose in such an altercation. Yet Rigby, in thus rebuking the

---

* Speech on Sarjeant Glynn's Motion for Enquiry into the Administration of Criminal Justice.—16 Parl. Deb. 1287.

† Sir James Caldwell.—Cavendish Debates.

chair, was himself disorderly, indecent, and presumptuous in the highest degree. He takes upon himself to lecture the Speaker, and at the same time to insult the counsel who was at the bar in the discharge of his duty. If any member during the present generation could have so far forgotten himself as to commit such an outrage as this, the House would not have failed to vindicate its dignity, and protect the authority of the chair. During the sessions of 1768-9-70 there were frequent wrangles between the Speaker and members of the House. Sometimes the Speaker was called to order, and on one occasion his words were taken down.

The chief complaint against modern Parliaments is the inordinate length of their debates. The great publicity given to the proceedings of Parliament by means of the daily press; the increased responsibility of the House of Commons to its constituents since the Reform Act, the accumulation of business, and the interest which all classes of the community take in the discussion of public affairs;—are causes which have concurred in protracting the debates, or rather, in multiplying speeches in the Lower House. But the comparison, even in this respect, with former times, is not altogether so unfavourable to modern practice. Long before the reporters of the daily press were admitted to the galleries, it was not uncommon for the House to sit ten or twelve hours without intermission. The debate on the Convention with Spain, in 1739, lasted from half-past eleven in the morning until half-past twelve at night. The motion of Mr. Sandys for the removal of Sir Robert Walpole, in 1741, was debated for thirteen hours. The debate on General Warrants, in 1765, was continued for seventeen hours. The House frequently sat during the whole night. It rarely happens in these days that the sitting of the House is prolonged much beyond midnight merely for the purpose

Length of modern debates.

of debate; but the evil of excessive discussion has been aggravated by the practice, which of late years has obtained, of delivering a series of speeches on important or interesting questions (for these are not convertible terms) by means of adjournment from day to day.

Many persons, both in and out of Parliament, disgusted at this waste of time in useless oratory, are inclined to regard debate altogether as an obstruction to public business. No man's vote, it is said, was ever affected by a speech, nor is the result of a division ever calculated upon the course of a debate. But even if both of these propositions are admitted, it does not follow that the practice of debating should be dispensed with in the British Parliament. The debates of both Houses are eagerly read throughout the country; and many a speech, which nobody listened to but a reporter, is perused by thousands out of doors. The speeches of those members who derive authority from office, or from their general reputation, are sure to be considered and canvassed by the public with the greatest attention and interest. From the consideration of the parliamentary debates by every class of the community, giving rise as they do to innumerable other debates in every haunt of business or pleasure—in every club, at every market-room, at the dinner-table, in the ball-room, in the beer-shop, at the cover side, at the corners of the street, in every family circle—from this manifold discussion, public opinion is to a great extent formed, and re-acts upon Parliament itself. It is not true, however, that debate does not immediately influence the vote. Even on occasions when the fate of a cabinet is to be decided, and each party musters all its strength, some stragglers there are who address themselves only to the merits of the particular question upon which the battle is fought, and reserve their decision until they have heard the

arguments on either side. These uncertain votes
frequently turn the scale. The general business of
Parliament is materially affected by the course of
debate, and frequently by particular speeches.* This
independent action of the House of Commons, which
is of recent growth, is to be attributed mainly to the
increased freedom and purity of election. A member
who is returned by the nomination of one or more
great proprietors follows, as of course, his party or
his patron. A man who has purchased his seat has
commonly some personal object in view, and can be
accounted for accordingly in an estimate of the effective strength of a government or an opposition. But
the representative who has been chosen by fair and
open election is seldom attached to either party; and
except, perhaps, on some cardinal points, is free and
willing to act as his own judgment, or any accidental
influence, may direct him. This tendency of the
House of Commons has, in latter years, no doubt increased the difficulty of administration; it renders,
perhaps, the formation of a strong and enduring
government an impossibility; and thus imparts, to a
certain degree, a character of waywardness and indecision to Parliament itself. On the other hand, the
old fashion of government by party is gone by. In
an age when the people were wholly uninstructed,
nor had yet learned to claim an independent position
in the political system—when the middle classes were
still, for the most part, rude and ignorant—the phrases

---

* Among numerous instances which have fallen under my own observation, during my experience of Parliament, I may mention a bill for disqualifying persons holding certain judicial offices for seats in the House of Commons. The bill was carried through its first stage by a considerable majority, notwithstanding the opposition of the Government. But on the second reading the bill was rejected by a majority as decisive. This result was entirely owing to a speech from Mr. Macaulay. No attempt was made by the supporters of the bill to answer his argument; and its effect was manifest in the division which almost immediately ensued.

Whig and Tory were, perhaps, the only intelligible expressions of public opinion. But these words have long lost their charm; and candidates, in the interest of party, are driven to every kind of fantastic paraphrase for the purpose of disguising a character with which the people have no longer any sympathy. The elements of political and religious strife nevertheless still exist among us; and threaten, at no distant day, unless happily the counsels of wisdom and moderation shall disperse them, or mitigate their fury, to shake the pillars of the State, and agitate society itself by their malignant influence.

END OF THE FIRST VOLUME.

INDEX.

	PAGE
Arnott on Sight and Touch	12
Acton's Modern Cookery	17
Aikin's Select British Poets	5
—— Memoirs and Remains	4
Alcock's Residence in Japan	23
Allies on Formation of Christianity	18
Alpine Guide (The)	23
Apjohn's Manual of the Metalloids	12
Arago's Biographies of Scientific Men	4
—— Popular Astronomy	10
—— Meteorological Essays	10
Arnold's Manual of English Literature	7
Arnott's Elements of Physics	11
Arundines Cami	25
Atherstone Priory	24
Atkinson's Papinian	5
Autumn holidays of a Country Parson	6
Ayre's Treasury of Bible Knowledge	19

Bacon's Life of a Philosopher	4
—— Essays, by Whately	5
—— Life and Letters, by Spedding	4
—— Works, by Ellis, Spedding, and Heath	3
Bain on the Emotions and Will	10
—— on the Senses and Intellect	10
—— on the Study of Character	10
Baines's Explorations in S. W. Africa	22
Ball's Guide to the Central Alps	23
—— Guide to the Western Alps	23
Bawdon's Rents and Tillages	18
Black's Treatise on Brewing	18
Blackley and Friedlander's German and English Dictionary	
Blaine's Rural Sports	25
Blight's Week at the Land's End	23
Bonney's Alps of Dauphiné	22
Bourne's Catechism of the Steam Engine	17
—— Handbook of Steam Engine	17
—— Treatise on the Steam Engine	17
Bowdler's Family Shakespeare	25
Boyd's Manual for Naval Cadets	17
Bramley-Moore's Six Sisters of the Valleys	21
Brande's Dictionary of Science, Literature, and Art	13
Bray's (C.) Education of the Feelings	10
—— Philosophy of Necessity	10
—— (Mrs.) British Empire	13
Brinton on Food and Digestion	20
Bristow's Glossary of Mineralogy	12
Brodie's (Sir C. B.) Psychological Inquiries	10
—— Works	10
—— Autobiography	4
Browne's Ice Caves of France and Switzerland	23
—— Exposition 39 Articles	19
—— Pentateuch	19

	PAGE
Buckle's History of Civilisation	3
Bull's Hints to Mothers	20
—— Maternal Management of Children	20
Bunsen's Analecta Ante-Nicæna	20
—— Ancient Egypt	3
—— Hippolytus and his Age	20
—— Philosophy of Universal History	20
Bunyan on Apocrypha	20
Bunyan's Pilgrim's Progress, illustrated by Bennett	18
Burke's Vicissitudes of Families	4
Burton's Christian Church	3

Cabinet Lawyer	24
Calvert's Wife's Manual	21
Campaigner at Home	6
Cats and Farlie's Moral Emblems	18
Chorale Book for England	21
Colenso (Bishop) on Pentateuch and Book of Joshua	19
Columbus's Voyages	22
Commonplace Philosopher in Town and Country	6
Conington's Handbook of Chemical Analysis	14
Contanseau's Pocket French and English Dictionary	8
—— Practical ditto	8
Conybeare and Howson's Life and Epistles of St. Paul	19
Cook's Voyages	22
Copland's Dictionary of Practical Medicine	15
—— Abridgment of ditto	15
Cox's Tales of the Great Persian War	2
—— Tales from Greek Mythology	24
—— Tales of the Gods and Heroes	24
—— Tales of Thebes and Argos	24
Cresy's Encyclopædia of Civil Engineering	16
Critical Essays of a Country Parson	6
Crowe's History of France	2

D'Aubigné's History of the Reformation in the time of Calvin	3
Dead Shot (The), by Marksman	25
De la Rive's Treatise on Electricity	12
Delaband's Village Life in Switzerland	23
De la Pryme's Life of Christ	20
De Tocqueville's Democracy in America	2
Diaries of a Lady of Quality	4
Dobson on the Ox	25
Dove's Law of Storms	11
Doyle's Chronicle of England	3

Ellice, a Tale	24
Elliott's Broad and Narrow Way	19
—— Commentary on Ephesians	19
—— Destiny of the Creature	19
—— Lectures on Life of Christ	19

NEW WORKS PUBLISHED BY LONGMANS AND CO.

	PAGE
ELLICOTT'S Commentary on Galatians	19
——— Pastoral Epist.	19
——— Philippians, &c.	19
——— Thessalonians	19
Essays and Reviews	20
——— on Religion and Literature, edited by MANNING	
——— written in the Intervals of Business	9
FAIRBAIRN'S Application of Cast and Wrought Iron to Building	17
——— Information for Engineers	17
——— Treatise on Mills & Millwork	17
FROUDE'S Christendom's Divisions	10
First Friendship	24
FITZ ROY'S Weather Book	16
FOWLER'S Collieries and Colliers	17
FRESHFIELD'S Alpine Byways	23
——— Tour in the Grisons	23
Friends in Council	9
FROUDE'S History of England	1
GARRATT'S Marvels and Mysteries of Instinct	12
GEE'S Sunday to Sunday	21
Geological Magazine	12
GILBERT and CHURCHILL'S Dolomite Mountains	23
GILLY'S Shipwrecks of the Navy	22
GOSSE'S Second Feast, by Anster	24
GOODEVE'S Elements of Mechanism	
GOULT'S Questions on BROWN'S Exposition of the 39 Articles	18
Graver Thoughts of a Country Parson	9
GRAY'S Anatomy	15
GOSSE'S Corals and Sea Jellies	12
——— Sponges and Animalcules	12
Grove on Correlation of Physical Forces	12
GWILT'S Encyclopædia of Architecture	16
Handbook of Angling, by EPHEMERA	25
HARRIS on Election of Representatives	7
HARTWIG'S Sea and its Living Wonders	12
——— Tropical World	12
HAWKER'S Instructions to Young Sportsmen	25
HEATON'S Notes on Rifle Shooting	25
HELPS'S Spanish Conquest in America	2
HERSCHEL'S Essays from the Edinburgh and Quarterly Reviews	13
——— Outlines of Astronomy	10
HEWITT on the Diseases of Women	14
HINCHLIFF'S South American Sketches	28
Hints on Etiquette	29
HOLCROFT'S Time and Space	10
HOLLAND'S Chapters on Mental Physiology	9
——— Essays on Scientific Subjects	13
——— Medical Notes and Reflections	14
HOLMES'S System of Surgery	
HOOKER and WALKER-ARNOTT'S British Flora	13
HORNE'S Introduction to the Scriptures	19
——— Compendium of ditto	19
HOSKYN'S Talpa	27
How we Spent the Summer	22
HOWITT'S Australian Discovery	22
——— History of the Supernatural	9
——— Rural Life of England	23
——— Visits to Remarkable Places	23
HOWSON'S Hulsean Lectures on St. Paul	18
HUGHES'S (W.) Geography of British History	11
——— Manual of Geography	11
HULLAH'S History of Modern Music	7
——— Transition Musical Lectures	7
HUMPHREYS' Sentiments of Shakspeare	16

	PAGE
Hunting Grounds of the Old World	25
Hymns from Lyra Germanica	21
INGELOW'S Poems	26
JAMESON'S Legends of the Saints and Martyrs	16
——— Legends of the Madonna	16
——— Legends of the Monastic Orders	16
JAMESON and EASTLAKE'S History of Our Lord	16
JOHNS'S Home Walks and Holiday Rambles	12
JOHNSON'S Painters' Manual	17
——— Practical Draughtsman	17
JOHNSTON'S Gazetteer, or Geographical Dictionary	11
JONES'S Christianity and Common Sense	10
KALISCH'S Commentary on the Old Testament	7
——— Hebrew Grammar	7
KENNEDY'S Hymnologia Christiana	21
KESTEVEN'S Domestic Medicine	15
KIRBY and SPENCE'S Entomology	13
KNIGHTON'S Story of Elihu Jan	24
KÜLLER'S Notes to Lyra Germanica	21
KOENIG on Pentateuch and Joshua	19
Lady's Tour Round Monte Rosa	22
LANDON'S (L. E. L.) Poetical Works	26
Late Laurels	24
LATHAM'S English Dictionary	7
LECKY'S History of Rationalism	3
Leisure Hours in Town	9
LEWES'S Biographical History of Philosophy	4
LEWIS on the Astronomy of the Ancients	9
——— on the Credibility of Early Roman History	4
——— Dialogue on Government	4
——— on Egyptological Method	4
——— Essays on Administrations	4
——— Fables of Babrius	4
——— on Foreign Jurisdiction	4
——— on Irish Disturbances	4
——— on Observation and Reasoning in Politics	4
——— on Political Terms	4
——— on the Romance Languages	4
LIDDELL and SCOTT'S Greek-English Lexicon	8
——— Abridged ditto	8
LINDLEY and MOORE'S Treasury of Botany	13
LONGMAN'S Lectures on the History of England	2
LOUDON'S Encyclopædia of Agriculture	16
——— Cottage, Farm, and Villa Architecture	16
——— Gardening	16
——— Plants	13
——— Trees & Shrubs	13
LOWNDES'S Engineer's Handbook	16
Lyra Domestica	16
——— Eucharistica	21
——— Germanica	21
——— Messianica	21
——— Mystica	21
——— Sacra	21
MACAULAY'S (Lord) Essays	3
——— History of England	1
——— Lays of Ancient Rome	26
——— Miscellaneous Writings	9
——— Speeches	7
——— Speeches on Parliamentary Reform	7
MACDOUGALL'S Theory of War	17
MARSHMAN'S Life of Havelock	4

NEW WORKS PUBLISHED BY LONGMANS AND CO. 31

	PAGE
McCulloch's Dictionary of Commerce	17
—— Geographical Dictionary	11
Macfie's Vancouver Island	10
Maguire's Life of Father Mathew	4
—— Rome and its Rulers	4
Maling's Indoor Gardener	13
Massey's History of England	1
Maunder's History of the Reformation	2
Maunder's Biographical Treasury	9
—— Geographical Treasury	11
—— Historical Treasury	9
—— Scientific and Literary Treasury	16
—— Treasury of Knowledge	20
—— Treasury of Natural History	13
Maury's Physical Geography	11
May's Constitutional History of England	
Melville's Digby Grand	24
—— General Bounce	24
—— Gladiators	24
—— Good for Nothing	24
—— Holmby House	24
—— Interpreter	24
—— Kate Coventry	24
—— Queen's Maries	24
Mendelssohn's Letters	5
Merrill' Windsor Great Park	16
—— on Sewage	10
Merivale's (H.) Colonisation and Colonies	11
—— Historical Studies	3
—— (C.) Fall of the Roman Republic	3
—— Romans under the Empire	
—— on Conversion of Roman Empire	3
Miles on Horse's Foot	25
—— On Horses' Teeth	25
—— on Horse Shoeing	25
—— on Stables	25
Mill on Liberty	6
—— on Representative Government	6
—— on Utilitarianism	6
Mill's Dissertations and Discussions	6
—— Political Economy	6
—— System of Logic	6
—— Hamilton's Philosophy	6
Miller's Elements of Chemistry	14
Monsell's Spiritual Songs	21
—— Beatitudes	21
Montagu's Experiments in Church and State	19
Monteagle on the Signs and Symptoms of Freemasonry	14
Moore's Irish Melodies	23
—— Lalla Rookh	23
—— Memoirs, Journal, and Correspondence	6
—— Poetical Works	23
Morell's Elements of Psychology	9
—— Mental Philosophy	9
Morning Clouds	20
Morton's Prince Consort's Farms	17
Mosheim's Ecclesiastical History	20
Müller's (Max) Lectures on the Science of Language	7
—— (K. O.) Literature of Ancient Greece	
Murchison on Continued Fevers	15
Mure's Language and Literature of Greece	3
New Testament, Illustrated with Wood Engravings from the Old Masters	18
Newman's History of his Religious Opinions	4
Nightingale's Notes on Hospitals	20
Odling's Course of Practical Chemistry	14
—— Manual of Chemistry	14
Ormsby's Rambles in Algeria and Tunis	23
Owen's Comparative Anatomy and Physiology of Vertebrate Animals	19
Oxenham on Atonement	21

	PAGE
Packe's Guide to the Pyrenees	23
Paget's Lectures on Surgical Pathology	15
—— Camp and Cantonment	17
Pereira's Elements of Materia Medica	15
—— Manual of Materia Medica	15
Perkins's Tuscan Sculptors	18
Phillips's Guide to Geology	13
—— Introduction to Mineralogy	13
Piesse's Art of Perfumery	17
—— Chemical, Natural, and Physical Magic	17
—— Laboratory of Chemical Wonders	17
Playtime with the Poets	23
Practical Mechanic's Journal	17
Prescott's Scripture Difficulties	19
Preston's Saturn	10
Pycroft's Course of English Reading	7
—— Cricket Field	25
—— Cricket Tutor	25
—— Cricketana	25
Reade's Poetical Works	23
Recreations of a Country Parson, Second Series	
Reilly's Map of Mont Blanc	9
Riddle's Diamond Latin-English Dictionary	8
—— First Sundays at Church	21
Rivers's Rose Amateur's Guide	18
Ronalds's Correspondence of Greyson	9
—— Eclipse of Faith	9
—— Defence of ditto	9
—— Essays from the Edinburgh Review	9
—— Fullerians	9
Roget's Thesaurus of English Words and Phrases	7
Ronalds's Fly-Fisher's Entomology	25
Rowton's Debater	7
Russell on Government and Constitution	1
Saxby's Study of Steam	17
—— Weather System	11
Scott's Handbook of Volumetrical Analysis	14
Scrope on Volcanos	13
Senior's Biographical Sketches	5
—— Historical and Philosophical Essays	5
—— Essays on Fiction	8
Sewell's Amy Herbert	24
—— Ancient History	3
—— Cleve Hall	24
—— Earl's Daughter	24
—— Experience of Life	24
—— Gertrude	24
—— Glimpse of the World	24
—— History of the Early Church	3
—— Ivors	24
—— Katharine Ashton	24
—— Laneton Parsonage	24
—— Margaret Percival	24
—— Night Lessons from Scripture	20
—— Passing Thoughts on Religion	20
—— Preparation for Communion	20
—— Readings for Confirmation	20
—— Readings for Lent	20
—— Self-Examination before Confirmation	20
—— Stories and Tales	24
—— Thoughts for the Holy Week	20
—— Ursula	20
Shaw's Work on Wine	17
Shedden's Elements of Logic	7
Short Whist	25
Short's Church History	2
Sieveking's Amalie: Life, by Winkworth	4
Simpson's Handbook of Dining	17
Smith's (Southwood) Philosophy of Health	21
—— (J.) Voyage and Shipwreck of St. Paul	18

	Page		Page
Smith's (G.) Wesleyan Methodism	5	Vaughan's (R.) Revolutions in English History	1
—— (Sydney) Memoir and Letters	5	—— (R. A.) Hours with the Mystics	10
—— Miscellaneous Works	9	Villari's Savonarola	4
—— Sketches of Moral Philosophy	9		
—— Wit and Wisdom	9	Watson's Principles and Practice of Physic	14
Smith on Cavalry Drill and Manœuvres	17	Watts's Dictionary of Chemistry	14
Southey's (Doctor)	7	Webb's Celestial Objects for Common Telescopes	4
—— Poetical Works	25	Webster & Wilkinson's Greek Testament	11
Spohr's Autobiography	4	Weld's Last Winter in Rome	22
Spring and Autumn	20	Wellington's Life, by Brialmont and Gleig	4
Stanley's History of British Birds	13	—— by Gleig	4
Stebbing's Analysis of Mill's Logic	7	West on the Diseases of Infancy and Childhood	14
Stephenson's (R.) Life by Jeaffreson and Pole	4	Whately's English Synonymes	5
Stephen's Essays in Ecclesiastical Biography	5	—— Logic	6
—— Lectures on the History of France	2	—— Remains	5
Stirling's Secret of Hegel	10	—— Rhetoric	6
Stonehenge on the Dog	25	—— Sermons	22
—— on the Greyhound	25	—— Paley's Moral Philosophy	13
		Wewell's History of the Inductive Sciences	3
Tabb's Jerusalem, by James	25	Whist, what to lead, by Cam	24
Taylor's (Jeremy) Works, edited by Eden	20	Witts and Riddle's Latin-English Dictionary	6
Tennent's Ceylon	12	Wilberforce (W.) Recollections of, by Harford	5
—— Natural History of Ceylon	12	Williams's Superstitions of Witchcraft	5
Thirlwall's History of Greece	3	Willich's Popular Tables	24
Thomson's (Archbishop) Laws of Thought	7	Wilson's Bryologia Britannica	12
—— (J.) Tables of Interest	25	Wood's Homes without Hands	12
—— Conspectus, by Birkett	15	Woodward's Historical and Chronological Encyclopædia	3
Todd's Cyclopædia of Anatomy and Physiology	15		
—— and Bowman's Anatomy and Physiology of Man	15	Yonge's English-Greek Lexicon	8
Trollope's Barchester Towers	23	—— Abridged ditto	8
—— Warden	23	Youatt's Nautical Dictionary	17
Twiss's Law of Nations	17	Youatt on the Dog	27
Tyndall's Lectures on Heat	11	—— on his Horse	27
Ure's Dictionary of Arts, Manufactures, and Mines	18		
Van der Hoeven's Handbook of Zoology	12		

www.ingramcontent.com/pod-product-compliance
Lightning Source LLC
Chambersburg PA
CBHW022147300426
44115CB00006B/377